Artificial Life

DATE DUE

		WITHDRAWN	

Complex Adaptive Systems

John H. Holland, Christopher Langton, and Stewart W. Wilson, advisors

Artificial Life
An Overview

edited by Christopher G. Langton

A Bradford Book

The MIT Press
Cambridge, Massachusetts
London, England

Fifth printing, 2000

First MIT Press paperback edition, 1997

© 1995 Massachusetts Institute of Technology

Printed and bound in the United States of America.

Library of Congress Cataloging-in-Publication Data

Artificial Life: an overview / edited by Christopher G. Langton.
    p.   cm.—(Complex adaptive systems)
  "A Bradford Book."
  Includes bibliographical references (p.) and index.
  ISBN 0-262-12189-1 (HB), 0-262-62112-6 (PB)
  1. Biological systems—Computer simulation. 2. Biological systems—Simulation methods. 3. Artificial
Intelligence. I. Langton, Christopher G. II. Series.
QH324.2.A74   1995
574´.01´13—dc20

                    94–46217
                    CIP

Contents

Contents

Foreword

Christopher G. Langton
Editor-in-Chief
Santa Fe Institute

This book is intended as a high-level index to the Artificial Life enterprise. It provides a point of entry to the field for both the newcomer and the seasoned researcher alike. The essays in this book introduce the many subdisciplines of Artificial Life and organize a large body of citations to the literature in the field.

I would recommend this book as an excellent text for a graduate seminar on Artificial Life, accompanied by readings drawn from the citations tailored to the professor's or the student's interests.

As Artificial Life is a highly interdisciplinary field, drawing researchers from across the academic and scientific spectrum, the authors have made an extra effort to make their essays comprehensible to readers from outside their own particular disciplines. They have defined technical terms where needed and provided background motivation for techniques and approaches that might otherwise require in-depth knowledge of some highly specialized body of theory. Thus, this book should prove accessible to anyone with a moderate background in the sciences.

I have made a special effort to include not only scientific and engineering papers, but also reviews of some of the philosophical and social issues, as it is just as important to understand how a field fits into the web of science and society as it is to understand the internal details of the field.

Christopher G. Langton

Editor's Introduction

Christopher G. Langton
Editor-in-Chief
Santa Fe Institute

This book consists of the first three issues of *Artificial Life*. These initial issues contain a special set of overview articles contributed by members of the editorial board of the journal. In these articles, each editor has attempted to review his or her own thread of special interest within the broad and diverse tapestry of research efforts that have come to be associated with the term "Artificial Life." In general, each article contains a bit of history on a particular research topic, a review of some of the more important problems, a description of the most promising techniques and methods for addressing these problems, and a view toward the future, with suggestions of the impact that Artificial Life techniques will have on our understanding of the biological phenomena under study.

The primary purpose of this initial set of overview articles is to "prime the pump" for future research in the field of Artificial Life, thereby stimulating future contributions to the journal itself. They are also intended to help define and delineate the field of Artificial Life more thoroughly than has been done until now.

The term Artificial Life literally means "life made by humans rather than by nature." As you will see in these articles, Artificial Life is many things to many people, and I will not attempt to give a concise definition of it here. In fact, Artificial Life is not yet ready to be constrained by quick and short definitions—the field is still in the process of defining itself, as is proper for any new discipline. The articles in this volume carefully stake out claims to certain areas of study, but there is far more intellectual territory out there waiting to be discovered and laid claim to.

Among all of the things that Artificial Life is or will come to be, however, it is probably safe to say that the field as a whole represents an attempt to increase vastly the role of synthesis in the study of biological phenomena. Synthesis has played a vital role in the grounding of many scientific disciplines, because it extends the empirical database upon which the theory of the discipline is built beyond the often highly accidental set of entities that nature happened to leave around for us to study.

Take the field of chemistry as an example: In the earliest stages of research into the constitution of matter, people took stock of the kinds of chemical compounds that nature had provided them with, catalogued and classified them, analyzed them by taking them apart into their constituent pieces, and then analyzed the pieces. This was fine as far as it went, but there was a great deal of accident and historical process involved in the determination of the kinds of chemical compounds that nature happened to leave around for study, and it would have been very difficult to observe the law-regularities in the highly irregular and unique set of compounds that early researchers happened to have available for study. It was only through the process of synthesis—putting the constituent pieces of matter together in new and different ways—that researchers were able to extend the set of chemical compounds available for study far beyond the irregular set provided to them by nature. It was only within the context of this much larger set of "possible" chemical compounds that researchers were able to see beyond the accidental nature of the "natural" chemical compounds, and glimpse the regularities in the constitution of matter. To have a theory of the actual, it is necessary to understand the possible.

The situation is much the same in biology. The set of biological entities provided to us by nature, broad and diverse as it is, is dominated by accident and historical contingency. We trust implicitly that there were lawful regularities at work in the determination of this set, but it is unlikely that we will discover many of these regularities by restricting ourselves only to the set of biological entities that nature actually provided us with. Rather, such regularities will be found only by exploring the much larger set of possible biological entities.

Many biologists have speculated wistfully about "rewinding the tape" of evolution, starting the process over again from slightly different initial conditions. What would emerge? What would be the same? What would be different? We sense that the evolutionary trajectory that did in fact occur on earth is just one out of a vast ensemble of possible evolutionary trajectories—each leading to a biology that could have happened in principle, but didn't in fact solely for reasons of accident combined with common genetic descent. We sense that the regularities we seek would be revealed to us if we could just get a glimpse of that space of possible biologies.

Just as chemistry did not become lawful until the set of compounds under study was extended beyond the set originally provided by nature, so it is likely that biology will not become lawful until the set of biological entities under study is vastly extended beyond the set originally provided to us by nature. This is the role of synthesis, and this is the primary motivation for the field of Artificial Life: to give us a glimpse of that wider space of possible biologies.

Not only did the synthetic method in chemistry lead to a more solid theoretical grounding of the field itself, but the very nature of synthesis led to novel chemical compounds with many practical industrial and engineering applications, such as synthetic rubber, plastics, medicinal compounds, and so forth. Likewise, a major motivation for the field of Artificial Life, besides the desire for a firmer theoretical grounding for biology, is the promise it holds for the synthesis of biological phenomena in forms that will be of great practical use in our industrial and engineering endeavors. Nature has discovered ingenious solutions to many hard engineering problems, problems that we have not been able to solve by our traditional engineering methods. The synthetic process of attempting to recreate these biological solutions in other materials will be of great practical use. Furthermore, we may even borrow the engineering method nature used to come up with these ingenious solutions in the first place: the process of evolution. By synthesizing the mechanisms underlying the evolutionary process in computers and in other "nonbiological" media, we can discover solutions to engineering problems that have long resisted our traditional approaches.

However, as was the case with synthetic chemistry, we need not restrict ourselves to attempting merely to recreate biological phenomena that originally occurred naturally. We have the entire space of possible biological structures and processes to explore, including those that never did evolve here on earth. Thus, Artificial Life need not merely attempt to recreate nature as it is, but is free to explore nature as it could have been—as it could still be if we realize artificially what did not occur naturally. Of course, we must constantly be aware of which of our endeavors are relevant to biology, and which break ground that is ultimately outside of the domain of biological relevancy. However, much of the latter will be of interest on its own right, regardless of whether or not it teaches us anything about biology as it is understood today. Artificial Life will teach us much about biology—much that we could not have learned by studying the natural products of biology alone—but Artificial Life will ultimately reach beyond biology, into a realm that we do not yet have a name for, but which must include culture and our technology in an extended view of nature.

I don't want merely to paint a rosy picture of the future of Artificial Life. It will not solve all of our problems. Indeed, it may well add to them. The potential that Artificial Life holds for unlocking the secrets of life is great, but in unlocking those secrets we run the risk of unlocking a Pandora's box. As has been the case with our mastery of any new technology in the past, the mastery of the technology of life holds tremendous potential for beneficial use, but it also holds tremendous potential for abuse, whether accidental or intentional. Perhaps the simplest way to emphasize this point is by merely pointing out that Mary Shelley's prophetic story of Dr. Frankenstein can no longer be considered to be merely science fiction. We are on the verge of duplicating Dr. Frankenstein's feat and, therefore, of duplicating the consequences that lead to his ultimate ruin. Mary Shelley's genius was to paint the scientist Frankenstein as the real monster of the story, by his refusal to accept responsibility for the potential consequences of his pursuit of knowledge for its own sake. There is a lesson here for all science, not just Artificial Life, but it is especially poignant when one considers what it is that Artificial Life is attempting to accomplish.

Artificial Life will have a tremendous impact on the future of life on earth as well as on our view of ourselves and the "role" of human beings in the greater overall scheme of the universe. In addition to scientific and technical issues, Artificial Life raises many questions more appropriately treated by the disciplines of philosophy and ethics. What is the ontological status of artificially created "living" entities? What rights do they have? What is the nature of the relationship between ourselves as creators and our artifacts as living creations? How will Artificial Life impact society? How, if at all, can we guarantee peaceful coexistence with autonomously evolving synthetic life forms sharing our physical environment? What is the future of life, natural and artificial?

Obviously, the domain of discourse concerning Artificial Life is potentially very large, involving virtually all of the academic disciplines. This is quite a diverse area for a single field to cover, including research in wetware, hardware, software, and more. It is expected that the "bread and butter" of the field will consist in computational approaches to open problems in biological theory and in the application of biological principles to engineering domains. However, we cannot ignore the impact that our studies will have on life itself, on us as living things, or on our understanding of ourselves and our place in the universe.

This volume should serve as an initial orientation to the diverse territory of Artificial Life research, but it is only a crude map pieced together through the efforts of these early explorers. There is much more to be discovered, and there is much more to be learned even about the territories reviewed here. My hope is that this early map will inspire others to further explorations.

Artificial Life as a Tool for Biological Inquiry

Charles Taylor
Department of Biology
University of California at
Los Angeles
Los Angeles, CA 90024
taylor@cs.ucla.edu

David Jefferson
Department of Computer
Science
University of California at
Los Angeles
Los Angeles, CA 90024
jefferson@cs.ucla.edu

Abstract Artificial life embraces those human-made systems that possess some of the key properties of natural life. We are specifically interested in artificial systems that serve as models of living systems for the investigation of open questions in biology. First we review some of the artificial life models that have been constructed with biological problems in mind, and classify them by medium (hardware, software, or "wetware") and by level of organization (molecular, cellular, organismal, or population). We then describe several "grand challenge" open problems in biology that seem especially good candidates to benefit from artificial life studies, including the origin of life and self-organi- zation, cultural evolution, origin and maintenance of sex, shifting balance in evolution, the relation between fitness and adaptedness, the structure of ecosystems, and the nature of mind.

Keywords
artificial life, evolution, natural selection, origin of life, development,
wetware, emergent properties

The question of what the major current problems of Biology are cannot be answered, for I do not know of a single biological discipline that does not have major unresolved problems. . . . Still, the most burning and as yet most intractable problems are those that involve complex systems.

Ernst Mayr [42]

I Introduction

Natural life on earth is organized into at least four fundamental levels of structure: the molecular level, the cellular level, the organism level, and the population-ecosystem level. A living thing at any of these levels is a complex adaptive system exhibiting behavior that emerges from the interaction of a large number of elements from the levels below. Understanding life in any depth requires knowledge at all these levels.

To deal with this multilevel complexity, a broad methodological shift is in progress in the biological sciences today as a new collection of Artificial Life models of natural biological systems become available for the first time. These modeling tools, some expressed as software, some as hardware, and some as wet-bench lab techniques (wetware), are powerful enough to capture much of the complexity of living systems, yet in a form that is more easily manipulable, repeatable, and subject to precisely controlled experiment than are the corresponding natural systems.

In Artificial Life there is a major intellectual divide, similar to the one in the field of Artificial Intelligence, between "engineered" systems designed to accomplish some complex task by any means the designer can devise, even if only distantly related to the way natural systems accomplish it, and systems meant to accurately model biological systems and intended for testing biological hypotheses. For example, most of the literature on genetic algorithms [26] has centered on function optimization, and the technical concerns have been about which algorithm variations are most efficient for which class of optimization problems. While these issues are important for many purposes, they are not central to the behavior of living systems.

We are specifically interested in those Artificial Life systems that tell us something about natural life. In this review, we will describe some of the modeling techniques under development for biological problems in order to survey the breadth of research in those areas. Then we will describe a number of open problems in biology that seem especially good candidates to benefit from the tools that Artificial Life is beginning to offer.

2 Brief Survey of Artificial Life Models Applied to Problems in Biology

Researchers have produced Artificial Life models at each of the levels of organization recognized in natural life, from the molecular to the population level, sometimes covering two or three levels in a single model. At present there is a tendency to study the molecular level through wetware experiments, the cellular and population levels with software experiments, and the organismic level with hardware (robotic) studies, although that may change in the future. We will classify the Artificial Life systems we discuss by medium: wetware, hardware, or software.

2.1   The Molecular Level: Wetware Systems

Wetware Artificial Life systems are the most similar to natural life and indeed are actually derived from natural life, today at least. Most of the experiments are attempts to direct an artificial evolutionary process toward the production of ribonucleic acid (RNA) molecules with specific catalytic properties. Experiments typically begin with a pool of 10^{13} to 10^{15} variant RNA molecules, placed in a solution of substrates for a specific reaction that the experimenter wishes to catalyze. Because initially the sequences are almost all distinct, and there are trillions of them, some will presumably "accidentally" catalyze the reaction at least weakly. The more "successful" RNA molecules, those that promote the target reaction more strongly than others, are then selected and separated from the "unsuccessful" and replicated many times, with mutations inserted, by using a variant of the polymerase chain reaction (PCR)—a relatively new technique for creating vast numbers of copies of nucleic acid sequences. These new daughter sequences are then tested and selected again, and the whole cycle is repeated for a number of generations until RNA sequences with sufficiently strong catalytic properties are evolved.

Examples of wetware research along these lines include work by (a) Beaudry and Joyce, where RNA ribozymes that normally cleave specific RNA sites were evolved to cleave DNA as well; by (b) Bartel and Szostak [2], who evolved catalytic RNAs from a pool of random-sequence RNAs; and by (c) Lehman and Joyce [36], who evolved RNA sequences to work with different metal ions than they normally would. So far the RNA sequences produced artificially have been similar to natural sequences; however, they have enzymatic functions not possessed by any preexisting natural RNA, so far as we know, indicating an obvious potential for evolving chemically useful RNA molecules. And someday, perhaps, if the RNA molecules are selected not on the basis of their own catalytic behavior but on that of the proteins they code for, then we can look forward to evolving artificial genes for medically useful protein molecules.

If we view the direct goal of these experiments as producing some particular catalytic properties in RNA, the experiments are not biological modeling as we have defined it. But taken collectively, they do have a biological significance well beyond their potential economic and medical value. They help us calibrate the degree to which RNA can catalyze biochemical reactions, a job normally done by proteins, and they lend strong credibility to the hypothesis of the "RNA world" [30], one of the most important theories about the origin of life. This RNA world hypothesis asserts that there was a time early in the earth's history when there were few if any deoxyribonucleic acid (DNA) or protein molecules, and the primordial soup was instead dominated by RNA molecules that were able to accomplish both replication and catalysis. By demonstrating that pure replicating RNA systems are capable of evolving specific catalytic behaviors, these Artificial Life studies are providing evidence for the plausibility of the RNA world that is more direct than any other line of research so far.

2.2   The Cellular Level: Software Systems

It is customary to distinguish between *chemical evolution*, which refers to evolutionary history from the stage of self-replicating molecules to the stage of encapsulated cells, and *organic evolution*, which refers to evolution since life became organized almost exclusively into cells that, either alone or in assemblages, behave and reproduce as clearly defined units. Much research in Artificial Life is directed at understanding just how a differentiated multicellular assemblage can replicate itself, and how such replication might have evolved.

John von Neumann was the first to characterize conditions for self-replication in cellular automata systems [6, 58]. He constructed self-replicating systems that possess the full computational power of universal Turing machines using a very large number of cells, each with 29 possible states. Langton [33] dropped the requirement of universality (after all, natural cells do not seem to have that) and found very much simpler systems that are capable of self-replication, nicely displayed in Langton [34]. Reggia, Armentrout, Chou, and Peng [53] have identified a number of even simpler self-replication patterns in cellular automata.

Whatever the first self-replicating molecules may have been, their organization into cells must have required the evolution of mechanisms for spatial segregation in a chemical environment. How this occurred has been an open question in chemical evolution since Oparin posited a role for coacervates in the 1920s (see Chang, DeMarais, Mack, Miller, & Strathern [8]). Recently Boerlijst and Hogeweg [4] have studied cellular automata that generate hypercycles and seem to generate spatial diversity spontaneously. While it is still too early to know just how directly this corresponds to the actual evolution of cells, these studies serve to enlarge the set of possible explanations.

It took only 1 billion years or so for the first cells to form on earth but about 3 billion more years for these to evolve into metazoans (multicellular organisms) shortly before the Cambrian period. There are many questions about how this might have been accomplished, and it appears that several major steps were involved. One step was the formation of endosymbiotic associations, where distinct types of cells associate, with one inside the cell membrane of the other (as apparently happened in the formation of chloroplasts and mitochondria within eucaryotic cells). Another step was the association of genetically related cells to form multicellular organisms, in which only some of the cells reproduce. These issues are only partly understood. While there have been a number of fine studies on symbiotic associations generally (e.g., [28,59]), there has been much less work directed at endosymbiosis, although there has been some [56]. And while there have been several studies of how individual cells might reproduce to form the next higher level of organization [37,44,51], these have been clearly exploratory. The cellular level of life is an area where it would seem that artificial life research has only begun.

2.3   The Organism Level: Hardware Systems

To model the behavior of living things at the organism level, for example, of insects, one must model the organism's sensory and nervous system, its body, and its environment. Although we are quite used to thinking of nervous systems as fantastically complex, we tend to ignore the fact that animals' bodies are highly complex as well, with extremely complicated geometries, mechanical, dynamical and thermal properties, energy constraints, growth and developmental programs, etc.

In principle all of the components of an animal—nervous system, body, environment—can be simulated in software. In practice, however, the amount of computation required to reasonably model the properties of sound or light in a complicated environment, or the mechanical properties of an organism with 100 coupled elastic parts, is vast and effectively beyond the capacity of computational technology for some time to come.

However, it is now becoming possible to let the real physical environment model itself, and to represent the bodies of animals and their interactions with the environment by using small, computer-controlled, autonomous mobile robots (mobots). With this technology, we can now model how organisms accomplish the integration of various perceptual modalities, how they navigate in space, how they control their senses and muscles to accomplish precisely coordinated movements, and how they do all these things in real time.

One research project of this kind involved the mobot Genghis, developed by Angle [1] and programmed by Maes and Brooks [41] to learn to walk. Genghis is a six-legged robot, approximately 1 foot long and 1 food wide, designed to traverse rugged terrain. Each leg is powered by two motors and there are two sensors, one in front and one in back, to detect whether the body is touching the ground, and another sensor to measure the distance Genghis has traveled. In most such systems, coordination for tasks such as walking is statically programmed; Genghis, however, has to learn to walk. The leg modules are coordinated by a network of finite automata that receives feedback from the sensors about stability and forward movement, and produces output to the motors. Starting from a random neural network, Genghis learns how to achieve a reliable tripod gait in just few minutes.

Several features of the Genghis experiments and others like it are worth noting: (a) Emergent functionality of control: Control of Genghis' gait is an emergent property, in that no individual part of the neural net "knows" how to walk. (b) Task-level decomposition: The agents that govern behavior are essentially autonomous. At the lowest level, one simple task is accomplished (e.g., standing up), upon which is superimposed the next layer (e.g., moving), upon which is superimposed another (e.g., obstacle avoidance), and so on. This layering of behaviors, each one making use of others that preexist, is analogous to the way that task proficiency might be accomplished by evolution in natural life. (c) Low-level processing: Because there is no global model, much of the reasoning is accomplished at a low level, close to the perception level, in much the same way that visual information seems to be processed in the mammalian retina. These points are discussed in Maes [40] and Brooks [5]. Adherents to this approach make the narrow claim that it is a good way to control mobile robots for complex tasks, and the broader claim that it is a good way to engineer intelligent systems generally. If so, then using mobots to model animals will aid in extracting some of the principles of intelligent behavior generally, whether natural or artificial.

2.4 Software Life at the Population Level: Equational Models versus Artificial Life Models

Models of population behavior for the study of ecosystem organization, population genetics, macroevolution, geographic dispersal, etc. have traditionally been expressed formally as systems of algebraic or differential equations. Unfortunately, equational models are subject to many limitations. For example, in many models it is common to refer to the derivative of a variable with respect to population size N. This in turn implies the assumption of very large populations in order for such a derivative to make sense, which has the effect of washing out small population effects, such as genetic drift, or extinction. Another difficulty is that it would take tens to hundreds of lines of equations to express even a simple model of an organism's behavior as a function of the many genetic, memory, and environmental variables that affect its behavior, and there are simply no mathematical tools for dealing with equational systems of that complexity. Furthermore, equational models are generally poor at dealing with highly nonlinear effects such as thresholding or if-then-else conditionals, which arise very frequently in the description of animal behavior.

One of the most fundamental and successful insights of the field of Artificial Life has been the development of an alternative population modeling paradigm that dispenses with equations entirely, and represents a population procedurally, that is, as a set of coexecuting computer programs, one for each cell or one for each organism. We consider this feature, the representation of organisms by programs, to be the defining feature of "artificial life" models of population behavior, the property that distinguishes them from other mathematical or computational models of populations.

Artificial Life models offer the advantage of coding an organism's behavior explicitly as a program, rather than implicitly as the solution to equations that must be integrated. This directness of encoding typically makes Artificial Life systems much easier to use and modify, as new information is obtained or new hypotheses are entertained, than is possible with equational models. Today most Artificial Life models represent each organism as a Lisp program, a finite automaton, or a neural net. The genes of the organism are represented variously as bit strings, character strings, or list structures, either contained within the organism or stored as a separate data object that serves to encode the structure or behavior of the organism. Software organisms can reproduce either asexually, with point mutations altering the genetic data passed from parent to child, or sexually, with the child's genome derived by combining information from two parent genomes.

An early example of the artificial life modeling approach is the RAM system [55], developed by Taylor, Jefferson, Turner, and Goldman, in which animal-like processes (parameterized Lisp programs) and environment-like processes could execute concurrently and synchronously. A RAM animal's program is a Lisp routine whose parameters serve as genes. RAM animals reproduce asexually but live in a common environment in which they interact and compete ecologically. The RAM system was relatively limited in two ways: (a) The "genes" defined a relatively small parameter space within which variation could occur, leaving limited scope for innovation and evolution; and (b) because at the time it was built only a few hundred individuals could be simulated for a few tens of generations per hour of workstation time, so the process of natural selection was subject to drift unless the selection forces were exceptionally strong.

Jefferson et al. [29] drastically extended and scaled up the idea of representing organisms as programs with such systems as Genesys. In that system, executed on a Connection Machine, animals were represented as neural nets in some cases or as finite automata in others. The genes of each organism were represented as bit strings that encoded either the weights of a neural net, or the transition table of a finite automaton. With a population of 64K individuals evolving at the rate of one generation per minute, and starting from a population of random bit strings, Genesys was able to evolve the ability to follow a broken rectilinear trail in a grid environment in 100–200 generations.

Since RAM and Genesys, many other systems representing organisms as programs have been developed to explore problems in biology. We can illustrate the diversity of this approach by classifying these systems according to the general purposes for which they were developed—the study of evolution, behavior, ecology, developmental biology, or teaching.

Evolution. Artificial Life models are especially well suited for studying the dynamics of natural evolution and were originally invented for this purpose. Imagine a genetic algorithm in which each genome encodes a computer program, and the programs in the population are selected and bred on the basis of their ability to survive and prosper in some environment. One would expect that the future generations of programs will perform better than their progenitors, and, indeed, in practice this is typically the case— although it depends on how the programs are represented, as Collins and Jefferson [10] have argued. For a number of reasons, artificial neural networks, encoded in various ways into bit strings, seem to be especially good representations for evolution.

Sexual selection is an evolutionary phenomenon recognized by Darwin and emphasized by Fisher [19] in the 1930s. If a female produces sons who are extreme for some trait (e.g., wattle color) and also daughters who have a preference for that extreme— through linkage, pleiotropy, or some other mechanism—then that trait will be selected to a high frequency in the population even if it has very disadvantageous side effects. It has been suggested that chance differences in traits subject to such runaway selection might underlie the tremendous diversity of secondary sexual characters in many tropical birds. The mathematical analysis of this phenomenon, however, requires a system of several nonlinear differential equations, so it is very complex and has been successful for only a few special cases.

Collins and Jefferson [11] constructed an Artificial Life model of sexual selection, endowing the organisms with the relevant heritable traits and preferences. They explored this system in some generality, identifying where such explanations are plausible and where they are not. In particular, they were able to show that certain propositions that had been demonstrated analytically under very restrictive assumptions were actually true under a much broader set of circumstances than was provable by mathematical analysis. There are many other problems in sexual selection (see, e.g., Williams [60]) where similar methods would appear to be useful.

Behavior. Even Darwin was impressed by how exquisitely adapted animals seem to be to their environments. Indeed, when it has been possible to develop models of optimal behavior from theoretical principles and then compare these to the way animals actually behave, the fit is often striking. How is that accomplished? Do animals figure out the relevant formulae, differentiate them, and solve for zero?

Koza, Rice, and Roughgarden [32] have recently examined the feeding behavior of *Anolis* lizards, a small, well studied group that inhabits the Caribbean region, and compared their actual foraging behavior to optimal foraging behavior as determined by a theoretical analysis, noting that the fit was quite close. They then compared that to the foraging behavior of simulated lizards that they evolved via genetic algorithms, and found that it was not difficult for the evolution to endow the lizard with behavioral strategies that closely approximate the optimal.

In a similar vein, Gibson, Taylor, and Jefferson [22] used the RAM system described earlier to model the peculiar mating behavior of sage grouse in which the females choose from among male suitors. Dozens of males will gather to form leks (local mating markets) in which they display and attract the attention of females. Gibson et al. were trying to discover what influenced the females in selecting males. By searching a space of parameterized Artificial Life models, they found that if females, when choosing a mating lek, considered the distance from their nest, the number of males there, and the expected waiting time for the top male, most of the variance in their observed behavior was explainable. Similar work by Denoubourg, Theraulaz, and Beckers [15] on "swarm intelligence" has identified plausible sets of rules that are sufficient to explain much of the complex behavior used by ants and other social insects.

In a more theoretical direction, Lindgren and Nordahl [39] examined how the outcomes of iterative games of the Prisoner's Dilemma, a widely used model for the evolution of cooperation, might differ when there is misinformation among the players. Their analysis is remarkable because it lends credence to the position that social behavior will by itself lead to increased complexity in participant behavior. This approach is described more fully in Lindgren [38].

Ecology. Behavioral and ecological phenomena are often closely related, and both are rich with examples of collective action and emergent phenomena. At an abstract level, Ray [52] has shown how several trophic levels might emerge as a general property of ecological systems. Similarly, Ikegami [27] used variations of the Prisoner's Dilemma analogous to symbiosis and host/predator or predator/prey interactions to examine this evolution of interspecies associations.

Toquenaga, Ichinose, Hoshino, and Fuji [57] and Fry, Taylor, and Devgan [21] have used Artificial Life models to examine complex modes of behavior and population growth. By programming empirically-derived rules of behavior into the artificial animals, they observed the consequences of the collective behavior that was exhibited by ensembles of animals and the environments with which they interacted.

Developmental biology. Emergent phenomena are nowhere more evident than in developmental biology, where large numbers of cells, following presumably simple rules of behavior, collectively generate complex and interesting patterns. Prusinkiewicz [50] has explored the use of algebraic formulae for cell division and differentiation. These generate some stunning visual representations as well as realistic botanical patterns. Recently, Fleischer and Barr [20] have developed a system where cells change state and/or produce fields that mimic diffusion of growth regulators.

Because there is such a large amount of new information accumulating, consistent with simple collective behavior both within and between cells, it seems likely to us that Artificial Life systems will prove invaluable in the future for precisely formulating and testing hypotheses about development.

Teaching. It is sobering to reflect that 40% of Americans do not believe in Darwinian evolution and that this is true for 25% of all college-educated Americans as well. Religious convictions seem to be only part of the problem. Rather, it appears that the major obstacle is failure to understand the theory of evolution itself, aggravated by the fact that even many secondary school biology teachers have serious misunderstandings. It is well established that students are less likely to understand and absorb when they are passively presented with facts than when they are actively involved in construction and experimentation.

Artificial Life, however, offers a student the possibility of watching evolution in action, actively intervening with it and creating his or her own microworld. The Blind Watchmaker program by Dawkins [14] is especially noteworthy in this regard, as are the efforts of Resnick [54] to explore how children learn about collective behavior, and of the Apple Vivarium group (A. Kay [personal communication]), who are exploring Artificial Life systems to provide better ways of teaching ecology, evolution, and biology in general, in a classroom setting.

Papert [47], whose earlier Mindstorms was so influential for introducing computers to the K-12 classrooms, has recently advocated [48] a cybernetic approach to teaching science in the early grades. The argument he makes is compelling, and if generally adopted, then we may see a major influence of Artificial Life on the next generation of scientists.

3   Open Problems in Biology that Are Amenable to Study by Artificial Life Modeling

The opening quotation by Ernst Mayr concerns the need for understanding biological systems as complex adaptive systems. In the past, despite several brave attempts, discussion of holistic properties and emergence in biology typically devolved into mysticism or obfuscation. The study of Artificial Life, if it accomplishes nothing else, is providing a platform for more informed discussion of those issues.

We believe that several of the major outstanding problems in biology, especially in the study of evolution, are likely to benefit from the study of Artificial Life. In this section a few such problems are described. We will focus on evolution simply because it is the foundation upon which so much of biology is based, because it is permeated with problems of emergence, and because we are more familiar with this area.

3.1 Origin of Life and Self-Organization

Questions abound when one attempts to understand how life originated on earth and possibly elsewhere in the universe as well. If we restrict our attention to the origin of life on earth, those problems involve reconstructing the physical, chemical, geologic, and competitive forces that shaped the peculiar history of life on earth, the sequence of chemical reactions that may have occurred, the manner in which they became packaged and encapsulated so that organic evolution could supplant that which occurred previously, etc. Work along theoretical lines, such as that by Langton [35]; Farmer, Kauffman, and Packard [18,31]; or Eigen and Schuster [17] will be required, as well as experimental work [30]. As yet there has been little research in Artificial Life directed toward the actual constraints that operate on the other planets in our solar system and prevented (or at least constrained) the origin of life there. Most is directed at learning the minimal chemical requirements for replication to get started.

3.2 Cultural Evolution

Ideas and other atomic particles of human culture often seem to have a life of their own—origination, mutation, reproduction, spreading, and dying. In spite of several bold attempts to construct theories of cultural evolution (e.g., [7,13]), an adequate theory remains elusive. The financial incentive to understand any patterns governing fads and fashion is enormous, and because cultural evolution has contributed so much to the uniqueness of human nature, the scientific motivation is equally great.

Much of the problem with cultural evolution is similar to that for prebiotic evolution—the difficulty of identifying just what evolves (the "units of evolution"), how these units maintain their identity, and how they interact with one another. This area would seem to benefit from the same sorts of considerations that govern the origin of life.

3.3 Origin and Maintenance of Sex

Few problems in contemporary evolutionary theory are attracting as much attention as is the evolution of sex, sometimes referred to as "the cost of meiosis" [43]. All else being equal, a female who reproduces asexually will leave twice as many genes in her offspring as will a female who reproduces with a male. This would seem to impose a tremendous hurdle for sexuality to overcome, yet it persists, and sex is widespread in the natural world. Why? The answer almost certainly involves complex interactions among linkage, pleiotropy, epistasis, parasitism, and nonlinear relations between genotype and fitness. There are many qualitative theories but little in the way of testable quantitative research.

The ability to construct and examine large, but finite, populations with a variety of arbitrary constraints makes Artificial Life systems an excellent platform from which to study the theoretical side of this problem. We have observed, for example, that the ability of sexual systems to rid themselves of maladaptive mutations (Muller's ratchet) can be significant in populations of bit strings that evolve by genetic algorithm [12]. The genetic algorithm literature also has many examples where these issues are addressed in the context of optimization problems [23].

3.4 Shifting Balance Paradigm

Wright, in his four-volume treatise on population genetics [61], argued that the key issues in evolution today had their roots in the disagreements of the 1930s–1950s among Fisher, Haldane, and himself. This related particularly to how populations of organisms traversed their adaptive landscape—through gradual fine-tuning by natural selection on large populations, or alternatively in fits and starts with a good bit of chance to "jump" adaptive valleys in order to find more favorable epistatic combinations. The traditional mathematical models of population genetics and evolution require extensive linearization and so are not very good for exploring the nonlinear interactions that this problem requires. On the other hand, Artificial Life models are ideal for studying this problem, and several studies have begun on the importance of population size for evolving solutions with arbitrary degrees of epistasis. It may be that the rules that govern adaptation in artificial systems are different from those for natural systems, but these studies will certainly highlight which issues are most important, and there will certainly be some generalizations that pertain to both worlds.

3.5 Fitness and Adaptedness

Even before Darwin, it was recognized that there is some degree of direction or progress toward more complex forms over geologic time—the "chain of being," although how much direction there might be and how that effect is produced by natural selection remain murky. This concern can be compressed essentially into one question, What is the relation between adaptedness and fitness, that is, between adaptation and what is selected for? This question has occupied some of the greatest evolutionists of this century [16] and remains quite open [60]. It is now well understood that natural selection does not necessarily maximize adaptedness, even in theory [45]. Yet field biologists are constantly impressed by just how good the fit seems to be, and optimization arguments abound in population ecology (see Koza et al. [32]). In a classic essay, Gould and Lewontin [24] assailed the widespread use of optimization, pointing out that chance, structural necessity, pleiotropy, historical accident, and a host of other contributors will detract from making this "the best of all possible worlds."

The analysis of artificially living systems is beginning to shed needed light on this issue. Miglino, Nolfi, and Parisi [44] studied the evolution of generating functions that produced neural nets, which then determined the behavior of organisms, which in turn determined the fitness of artificial organisms in their environments. They found that a variety of genotypes coded for identical neural nets, that a variety of neural nets coded for the same behavior, and that a variety of behaviors achieved the same fitness in their system. However, the opportunities these various solutions offered for future evolution differed significantly. Similar observations were made by Hinton and Nowlan [25] in their study of the Baldwin effect in evolved learning by neural networks.

As research in Artificial Life acquires greater ability to capture development of organisms and intervening levels of organization between molecules and populations, the field is likely to contribute to the analysis of this problem that Dobzhansky characterized as "the most important theoretical problem in the study of evolution" (personal communication).

3.6 Structure of Ecosystems

In natural ecosystems there are a number of patterns that seem fairly general. For example, in their study of many food webs, Pimm, Lawton, and Cohen [49] observed a number of patterns, among them (a) the average proportion of top predators, intermediate species, and basal species remained roughly constant; (b) linkage density is approximately constant; and (c) the modal number of trophic levels is three to four.

There are others that also point to emergent properties of natural ecosystems. The reasons underlying these regularities are seldom understood.

As Artificial Life develops and ecosystems are evolved, perhaps along the lines of Ray [52] or Holland [26], it will be interesting to see if the same patterns evolve. Perhaps others will emerge, such as the intermediate connectedness of complex adaptive systems and their posture near the edge of chaos [31,35].

3.7 Mind in Nature

No problems in science are more venerable or profound than those surrounding the nature of mind. Will it be possible to design or evolve robots that experience the same sensations that we do? Do radically different life forms experience equally different forms of consciousness? Or is consciousness a universal property that organisms experience to various degrees but fundamentally alike in kind (and how can we tell)? How could mind and consciousness be produced by Darwinian evolution? Two recent and lucid accounts of these problems are those by Nagel [46] and Churchland [9].

Like most people, we have our own views on these problems. But unless these views are subject to rigorous definition, testing, and verification, they cannot be considered scientific. As the ability to construct Artificial Life systems improves, it may well become possible to construct systems that exhibit behavior that is typically ascribed to "mind." Such systems will, in a sense, play a role analogous to that played by *Escherechia coli* or *Drosophila melanogaster* that have permitted manipulation and dissection of mechanisms in natural living systems. If that happens, and we believe it will, then the field of Artificial Life will have contributed to what is surely one of the scientific grand challenges of all time.

References

1. Angle, C. M. (1989). *Genghis, a six-legged autonomous walking robot*. Bachelor's thesis, Department of EECS, Massachusetts Institute of Technology, Cambridge, MA.

2. Bartel, D. P., & Szostak, J. W. (1993). Isolation of new ribozymes from a large pool of random sequences. *Science, 261*, 1411–1418.

3. Beaudry, A. A., & Joyce, G. F. (1992). Directed evolution of an RNA enzyme. *Science, 257*, 635–641.

4. Boerlijst, M., & Hogeweg, P. (1992). Self-structuring and selection: Spiral waves as a substrate for prebiotic evolution. In C. Langton, C. E. Taylor, J. D. Farmer, & S. Rasmussen (Eds.), *Artificial life II*, 255–276. Reading, MA: Addison-Wesley.

5. Brooks, R. A. (1991). New approaches to robotics. *Science, 253*, 1227–1232.

6. Burks, A. (1970). *Essays on cellular automata*. Urbana, IL: University of Illinois Press.

7. Cavalli-Sforza, L. L., & Feldman, M. W. (1981). *Cultural transmission and evolution: A quantitative approach*. Princeton, NJ: Princeton University Press.

8. Chang, S., DeMarais, D., Mack, R., Miller, S. L., & Strathern, G. E. (1983). Prebiotic organic syntheses and the origin of life. In J. W. Schopf (Ed.), *Earth's earliest biosphere: Its origin and evolution*, 53–92. Princeton, NJ: Princeton University Press.

9. Churchland, P. (1990). *Matter and consciousness: A contemporary introduction to the philosophy of mind*. Cambridge, MA: The MIT Press,

10. Collins, R., & Jefferson, D. (1991). Representations for artificial organisms. In J.-A. Meyer & S. Wilson (Eds.), *Proceedings of the Simulation of Adaptive Behavior* (pp. 382–390). Cambridge, MA: The MIT Press.

11. Collins, R., & Jefferson, D. (1992). The evolution of sexual selection and female choice. In F. J. Varela and P. Bourgine (Eds.), *Toward a practice of autonomous systems: Proceedings of the First European Conference on Artificial Life* (pp. 327–336). Cambridge, MA: The MIT Press.

12. Daghat, M., & Taylor, C. Unpublished manuscript.

13. Dawkins, R. (1976). *The selfish gene*. New York: Oxford University Press.

14. Dawkins, R. (1989). *The evolution of evolvability*. In C. G. Langton (Ed.), *Artificial life* (pp. 201–220). Reading, MA: Addison-Wesley.

15. Denoubourg, J.-L., Theraulaz, G., & Beckers, R. (1992). Swarm-made architectures. In F. J. Varela & P. Bourgine (Eds.), *Toward a practice of autonomous systems: Proceedings of the First European Conference on Artificial Life*, 123–133. Cambridge, MA: The MIT Press.

16. Dobzhansky, T. (1970). *Genetics of the evolutionary process*. New York: Columbia University Press.

17. Eigen, M., & Schuster, P. (1979). *The hypercycle: A principle of natural self-organization*. New York: Springer Verlag.

18. Farmer, J. D., Kauffman, S. A., & Packard, N. H. (1986). Autocatalytic replication of polymers. *Physica D*, *22*, 50–67.

19. Fisher, R. A. (1930). *The genetical theory of natural selection*. Oxford, UK: Clarendon.

20. Fleischer, K., & Barr, A. (1994). The multiple mechanisms of morphogenesis: A Simulation testbed for the study of multicellular development. In C. Langton (Ed.), *Artificial life III*, 389–416. Reading, MA: Addison-Wesley.

21. Fry, J., Taylor, C. E., & Devgan, U. (1989). An expert system for mosquito control in Orange County, California. *Bull. Soc. Vector Ecol.*, *2*, 237–246.

22. Gibson, R., Taylor, C., & Jefferson, D. (1990). Lek formation by female choice: a simulation study. *Journal of the International Society for Behavioral Ecology*, *1*(1), 36–42.

23. Goldberg, D. (1989). *Genetic algorithms in search, optimization, and machine learning*. Reading, MA: Addison-Wesley.

24. Gould, S. J., & Lewontin, R. C. (1979). The spandrels of San Marco and the Panglossian paradigm: A critique of the adaptationist programme. *Proceedings of the Royal Society B*, *205*, 581–598.

25. Hinton, G. E., & Nowlan, S. J. (1987). How learning can guide evolution. *Complex Systems*, *1*, 495–502.

26. Holland, J. H. (1992). *Adaptation in natural and artificial systems*. Cambridge, MA: The MIT Press.

27. Ikegami, T. Ecology of evolutionary game strategies. Unpublished manuscript.

28. Ikegami, T., & Kaneko, K. (1990). Computer symbiosis—emergence of symbiotic behavior through evolution. *Physica D*, *42*, 235–243.

29. Jefferson, D., Collins, R., Cooper, C., Dyer, M., Flowers, M., Korf, R., Taylor, C., & Wang, A. (1992). The Genesys system: Evolution as a theme in artificial life. In C. G. Langton, J. D. Farmer, S. Rasmussen, & C. E. Taylor (Eds.), *Artificial life II* (pp. 549–578). Reading, MA: Addison-Wesley.

30. Joyce, G. F. (1989). RNA evolution and the origins of life. *Nature*, *338*, 217–224.

31. Kauffman, S. (1993). *Origins of order: Self-organization and selection in evolution*. New York: Oxford University Press.

32. Koza, J. R., Rice, J. P., & Roughgarden, J. (1992). Evolution of food-foraging strategies for the Caribbean *Anolis* lizard using genetic programming. *Adaptive Behavior*, *1*, 171–200.

33. Langton, C. G. (1984). Self-reproduction in cellular automata. *Physica D*, 10, 135–144.

34. Langton, C. G. (1992). Self-reproducing loops and virtual ants. In C. Langton (Ed.), *Artificial Life II Video Proceedings*. Reading, MA: Addison-Wesley.

35. Langton, C. G. (1990). Computation at the edge of chaos: Phase transitions and emergent computation. *Physica D*, *42*, 12–37.

36. Lehman, N., & Joyce, G. F. (1993). Evolution in vitro of an RNA enzyme with altered metal dependence. *Nature, 361*, 182–185.

37. Lindenmeyer, A., & Prusinkiewicz, P. (1989). Developmental models of multicellular organisms: A computer graphics perspective. In C. G. Langton (Ed.), *Artificial life* (pp. 221–250). Reading, MA: Addison-Wesley.

38. Lindgren, K., & Nordahl, M. G. (1994). Cooperation and community structure in artificial ecosystems. *Artificial Life, 1*, 15–37.

39. Lindgren, K., & Nordahl, M. G. (in press). Artificial food webs. In C. Langton (Ed.), *Artificial life III*, 73–104. Reading, MA: Addison-Wesley.

40. Maes, P. (1990). Designing autonomous agents: Theory and practice from biology to engineering and back. *Robotics and Autonomous Systems, 6*, 1–2.

41. Maes, P., & Brooks, R. A. (1990). Learning to coordinate behaviors. In *Proceedings of the American Association of Artificial Intelligence* (pp. 796–802), Boston. Los Altos, CA: Morgan Kauffman.

42. Mayr, E. (1982). *The growth of biological thought* (pp. 131–132). Cambridge, MA: Harvard University Press.

43. Michod, R. E., & Levin, B. R. (1988). *The evolution of sex*. Sunderland, MA: Sinauer Associates.

44. Miglino, O., Nolfi, S., & Parisi, D. (in press). Discontinuity in evolution: How different levels of organization imply pre-adaptation. In R. Belew and M. Mitchell (Eds.), *Plastic individuals in evolving populations: Models and algorithms*.

45. Mueller, L. D., & Feldman, M. W. (1988). The evolution of altruism by kin selection: New phenomena with strong selection. *Ethology and Sociobiology, 9*, 223–240.

46. Nagel, T. (1986). *The view from nowhere*. New York: Oxford University Press.

47. Papert, S. (1980). *Mindstorms: Children, computers, and powerful ideas*. New York: Basic Books.

48. Papert, S. (1993). *The children's machine*. New York: Basic Books.

49. Pimm, S. L., Lawton, J. H., & Cohen, J. E. (1991). Food web patterns and their consequences. *Nature, 350*, 669–674.

50. Prusinkiewicz, (1994). Visual models of morphogenesis. *Artificial Life, 1*, 61–80.

51. Prusinkiewicz, P., & Lindenmeyer, A. (1990). *The algorithmic beauty of plants*. New York: Springer Verlag.

52. Ray, T. (1994). An evolutionary approach to synthetic biology. *Artificial Life, 1*, 185–215.

53. Reggia, J. A., Armentrout, S. L., Chou, H.-H., & Peng, Y. (1993). Simple systems that exhibit self-directed replication. *Science, 259*, 1282–1287.

54. Resnick, M. (1992). *Beyond the centralized mindset*. Unpublished doctoral dissertation, Massachusetts Institute of Technology, Cambridge, MA.

55. Taylor, C. E., Jefferson, D. R., Turner, S. R., & Goldman, S. R. (1989). RAM: Artificial life for the exploration of complex biological systems. In C. G. Langton (Ed.), *Artificial life* (pp. 275–295). Reading, MA: Addison-Wesley.

56. Taylor, C. E., Muscatine, L., & Jefferson, D. R. (1989). Maintenance and breakdown of the Hydra-Chlorella symbiosis: A computer model. *Proceedings of the Royal Society of London B, 238*, 277–289.

57. Toquenaga, Y., Ichinose, M., Hoshino, T., & Fuji, K. (1994). Contest and scramble competition in an artificial world. In C. Langton (Ed.), *Artificial life III*, 177–199. Reading, MA: Addison-Wesley.

58. von Neumann, J. (1966). *The theory of self-reproducing automata*. Urbana, IL: University of Illinois Press.

59. Weisbuch, G., & Duchateau, G. (1992). *Emergence of mutualism: Application of a differential model to the coelenterates-algae associations.* (Tech. Rep. No. 92-06-030). Santa Fe, NM: Santa Fe Institute.

60. Williams, G. C. (1992). *Natural selection: Domains, levels, and challenges.* New York: Oxford University Press.

61. Wright, S. (1969–1978). *Evolution and the genetics of populations* (Vols. I–IV). Chicago, IL: University Chicago Press.

Cooperation and Community Structure in Artificial Ecosystems

Kristian Lindgren
Institute of Physical Resource Theory
Chalmers University of Technology
S-412 96 Göteborg, Sweden

Mats G. Nordahl*
Santa Fe Institute
1660 Old Pecos Trail, Suite A
Santa Fe, NM 87501 USA

Abstract We review results on the evolution of cooperation based on the iterated Prisoner's Dilemma. Coevolution of strategies is discussed both in situations where everyone plays against everyone, and for spatial games. Simple artificial ecologies are constructed by incorporating an explicit resource flow and predatory interactions into models of coevolving strategies. Properties of food webs are reviewed, and we discuss what artificial ecologies can teach us about community structure.

Keywords
evolution, Prisoner's Dilemma, co-operation, community structure, food webs, lattice games

1   Introduction

Artificial ecologies consisting of artificial organisms are likely to become useful tools for understanding general principles for how ecological communities are organized. In particular they could be used to study phenomena on scales in time and space that cannot be accessed in ordinary experiments and field studies.

Many of the artificial ecologies discussed in this paper are based on the iterated Prisoner's Dilemma (IPD). This game simultaneously provides an abstract model for the evolution of cooperation and a very complex coevolutionary landscape.

The path followed in this review starts out with a discussion of different mechanisms for the evolution of cooperation and altruistic behavior. We then discuss the IPD in detail. Models of coevolution of strategies are reviewed, both in situations where everyone plays against everyone and in spatial settings where interactions are localized.

Populations of coevolving strategies can be viewed as simple artificial ecological communities. An important aspect of community structure is who is eaten by whom. We review some basic facts about the structure of food webs and briefly discuss mathematical models of community structure and assembly. Finally we discuss how explicit resource flows can be combined with coevolution of strategies, which allows us to include predatory as well as cooperative interactions. This route is different from that followed in most investigations of community structure, where predation often is the only interaction considered.

2   The Evolution of Cooperation

Altruistic behavior, that is, behavior that benefits another individual or organism (not necessarily a relative), while being apparently detrimental to the organism itself, is an important phenomenon both in nature and human society. Cooperative behavior often depends on a certain amount of altruism, in that the participants need to refrain from

---

* present address: Institute of Theoretical Physics, Chalmers University of Technology, S-41296 Göteborg, Sweden.

taking advantage of others by acting according to short-term self-interest. In other cases, cooperation could be profitable enough that it is dictated even by shortsighted selfishness.

In the early history of evolutionary theory, the emphasis appears to have been mostly on the struggle for existence. (See Cronin [19] for a discussion.) Some early writers, such as the anarchist Kropotkin [47], did, however, stress the importance of cooperative interactions both in a biological context and in society. A number of scenarios for how altruistic and cooperative behavior could be established have later been suggested. The main difficulty in the evolution of altruistic behavior and cooperation is explaining how this behavior could be stable against cheaters who enjoy the benefits without giving something in return.

One case, which will not be discussed further in this article, is when the altruistic behavior is directed toward relatives (e.g., [34]). From the viewpoint of reproduction of genes, an individual is equivalent to two of his brothers or eight of his cousins. In the terminology of biologists, this is called kin selection. A number of cases of altruistic behavior in biology, such as eusociality among ants, bees, and wasps (e.g., [2]), have been claimed to at least in part depend on kin selection.

Another important mechanism is reciprocal altruism (e.g., [98]). In this case favors are given, and favors are expected back in return. In many cases, this could be viewed as enlightened self-interest that takes the shadow of the future into account. The game theoretic models discussed later mostly fall under this heading.

A third mechanism could be group selection, where selection can be viewed as operating at higher levels. A simple mathematical example where clearly defined higher units of selection (different kinds of spiral waves) appear is the spatial hypercycle model studied by Boerlijst and Hogeweg [10,11].

Another case where cooperative behavior can occur is when cooperation follows from immediate self-interest. This was called by-product mutualism in Dugatkin, Mesterton-Gibbs, and Houston [24]; in a game theoretic framework, parameters have changed so that the game is no longer a Prisoner's Dilemma (PD) (see section 2.1), but the trivial game where both players prefer cooperation. For example, this could be the case if the profit of a group grows faster than linearly with the number of participants. Cooperative hunting of larger prey among lions has been suggested as one example [24] (but see also [18]).

Finally, explanations of cooperation in human society could take cultural as well as genetic transmission into account, and could involve, for example, explicit modeling of societal norms (e.g., [5,14,93]).

This list of scenarios is undoubtedly incomplete, and many examples may be hard to classify as one scenario or the other. Consider, for example, the case of cleaning symbiosis discussed in Trivers [98], where certain small fish (cleaners) clean larger fish (e.g., a grouper, which serves as host) of ectoparasites.

The large fish appears to have very strong barriers against feeding on the cleaners— the cleaner, which is comparable in size to the ordinary prey of the larger fish, even works in the mouth of its customer. Cleaners are identified, for example, by their swimming pattern. Species that mimic cleaners but instead bite off pieces of the fins of the large fish also exist.

This is certainly a reciprocal relationship—both species obviously benefit from it. But whether the benefit (e.g., of having parasites removed) is large enough that this is a case of an interaction in both players' short-term interest is not immediately obvious. An IPD model would have the property that a single defection by the large fish ends the game; it also fails to include evolution of signals that are clearly important. (An example of a model of mutualism where recognition is included is given by Weisbuch and Duchateau [102]).

Table 1. Payoff Matrix M for the Prisoner's Dilemma.

$$
\begin{array}{c}
\text{Player 2} \\
\begin{array}{cc}
C & D
\end{array}
\end{array}
$$

$$
\text{Player 1} \quad
\begin{array}{c}
C \\
D
\end{array}
\left(
\begin{array}{cc}
(R, R) & (S, T) \\
(T, S) & (P, P)
\end{array}
\right)
$$

In the rest of this section, we concentrate on models of the evolution of cooperation based on the IPD. The previous examples should, however, serve as a reminder that the PD by no means covers all aspects of the evolution of cooperation.

2.1 The Prisoner's Dilemma

The Prisoner's Dilemma (PD) provides a useful framework for studying how cooperation can become established in a situation where short-range maximization of individual utility leads to a collective utility (welfare) minimum. This is a two-person game where the players simultaneously choose between the two actions "cooperate" and "defect," which we denote by C and D (or equivalently 1 and 0).

The game was first studied by Flood and Dresher at Rand Corporation in 1950 [30]. (An account of the first iterated Prisoner's Dilemma-like game played can also be found in Poundstone [85].) The name is derived from an anecdote by Tucker, which goes more or less as follows:

Two persons have been caught, suspected of having committed a crime together. Unless one of them confesses, there is no evidence to sentence them. The prosecutor offers a reward to the one that confesses; the other will in this case get a severe sentence. If both confess, they will be imprisoned, but for a shorter time. If they stay quiet, they will be released in the absence of evidence.

The results of the players' choices are quantified by the payoff matrix of Figure 1. Here R is the reward for mutual cooperation (i.e., keeping quiet), and T is the temptation to defect against a cooperating opponent, who then gets the sucker's payoff S. In the case of mutual defection, both get the penalty P. The PD is defined by the inequalities $T > R > P > S$ and $2R > T + S$. $R = 3$, $T = 5$, $S = 0$, and $P = 1$ is a common choice in the literature. The PD is a non-zero-sum game, that is, the total score distributed among the players depends on the actions chosen.

If the game is only played once, a player maximizes her score by defecting, regardless of the move of the opponent. Thus, two rational players share the lowest total payoff for mutual defection. This is the Nash equilibrium of economic theory—none of the players is willing to change to cooperation.

If, on the other hand, the game is played more than once, that is, there is a high probability that a player encounters the same opponent again, cooperating strategies may be more successful. (We assume that the objective is maximizing the score, rather than beating the opponent.) This is the iterated Prisoner's Dilemma (IPD).

A computer tournament arranged by Axelrod [3–5,8] showed that a very good strategy is given by cooperating unless your opponent defected in the previous round. This strategy that mimics the opponent's last action is called Tit-for-Tat (TfT).

For a game consisting of a known fixed number of rounds, the cooperative behavior is destabilized [87]. In the last round, the single-round dilemma appears, and both players should defect—but then the same reasoning applies to the next to last round, and so on. In this particular situation, defection is the unique Nash equilibrium. This somewhat pathological behavior can be avoided by considering an infinitely iterated game or by choosing the number of rounds stochastically.

One complicating factor in a repeated game is the possibility of mistakes by the players (noise). These could be either mistakes where the action performed by a player is different from the intended one, or misinterpretations of the opponent's action (which leads to the players seeing different histories).

Noise in the iterated game destroys the cooperative pattern between two TfT players. An accidental defection causes a sequence of alternating revenges; another mistake can then result in either mutual cooperation or defection. In the infinitely iterated game, the score for TfT playing against itself drops from R to $(R + S + T + P)/4$ for any non-zero noise level.

A strategy that defects only if the opponent defects twice in a row (Tit-for-two-Tats, Tf2T) is stable against a low noise rate but can be exploited by a strategy that cooperates only every second round. Another possibility is the strategy called Simpleton by Rapoport and Chammah [87]: change action if the score received in the previous round was less than R, that is, cooperate when the actions of the previous round are identical. For an accidental defection D* during a period of mutual cooperation, the players return to cooperation after a single round of mutual defection, that is, $(\ldots, CC, CC, CD^*, DD, CC, CC, \ldots)$.

Whether this strategy can be exploited or not depends on the payoff matrix. When $T + P < 2R$ (to 0th order in the mistake probability p_{err}), defection scores less than cooperation against Simpleton; for the standard parameter values, equality holds, and Simpleton can be exploited by uncooperative strategies.

The strategies discussed so far depend only on a finite portion of the history of the game. TfT, Simpleton, and Tf2T can be classified in terms of the maximal number of history bits used by the strategy as memory 1, 2, and 3, respectively. They are also deterministic, which means that the history determines the action uniquely. Some successful deterministic strategies of higher memory will be discussed below.

A strategy that makes a stochastic choice of action with probabilities depending on the history is called probabilistic. A TfT-like strategy that forgives defections with a suitably tuned probability can both resist exploitation and cooperate with its own kind in a manner stable against accidental defections [69,75]. Probabilistic strategies with tunable random number generators appear to be rare in nature, however.

The PD has been applied to explain the emergence of altruistic behavior in a number of situations, both in biology and in human society.

Axelrod [5] discusses cooperative behavior between British/French and German soldiers in the trench warfare of World War I. During the first years of the war, the same units faced each other for long periods, which placed them in a situation reminiscent of an IPD, and a TfT behavior was established (quotation from Hay [37]): "It would be child's play to shell the road behind the enemy's trenches, crowded as it must be with ration wagons and water carts, into a bloodstained wilderness ... but on the whole there is silence. After all, if you prevent your enemy from drawing his rations, his remedy is simple; he will prevent you from drawing yours."

In many other applications to human society, it is natural to consider a similar game with a larger number of players—an n-person PD. One situation where this occurs is in the sharing of a common resource (the tragedy of the commons), such as air and water in an environmental context.

Another situation, where cooperation is a less desirable outcome, is an oligopoly consisting of a small number of firms that sell almost identical products (such as coffee, gasoline, or airline tickets), and compete by adjusting prices (e.g., [57]). Two strategy tournaments for this situation modeled by a three-person generalized PD with continuous actions were organized at MIT by Fader and Hauser; see [28] for details.

Game theory [100, 101] has found a number of applications in biology [62]. Some cases where interpretations of altruistic behavior in terms of the PD have been attempted are food (blood) sharing among vampire bats [103,104], interactions between breeding adults and nonbreeders in tree swallows [53], and cooperative inspection of approaching predators in small fish such as sticklebacks [66]. The identification of the game and strategy followed (e.g., [67,76]) is often somewhat uncertain in these examples.

In biological applications of game theory, the analysis has often focused on finding evolutionarily stable strategies. An evolutionarily stable strategy (ESS) [62] is a strategy that cannot be invaded by any other strategy present in arbitrarily small amounts. (Other, less intuitive definitions involving invasion by a group of strategies also appear in the literature [13].) A distinction is often made between the case where strategies exist that achieve equal scores to the strategy in question, and can invade through genetic drift, and the case where a strategy dominates strictly.

In the PD, a number of results about ESSs are known: In the error-free case, no deterministic strategy or finite mixture of such can be an ESS in the infinitely iterated game [13,29]; for general probabilistic strategies, the same result has been shown except in the still open case of no discounting of the future [54]. When mistakes occur, ESSs can exist ([12]; see also later).

An analysis of a system in terms of evolutionary stability should not be viewed as complete. Knowledge of the fixed points of a dynamical system and their stability is not the same as a complete understanding of the system. The artificial life perspective could contribute to a greater understanding of the evolutionary dynamics of many different systems.

Let us finally remark that in some of the evolutionary models discussed later, the PD provides not only a model of the evolution of cooperation, but it also generates an interesting example of a complex coevolutionary landscape [44, 71], which can serve as a simple prototype model for the study of coevolutionary phenomena.

2.2 Evolutionary Dynamics

Evolutionary dynamics can be imposed on the space of strategies by viewing strategies as interacting individuals in a population. All pairwise interactions in the population could be included, or individuals could interact only with some subset of the population, such as their neighbors in space. Through these interactions, each individual receives a score that represents the success in the game. We can introduce population dynamics by letting successful strategies produce more offspring in the next generation. If strategies are represented as individuals, births and deaths could be given by a stochastic process. Species could also be represented by their population size; in this case the dynamics is given by a set of differential equations.

An evolutionary process requires a mechanism for generating variation as well as a mechanism for selection. This can be arranged by including mutations in the step where strategies are reproduced. The exact nature of these will depend on the representation scheme used.

A number of evolutionary simulations of this type have been performed for the IPD: Axelrod [6] applied a genetic algorithm (e.g., [38]) to evolve PD strategies of fixed memory length 6. The strategies played games of 151 rounds against eight selected strategies from his tournament [5]. A coevolutionary simulation, in which the strategies played against each other, was also discussed.

In another experiment, Miller [68] represented strategies as 15-state finite automata with 148-bit genotypes. Here a coevolutionary model, where each generation was evaluated by playing all pairwise games, was studied more extensively. A population of 30 individuals was followed for 50 generations; games consisted of 150 rounds. Three cases were studied: perfect information, and a probability for misunderstanding of 0.01 or 0.05. No successful error-correcting strategies were discovered, possibly because of the very short evolutionary time scale of the simulations.

Several other experiments of this kind have been performed. (We are probably not aware of them all; we also do not attempt to discuss models of dynamics in strategy spaces containing only a small number of strategies.) Interesting examples are, for example, the work by Fujiki and Dickinson [32], who used a representation in terms of Lisp programs (a representation later used by Koza in his genetic programming approach [46]), the work by Marks [57] where strategies for the three-person generalized PD discussed earlier also were considered, and work by Fogel [31] which suggested that the initial moves in the game may become a tag that allows strategies to recognize each other.

A model introduced by one of us [49] uses the infinitely IPD with noise as an interaction between individuals and considers the evolution of deterministic finite memory strategies with an initial population containing only memory 1 strategies. The memory length is allowed to change through neutral gene duplications and split mutations.

The genomes in the model represent strategies in the game, which determine the next move of a player given the history $h = ((x_0, y_0), \ldots, (x_t, y_t))$ of the game. Here (x_t, y_t) are the moves of the player and the opponent at time t. We consider deterministic strategies of finite memory $m \geq 0$. For m even, the strategy depends on the last $m/2$ moves of both players; for m odd on the last $[\frac{m+1}{2}]$ moves of the opponent and the last $[\frac{m-1}{2}]$ moves of the player herself.

If we let 1 denote the action C, and 0 the action D, a strategy of memory m can be represented as a binary string s of length 2^m (see Figure 1).

In the reproduction of a strategy, three types of mutations can occur: point mutations, gene duplications, and split mutations. Point mutations flip single bits in the genome with frequency p_{mut}. Gene duplications increase the memory from m to $m + 1$ (with frequency p_{dupl}) while leaving the actual strategy unchanged. This corresponds to duplicating the genome, for example, $1011 \rightarrow 10111011$. Gene duplication is a neutral mutation, which increases the size of the evolutionary search space without affecting the phenotype. Additional point mutations can then give rise to new strategies without shorter memory equivalents. Finally, the split mutation keeps only a randomly chosen half of the genome with frequency p_{split}.

Each strategy i has a real-valued population size x_i. The population densities evolve in time according to

$$\Delta x_i = \alpha x_i \left(\sum_j g_{ij} x_j - \Phi \right), \tag{1}$$

where the term (identical to the average score of the population)

$$\Phi = \sum_{i,j} g_{ij} x_i x_j \tag{2}$$

ensures that the total population stays constant.

The interaction coefficient g_{ij} is the score obtained when strategy i plays the noisy infinitely iterated PD against strategy j. The infinite game can be viewed as a Markov chain of finite memory, which means that the result of the game can be calculated analytically. (See Lindgren [49] for details.)

At each time step, mutations act in the way described previously. In this way new species can be introduced. Species are removed from the system if their population falls below a threshold value.

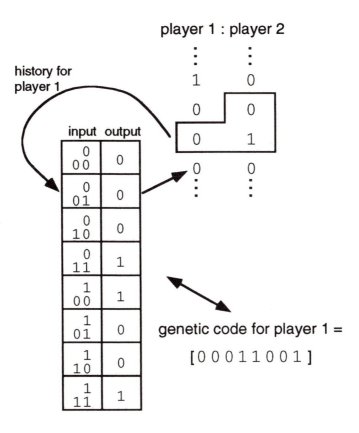

Figure 1. The representation of strategies in the model of Lindgren [49] is illustrated for the memory 3 strategy 00011001.

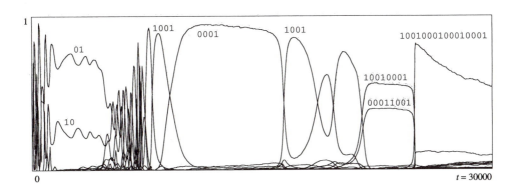

Figure 2. A typical simulation of the coevolving strategy model of Lindgren [49]; 30,000 generations of the simulation are shown.

A typical example of a simulation of the model is shown in Figure 2. In general, a succession of stable periods separated by periods of rapid evolution are seen (reminiscent of punctuated equilibria [26]).

Cooperation can be observed at several levels in the model. The elementary actions C and D represent cooperation at the lowest level. In an application of the PD, they would be an abstraction of behavior with a more interesting substructure. The average score tends to increase in the time evolution (although not monotonically), which indicates an increasing degree of cooperation at the level of elementary actions.

But we also observe cooperative behavior at the level of strategies. Consider, for example, the first period of stasis, where TfT (01) and ATfT (10) coexist. This coexistence is possible because TfT suppresses invasion attempts by AllD (00), which otherwise would outcompete ATfT, and similarly ATfT suppresses invasion attempts by AllC (11), which could outcompete TfT. In other words, the strategies cooperate through indirect effects where one suppresses the predators of the other, and vice versa. However, TfT and ATfT do not manage to get very high scores in the game.

The stable period at memory 3 is dominated by a symbiotic pair of strategies. This is an example of mutualism where the strategies achieve a fairly high score by cooperating to correct errors [49], something they cannot do when interacting with themselves.

The evolution of error correcting mechanisms is an interesting example of emergent higher level behavior in the model. The first error-correcting strategy that appears in the simulations is 1001 or Simpleton, which was discussed earlier. In case of an accidental defection, two strategies of this type return to cooperation after a single round of mutual defection. For the standard payoff matrix, this behavior is too forgiving, and defectors can invade. A strategy that defects twice before returning to cooperation, however, is sufficiently punishing to avoid exploitation.

This type of strategy requires memory 4 (a history of two rounds) and often appears as a very stable final state for the standard parameter values (see Figure 2). We denote this strategy type s_1; it is defined by fixing seven of the positions in the genome to 1xx10xxx0xxxx001, where the symbol x stands for undetermined actions that occur infrequently (order p_{err}^2) when s_1 plays itself. Several strategies that fit this template can in fact be shown to be ESSs (under reasonable assumptions about the allowed class of invading strategies for the infinite game).

The choices of representation and adaptive moves in this model, of course, are not unique. Another choice was made in the model studied by Ikegami [40], where strategies were represented as trees of unequal depth representing all contexts where the strategy defects. Mutations included genetic fusion [43], where a tree is attached to a leaf of another. This choice of representation favors the evolution of noncooperative strategies.

Probabilistic strategies could also be considered. Nowak and Sigmund [75,76] have studied the coevolution of probabilistic strategies in the memory 1 and memory 2 subspaces, respectively.

Extensions of the simple PD model are also possible, for example, in the form of tags and signals, communication, and control over whom to play. Stanley, Ashlock, and Tesfatsion [94] have studied evolution of strategies for the noise-free IPD, where strategies have the option of choosing and refusing partners depending on the results of the games between them. Models of the evolution of cooperation that go beyond the standard framework of the IPD, both by extending it and by focusing more in detail on actual mechanisms of interaction and cooperation so that a PD appears implicitly, are certainly worth pursuing.

2.3 Spatial Games

The fact that the physical world has three spatial dimensions did not enter into the evolutionary models discussed in the previous section. In some cases, this may be a reasonable approximation—we could consider organisms mobile enough that in a generation, all individuals in the population have time to interact with each other.

Table 2. Different Paradigms for Spatial Dynamics.

individuals

	discrete	continuous
discrete	CA	CML
continuous	Gas/Swarm	PDE

space-time

But in general the environment may provide barriers so that different evolutionary paths can be explored in different regions of the world, and it is essential to take spatial effects into account. In the context of explaining speciation, Mayr [63, 64] has argued for the importance of spatial separation (see also [26]). A typical case would involve a small founder population capable of rapid evolution separated off from the region inhabited by the majority of its species, for example, on an island.

The spatiotemporal dynamics of the system can also be important. Even in a homogenous environment, the dynamics of the system could generate spatial structure, which could influence evolutionary processes. As an example, Boerlijst and Hogeweg [10,11] studied a cellular automaton model of the hypercycle model of Eigen and Schuster [25] and found spiral wave dynamics that increased the stability against parasites. Selection for certain altruistic properties (catalytic support and faster decay rates) was observed—the introduction of spatial degrees of freedom allows localized structures to form, and selection can take place at the level of these structures as well.

The spatial dynamics could also affect the stability of ecological systems and in that way influence evolutionary processes. As an example, space-time chaos can allow locally unstable systems to persist with essentially constant global population levels (e.g., [35]).

Several different ways of introducing spatial degrees of freedom can be imagined. In Figure 2.3 we have classified these into four groups, depending on whether space and time are treated as continuous or discrete, and whether we consider separate individuals or a continuous local population density.

Let us first consider the case with discrete individuals and discrete space and time. In this case we obtain models that are essentially cellular automata (CA) (e.g., [107]) or lattice Monte Carlo simulations, depending on whether sites are updated simultaneously or asynchronously in random order.

One class of lattice games is obtained in the following way: Let each lattice site be occupied by a single strategy; empty lattice sites are not allowed. All lattice sites are updated simultaneously in the following manner: First, the score of a site is calculated as the sum of the average scores obtained when the strategy at the site plays the infinitely iterated game against the strategies in the neighborhood N_1 (e.g., the four nearest neighbors on a square lattice).

The score of a site is then compared to the scores in a neighborhood N_2 (e.g., the von

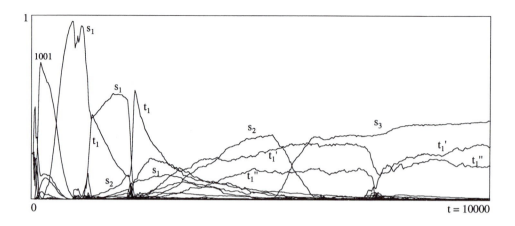

Figure 3. Species density curves from a simulation of the spatial version of coevolution of strategies for the iterated PD discussed in the text. The first 10,000 generations of the simulation are shown.

Neumann neighborhood consisting of the site itself and its four nearest neighbors), and the highest scoring strategy in N_2 is adopted at the site at the next time step. Ties are broken at random. In an evolutionary model, mutations can occur in the reproduction.

Because the scores of the nearest neighbors in turn depend on the strategies of their neighbors, the strategy at a certain site is updated depending on the strategies in a neighborhood of radius 2. If the set of allowed strategies is finite, the model is a cellular automaton.

Cellular automaton models of this kind (with a fixed set of strategies and without evolution) were introduced by Axelrod [5]. He found that the ranking of the strategies submitted to his second tournament changed completely in the spatial case. Complicated patterns of coexisting AllD and TfT players were also observed. In Nowak and May [72, 73] the dynamics of the memoryless strategies AllC and AllD on a lattice was studied in more detail; in particular spatiotemporal chaos was observed. A model closely related to a lattice PD was also studied in Wilson, Pollack, and Dugatkin [105].

A different approach to spatial games is to let all players on the lattice make simultaneous moves and to let strategies depend on the actions in a neighborhood on the lattice, which gives a genuine n-person game. This approach has been investigated by Matsuo and coworkers [58,1].

We [51] studied a spatial evolutionary model where the spatiotemporal dynamics was introduced as described earlier. The representation of strategies and adaptive moves were identical to those of Lindgren [49] (see previous section).

Figure 3 shows an example of a simulation of this model. The payoff matrix is given by the standard parameter values $(R, S, T, P) = (3, 0, 5, 1)$, the error rate is $p_{err} = 0.01$, and the mutation rates are $p_{mut} = 0.002$, and $p_{dupl} = p_{split} = 0.001$. In the initial state, the four memory 1 strategies appear with equal probability. The lattice size is 128×128.

This simulation shows several important differences between the spatial model and the differential equation model discussed above (see Figure 2), which from a physicist's perspective could be viewed as a mean-field approximation to the spatial model. At memory 1, a frozen state of AllC and AllD is found, where TfT is maintained at significant levels by spreading waves of activity generated by mutations from AllD to TfT (see Figure 4d). At memory 2, the strategy 1001 (Simpleton) takes over most of the lattice. The noncooperative strategies 00 and 0001 can coexist with 1001 at low levels by forming a network of mostly diagonal lines. In the mean-field model, the noncooperative strategy 0001 dominates at memory 2; on the lattice this strategy can only exploit its nearest neighbors, and the cooperative strategy 1001 has an advantage.

No analog of the symbiotic pair of strategies seen at memory 3 in Figure 2 is found in the spatial model. Memory 4 strategies of type s_1 often appear on the lattice as well; in the simulation shown in Figure 3, we see two closely related memory 4 strategies of this type (s_1 and s_2) appear, and then a similar memory 5 strategy s_3. In many simulations, the strategy s_3 takes over the entire lattice and forms a homogenous state. In Figure 3, however, we find another strategy $t_1 = 1001000000001111$ and some closely related strategies that are able to coexist with s_3. This coexistence is not observed in the mean field model.

An accidental defection in a game between two strategies of type t_1 results in the sequence $(\ldots, CC, CD^*, CC, DD, CC, CC, \ldots)$. The advantage of this pattern is that it reduces the score less than the error-correcting mechanism of, for example, s_2 or s_3. The strategy t_1 is at the same time more resistant than 1001 to exploitation by defectors.

This example illustrates how the introduction of spatial degrees of freedom allows coexistence of strategies through the formation of stable spatial domains.

For other values for the payoff matrix, a rich variety of dynamical behavior is observed. (See Lindgren and Nordahl [51] for a detailed description.) Even if we restrict ourselves to the space of memory 1 strategies, a number of different regions of qualitatively different spatiotemporal dynamics are found (typically with discontinuous transitions at the boundaries between them). Some examples of fixed-time configurations from simulations with memory 1 are shown in Figure 4. The payoff matrix can always be transformed to the normal form $(R, S, T, P) = (1, 0, p, q)$; the standard parameter values correspond to $(p, q) = (5/3, 1/3)$. The behavior in this case is similar to Figure 4d.

Figure 4a has $(p, q) = (1.4, 0.05)$. In this region we find spatiotemporal chaos involving AllD, TfT, and AllC. In Figure 4c we have $(p, q) = (1.9, 0.8)$. Here we find rather irregular wave activity and expanding patches with all four memory 1 strategies present. By decreasing q, we move into a region dominated by spiral waves (which break into smaller fragments because of mutations) (see Figure 4b).

Varying the payoff matrix also affects the nature of the evolutionary dynamics. A tendency toward constancy of the qualitative nature of the spatiotemporal dynamics during the evolutionary process is seen, so that one may, for example, have strategies that evolve toward longer memory while the dynamics constantly is spatiotemporally chaotic [51].

One of the more important properties of the spatial model is its capacity to support a larger diversity of species than the ordinary coevolution model. In particular, one can find very complex frozen states where a large number of different frozen patches coexist.

These are somewhat reminiscent of plant communities. There are around $3 \cdot 10^5$ known plant species on earth, which all depend on a quite small number of resources. This number is much larger than allowed by results based on ordinary population dynamics, which limit the number of species in terms of the number of resources [48, 55]. Static explanations in terms of varying equilibria in a heterogenous environment have been suggested (e.g., [96]). One may speculate that dynamical processes could generate diversity even in a homogenous spatial system.

Another option for modeling the spatiotemporal dynamics is to keep the discrete spatial lattice and discrete time, but to consider continuous population densities at each site. The sites could be coupled by diffusion. In this way one obtains a coupled map lattice (CML) (e.g., [43]), possibly with a variable number of degrees of freedom at each site if some mechanism for adding and deleting species is included. We have

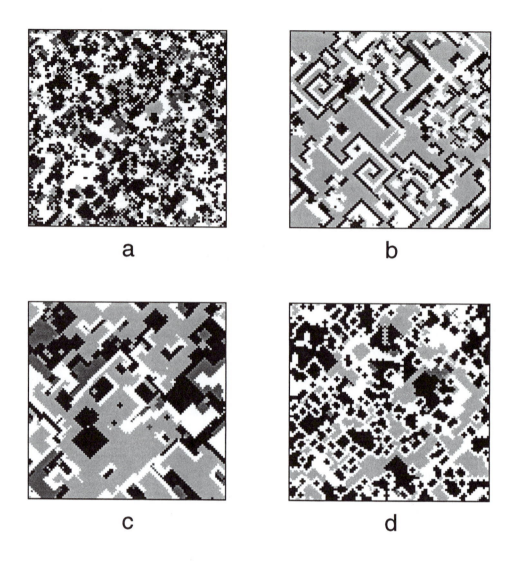

Figure 4. Examples of typical configurations from simulations with memory 1 strategies and a payoff matrix given by (a) $(p, q) = (1.4, 0.05)$, (b) $(p, q) = (1.9, 0.2)$, (c) $(p, q) = (1.9, 0.8)$, (d) $(p, q) = (1.4, 0.5)$. The coding of strategies is such that from light to dark we have the order AllD, TfT, ATfT, and AllC.

studied a one-dimensional model with a copy of the model of Lindgren [49] at each site [50]. For the standard payoff matrix, the dynamics of this system is rather similar to the mean-field model—successful new strategies typically propagate and take over the entire lattice as soon as they are discovered at one site.

The third option for modeling spatiotemporal dynamics is in terms of partial differential equations (PDE). For a finite number of strategies, one could consider the reaction-diffusion-like system obtained by adding a diffusion term to equation 1:

$$\partial_t x_i = \alpha x_i \left(\sum_j g_{ij} x_j - \Phi \right) + \beta \Delta x_i. \tag{3}$$

Finally, we have the case of moving or diffusing individuals in continuous space. (A case suitable for a Swarm simulation—studies of systems with strategies for motion as well as the game, e.g, avoidance behavior, would be particularly interesting.) We are not aware of any simulation of a spatial game of this kind.

Some recent work in the biology literature, however, is closely related—Enquist and Leimar [27] discussed a system where individuals form temporary associations while playing the game. Defectors are rejected after a short time compared to the average duration of a game between two cooperators and then search for a new partner to exploit. As expected, increased mobility favors defectors, which then more easily can find a new victim. Data from sphecid wasps, where in some species females cooperate by sharing nests, show that cooperation is less likely in species that form large population aggregations, which lowers the search time for defectors.

Unfortunately these authors only consider a mean-field approximation, not the actual spatial system, and only discuss the relative stability of a few chosen strategies instead of performing an evolutionary simulation. If an actual spatial system with local reproductive dynamics was studied, it is conceivable that domain formation could occur, so that mean field theory would not be a good approximation. This would favor cooperation.

3   Artificial Community Structure

Are ecological communities structured entities or just random collections of species that respond independently to the environment? Questions of this kind can be addressed through field studies of real ecosystems, through laboratory experiments that assemble artificial ecologies of real organisms and by making mathematical models.

In our opinion, there is also a niche for artificial life in the study of community structure. By creating artificial ecologies out of artificial rather than real organisms, many constraints on real experiments and field studies can be circumvented. Real ecological studies are severely limited in space and time. (See Pimm [82] for a discussion of time and length scales accessible and nonaccessible in ecological, biogeographical, and paleontological studies.) Given enough computer resources, artificial ecologies could be studied on a much wider range of scales. Artificial ecosystems can also be manipulated in many ways that are impossible for real communities.

On the other hand, compared with simple mathematical models, which may summarize the interaction between two species in terms of two real numbers as in the Lotka-Volterra approach, artificial ecologies could capture much more of the complexity of interactions in real biological systems. Individual variability can enter in a natural way; learning and individual adaptation can also be included.

As an example of the complexity of interactions, think of herbivores interacting with a plant community [41]. Not only do plants and trees provide food for the herbivore, they also provide shelter from sun and wind, escape routes and places to hide from predators, and branches and twigs to make nests and squats from. The grazing of herbivores also affects the plant community: Defoliation can stimulate grasses and trees to produce more leaves; dispersal of fruits, nuts, and seeds by herbivores may affect the spatial structure of the plant community. Apart from direct interactions, herbivores may interact indirectly with other herbivores through their effects on the vegetation, both by reducing resources for other species and by providing access to them (e.g., when elephants fell whole trees). Other indirect interactions may involve changing the risk of predation for other species. Larger species avoid predators by detecting them at a distance and benefit from reduced cover. On the other hand, smaller species that avoid predators by hiding would benefit from increased cover.

A crude classification of the interactions between species would label interactions depending on the signs of the couplings in an imagined set of Lotka-Volterra equations: predation, competition, and mutualism (if one assumes that all couplings are nonzero). In many cases, studies of community structure take only who-eats-whom into account for a number of exceptions (see Kawanabe et al. [45]). Our own approach has been rather different: Starting out from models of the evolution of cooperation, which provide complex interactions between individuals, we then attempt to extend the model to describe predation and resource flow.

In the next two sections, we discuss food webs and simple models of community structure. However, our own goal is not to make models of food webs. Instead, we attempt to build simple artificial ecologies with some degree of biological plausibility, and food webs are only one example of observables that could be measured (although a rather useful example, because a reasonable amount of experimental data exist, and a number of statistical regularities in the data have been suggested; see section 3.1).

Another issue that needs to be considered if artificial life models are going to make contributions to biology is that of physical realism. Real ecosystems are subject to constraints such as conservation of energy and matter. Many biological scaling laws that involve the body size of organisms (see, e.g., Johnson [42] for an overview) have a physical basis, even if they are not directly derivable from physical scaling.

In the coevolving strategy models of the previous section, there are no obvious conserved quantities, and who-eats-whom to some extent becomes a matter of interpretation. In principle, these models could be equally relevant to ecology, but observables related to energy flow are not easily studied. In section 3.3, we describe a model where resources are derived from an external environment, and the result of a game determines their distribution. We also discuss other artificial life models where resources have been explicitly included.

3.1 Food Webs

A food web is a graphical representation of who-eats-whom in an ecological community. In most cases food webs are compiled in a qualitative way by ecologists, so that a (directed) link from A to B is present if and only if species B eats species A. Quantitative data showing the relative importance of different links can sometimes also be found in the literature.

An example of an experimental food web from the literature is shown in Figure 5 (redrawn from Niering [70]), which shows the most significant feeding relationships among the species on the Kapingamarangi Atoll in Micronesia. This web has some features in common with many reported webs. Many species with similar feeding habits have been clustered into groups (e.g., insects), and there is a cutoff so that rare trophic links are not included (as an example, the fact that Polynesian rats occasionally feed on newly hatched sea turtles is not included).

A food web is obviously not a complete description of the community or even of the resource flow in the system. But food webs may still be useful observables to consider, both for real and artificial ecologies. A number of statistical regularities have been claimed to exist in the structure of food webs (e.g., [16, 81]):

- The average number of trophic links L is approximately proportional to the number of species S, $L \sim k \cdot S^{1+\epsilon}$, where ϵ is small.

- The fractions of top predators, intermediate species, and basal species are approximately constant across webs.

- The fractions of trophic linkages of different types: top–intermediate, top–bottom,

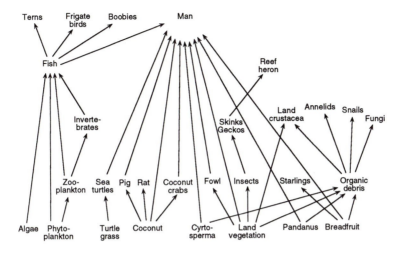

Figure 5. Food web from the Kapingamarangi atoll in Micronesia, drawn using the data of Niering [70].

intermediate–intermediate, and intermediate–bottom are also approximatively constant across webs.

- Averages of maximal food chain length are typically fairly low (approximately 3–4) and do not appear to depend on the productivity of the environment [80]. On the other hand, they do depend on the dimensionality of the environment; three-dimensional environments, such as pelagic water columns and forest canopies, appear to have longer food chains than do two-dimensional environments, such as grasslands and intertidal zones.

- Cycles are rare. Food webs in the literature typically do not include cycles due to cannibalism or cycles due to the presence of decomposers.

- Food webs can often be represented as interval graphs, that is, graphs that represent how a set of subintervals of the real line overlap each other.

Critiques of food web theory can be found, for example, in Paine [77] and Polis [83]. Most published food webs contain a fairly limited number of species, and trophically similar species are often considered as groups. Experimental studies that reflect more of the complexity of real ecosystems (e.g., [83, 106]) are likely to change some of these conclusions.

An example of a recent experimental study that disagrees with the link-species scaling law is the work by Havens [36], where power law scaling with $L \sim k \cdot S^{1.4}$ was found in a study of communities in small lakes and ponds. In this case the webs were resolved down to genus and species, but the interactions were not measured. Instead, diet information from other sources was used, which makes comparisons with other studies difficult. Multivariable scaling that also involves resolution should be investigated in this context.

The study of artificial ecologies might be useful in sorting out which regularities are real and which are artifacts of experimental procedures, because data are more easily available, and the artificial ecosystems can be freely manipulated.

In these cases, quantitative comparisons between real and artificial communities can be made via scaling laws. There are other types of statistical regularities in ecological systems where similar comparisons can be made. One of the most well known is the area-species law (e.g., [56]), a power law for the number of species on an island as a function of its area, $S \sim c \cdot A^z$, with an exponent $z \approx 0.3$. (The exponent does not appear to be universal.) Under certain assumptions, this power law can be related to a log-normal distribution of population abundances [61, 86]. Regularities in the patterns of resource flows have also been suggested [65].

3.2   Community Models

In this section we briefly discuss some food web and community assembly models that have been studied in the literature. These models fall into two classes: One could consider only static patterns (e.g., food webs), or one could attempt to model the dynamic process that creates these patterns.

An example of a model of the first kind is the cascade model of Cohen et al. [15,16]. This model essentially assumes that food webs are random feed-forward networks. This allows many of their statistical properties to be calculated analytically. No dynamics is involved, just assumptions about the probability measure on the space of webs (although extensions involving population dynamics have been studied [17]).

The work by Gardner and Ashby [33], May [59, 60], and others on the relation between complexity and stability led to some work on the dynamics of communities. If large systems with randomly generated interactions between species typically are unstable (as claimed by May), is it possible that communities generated by more realistic assembly processes would be more stable?

A number of authors (e.g., [84, 89, 90, 97, 108]) studied models where species were removed from and/or added to the system according to various principles (which unfortunately did not include integration of the population dynamics). Increased stability was typically found. Only more recently has integration of the Lotka-Volterra equations been used in this context [95]. Comparisons between communities structured by invasion and by coevolution were also attempted [91, 92].

More recent work (both theoretical and experimental) by Drake and others [20–23, 74, 82] has focused more on the dynamics of the assembly process. Are there multiple attractors for the assembly dynamics depending on the order in which species are introduced? What is the distribution of local extinction events caused by invasion, and is there a connection to self-organized criticality?

The interactions between species in these models are in many cases obtained by choosing invading species at random from a large, predefined food web. In artificial life models, one would in most cases design a reasonable interaction between species in a simple artificial world; a food web then emerges in a natural way from the underlying interaction (if one assumes that it includes some type of predation). Such models could also enable us to study the interplay between coevolution and spatial dispersal of species without making too many oversimplifying assumptions.

3.3   Artificial Ecologies

Models such as the coevolving strategy model described earlier can be interpreted as very simple artificial ecologies, where the result of the game directly determines the interaction between species. However, as we have pointed out before, the notions of resources and conservation laws are missing in these models (as well as in various coevolutionary landscape models [9, 44, 71]).

Explicit resource flows do appear in a number of artificial life models. Some of these may still not have any immediate ecological interpretation, for example, in the case of more ambitious models where the notion of individuality is intended to be an emergent

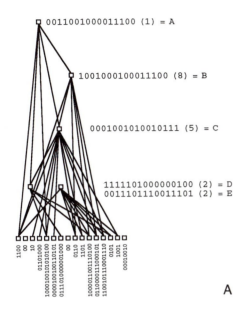

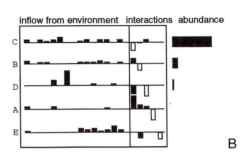

Figure 6. The food web and energy flow matrix after 33,600 generations in a simulation of model I of Lindgren and Nordahl [52]. The first part of the histogram represents energy inflows from the environment (always positive); the second energy flows between species (signs depend on the directions of the flows). The open bars show the energy dissipation for each species. The magnitude of the flow is shown relative to the total energy flow for the species in question.

property rather than being imposed from the outside (as in the models of Rasmussen and coworkers [87]). Examples of models with a more direct ecological interpretation include the models of Lindgren and Nordahl [52], Holland's Echo [38,39], the model studied by Johnson [42], and many more.

The interactions between individuals in the first model of Lindgren and Nordahl [52] (Model 1) are still based on the iterated Prisoner's Dilemma, but the result of the game now determines the distribution of a resource e ("energy"). Each strategy stores a certain amount of energy; the energy transfered in the interaction between two strategies is proportional to the score difference in the game between them (up to cutoff terms).

The system lives in an external environment consisting of a number of fixed strategies; energy can flow into the system as a result of playing the game against the environment strategies.

The conservation of energy in the interaction turns the game into a zero-sum game. The cooperative effects of the PD are reintroduced by letting the dissipation of energy for each species depend on the score in the game, so that high-scoring strategies utilize their resources more efficiently.

Figure 6 shows an example of a food web and matrix of energy flow between species generated in a simulation of this model. The species seen in the web are trophic species, that is, equivalence classes of genomes that interact in approximately the same way with all other genomes. Some of the proposed statistical features of real food webs, such as the approximately linear link-species scaling, are nicely reproduced by the model (see Lindgren & Nordahl [52]).

In the second model of Lindgren and Nordahl [52], the genomes consist of three parts: a strategy gene, a gene that indicates preferences for whom to play, and a tag gene on which other organisms base their choice. In this way a more distinct difference between genotype and phenotype is introduced—the tag gene can be regarded as the "visual appearance" of an organism. This model allows species to develop a higher degree of specificity in their dietary preferences. It also allows the evolution of phenomena such as camouflaged predators that hide among the environment strategies, and mimicry.

Introducing spatial degrees of freedom is at least as important in these models as in the ordinary model for coevolution of strategies. With a model that allows interactions with an external environment, phenomena that depend on having a heterogenous environment can be modeled. Extensions to cases with several different resources would also be interesting.

These models are rather similar in spirit to Holland's Echo [38, 39]—we use a more complex interaction between individuals (the IPD instead of simple pattern matching); Echo, on the other hand, has more emphasized multiple resources.

Another simpler model where hierarchical food webs are observed is that of Johnson [42]. This model incorporates some physical constraints by assigning a body size to each organism. The movement rate and metabolic costs scale as (externally imposed) power laws as function of body size. Organisms have genetically determined food preferences among the species smaller than the organism itself. The dynamics of the system is a Monte Carlo simulation, where individuals interact and move by diffusion on a lattice. This model could be viewed as a natural way of extending the cascade model of Cohen et al. to a dynamical system with discrete individuals.

4 Discussion

The problem of understanding the evolution of cooperation (at least when covered by the IPD) is a case where methods that could be classified as artificial life, in particular coevolutionary simulations, already have yielded significant results. We believe that in the future, an understanding of the underlying evolutionary dynamics will be reached for many biological problems. All problems that today are analyzed in terms of game theory and ESS are obvious candidates, but also many other problems where this approach is less suitable. The evolution of flocking behavior in birds is one example. In the case of understanding community structure, the ability to perform a large number of simulations and to sort out statistical patterns will be important.

Acknowledgments

This work was supported by the Swedish Natural Science Research Council.

References

1. Adachi, N., & Matsuo, K. (1992). Ecological dynamics of strategic species in Game World. *FUJITSU Scientific and Technical Journal, 28*, 543–558.

2. Andersson, M. (1984). The evolution of eusociality. *Annual Review of Ecology and Systematics, 15*, 165–189.

3. Axelrod, R. (1980). Effective choice in the Prisoner's Dilemma. *Journal of Conflict Resolution, 24*, 3–25.

4. Axelrod, R. (1980). More effective choice in the Prisoner's Dilemma. *Journal of Conflict Resolution, 24*, 379–403.

5. Axelrod, R. (1984). *The evolution of cooperation.* New York: Basic Books.

6. Axelrod, R. (1987). The evolution of strategies in the iterated Prisoner's Dilemma. In: L. Davis (Ed.); *Genetic algorithms and simulated annealing* (pp. 32–41). Los Altos, CA: Morgan Kaufmann.

7. Axelrod, R. (1986). Evolutionary approach to norms. *The American Political Science Review, 80,* 1095.

8. Axelrod, R., & Hamilton, W. (1981). The evolution of cooperation. *Science, 211,* 1390–1396.

9. Bak, P., Flyvbjerg, H., & Lautrup, B. (1992). Coevolution in a rugged fitness landscape. *Physical Review A, 46,* 6724–6730.

10. Boerlijst, M. C., & Hogeweg, P. (1991). Spiral wave structure in prebiotic evolution: hypercycles stable against parasites. *Physica D, 48,* 17–28.

11. Boerlijst, M. C., & Hogeweg, P. (1991). Self-structuring and selection: spiral waves as a substrate for prebiotic evolution. In: C. G. Langton, J. D. Farmer, S. Rasmussen, & C. Taylor (Eds.), *Artificial life II* (pp. 255–276). Redwood City, CA: Addison-Wesley.

12. Boyd, R. (1989). Mistakes allow evolutionary stability in the repeated Prisoner's Dilemma game. *Journal of Theoretical Biology, 136,* 47–56.

13. Boyd, R., & Lorberbaum, J. (1987). No pure strategy is evolutionarily stable in the repeated Prisoner's Dilemma game. *Nature, 327,* 58–59.

14. Boyd, R., & Richerson, P. J. (1985). *Culture and the evolutionary process.* Chicago: University of Chicago Press.

15. Cohen, J. E., & Newman, C. M. (1985). A stochastic theory of community food webs. I. Models and aggregated data. *Proceedings of the Royal Society of London [Biol], 224,* 421–448.

16. Cohen, J. E., Briand, F., & Newman, C. M. (1990). *Community food webs.* Berlin: Springer-Verlag.

17. Cohen, J. E., Luczak, T., Newman, C. M., & Zhou, Z.-M. (1990). Stochastic structure and nonlinear dynamics of food webs: qualitative stability in a Lotka-Volterra cascade model. *Proceedings of the Royal Society of London [Biol], 240,* 607–627.

18. Creel, S. (1993). Why cooperate? Game theory and kin selection. *Trends in Ecology and Evolution, 8,* 71–72.

19. Cronin, H. (1991). *The ant and the peacock.* Cambridge University Press.

20. Drake, J. A. (1988). Models of community assembly and the structure of ecological landscapes. In: T. Hallam, L. Gross, & S. Levin (Eds.) *Mathematical ecology* (pp. 584–604). Singapore: World Scientific Press.

21. Drake, J. A. (1990). The mechanisms of community assembly and succession. *Journal of Theoretical Biology, 147,* 213–233.

22. Drake, J. A. (1991). Communities as assembled structures: do rules govern patterns? *Trends in Ecology and Evolution, 5,* 159–164.

23. Drake, J. A. (1991). Community assembly mechanics and the structure of an experimental species ensemble. *American Naturalist, 137,* 1–26.

24. Dugatkin, L. A., Mesterton-Gibbs, M., & Houston, A. I. (1992). Beyond the Prisoner's Dilemma: toward models to discriminate among mechanisms of cooperation in nature. *Trends in Ecology and Evolution, 7,* 202–205.

25. Eigen, M., & Schuster, P. (1979). *The hypercycle: a principle of natural self-organization.* Berlin: Springer-Verlag.

26. Eldredge, N., & Gould, S. J. (1972). Punctuated equilibria: an alternative to phyletic gradualism. In T. J. M. Schopf (Ed.), *Models in paleobiology* (pp. 82–115). San Francisco: Freeman Cooper.

27. Enquist, M., & Leimar, O. (1993). The evolution of cooperation in mobile organisms. *Animal Behavior, 45,* 747–757.

28. Fader, P. S., & Hauser, J. R. (1988). Implicit coalitions in a generalized Prisoner's Dilemma. *Journal of Conflict Resolution, 32,* 553–582.

29. Farrell, J., & Ware, R. (1989). Evolutionary stability in the repeated Prisoner's Dilemma. *Theoretical Population Biology, 36,* 161–166.

30. Flood, M. M. (1952). *Some experimental games* (Report RM-789-1). Santa Monica, CA: The Rand Corporation.

31. Fogel, D. B. (1993). Evolving behaviors in the iterated prisoner's dilemma. *Evolutionary Computation, 1,* 77–97.

32. Fujiki, C., & Dickinson, J. (1987). Using the genetic algorithm to generate Lisp source code to solve the Prisoner's Dilemma. In J. Greffenstette (Ed.), *Genetic algorithms and their applications* (pp. 236–240). Hillsdale, NJ: Lawrence Erlbaum.

33. Gardner, M. R., & Ashby, W. R. (1970). Connectance of large dynamic (cybernetic) systems: critical values for stability. *Nature, 228,* 784.

34. Hamilton, W. D. (1964). The genetical evolution of social behaviour. *Journal of Theoretical Biology, 7,* 1–52.

35. Hassell, M. P., Comins, H. N., & May, R. M. (1991). Spatial structure and chaos in insect population dynamics. *Nature, 353,* 255–258.

36. Havens, K. (1992). Scale and structure in natural food webs. *Science, 257,* 1107–1109.

37. Hay, I. (1916). *The first hundred thousand.* London: Wm. Blackwood.

38. Holland, J. H. (1992). *Adaptation in natural and artificial systems* (2nd ed.). Cambridge, MA: The MIT Press.

39. Holland, J. H. (1993). *Echoing emergence: objectives, rough definitions, and speculations for Echo-class models.* Santa Fe Institute preprint 93-04-023.

40. Ikegami, T. (1993). *Ecology of evolutionary game strategies.* From genetic evolution to emergence of game strategies. To appear in *Physica D.*

41. Jarman, P. J. (1993). Plant communities and the social organization and community structure of herbivorous animals. In: H. Kawanabe, J. E. Cohen, & K. Iwasaki (Eds.), *Mutualism and community organization* (pp. 109–132). Oxford University Press.

42. Johnson, A. R. (1993). Evolution of a size-structured, predator-prey community. To appear In: C. G. Langton (Ed.), *Artificial life III.* Reading, MA: Addison-Wesley.

43. Kaneko, K. (1989). Pattern dynamics in spatiotemporal chaos: pattern selecton, diffusion of defect, and pattern competition intensity. *Physica D, 34,* 1–41.

44. Kauffman, S. A., & Johnsen, S. (1991). Coevolution to the edge of chaos: coupled fitness landscapes, poised states, and coevolutionary avalanches. In: C. G. Langton, J. D. Farmer, S. Rasmussen, & C. Taylor (Eds.), *Artificial life II* (pp. 325–369). Redwood City, CA: Addison-Wesley.

45. Kawanabe, H., Cohen, J. E., & Iwasaki, K. (Eds.) (1993). *Mutualism and community organization.* Oxford University Press.

46. Koza, J. R. (1992). *Genetic programming: on the programming of computers by means of natural selection.* Cambridge, MA: The MIT Press.

47. Kropotkin, P. (1902). *Mutual aid: a factor of evolution.* London.

48. Levin, S. A. (1970). Community equilibria and stability, an extension of the competitive exclusion principle. *American Naturalist, 104,* 413–423.

49. Lindgren, K. (1991). Evolutionary phenomena in simple dynamics. In: C. G. Langton, J. D. Farmer, S. Rasmussen, & C. Taylor (Eds.), *Artificial life II* (pp. 295–312). Redwood City, CA: Addison-Wesley.

50. Lindgren, K. Unpublished.

51. Lindgren, K., & Nordahl, M. G. (1993). Evolutionary dynamics of spatial games. To appear in *Physica D*.

52. Lindgren, K., & Nordahl, M. G. (1993). Artificial food webs. In C. G. Langton (Ed.), *Artificial Life III*. Addison-Wesley.

53. Lombardo, M. P. (1985). Mutual restraint in tree swallows. *Science, 227*, 1363–1365.

54. Lorberbaum, J. (1992). *No strategy is evolutionarily stable in the repeated Prisoner's Dilemma*. Preprint.

55. MacArthur, R. H., & Levins, R. (1964). Competition, habitat selection and character displacement in a patchy environment. *Proceedings of the National Academy of Sciences of the United States of America (Washington), 51*, 1207–1210.

56. MacArthur, R. H., & Wilson, E. O. (1967). *The theory of island biogeography*. Princeton, NJ: Princeton University Press.

57. Marks, R. E. (1989). Breeding hybrid strategies: optimal behavior for oligopolists. In: *Proceedings of the Third International Conference on Genetic Algorithms* (pp. 198–207). San Mateo, CA: Morgan Kauffman.

58. Matsuo, K. (1985). Ecological characteristics of strategic groups in "dilemmatic world." In *Proceedings of IEEE International Conference on Systems and Cybernetics* (pp. 1071–1075).

59. May, R. M. (1972). Will a large complex system be stable? *Nature, 238*, 413–414.

60. May, R. M. (1973). *Stability and complexity in model ecosystems*. Princeton, NJ: Princeton University Press.

61. May, R. M. (1988). How many species are there on earth? *Science, 241*, 1441–1449.

62. Maynard Smith, J. (1982). *Evolution and the theory of games*. Cambridge, UK: Cambridge University Press.

63. Mayr, E. (1954). Change of genetic environment and evolution. In J. Huxley, A. C. Hardy, & E. B. Ford (Eds.), *Evolution as a Process* (pp. 157–180). London: Allen and Unwin.

64. Mayr, E. (1976). *Evolution and the diversity of life*. Cambridge, MA: Harvard University Press.

65. McNaughton, S. J., Oesterheld, M., Frank, D. A., & Williams, K. J. (1989). Ecosystem-level patterns of primary productivity and herbivory in terrestrial habitats. *Nature, 341*, 142–144.

66. Milinski, M. (1987). Tit for Tat in sticklebacks and the evolution of cooperation. *Nature, 325*, 433–435.

67. Milinski, M. (1993). Cooperation wins and stays. *Nature, 364*, 12–13.

68. Miller, J. H. (1989). *The coevolution of automata in the repeated Prisoner's Dilemma*. Santa Fe Institute working paper 89-003.

69. Molander, P. (1985). The optimal level of generosity in a selfish, uncertain environment. *Journal of Conflict Resolution, 29*, 611–618.

70. Niering, W. A. (1963). Terrestrial ecology of Kapingamarangi Atoll, Caroline Islands. *Ecological Monographs, 33*, 131–160.

71. Nordahl, M. G. *A spin-glass model of coevolution*. Preprint.

72. Nowak, M. A., & May, R. M. (1992). Evolutionary games and spatial chaos. *Nature, 359*, 826–829.

73. Nowak, M. A., & May, R. M. (1993). The spatial dilemmas of evolution. *International Journal of Bifurcation and Chaos, 3*, 35–78.

74. Nee, S. (1990). Community construction. *Trends in Ecology and Evolution, 5*, 337–340.

75. Nowak, M. A., & Sigmund, K. (1992). Tit for tat in heterogenous populations. *Nature, 359*, 250–253.

76. Nowak, M. A., & Sigmund, K. (1993). A strategy of win-stay, lose-shift that outperforms tit-for-tat in the prisoner's dilemma game. *Nature, 364*, 56–58.

77. Paine, R. T. (1988). Food webs: road maps of interactions or grist for theoretical development? *Ecology, 69*, 1648–1654.

78. Paine, R. T. (1992). Food-web analysis through field measurement of per capita interaction strength. *Nature, 355*, 73–75.

79. Pimm, S. L. (1982). *Food webs*. London: Chapman and Hall.

80. Pimm, S. L., & Kitching, R. L. (1987). The determinants of food chain lengths. *Oikos, 50*, 302–307.

81. Pimm, S. L., Lawton, J. H., & Cohen, J. E. (1991). Food web patterns and their consequences. *Nature, 350*, 669–674.

82. Pimm, S. L. (1991). *The balance of nature?: ecological issues in the conservation of species and communities*. Chicago: The University of Chicago Press.

83. Polis, G. A. (1991). Complex trophic interactions in deserts: an empirical critique of food-web theory. *American Naturalist, 138*, 123–155.

84. Post, W. M., & Pimm, S. L. (1983). Community assembly and food web stability. *Mathematical Biosciences, 64*, 169–192.

85. Poundstone, W. (1992). *The Prisoner's Dilemma*. New York: Doubleday.

86. Preston, F. W. (1962). The canonical distribution of commonness and rarity: part I. *Ecology, 43*, 185–215; part II. *Ecology, 43*, 410–432.

87. Rapoport, A., & Chammah, A. M. (1965). *The Prisoner's Dilemma*. Ann Arbor, MI: The University of Michigan Press.

88. Rasmussen, S., Knudsen, C., & Feldberg, R. (1991). Dynamics of programmable matter. In: C. G. Langton, J. D. Farmer, S. Rasmussen, & C. Taylor (Eds.), *Artificial life II* (pp. 211–254). Redwood City, CA: Addison-Wesley.

89. Roberts, A., & Tregonning, K. (1980). The robustness of natural systems. *Nature, 288*, 265–266.

90. Robinson, J. V., & Valentine, W. D. (1979). The concepts of elasticity, invulnerability, and invadability. *Journal of Theoretical Biology, 81*, 91–104.

91. Rummel, J. D., & Roughgarden, J. (1983). Some differences between invasion-structured and coevolution-structured communities: a preliminary theoretical analysis. *Oikos, 41*, 477–486.

92. Rummel, J. D., & Roughgarden, J. (1985). A theory of faunal buildup for competition communities. *Evolution, 39*, 1009–1033.

93. Simon, H. A. (1990). A mechanism for social selection and successful altruism. *Science, 250*, 1665–1668.

94. Stanley, E. A., Ashlock, D., & Tesfatsion, L. (1993). Iterated Prisoner's Dilemma with choice and refusal of partners. To appear in C. G. Langton (Ed.), *Artificial life III*, Reading, MA: Addison-Wesley.

95. Taylor, P. J. (1988). The construction and turnover of complex community models having generalized Lotka-Volterra dynamics. *Journal of Theoretical Biology, 135*, 569–588.

96. Tilman, D. (1982). *Resource competition and community structure*. Princeton, NJ: Princeton University Press.

97. Tregonning, K., & Roberts, A. (1979). Complex systems which evolve towards homeostasis. *Nature, 281*, 563–564.

98. Trivers, R. (1971). The evolution of reciprocal altruism. *The Quarterly Review of Biology*, *46*, 35–57.

99. Yeager, L. (1993). Computational genetics, physiology, metabolism, neural systems, learning, vision, and behavior, or PolyWorld: life in a new context. In C. G. Langton (Ed.), *Artificial life III*. Reading, MA: Addison-Wesley.

100. von Neumann, J. (1928). Zur Theorie der Gesellschaftsspiele. *Mathematische Annalen*, *100*, 295–320.

101. von Neumann, J., & Morgenstern, O. (1944). *Theory of games and economic behavior*. Princeton, NJ: Princeton University Press.

102. Weisbuch, G., & Duchateau, G. (1993). Emergence of mutualism: application of a differential model to *endosymbiosis, Bulletin of Mathematical Biology*, *55*, 1063–1090.

103. Wilkinson, G. S. (1984). Reciprocal food sharing in the vampire bat. *Nature*, *308*, 181–184.

104. Wilkinson, G. S. (1985). The social organization of the common vampire bat. *Behavioral Ecology and Sociobiology*, *17*, 111–121.

105. Wilson, D. S., Pollock, G. B., & Dugatkin, L. A. (1992). Can altruism evolve in purely viscous populations? *Evolutionary Ecology*, *6*, 331–341.

106. Winemiller, K. O. (1990). Spatial and temporal variation in tropical fish trophic networks. *Ecological Monographs*, *60*, 331–367.

107. Wolfram, S. (Ed.) (1986). *Theory and applications of cellular automata*. Singapore: World Scientific.

108. Yodzis, P. (1981). The stability of real ecosystems. *Nature*, *284*, 674–676.

Extended Molecular Evolutionary Biology: Artificial Life Bridging the Gap Between Chemistry and Biology

P. Schuster

Institut für Molekulare
Biotechnologie,
Jena, Germany,
Institut für Theoretische
Chemie
der Universität Wien,
Austria, and
Santa Fe Institute,
Santa Fe, NM 87501, USA

Abstract   Molecular evolution provides an ample field for the extension of Nature's principles towards novel applications. Several examples are discussed here, among them are evolution in the test tube, nucleotide chemistry with new base pairs and new backbones, enzyme-free replication of polynucleotides and template chemistry aiming at replicating structures that have nothing in common with the molecules from nature.

Molecular evolution in the test tube provides a uniquely simple system for the study of evolutionary phenomena: genotype and phenotype are two features of one and the same RNA molecule. Then fitness landscapes are nothing more than combined mappings from sequences to structures and from structures to functions, the latter being expressed in terms of rate constants. RNA landscapes are presented as examples for which an access to phenomena in reality by mathematical analysis and computer simulations is feasible. New questions concerning stability of structures in evolution can be raised and quantitative answers are given.

Evolutionary biotechnology is a spin-off from molecular evolution. Darwin's principle of variation and selection is applied to design novel biopolymers with predetermined functions. Different approaches to achieve this goal are discussed and a survey of the current state of the art is given.

Keywords
evolutionary biotechnology, molecular evolution, quasi-species, RNA replication, RNA structure, shape space, template chemistry

I   Molecular Replication and Template Chemistry

In the early 1970s, molecular evolution became a discipline in its own right by Spiegelman's [1] pioneering experiments on evolution of RNA molecules in the test tube and Eigen's [2] seminal theoretical work on self-organization on biological macromolecules. Evolutionary phenomena, in particular selection and adaptation to changes in the environment, occur only at conditions far away from thermodynamic equilibrium. Spiegelman studied RNA molecules from small bacteriophages and created nonequilibrium conditions by means of the serial transfer technique (Figure 1). Material consumed by multiplication of RNA molecules is renewed, and the degradation products are removed at the end of constant time intervals by transfer of small samples into an excess of fresh stock solution. Continuous renewal and removal can be achieved in elaborate flow reactors [3,4]. Populations of RNA molecules adapt to the environmental conditions given by the stock solution through variation and selection of the most efficient variants in

RNA Sample

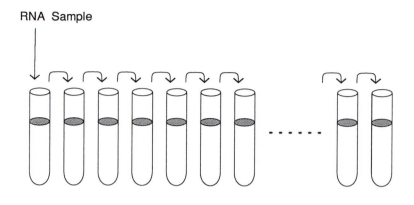

Stock Solution: RNA Replicase, ATP, UTP, GTP, CTP, Buffer

Figure 1. The serial transfer technique for test tube evolution. This technique was applied already by Spiegelman [1] in his pioneering studies. A suitable medium for replication of RNA molecules is prepared and filled into a large number of test tubes. At first Tube 1 is infected by a sample of RNA. Replication starts instantaneously. After a predetermined period of time, a small sample of the solution is transferred to Tube 2, and the procedure is repeated many times, usually in the order of hundreds of transfers. The rate of RNA synthesis increases during such a series, because faster growing variants produced from the original RNA by mutation are selected through competition for nutrients. They grow out their less efficient competitors by consuming the stock solution more quickly.

the sense of Darwin's principle. Another selection technique recently developed by McCaskill [5] makes use of spatial spreading of autocatalytic chemical reactions: Capillaries contain a medium suitable for replication, RNA is injected, and a wave front travels through the medium. The front velocity of the traveling wave increases with the replication rate, and, hence, faster replicating species are selected by the wave propagation mechanism.

In vitro replication of RNA molecules by means of specific enzymes, so-called replicases, proved to be sufficiently robust in order to allow for detailed kinetic studies on their molecular mechanism [6]. These investigations revealed the essential features of template-induced RNA synthesis by virus specific replicases, which, like the conventional photographic process, follows a complementarity rule:

$$activated\ monomers + plus\ strand \xrightarrow{replicase} minus\ strand + plus\ strand$$

$$activated\ monomers + minus\ strand \xrightarrow{replicase} plus\ strand + minus\ strand.$$

Both steps together yield the basis of multiplication at the molecular level. The replicating entity thus is the plus-minus ensemble. The molecular principle of replication is the complementarity of natural nucleotides in base pairs, $A = U$ and $G \equiv C$, which match with the geometry of the famous Watson-Crick double helix (Figure 2). In addition to

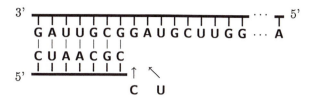

Point mutations: **GAUUG|C|GGAU** $\Longrightarrow$ **GAUUG|U|GGAU**

Insertions: **GAU|UGC|GGAU** $\Longrightarrow$ **GAU|UGCUGC|GGAU**

Deletions: **GAU|UGC|GGAU** $\Longrightarrow$ **GAU|GGAU**

Figure 2. The principle of RNA and DNA replication is the formation of complementary base pairs that fit into a rigid molecular backbone. The backbone is the famous Watson-Crick double helix. The formation of highly specific intermolecular complexes, $A = U$ or $G \equiv C$, respectively, introduces *yes-or-no* decision into biophysical chemistry and, thus, gives rise to a kind of *digital* or discrete chemistry that among other features makes replication feasible. In addition, we show the three main classes of mutations: *point mutations* or single base exchanges, *insertions* or internal partial duplications of the sequence, and *deletions*.

correct complementary replication, several fundamental side reactions were detected, for example,

- double-strand formation from plus and minus strand [7].

- *de novo* RNA synthesis [8,9].

- mutation [10,11] comprising in essence three classes of processes, point mutations, or single-base exchanges, deletions, and insertions (Figure 2).

Double-strand formation following the reaction

plus strand + minus strand $\rightleftarrows$ double strand

represents a deadend of replication because double strands are not recognized as templates by the enzyme. The probability that a plus-minus double strand dissociates into its components is practically zero under the conditions of a replication experiment. Efficient replication thus requires separation of the two complementary strands already in the course of the replication process. This is achieved by the enzyme that causes separation of the two strands and simultaneous formation of structure in both single strands (Figure 3).

De novo RNA synthesis by template-free $Q\beta$ replicase has been heavily disputed in the past [12,13]. *De novo* RNA synthesis turned out to be important for an understanding of the mechanism of replication because it provided the smallest molecules that were

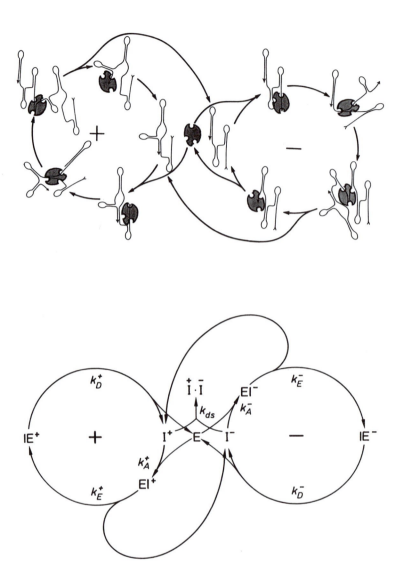

Figure 3. RNA replication through virus-specific enzymes like $Q\beta$ replicase uses a complementary mechanism. The upper part presents a sketch of the molecules involved in the replication process. In the lower part molecules are given as symbols: **E** is the replicase, **I** stands for RNA molecules, **EI** and **IE** are different types of protein-RNA complexes; plus and minus strands are symbolized by "+" and "−"; k_A, k_E, k_D and k_{ds} are the rate constants for association, chain elongation, dissociation and double-strand formation, respectively. The template and the newly synthesized strand are separated already during the replication process and fold into specific secondary structures that are prohibitive for double strand formation. (The figure is reproduced from ref. 6 by courtesy of the authors.)

accepted as templates by the replicase [14]. The role of mutation certainly is to provide sufficient variation for selection to act upon: *No mutation* (and no recombination in higher organisms) implies *no evolution*. Mutation in the in vitro experiments and error propagation in populations of RNA molecules will be discussed in the next section.

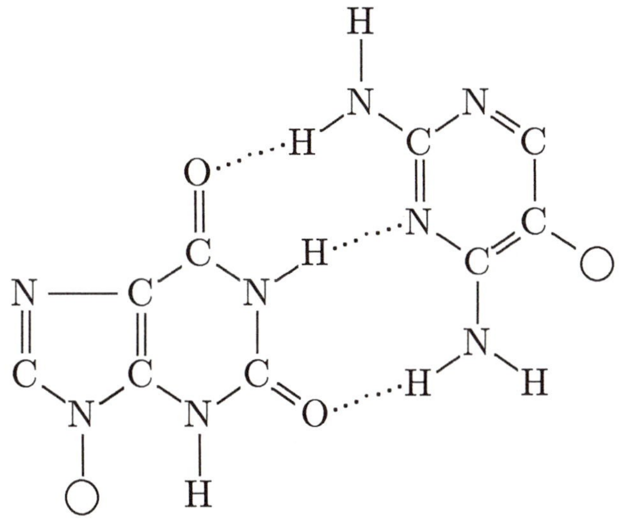

Figure 4. The xanthine–2,6-diaminopyridine base pair. It fits into the backbone of the Watson-Crick type double helix of nucleic acids. The corresponding nucleotides were indeed synthesized and incorporated into RNA and DNA by enzymatic reactions. There the two new bases form a third base pair $X \equiv K$ that is not in conflict with the two natural base pairs.

Benner and coworkers [15] have shown that nature's choice of the genetic alphabet can be extended by the scientists' intuition. They synthesized nucleotides that form base pairs of Watson-Crick type with a hydrogen bonding pattern that is different from both $A = U$ and $G \equiv C$ (Figure 4). Nucleotides carrying the new bases were successfully incorporated enzymatically into RNA and DNA, where they constitute a third base pair. The genetic alphabet has been extended to a new logic based on six letters. Why did evolution never make a successful attempt to use a third (or perhaps a fourth) base pair? A speculative explanation given by Szathmáry [16] sees in two base pairs a compromise between replication fidelity, decreasing with the number of base pairs, and catalytic capacity of RNA, which is supposed to increase with the number of base pairs. We shall provide an alternative less obvious explanation in section 3.

A series of highly interesting experiments on the backbone of conventional nucleic acids was carried out by Albert Eschenmoser [17]. He synthesized "homo-DNA" by replacing the natural carbohydrate residue 2-deoxy-ribofuranose by 2,3-dideoxy-glucopyranose which contains one more CH_2-group than the natural compound. The five-membered furanose ring in the nucleic acid backbone is thus changed into a six-membered ring. This change has a strong influence on the properties of the polynucleotides. The helix conformation of the natural backbone is replaced by an almost perfectly straight backbone geometry and this implies entirely different strengths of base pairs in double strands: **GC > AA > GG > AT > ⋯**. A biochemistry derived from (dideoxy)-glucose nucleic acids would indeed be very different from the natural ribose biochemistry, and more surprises are to be expected from further explorations of artificial polynucleotides.

As far as the principle of polynucleotide replication is concerned, there seems to be no reason why molecular replication should need a protein catalyst. Extensive studies by Orgel and coworkers (see ref. 18 and references 1–5 quoted therein) have indeed shown that template-induced synthesis of complementary strands of RNA can be achieved under suitable conditions without an enzyme. Enzyme-free, template-induced replication of RNA, however, is exceedingly difficult. In the early experiments with homopolymer templates (poly-U, poly-C), the conditions that allow for efficient synthesis of one strand are usually very poor conditions for the synthesis of the complementary strand. The synthesis commonly leads to formation of stable double helical plus-minus ensembles that do not dissociate and are also a deadend for enzyme-free replication. von Kiedrowski [19] did the first successful enzyme-free replication experiment involving two trinucleotides as building blocks and a self-complementary hexamer (plus and minus strands are identical) as template. The bond between the two trinucleotides is formed by means of a water soluble carbodiimide as condensating agent:

$$\begin{array}{c} \textbf{CCGCGG} \\ \cdot\ \cdot\ \cdot\ \cdot\ \cdot\ \cdot \\ \textbf{CCG} + \textbf{CGG} + \textbf{GGCGCC} \rightarrow \rightarrow \quad \textbf{GGCGCC} \quad \rightleftharpoons \quad 2\textbf{GGCGCC} \end{array}$$

At first the hexanucleotide forms a double-helical ternary complex with the two trinucleotides. Bond formation between the trinucleotides is facilitated by the geometry of the double helix, and a binary complex of two identical, self-complementary hexanucleotides is obtained. The reaction equation shown previously indicates already the intrinsic problem of template-induced replication: The double-helical binary complex formed in the copying process has to dissociate in order to provide templates for further replication. In the case of hexanucleotides, the dissociation constant is just sufficiently large to sustain some replication, which then follows a subexponential growth law. Analogous reactions with longer helices are unlikely to work because of the high stability of the double-helical intermediate shown previously. High stability implies very low dissociation constants. Thus, we recognize the crucial role of the enzyme in molecular evolution experiments that it plays by readily separating the double-helical replication complex into template and growing strand (Figure 3).

Recent studies have shown that template-induced molecular replication is not a priviledge of nucleic acids: Rebek and coworkers [20,21] use other classes of rather complex templates carrying the complementary units, and obtain replication under suitable conditions. There is again a backbone whose role is to bring the digits in such a rigid sterical position that they can be read by their complements. Complementarity is based on essentially the same principle as in nucleic acids: Specific hydrogen bonding patterns allow one to recognize the complementary digit and to discriminate all other letters of the alphabet. Sometimes the hydrogen bonding pattern is assisted by opposite electric charges carried by the complements [22]. Template chemistry and molecular replication are rapidly growing fields at present [23]. Organic chemistry provides an ample and rich source for the extension of principles from nature to new classes of compounds in the spirit of artificial life.

It seems necessary to stress a fact that is often overlooked or even ignored by theorists and epistemologists. Molecular replication is anything but a trivially occurring function of molecules. As we have seen earlier, even in cases were the (already hard to meet) molecular requirements for template action are fulfilled, replication still depends on low stability of the complex formed by association of the complementary, plus and minus, molecular species. There is no replication when the complex does not readily dissociate. This is a kind of *Scylla and Charybdis* problem because weak complex formation implies weak mutual recognition between complements tantamount to ineffectiveness in template reactions. There are three solutions to the problem at the present state of our knowledge:

1. The strength of complementary interaction weakens as a consequence of bond formation between the two units associated with the template (usually monomer and growing chain, or two oligoners).

2. The separation of plus and minus species is achieved by a third reaction partner (like the enzyme in present day replication of RNA viruses).

3. The plus-minus duplex is replicated as an entity as it happens with natural DNA replication (requiring, however, a highly elaborate machinery involving 30 enzymes or more).

Only the first solution seems to be achievable in prebiotic chemistry and early evolution.

Everybody who has experience with primitive computing machines knows that the copy instruction is a very simple function. Chemistry and early biological evolution are radically different from computer science in this respect: Replication has to find a simultaneous solution to all requirements, which is generally in conflict with common physical chemistry. Working compromises between contradicting demands are rare, and, hence, only highly elaborate structures might be able to replicate efficiently without specific help.

Returning to enzyme-assisted, template-induced replication, we reconsider correct replication and mutation. Both are initiated in the same way and represent parallel reactions that branch at some instant along the multistep reaction of template copying [2,24]. Virus-specific RNA replicases are much less accurate than the DNA replicating machinery. In vivo they make on the average about one error per replication of an entire viral genome. The populations of almost all RNA viruses are vastly heterogeneous, therefore, and contain a rich reservoir of variants. Such reservoirs are particularly important in variable environments that are provided, for example, by the host's immune system. The larger the genetic reservoir, the more likely a variant can be found that meets the challenge of the altered environmental conditions.

Adaptation to changes in environmental conditions has been studied also in test tube experiments. The replication medium was deteriorated by addition of substances that either' interfere with replication, reduce the lifetime of replicators, or do other nasty things to the replicating RNA molecules. Examples are studies of RNA replication by $Q\beta$ replicase in the presence of ethidium bromide [25] or in solutions containing a ribonuclease [26]. In both cases the rate of RNA synthesis drops dramatically at the deleterious change in the replication medium. After several serial transfers, however, one observes (at least partial) recovery of the original rate. Variants are isolated that are resistant to the reagents that interfered with replication. Changes in sequences and structures of the RNA molecules isolated before the deterioration of the replication assay and after the recovery can be interpreted as molecular adaptations to the environmental change. For example, mutants were isolated that have fewer binding or cleavage sites than the wild type and, thus, compensate for the change in the environment.

2   Mutation, Error-propagation, and Optimization

Replication errors lead to new molecular species whose replication efficiency is evaluated by the selection mechanism. The most frequently occurring molecular species, commonly called the wild types or the *master sequences*, are accompanied by clouds of mutants. The higher the error rate, the more mutations occur and the more viable mutants appear in the population. The mutant spectrum, in addition, is determined

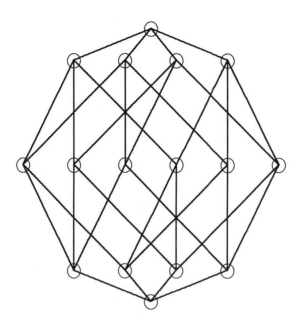

Figure 5. The sequence space of binary (*AU* or *GC*) sequences of chain length $n = 4$. Every circle represents a single sequence of four letters. All pairs of sequences with Hamming distance $d_h = 1$ (these are pairs of sequences that differ only in one position) are connected by a straight line. The geometric object obtained is a hypercube in four-dimensional space, and, hence, all positions (and all sequences) are topologically equivalent.

by the distribution of fitness values. In constant environments this distribution may be described by a fitness landscape. All possible sequences are ordered in a natural way according to their genetic relatedness. Distances between pairs of sequences are expressed in terms of the minimum number of mutations converting the two sequences into each other. (As an example, we show in Figure 5 the geometry of the sequence space created by point mutations on binary sequences that is identical to that of a hypercube whose dimension is the same as the length (n) of the sequences.) A landscape is obtained by assigning a value, for example, a fitness value, to every sequence. In general, an equilibrated or stationary mutant spectrum is broader, the more shallow the fitness landscapes are.

The stationary mutant distribution is characterized as *quasispecies* [2,10,11,24], because it represents the genetic reservoir of asexually replicating populations. An increase of the error rate in the replication on a given fitness landscape leads to a broader spectrum of mutants and, thus, makes evolutionary optimization faster and more efficient in the sense that populations are less likely caught in local fitness optima. There is, however, a critical error threshold [2,24,27]: If the error rate exceeds the critical limit, heredity breaks down, populations are drifting in the sense that new RNA sequences are formed steadily, old ones disappear, and no evolutionary optimization according to Darwin's principle is possible (Figure 6).

Variable environments require sufficiently fast adaptation, and populations with tunable error rates will adjust their quasispecies to meet the environmental challenge. In constant environments, on the other hand, such species will tune their error rates to the smallest possible values in order to maximize fitness. Viruses are confronted with

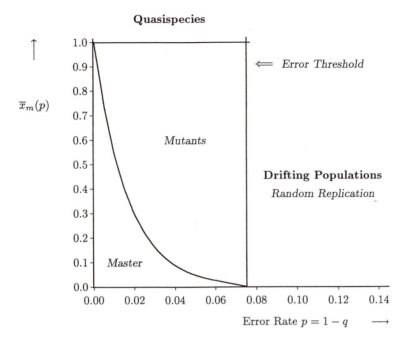

Figure 6. Evolution at the error threshold of replication. The fraction of the most frequent species in the population, called the *master sequence*, is denoted by $x_m(p)$. It becomes very small at the error threshold. Accordingly, the total fraction of all mutants, $1 - x_m(p)$, approaches one at the critical mutation rate.

extremely fast-changing environments because their hosts develop a variety of defense mechanisms ranging from the restriction enzymes of bacteria to the immune system of mammals and man. RNA viruses have been studied extensively. Their multiplication is determined by enzymes that do not allow large-scale variations of replication accuracies. They vary, however, the cumulative error rate by changing the length of their genomes. It is adjusted to optimal values that often correspond to maximal chain lengths [2,24]:

$$n_{\max} = \frac{\ln \sigma}{p} \ .$$

Herein $n_{\max}$ is the maximal chain length that a master sequence can adopt and still allow for stable replication over many generations, $\sigma \geq 1$ is the superiority of this master sequence in the stationary population, and p is the error rate per (newly incorporated) base and replication event. The superiority expresses differential fitness between the master sequence and the average of the remaining population. Thus, it is a function of both, the fitness landscape and the distribution of mutants. In the limit $\lim \sigma \to 1$, we are dealing with *neutral evolution* [28]. Experimental analysis of several RNA virus populations has shown that almost all chain lengths are adjusted to yield error rates close to the threshold value. Thus, RNA viruses appear to adapt to their environments by driving optimization efficiency toward the maximum.

The quasi-species concept has been derived from kinetic differential equations [2,24], and, thus, it is strictly valid in infinite populations only. It turned out, however, to be also a good approximation for realistic stationary populations at sufficiently low error rates below the threshold value. Replication-mutation dynamics has been studied also in finite populations. Analytical expressions were derived for error threshold on simple model landscapes: In order to sustain a stationary population, replication has to be more accurate in smaller populations. In sufficiently large populations, the critical minimal replication accuracy ($q_{min} = 1 - p_{max}$) depends on the reciprocal square root of the population size [29]:

$$q_{min}(N) = q_{min}(\infty) \left(1 + \frac{2\sqrt{\sigma - 1}}{n\sqrt{N}} + \cdots \right).$$

The higher accuracy required for stable replication in small populations is easily interpreted by the fact that the master sequence can be lost in future generations not only by error propagation but also by random fluctuations.

Evolutionary optimization is viewed appropriately as an adaptive walk on a rugged fitness landscape [30]. A few examples of studies on different types of such landscapes are mentioned here. Replication-mutation dynamics on landscapes derived from spin-glass Hamiltonians yielded interesting multimodal population distributions at error rates above the critical error rate for the conventional single-peak quasi-species [31]. Population dynamics on realistic landscapes based on RNA folding has been studied by computer simulations [32,33]. Error thresholds were detected on these rather very rugged landscapes, too. On completely flat fitness landscapes, a new phenomenon was observed [34]: At sufficiently high replication accuracy populations move as coherent peaks in sequence space. There is, however, again a critical error rate. If it is exceeded, the population loses its coherence in sequence space and becomes disperse. It is suggestive, therefore, to call this second critical error rate the *dispersion threshold*.

3 Mutational Stability of Structures

Stability against mutation has also a second, less strict meaning: Assume we have a change in the sequence that does not alter the structure and the properties of the RNA molecule. We would not be able to detect such a *neutral mutation* unless we compare the sequences. Given a certain mutation rate, we may ask, therefore, what are the differences in stability of RNA structures against mutations in the corresponding sequences. How likely does a change in the sequence result in an actual change in the structure? In other words, we try to estimate the fraction of neutral mutants in the neighborhood of a typical sequence. (Neutral is commonly used for sequences that have properties that are indistinguishable for the selection process; we shall use the term here in the narrower sense of identical structures.) This question is of statistical nature and can be answered only by proper application of statistical techniques.

RNA secondary structures are first approximations to the spatial structures of RNA molecules. They are understood as listings of the Watson-Crick-type base pairs in the actual structure and may be represented as planar graphs (Figure 7). We consider RNA secondary structures as elements of an abstract *shape space*. As in the case of sequences (where the Hamming distance d_h represents a metric for the sequence space), a measure of relationship of RNA structures can be found that induces an metric on the shape space [35–37]. We derived this distance measure from trees that are equivalent to the structure graphs, and accordingly it is called the *tree distance*, d_t. Thus, RNA folding can be understood as a mapping from one metric space into another, in particular, from sequence space into shape space. A path in sequence space corresponds uniquely to a

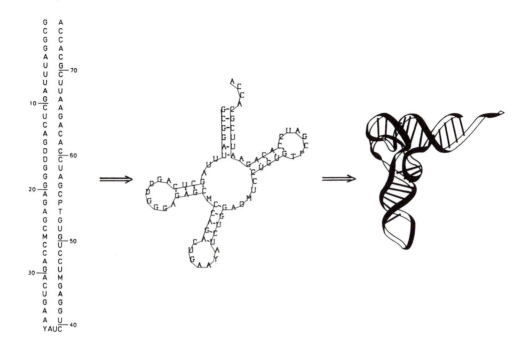

Figure 7. Folding of an RNA sequence into its spatial structure. The process is partitioned into two phases: In the first phase only the Watson-Crick-type base pairs are formed (which constitute the major fraction of the free energy), and in the second phase the actual spatial structure is built by folding the planar graph into a three-dimensional object. The example shown here is phenylalanyl-transfer-RNA (t-RNA^phe) whose spatial structure is known from X-ray crystallography.

path in shape space. (The inversion of this statement, however, is not true as we shall mention in the section 4.)

The whole machinery of mathematical statistics and time series analysis can now be applied to RNA folding. In particular, an autocorrelation function of structures based on tree distances (d_t) is computed from the equation

$$\varrho_t(b) = 1 - \frac{\langle d_t^2(b) \rangle}{\langle d_t^2 \rangle} \ .$$

Mean square averages are taken over sequences in sequence space ($\langle d_t^2 \rangle$), or over sequences in the mutant class b of the reference sequence ($\langle d_t^2(b) \rangle$, that is, over all sequences at Hamming distance b from the reference). The autocorrelation functions can be approximated by exponential functions, and correlation lengths (ℓ_t) are estimated from the relation: $\ln(\varrho_t(\ell_t)) = -1$.

The correlation length is a statistical measure of the hardness of optimization problems (see, e.g., [11]). The shorter the correlation length, the more likely is a structural change occurring as a consequence of mutation. Thus, the correlation length measures stability against mutation. In Figure 8 correlation lengths of RNA structures are plotted against chain lengths. An almost linear increase is observed. Substantial differences are found in the correlation lengths derived from different base pairing alphabets. In particular, the structures of natural ($AUGC$) sequences are much more stable against

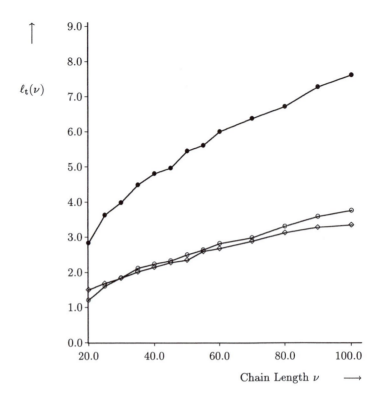

Figure 8. Correlation lengths of structures (ℓ_t) of RNA molecules in their most stable secondary structures as functions of the chain length ν. Values are shown for binary pure GC sequences (◇), for binary pure AU sequences (○), and for natural $AUGC$ sequences (●). The correlation lengths are computed from (ln $\varrho_t(h)$, h) plots by means of a least root mean square deviation fit.

mutation than pure GC sequences or pure AU sequences. This observation is in agreement with structural data obtained for ribosomal RNAs [38]. It provides also a plausible explanation for the use of two base pairs in nature: Optimization in an RNA world with only one base pair would be very hard, and the base pairing probability in sequences with three base pairs is rather low, so that most random sequences of short chain lengths ($n < 50$) do not form thermodynamically stable structures. The choice of two base pairs appears to be a compromise between stability against mutation and thermodynamic stability.

4   Shape Space Covering

The sequence space is a bizarre object: It is of very high dimension (because every nucleotide can be mutated independently, its dimension coincides with the chain length of RNA: $25 < n < 500$ for RNA molecules in test tube experiments, $250 < n < 400$ for viroids, and $3,500 < n < 20,000$ for (most) RNA viruses), but there are only a few points on each coordinate axis (κ points; κ is the number of digits in the alphabet: $\kappa = 2$ for AU and GC, $\kappa = 4$ for $AUGC$). The number of secondary structures that are acceptable as minimum free energy structures of RNA molecules is much smaller than the number of different sequences and can be estimated by means of proper combinatorics [39]: In case of natural $(AUGC)$ molecules we have about $1.485 \times n^{-3/2}(1.849)^n$ structures for 4^n sequences. The mapping from sequence space into shape space is not invertible: Many sequences fold into the same secondary structure. We cannot expect that our intuition, which is well trained with mostly invertible maps in three-dimensional space, will guide us well through sequence and shape spaces. In order to get a feeling for the problem, search algorithms for the optimization of RNA structures and properties were conceived [32,33,40], and computer simulations were carried out on realistic landscapes based on RNA folding [32,33]. Here we shall adopt another strategy to obtain information on sequences and structures and use proper statistical techniques for the analysis of such an abstract object as the RNA shape space.

The information contained in the mapping from sequence space into shape space is condensed into a two-dimensional, conditional probability density surface,

$$S(t, h) = \mathrm{Prob}\left(d_t = t \mid d_h = h\right) \ .$$

This structure density surface (SDS) expresses the probability that the secondary structures of two randomly chosen sequences have a structure distance t provided their Hamming distance is h. An example of a structure density surface for natural sequences of chain length $n = 100$ is shown in Figure 9. We recognize an overall shape that corresponds to one half of a horseshoe with rugged details superimposed upon it. The contour plot illustrates an important property of the structure density surface: At short Hamming distances ($1 \leq n < 16$), the probability density changes strongly with increasing Hamming distance, but further away from the reference sequence ($16 < n < 100$), this probability density is essentially independent of the Hamming distance h. The first part reflects the local features of sequence–structure relations. Up to a Hamming distance of $h = 16$, there is still some memory of the reference sequence. Then, at larger Hamming distances the structure density surface contains exclusively global information that is independent of the reference.

In order to gain more information on the relationship between sequences and structures, an inverse folding algorithm that determines the sequences that share the same minimum free energy secondary structure was conceived and applied to a variety of different structures [39]. The frequency distribution of structures has a very sharp peak: Relatively few structures are very common, and many structures are rare and play no statistically significant role. The results obtained show in addition that sequences folding into the same secondary structure are, in essence, randomly distributed in sequence space. For natural sequences of chain length $n = 100$, a sphere of radius $h \approx 20$ (in Hamming distance) is sufficient to yield the global distribution of structure distances. We conjecture that all common structures are found already in these relatively small patches of sequence space. This conjecture was proven by a suitable computer experiment: We choose a test and a target sequence at random; both have a defined structure. Then we determine the shortest Hamming distance between the two structures by approaching the target sequence with the test sequence following a path through sequence space along which the test sequence changes, but its structure remains constant. (As shown in the next paragraph, such a path is neutral.) The result for the case considered here yields an average minimum distance of two arbitrary structures around a Hamming distance of 20. In order to find a given common structure of an RNA molecule of chain length $n = 100$, one has to search at maximum a patch of radius 20 that contains about 2×10^{30} sequences. This number is certainly not small, but it is negligible compared to the total number of sequences of this chain length: 1.6×10^{60}!

In order to complement this illustration of the RNA shape space, a second computer experiment was carried out that allows an estimate of the degree of selective neutral-

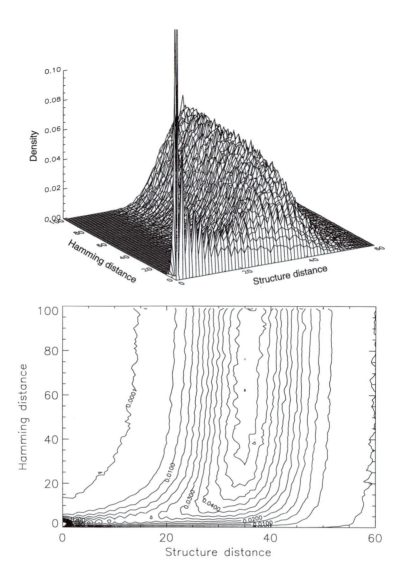

Figure 9. The structure density surface $S(t, h)$ of natural *AUGC* sequences of chain length $n = 100$. The density surface (upper part) is shown together with a contour plot (lower part). In order to dispense from confusing details, the contour lines were smoothened. In this computation, a sample of 1,000 reference sequences was used, which amounts to a total sample size of 10^6 individual RNA foldings.

ity. (Two sequences are considered neutral here if they fold into the same secondary structure.) As indicated in Figure 10, we search for *neutral paths* through sequence space. The Hamming distance from the reference increases monotonously along such a neutral path, but the structure remains unchanged. A neutral path ends when no further neutral sequence is found in the neighborhood of the last sequence. The length ℓ of a path is the Hamming distance between the reference sequence and the last sequence. Clearly, a neutral path cannot be longer than the chain length n ($\ell \leq n$). The length distribution of a neutral path in the sequence space of natural RNA molecules

Plate A

Plate 1. A photograph and a model of *Natica enzona* (Fowler, Meinhardt, & Prusinkiewicz, 1992).

Plate 2. Three shell models with pigmentation patterns generated using the reaction-diffusion models: *Volutoconus bednalli*, *Oliva porphyria*, and *Conus marmoreus* (Fowler, Meinhardt, & Prusinkiewicz, 1992).

Plate B

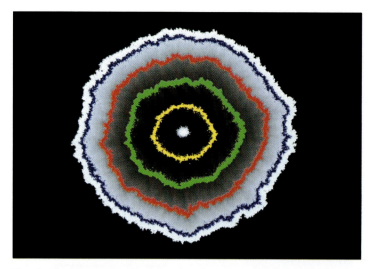

Plate 3. The Eden model of accretive growth. Colors indicate the times in which cells are adjoined to the cluster (James & Prusinkiewicz, 1993).

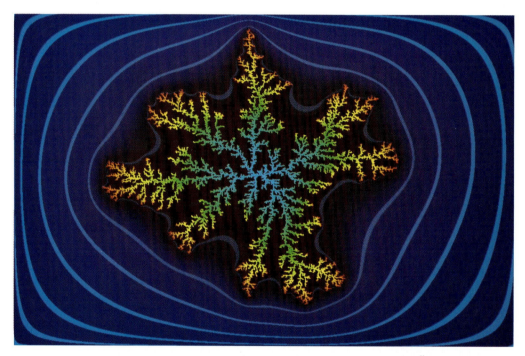

Plate 4. Diffusion-limited growth. Colors indicate concentrations of nutrients in the medium (James & Prusinkiewicz, 1993).

Plate C

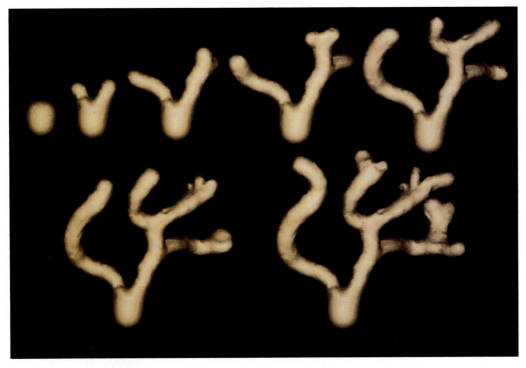

Plate 5. A model of a sponge-like structure (Kaandorp, 1992).

Plate 6. A model of a tree trunk with roots (Greene, 1991).

Plate D

Plate 7. Developmental model of *Mycelis muralis* (Prusinkiewicz & Hanan, 1987).

Plate 8. Development of a hawkweed flower *Hieracium umbellatum* simulated using a differential L-system (Hammel & Prusinkiewicz, 1993).

Plate E

Plate 9. Spruce trees synthesized using a particle system model expressed as a stochastic L-system (Orth, 1993).

Plate 10. A garden with trimmed trees (MacKenzie, 1993).

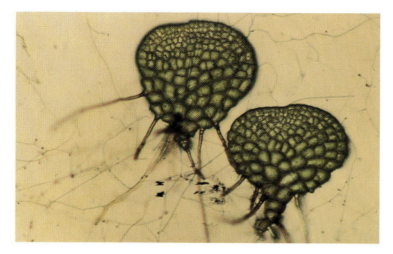

Plate 11. A photograph of thalli of *Microsorium linguaeforme* (de Boer, 1988).

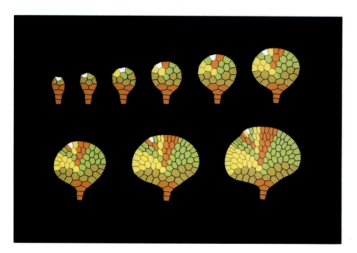

Plate 12. Development of a thallus of *Microsorium linguaeforme* simulated using a map L-system (Fracchia, Prusinkiewicz, & de Boer, 1990).

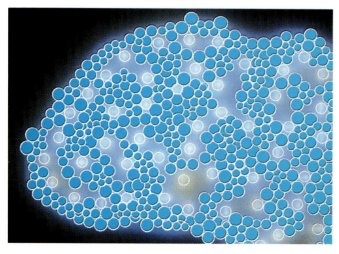

Plate 13. Simulation of mobile cells interacting in a continuous medium (Fleischer & Barr, 1993).

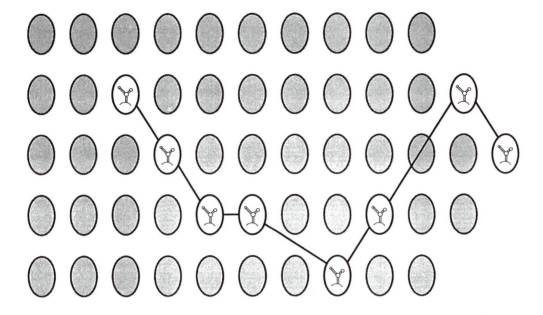

Figure 10. Percolation of sequence space by *neutral networks*. A neutral path connects sequences of Hamming distance $h = 1$ (single base exchange) or $h = 2$ (base pair exchange) that fold into identical minimum free energy structures. The sketch shows a neutral path of length $h = 9$. The path ends because no identical structure was found with $h = 10$ and $h = 11$ from the reference.

of chain length $n = 100$ is shown in Figure 11. It is remarkable that about 20% of the neutral paths have the maximum length and lead through the whole sequence space to one of the sequences that differ in all positions from the reference, but have the same structure.

Combination of information derived from Figures 9 and 11 provides insight into the structure of the shape space of RNA secondary structures, which is basic to optimization of RNA molecules already in an RNA world. Our results can be summarized in four statements:

1. Sequences folding into one and the same structure are distributed randomly in sequence space.

2. The frequency distribution of structures is sharply peaked. (There are comparatively few common structures and many rare ones.)

3. Sequences folding into all common structures are found within (relatively) small neighborhoods of any random sequence.

4. The shape space contains extended neutral networks joining sequences with identical structures. (A large fraction of neutral path leads from the initial sequence through the entire sequence space to a final sequence on the opposite side—there are $(\kappa - 1)^n$ sequences that differ in all positions from an initial sequence.)

Combining the two statements (1) and (3), we may visualize the mapping from sequences into structures as illustrated by the sketch shown in Figure 12.

These results suggest straightforward strategies in the search for new RNA structures. It provides little advantage to start from natural or other preselected sequences

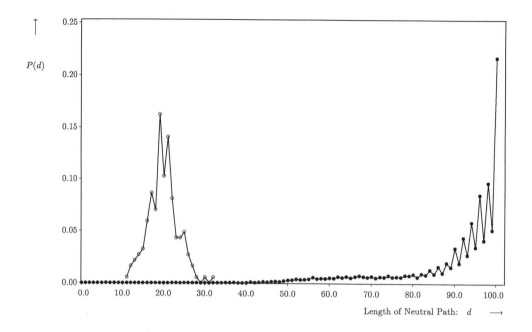

Figure 11. Length distribution of neutral paths starting from random *AUGC* sequences of chain length $n = 100$. A neutral path connects pairs of sequences with identical structures and Hamming distance $d_h = 1$ (single base exchange) or $d_h = 2$ (base pair exchange). The Hamming distance to the reference sequence is monotonously increasing along the path.

because any random sequence would do equally well as the starting molecule for the selection cycles of evolutionary biotechnology shown in Figures 13 and 14. Any common secondary structure with optimal functions is accessible in a few selection cycles. The secondary structure of RNA is understood as a crude first-order approximation to the actual spatial structure. Fine-tuning of properties by choosing from a variety of molecules sharing the same secondary structure will often be necessary. In order to achieve this goal, it is of advantage to adopt alternations of selection cycles with low and high error rates. At low error rates, the population performs a search in the vicinity of the current master sequence (the most common sequence, which is usually also the fittest sequence). If no RNA molecule with satisfactory properties is found, a change to high error rate is adequate. Then the population spreads along the neutral network to other regions in sequence space, which can be explored in detail after tuning the error rate low again.

The structure of shape space is highly relevant for evolutionary optimization in nature too. Because long neutral paths are common, populations drift readily through sequence space whenever selection constraints are absent. This is precisely what is predicted for higher organisms by the neutral theory of evolution [28] and what is observed in molecular phylogeny by sequence comparisons of different species. The structure of shape space provides also a rigorous answer to the old probability argument against the possibility of successful adaptive evolution [41]. How should nature find a given biopolymer by trial and error when the chance to guess it is as low as $1/\kappa^n$? Previously given answers [42] can be supported and extended by precise data on the RNA shape space. The numbers of sequences that have to be searched in order to find

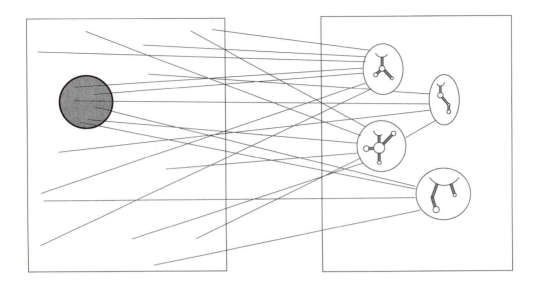

Sequence Space   Shape Space

Figure 12. A sketch of the mapping from sequences into RNA secondary structures as derived here. Any random sequence is surrounded by a ball in sequence space that contains sequences folding into (almost) all common structures. The radius of this ball is much smaller than the dimension of sequence space.

adequate solutions are many orders of magnitude smaller than those guessed on naive statistical grounds. If one of the common structures has a property that increases the fitness of the corresponding sequence, it can hardly be missed in a suitably conducted evolutionary search.

5 Evolutionary Biotechnology

The application of RNA-based molecular adaptive systems to solve problems in biotechnology by Darwin's selection principle was proposed in 1984 by Eigen and Gardiner [43]. Somewhat later a similar suggestion was made by Kauffman [44] for large-scale screening of proteins based on recombinant DNA techniques and selection methods. Meanwhile, many research groups started to apply evolutionary concepts to produce biomolecules with new properties. (For two recent reviews, see Joyce [45] and Kauffman [46].) At present molecular evolution seems to give birth to a novel branch of applied biosciences.

The essence of evolutionary biotechnology is shown in Figures 13 and 14. Experiments are carried out on the level of populations of molecules. Replication of nucleic acid molecules is used as an amplification factor. Variation is introduced into the populations either by artificially increased mutation rates or by partial randomization of RNA or DNA sequences. The synthesis of oligonucleotides with random sequences has become routine by now. The two techniques differ with respect to the selection procedure. The first approach to the problem is suitable for *batch experiments* (Figure 13). The essential trick of this technique is to encode the desired functions into the selection constraint. Several examples of successful applications of such molecular selection

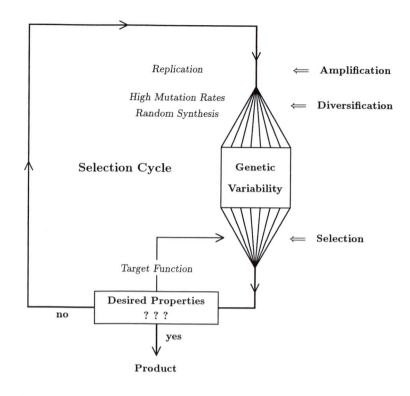

Figure 13. A selection technique of evolutionary biotechnology based on encoding of the function to be developed into the selection constraint.

techniques to biochemical problems are found in the current literature [47–50]. In reality it will often be impossible to encode the desired function directly into the selection constraint. Then spatial separation of individual genotypes and massively parallel screening provide a solution (Figure 14). This technique, however, requires highly sophisticated equipment that is currently under development [51,52]. Evolutionary biotechnology provides also new challenges for the design of high-tech equipment that is required to carry out massively parallel experiments under precisely controlled conditions.

The results on RNA shape space derived in the previous section suggest straightforward strategies in the search for new RNA structures. It is of little advantage to start from natural or other preselected sequences, because any random sequence would serve equally well as the starting molecule for the selection cycles shown in Figures 13 and 14. Any common secondary structure with suitable properties is accessible within a few selection cycles. Because the secondary structure is only a crude first approximation to the actual three-dimensional structure, fine tuning of properties by choosing from a variety of molecules sharing the same secondary structure will be necessary. In order to achieve this goal, it is advantageous to adopt alternations of selection cycles with low and high error rates. At low error rates, the population performs a search in the vicinity of the current master sequence (the most common sequence, which usually is the fittest sequence as well). If no RNA molecule with satisfactory properties is found, a change to high error rate is adequate. Then the population spreads along the neutral network to other regions of sequence space, which are explored in detail after tuning the error rate low again.

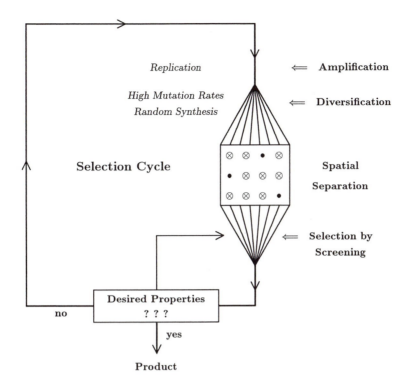

Figure 14. A selection technique of evolutionary biotechnology based on spatial separation of individual genotypes and massively parallel molecular screening.

6   The Theory of Evolution and Artificial Life

Molecular evolution has become an established field and produces already spin-offs with interesting technological aspects. What has it contributed to the theory of evolution? First, it has shown that replication and evolutionary adaptation are not exclusive priviledges of cellular life. Polynucleotides were found to replicate with suitable enzymes in cell-free assays. Small oligonucleotides can be replicated even without protein assistance. Other replicators that are not based on nucleotide chemistry were found as well. Template chemistry starts to become a field in its own right.

Second, the old tautology debate on biological fitness has come to an end. Fitness in molecular systems can be measured independently of the survival in an evolution experiment. Evolutionary processes may be described and analyzed in the language of physics.

Third, the probability argument against a Darwinian mechanism of evolution [41], as mentioned in section 4, is invalidated by the experimental proof of target-oriented adaptation, found, for instance, in the ribonuclease experiments [26]. Evolutionary search is substantially facilitated by the properties of sequence space and shape space [39].

The knowledge acquired in molecular evolution allows ample extensions. In the near future, many more nonnatural systems will be designed and synthesized that fulfill the principles of molecular genetics and are thus capable of evolution but, apart from that, have little in common with their living counterparts.

Molecular evolution, in essence, has established the basic kinetic mechanisms of genetics. In the case of RNA replication and mutation, the reaction mechanisms were resolved to about the same level of details as with other polymerization reactions in physical chemistry. Several aspects of a comprehensive theory of evolution, however, are still missing. For example, the integration of cellular metabolism and genetic control into a comprehensive theory of molecular genetics has not yet been achieved. Morphogenesis and development of multicellular organisms need to be incorporated into the theory of evolution. No satisfactory explanations can be given yet for the mechanisms leading to the origin of real novelties often addressed as the great jumps in evolution [53].

Nevertheless, the extension of molecular biology into organic and biophysical chemistry as described here is predestined to be part of the still heterogeneous discipline of artificial life. Principles are still taken from the living world, but the material carriers of the essential properties are new and unknown in the biosphere. At the same time, this very active area of research spans a bridge from chemistry to biology and also sheds some light on burning questions concerning the origin of life.

Acknowledgments

The statistical analysis of the RNA shape space presented here is joint work with Drs. Walter Fontana and Peter F. Stadler and will be described elsewhere in detail. Financial support by the Austrian *Fonds zur Förderung der wissenschaftlichen Forschung* (Projects S5305-PHY, P8526-MOB, and P9942-PHY) and by the Commission of the European Communities (Contract PSS*0396) is gratefully acknowledged.

References

1. Spiegelman, S. (1971). An approach to the experimental analysis of precellular evolution. *Quarterly Reviews of Biophysics*, *4*, 213–253.

2. Eigen, M. (1971). Self-organization of matter and the evolution of biological macromolecules. *Naturwissenschaften*, *58*, 465–523.

3. Husimi, Y., Nishgaki, K., Kinoshita, Y., & Tanaka, T. (1982). Cellstat—a continuous culture system of a bacteriophage for the study of the mutation rate and the selection process at the DNA level. *Review of Scientific Instruments*, *53*, 517–522.

4. Husimi, Y., & Keweloh, H.-C. (1987). Continuous culture of bacteriophage Qβ using a cellstat with a bubble wall-growth scraper. *Review of Scientific Instruments*, *58*, 1109–1111.

5. Bauer, G. J., McCaskill, J. S., & Otten, H. (1989). Traveling waves of in vitro evolving RNA. *Proceedings of the National Academy of Sciences of the United States of America (Washington)*, *86*, 7937–7941.

6. Biebricher, C. K., & Eigen, M. (1988). Kinetics of RNA replication by Qβ replicase. In E. Domingo, J. J. Holland, & P. Ahlquist (Eds.), *RNA genetics*. Vol. I: RNA directed virus replication (pp. 1–21). Boca Raton, FL: CRC Press.

7. Biebricher, C. K., Eigen, M., & Gardiner Jr., W. C. (1984). Kinetics of RNA replication: plus-minus asymmetry and double-strand formation. *Biochemistry*, *23*, 3186–3194.

8. Sumper, M., & Luce, R. (1975). Evidence for *de novo* production of self-replicating and environmentally adapted RNA structures by bacteriophage Qβ replicase. *Proceedings of the National Academy of Sciences of the United States of America (Washington)*, *72*, 162–166.

9. Biebricher, C. K., Eigen, M., & Luce, R. (1981). Product analysis of RNA generated *de novo* by Qβ replicase. *Journal of Molecular Biology*, *148*, 369–390.

10. Eigen, M., McCaskill, J., & Schuster, P. (1988). The molecular quasispecies—an abridged account. *Journal of Physical Chemistry*, *92*, 6881–6891.

11. Eigen, M., McCaskill, J., & Schuster, P. (1989). The molecular quasispecies. *Adv. Chem. Phys.*, *75*, 149–263.

12. Hill, D., & Blumenthal, T. (1983). Does $Q\beta$ replicase synthesize RNA in the absence of template? *Nature, 301*, 350.

13. Biebricher, C. K., Eigen, M., & Luce, R. (1986). Template-free RNA synthesis by $Q\beta$ replicase. *Nature, 321*, 89–91.

14. Biebricher, C. K., & Luce, R. (1993). Sequence analysis of RNA species synthesized by $Q\beta$ replicase without template. *Biochemistry, 32*, 4848–4854.

15. Piccirilli, J. A., Krauch, T., Moroney, S. E., & Benner, A. S. (1990). Enzymatic incorporation of a new base pair into DNA and RNA extends the genetic alphabet. *Nature, 343*, 33–37.

16. Szathmáry, E. (1991). Four letters in the genetic alphabet: a frozen evolutionary optimum? *Proceedings of the Royal Society of London B, 245*, 91–99.

17. Eschenmoser, A. (1993). Hexose nucleic acids. *Pure and Applied Chemistry, 65*, 1179–1188.

18. Wu, T., & Orgel, L. E. (1992). Nonenzymatic template-directed synthesis on oligodeoxycytidylate sequences in hairpin oligonucleotides. *Journal of the American Chemical Society, 114*, 317–322.

19. von Kiedrowski, G. (1986). A self-replicating hexadeoxynucleotide. *Angewande Chemie, International Edition in English, 25*, 932–935.

20. Tjivikua, T., Ballester, P., & Rebek, J., Jr. (1990). A self-replicating system. *Journal of the American Chemical Society, 112*, 1249–1250.

21. Nowick, J. S., Feng, Q., Tjivikua, T., Ballester, P., & Rebek, J., Jr. (1991). Kinetic studies and modeling of a self-replicating system. *Journal of the American Chemical Society, 113*, 8831–8839.

22. Terfort, A., & von Kiedrowski, G. (1992). Self-replication at the condensation of 3-amino-benzamidines with 2-formyl-phenoxy acetic acids. *Angewande Chemie, International Edition in English, 31*, 654–656.

23. Orgel, L. E. (1992). Molecular replication. *Nature, 358*, 203–209.

24. Eigen, M., & Schuster, P. (1977). The hypercycle. A principle of natural self-organization. Part A: Emergence of the hypercycle. *Naturwissenschaften, 64*, 541–565.

25. Kramer, F. R., Mills, D. R., Cole, P. E., Nishihara, T., & Spiegelman, S. (1974). Evolution in vitro: sequence and phenotype of a mutant resistent to ethidium bromide. *Journal of Molecular Biology, 89*, 719–736.

26. Strunk, G. (1993). *Automatisierte Evolutionsexperimente in vitro und natürliche Selektion unter kontrollierten Bedingungen mit Hilfe der Serial-Transfer-Technik.* Unpublished doctoral dissertation: Universität Braunschweig (B.R.D.). Available from university library upon request.

27. Swetina, J., & Schuster, P. (1982). Self-replication with errors—a model for polynucleotide replication. *Biophysical Chemistry, 16*, 329–345.

28. Kimura, M. (1983). *The neutral theory of molecular evolution.* Cambridge, UK: Cambridge University Press.

29. Nowak, M., & Schuster, P. (1989). Error thresholds of replication in finite populations. Mutation frequencies and the onset of Muller's ratchet. *Journal of Theoretical Biology, 137*, 375–395.

30. Kauffman, S. A., & Levin, S. (1987). Towards a general theory of adaptive walks on rugged landscapes. *Journal of Theoretical Biology, 128*, 11–45.

31. Tarazona, P. (1992). Error thresholds for molecular quasispecies as phase transitions: from simple landscapes to spin-glass models. *Physical Review A, 45*, 6038–6050.

32. Fontana, W., & Schuster, P. (1987). A computer model of evolutionary optimization. *Biophysical Chemistry, 26*, 123–147.

33. Fontana, W., Schnabl, W., & Schuster, P. (1989). Physical aspects of evolutionary optimization and adaptation. *Physical Review A, 40*, 3301–3321.

34. Derrida, B., & Peliti, L. (1991). Evolution on a flat fitness landscape. *Bulletin of Mathematical Biology, 53*, 355–382.

35. Fontana, W., Griesmacher, T., Schnabl, W., Stadler, P. F., & Schuster, P. (1991). Statistics of landscapes based on free energies, replication and degradation rate constants of RNA secondary structures. *Monatshefte fuer Chemie, 122*, 795–819.

36. Fontana, W., Stadler, P. F., Bornberg-Bauer, E. G., Griesmacher, T., Hofacker, I. L., Tacker, M., Tarazona, P., Weinberger, E. D., & Schuster, P. (1993). RNA folding and combinatory landscapes. *Physical Review E, 47*, 2083–2099.

37. Fontana, W., Konings, D. A. M., Stadler, P. F., & Schuster, P. (1993). Statistics of RNA secondary structures. *Biopolymers, 33*, 1389–1404.

38. Wakeman, J. A., & Maden, B. E. H. (1989). 28 S Ribosomal RNA in vertebrates. Location of large-scale features revealed by electron microscopy in relation to other features of the sequences. *Biochemical Journal, 258*, 49–56.

39. Schuster, P., Fontana, W., Stadler, P. F., & Hofacker, I. L. (1993). *From sequences to shapes and back. A case study on RNA secondary structures.* Preprint. Santa Fe, NM.

40. Wang, Q. (1987). Optimization by simulating molecular evolution. *Biological Cybernetics, 57*, 95–101.

41. Wigner, E. (1961). The logic of personal knowledge. In E. Shils (Ed.), *Essays presented to Michael Polanyi on his seventieth birthday 11th March 1961.* Free Press: Glencoe, IL.

42. Eigen, M., & Schuster, P. (1979). *The hypercycle—a principle of natural self-organization.* Berlin: Springer-Verlag.

43. Eigen, M., & Gardiner, W. (1984). Evolutionary molecular engineering based on RNA replication. *Pure & Applied Chemistry, 56*, 967–978.

44. Kauffman, S. A. (1986). Autocatalytic sets of proteins. *Journal of Theoretical Biology, 119*, 1–24.

45. Joyce, G. F. (1992). Directed molecular evolution. *Scientific American, 267*(6), 48–55.

46. Kauffman, S. A. (1992). Applied molecular evolution. *Journal of Theoretical Biology, 157*, 1–7.

47. Horwitz, M. S. Z., Dube, D. K., & Loeb, L. A. (1989). Selection of new biological activities from random nucleotide sequences: evolutionary and practical considerations. *Genome, 31*, 112–117.

48. Ellington, A. D., & Szostak, J. W. (1990). In vitro selection of RNA molecules that bind to specific ligands. *Nature, 346*, 818–822.

49. Tuerk, C., & Gold, L. (1990). Systematic evolution of ligands by exponential enrichment: RNA ligands to bacteriophage T4 DNA polymerase. *Science, 249*, 505–510.

50. Beaudry, A. A., & Joyce, G. F. (1992). Directed evolution of an RNA enzyme. *Science, 257*, 635–641.

51. Bauer, G. J., McCaskill, J. S., & Schwienhorst, A. (1989). Evolution im Laboratorium. *Nachrichten aus Chemie, Tecknik und Laboratorium, 37*, 484–488.

52. Bauer, G. J. (1990). *Biochemische Verwirklichung und Analyse von kontrollierten Evolutionsexperimenten mit RNA-Quasispezies in vitro.* Unpublished doctoral dissertation, Universität Braunschweig (B.R.D.) 1990.

53. Eigen, M., & Schuster, P. (1985). Stages of emerging life—five principles of early organization. *Journal of Molecular Evolution, 19*, 47–61.

Visual Models of Morphogenesis

Przemyslaw Prusinkiewicz
Department of Computer
Science
University of Calgary
Calgary, Alberta
Canada T2N 1N4
pwp@cpsc.ucalgary.ca

Abstract Rapid progress in the modeling of biological structures and simulation of their development has occurred over the last few years. It has been coupled with the visualization of simulation results, which has led to a better understanding of morphogenesis and given rise to new procedural techniques for realistic image synthesis. This paper reviews selected models of morphogenesis with a significant visual component.

Keywords
morphogenesis, simulation and visualization of biological phenomena, developmental model, reaction-diffusion, diffusion-limited growth, cellular automaton, L-system, realistic image synthesis

> If a natural object or organism demonstrates consistency of form ..., such symmetry is the consequence of Something rather than Nothing.
>
> Adrian D. Bell [3]

I Introduction

In the 1984 paper, "Plants, Fractals, and Formal Languages" [60], addressed to the computer graphics audience, Smith coined the term *database amplification* to denote the synthesis of complex images from small data sets. A generalization of this notion, called *emergence*, became a central concept of *Artificial Life*. According to Taylor [62, p. 31], emergence is a process in which a collection of interacting units acquires qualitatively new properties that cannot be reduced to a simple superposition of individual contributions. A well-known example of emergence is given by the *game of life* [19, 20], where complex patterns develop in an array of square cells governed by strikingly simple local rules. The development of patterns and forms in the domain of living organisms has been termed *morphogenesis*.

The relationship between the rules expressing the behavior of individual components and the resulting developmental processes, patterns, and forms is often nonintuitive and difficult to grasp. Consequently, computer simulations play an essential role in the study of morphogenesis. The objectives of such simulations were analyzed and illustrated using many examples by Bell [4], who grouped them as follows:

- analysis of the nature and complexity of the mechanisms that control the developmental processes,

- a better understanding of the form and development of specific organisms, acquired in the process of constructing models faithful to the biological reality,

- analysis of the impact of individual parameters on the overall form or pattern; this leads to a better appreciation of their relationship, and gives an insight into the direction of evolutionary changes,

- computer-assisted teaching,

- graphic design, computer art, and landscape architecture.

Visualization techniques offered by computer graphics facilitate the interpretation and evaluation of simulation results. In the absence of a formal measure of what makes two patterns or forms look alike, it is often necessary to rely on visual inspection while comparing the models with the reality. For example, Plate 1 shows a photograph and a model of the shell *Natica enzona*, juxtaposed to facilitate the comparison. The natural and synthetic pigmentation patterns differ in details, yet we perceive them as similar. Photorealistic presentation adds credibility to this observation by removing artifacts that might affect the comparison. We conclude that the underlying mathematical model of shell pigmentation pattern is plausible, although visual inspection obviously does not constitute a definitive validation.

This paper reviews mathematical models of morphogenesis capable of producing realistic images of biological patterns and forms. It begins with a list of notions useful in characterizing these models, then presents selected case studies. An extension of this work may lead to a taxonomy of the models of morphogenesis, systematically contrasting their underlying assumptions and exposing approaches that require further exploration.

2   Features of Models of Morphogenesis

Historically, the study of morphogenesis has been approached from two directions. The first one consists of viewing form as a derivative of growth, and was formulated by d'Arcy Thompson [63, p. 79]: "It is obvious that the *form* of an organism is determined by its rate of *growth* in various directions; hence rate of growth deserves to be studied as a necessary preliminary to the theoretical study of form."

The second direction focuses on the flow of substances through a medium and was initiated by Turing [65, p. 38]: "The systems considered consist of masses of tissues which are *not growing*, but within which certain substances are reacting chemically, and through which they are diffusing. These substances are called *morphogens*, the word being intended to convey the idea of a form producer."

The distinction between these two directions is captured as the first characteristic of the models, presented in the following list. Other characteristics also determine the essential properties of the models and influence the design of the simulation software.

1. Models may occupy constant space or may expand (and contract) over time. In the latter case, the expansion may be limited to the boundary of the structure or may take place in the interior as well.

2. Models may be structure-oriented, focusing on the components (modules) of the developing structure, or space-oriented, capturing the whole space that embeds this structure. A model in the first category typically describes where each component of the structure is located. A model in the second category describes what is located at (or what is the state of) each point of space.

3. The developing structure and the space that embeds it may be continuous or discrete. The state characterizing each module or point in space may be chosen from a continuous or discrete domain. The model may operate in continuous or discrete time.

4. Models may have different topologies, such as a nonbranching filament (a linear

arrangement of components), a branching structure, a network (graph with cycles), a two-dimensional surface, or a three-dimensional solid object.

5. The neighborhood relations between modules may be fixed at the time of their creation (determined by the division pattern of modules), or the modules may be mobile. By analogy, in the case of continuous structures, the developmental processes may be viewed as taking place in an elastic medium or in a fluid.

6. Communication between the modules may have the form of lineage (information transfer from the parent module to its offspring) or interaction (information transfer between coexisting modules). In the latter case, the information flow may be endogenous (between adjacent components of the model) or exogenous (through the space embedding the model). Similar notions can be applied to continuous structures.

The last categorization captures the crucial aspects of the flow of control information during morphogenesis, first emphasized by Lindenmayer [34, 35]. Refering to branching structures, Bell [4] proposed to call patterns created using these modes of communication blind, self-regulatory, or sighted, and offered the following intuitive descriptions:

- In blind patterns, branch initiation is controlled by the parent module, independently of the remainder of the structure and the environment in which this structure develops.

- In self-regulatory patterns, branch initiation is controlled potentially by the whole developing structure, using communication via the existing components of this structure.

- In sighted patterns, the initiation of a new branch is influenced by factors detected by its parent in the immediate neighborhood, such as proximity of other organisms or parts of the same organism.

In the following survey of selected models of morphogenesis, the distinction between space- and structure-oriented models serves as the main key, while the communication modes further characterize the structure-oriented models.

3 Space-Oriented Models

3.1 Reaction-Diffusion Pattern Models

Reaction-diffusion models were developed by Turing [65] to explain the "breakdown of symmetry and homogeneity," leading to the emergence of patterns in initially homogeneous, continuous media. The patterns result from the interaction between two or more morphogens that diffuse in the medium and enter into chemical reactions with each other. Mathematically, this process is captured by a system of partial differential equations. For properly chosen equations and parameter values, the uniform distribution of morphogens is unstable. Random fluctuations are amplified and produce a stable pattern of high and low concentrations.

Reaction-diffusion models have been extensively studied in theoretical biology, where they provide plausible explanations of many observed phenomena [28, 42, 47]. Ouyang and Swinney [49] recently validated the basic assumptions of these models by realizing reaction-diffusion processes in chemical experiments. In computer graphics, Turk [66] applied the original Turing equations to generate spot patterns, and a five-morphogen system proposed by Meinhardt [42, chap. 12] to generate stripe patterns

Figure 1. A venation pattern generated using Meinhardt's model of netlike structures on a hexagonal grid.

covering three-dimensional models of animals. Meinhardt and Klinger [43–45] applied the reaction-diffusion model to capture pigmentation patterns in shells. In this case, an observable pattern does not reflect a steady-state distribution of morphogens on the surface of the shell, but depicts the evolution of morphogen concentrations on the growing edge over time. Meinhardt's model has been applied by Fowler, Meinhardt, and Prusinkiewicz [15] to synthesize realistic images of shells (Plate 2). Pigmentation patterns have also been synthesized by Ermentrout, Campbell, and Oster [10], assuming that the concentration of the pigment is controlled by neural activities of the mollusc's mantle. As noted by Murray [47, p. 518], the reaction-diffusion and the neural activity models postulate similar types of information exchange along the shell edge (short-range activation and long-range inhibition).

Reaction-diffusion models may also be suitable for explaining and synthesizing the visually attractive arrangements of fish and reptile scales, patterns on butterfly wings, and coloring of flower petals. The generation of these patterns remains, to a large extent, an open problem.

3.2   A Reaction-Diffusion Model of Differentiation

Meinhardt [41] (see also [42, chap. 15]) extended reaction-diffusion models to capture differentiation of netlike structures from an undifferentiated medium. Figure 1 shows a venation pattern produced using his model. The reaction-diffusion equations are solved on a hexagonal grid (in this case). The state of each cell is characterized by concentrations of four morphogens, one of which determines whether a cell is in a differentiated state and belongs to the structure or in a nondifferentiated state and belongs to the medium. The simulation begins with the creation of a filamentous succession of differentiated cells, extending at the growing tip of the filament. During the development, the tip may split, creating dichotomous branches. At a sufficient distance from the tip (monitored by decreasing concentration of another morphogen, the inhibitor, produced by the tip), the filament initiates lateral branches. Next-order branches are formed in a similar way if no growing tips are nearby.

This model combines continuous and discrete components. On the one hand, the diffusion of morphogens is described using a set of differential equations, if one assumes a conceptually continuous medium. On the other hand, differentiation is described at the level of discrete cells.

3.3 Diffusion-Limited Accretive Growth

In many developmental processes, there is an obvious distinction between the structure and the surrounding medium. The focus of the model is then on the structure and its gradual expansion along the border, termed *accretive growth* [31].

Eden [9] simulated the accretive growth of a cell cluster in a square lattice by sequentially adjoining randomly selected cells to the structure formed during previous steps (Plate 3). Meakin [40] (see also [68]) improved this model by assuming that the growth rate (the probability of adjoining a new cell) depends on the local concentration of nutrients that diffuse from a surrounding exterior source and are consumed by the growing structure. The structure generated by this diffusion-limited growth model depends on the choice of parameters and may display a branching fractal character common with the diffusion-limited aggregation models (Plate 4), discussed later. Fujikawa and Matsushita [18, 39] showed that these models faithfully capture the growth of colonies of a bacterial species *Bacillus subtilis* on agar plates. Kaandorp [31, 32] applied a three-dimensional variant of the diffusion-limited growth to simulate and visualize the development of corals and sponges that expand in the direction of the largest concentration of nutrients (Plate 5). A branching topology is an emerging property of these structures, resulting from the higher gradient of nutrient concentration near the tips of the branches than near the origin of the structure.

3.4 Diffusion-Limited Aggregation

Witten and Sander [70] proposed a discrete counterpart of diffusion-limited growth, called *diffusion-limited aggregation* (DLA) (see also [68]), which captures diffusion of nutrients by simulating random movement of particles in a grid. The growing structure originates with a single fixed cell. Free particles move in the grid, with the displacement direction chosen at random on each simulation step. Once a moving particle touches the structure, it sticks to it rigidly.

Diffusion-limited aggregation has attracted considerable research interest, due in part to the fractal character of the emerging branching structures. It is a faithful model of many physical phenomena, such as the deposition of metallic ions on an electrode. It neglects, however, the active role of the organism using nutrients to build its body.

3.5 Cellular Automata

Cellular automata [64] can be considered a discrete-space counterpart of reaction-diffusion models. The space is represented by a uniform grid, with each site or cell characterized by a state chosen from a finite set. Time advances in discrete steps, and all cells change their states according to the same rule, which describes the next state as a function of the previous state of a cell and its close neighbors.

Young [71] proposed a cellular-automaton model of animal coat patterns using only two cell states: pigmented or not (Figure 2). Camazine [5] applied a cellular automaton to convincingly reproduce the pattern of a rabbit fish. The resulting patterns are similar to those obtained using continuous reaction-diffusion equations.

In general, the next-state function need not be related to the diffusion of morphogens. Ulam [67] pioneered the application of cellular automata to the simulation of the development of branching structures, where the discrete space provides a medium

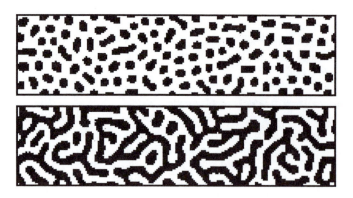

Figure 2. Patterns generated using a discrete counterpart of the reaction-diffusion model, proposed by Young.

Figure 3. A branching structure generated by Ulam's cellular automaton operating on a square grid.

for detecting collisions between branches. Figure 3 shows a pattern he termed *Maltese crosses*. The structure begins with a single seed cell and spreads within the (conceptually infinite) square grid of automata. In each iteration, the pattern expands to the adjacent cells, unless the resulting branches would collide. Figure 4 illustrates the same principle on a triangular grid. A slice of this pattern contained in a 60° wedge is reminiscent of a tree; as noticed by Stevens [61, pp. 127–131], this appearance can be reinforced by modifying branching angles while preserving the topology of the model.

3.6 Voxel Automata

Three-dimensional extensions of cellular automata, called *voxel automata* [24], have been used in computer graphics to model aspects of plant development strongly affected by the environment. Arvo and Kirk [2] and Greene [23] applied them to simulate the growth of climbing plants, attaching themselves to predefined objects in space.

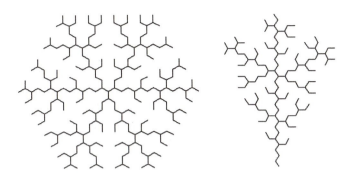

Figure 4. Branching structures generated by Ulam's cellular automaton operating on a triangular grid. Lines connect the centers of cells occupied by the growing structure.

Subsequently, Greene [24] extended this technique to capture variations in the diameter of branches and roots of a tree, and applied it to simulate the growth of roots searching their path through rocks in the ground, as shown in Plate 6. In this case, the voxels do not represent elements of the structure on the "all or nothing" basis but hold information about the run of the individual strands that compose branches and roots of the tree. This information is used to keep groups of strands together and guide their development between obstacles in the environment.

3.7 Development in Expanding Space

The models discussed so far can grow only on their boundary. Gottlieb [22] overcame this limitation by proposing a geometric model of development, in which the space expands uniformly. A predefined starting structure is placed in a small square grid (e.g., consisting of 2 × 2 cells). New branches are created by connecting the centers of grid cells to the structure, provided that the Euclidean distance between a particular center point and the structure is greater than a given threshold. The structure and the cellular space are then scaled twofold, the cells are subdivided, and connections to the centers of the new cells are made as in the previous step. This process is equivalent to the subdivision of the grid combined with the reduction of the threshold distance. The construction is repeated until the desired level of detail is reached, as presented on the left side of Figure 5. The right side of this figure shows the result of applying Gottlieb's method to model leaf venation. This application has a clear biological justification: As a leaf grows, its vascular system is developing in order to maintain the capacity for translocating water, nutrients, and products of photosynthesis to and from all parts of the blade. The model exhibits the hierarchical organization of the veins, but there is still a discrepancy between their layout and patterns observed in nature. Faithful modeling of leaf venation remains an open problem.

4 Structure-Oriented Models

In contrast to space-oriented models, which describe the entire space including the modeled structure, structure-oriented models focus only on the development of components that constitute the structure.

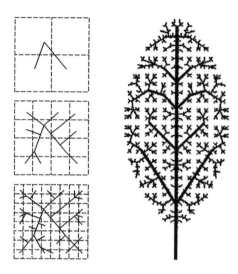

Figure 5. Principle of Gottlieb's method for pattern generation, and a venation pattern obtained using this method.

4.1 L-Systems

L-systems simulate the development of linear and branching structures built from discrete modules [34]. The development can be controlled by lineage (in context-free, or 0L-systems) and by endogenous interaction (in context-sensitive, or IL-systems). The modules represent individual cells of simple multicellular organisms, or larger modules of higher plants (e.g., internodes, apices, leaves, and branches). L-systems were originally limited to the specification of the topology of branching structures, but subsequent geometric interpretations have made it possible to visualize simulation results [52, 53]. For example, Plate 7 shows a simulated development of the herbaceous plant *Mycelis muralis*.

Although L-systems were introduced as a purely discrete model [36], practical applications revealed the need for shifting their various aspects to the continuous domain. Parametric L-systems [27, 52] have made it possible to assign continuous attributes to modules, such as the concentrations of substances propagating in a structure. Differential L-systems [51] extended this formalism to the continuous time domain, facilitating computer animation of developmental processes. For example, Plate 8 shows selected phases of the development of the hawkweed flower *Hieracium umbellatum*, simulated using differential L-systems.

L-systems are related to several other plant models. As shown by Prusinkiewicz and Lindenmayer [52, chap. 2], parametric L-systems can reproduce the tree models developed by Aono and Kunii [1], which in turn were based on models by Honda [29]. Françon [17] observed that L-systems can also capture the models of tree architecture classified by Hallé, Oldeman, and Tomlinson [26], and the AMAP models originated by de Reffye and his collaborators (for example, see [8]). Orth [48] constructed stochastic L-systems that approximately emulate the particle-system models of trees and grass proposed by Reeves and Blau [56] (Plate 9). Further analysis is needed to establish detailed relationships between all these models.

4.2   Branching Structures with Exogenous Control

While L-systems do not capture, in principle, the exogenous control mechanisms (the models are not "sighted"), such mechanisms were included in a number of other models of branching structures. Historically, the first model was proposed in 1967 by Cohen [6], who considered the development of a two-dimensional branching structure guided by a continuous "density field." The gradient of the density function indicated the least crowded regions available for the apical growth of each branch. Cohen suggested that his model may approximate the venation patterns in leaves, and the growth and branching of neural axons. A related model of the axon growth was proposed by Gierer [21]. Bell [3] and Ford [14] investigated idealized models of branching structures that included a mechanism for aborting the development of modules surrounded by an excess of neighbors. Honda, Tomlinson, and Fisher [30] used a similar technique to capture branch interactions in the trees *Terminalia catappa* and *Cornus alternifolia*. An interesting aspect of their study was a comparison of the exogenous limitation of branching (by proximity to other branches) with an endogenous mechanism (accumulation of regulatory substances propagating through the growing structure). The inhibition of branch production due to local overcrowding was also included in a model of *Pinaceae* by Ford, Avery, and Ford [13]. A model of treelike structures that developed according to the amount and direction of incoming light was proposed by Kanamaru and Takahashi [33]. This model generated fairly realistic crown shapes, thus illustrating the crucial impact of light on tree morphogenesis. Bell [4] outlined a model of clover, which integrated exogenous and endogenous control factors. Growth of buds was controlled by photosynthate exported from leaflets, but leaflets failed to produce photosynthate if they were shaded by other leaflets. Bell noted that the outcome of the simulation was difficult to predict, and simulation played an important role in understanding the resulting form. Combinations of exogenous and endogenous factors were subsequently incorporated in a comprehensive model of poplar trees [55]. Prusinkiewicz and McFadzean [54] and MacKenzie [38] reported preliminary results on incorporating exogenous control mechanisms into L-systems. The captured phenomena included collisions between pairs of branches, the branches and the environment, the removal of leaves shaded by other leaves and branches, and the response of plants to trimming. This work may lead to practical applications in the modeling of gardens for landscape design purposes (Plate 10). Recent surveys of models of plants have been given by Fisher [11] and Room, Maillette, and Hanan [58].

4.3   Map L-Systems

Map L-systems [37] extend the expressive power of L-systems beyond branching structures to graphs with cycles, called *maps*, representing cellular layers. Their geometrical interpretation is more difficult than that of branching structures, because the presence of cycles makes it impossible to assign metric properties to the model using local rules. For example, the angles between the edges of a quadrilateral cycle must sum to 360° and, therefore, cannot be specified independently from each other. Fracchia, Prusinkiewicz, and de Boer [16] (see also [52, chap. 7]) proposed a physically based solution to this problem. The cells are assumed to have physical properties, osmotic pressure and wall tension, and they form a final configuration by mechanically pushing each other until an equilibrium is reached.

Map L-systems have been successfully applied to model fern gametophytes [7, 52]. For example, Plates 11 and 12 compare a microphotograph and computer-generated images of the fern thallus *Microsorium linguaeforme*. The natural and the simulated shapes look alike, which supports the hypothesis that the timing and orientation of cell divisions are the dominant factors determining the global thallus shape.

Map L-systems with geometric interpretation operate by first establishing the neighborhood relations between the cells, then assigning geometric parameters to the resulting graph. This approach is biologically justified in multicellular plant structures, because plant cells are tightly cemented together, but is inappropriate in models of animal tissues, because animal cells can move with respect to each other. A model of morphogenesis addressing this problem is described next.

4.4   Mobile Cells in a Continuous Medium

Fleischer and Barr [12] proposed an extensible simulation framework for studying morphogenesis that focused on the generation of connectivity patterns during neural development. Their model consists of discrete cells embedded in a continuous substrate. The actions of the cells are divided into continuous processes (grow, move) and discrete events (divide, create a dendrite, die). The cells move in response to physical forces and interact with other cells and the substrate through mechanical, chemical, and electrical means. Internally, the activity of each cell is governed by a set of differential equations that depend on the cell's state and the local environment. These equations represent the "genetic information" of the cell and describe the changes to an array of variables controlling the cell's behavior (movements, growth, divisions). The substrate acts as a medium in which chemical substances diffuse, dissipate, and enter into reactions. A sample frame from a simulation carried out in this environment is shown in Plate 13. The yellow cells appear first, then some of them differentiate into blue cells. The blue cells grow and gradually form a connected skeleton.

Map L-systems and the Fleischer-Barr model present opposite approaches to the definition of multicellular structures. In map L-systems, grammar-based rules specify a model's topology, which subsequently determines its geometry. The cells cannot move with respect to each other. On the other hand, in the Fleischer-Barr model, cell movements determine their relative positions; the resulting clusters of adjacent cells indirectly specify topological properties of the emerging structure. The work of Mjolsness, Sharp, and Reinitz [46] presents a step toward a synthesis of both approaches: a model in which spatial relationships between the cells *and* grammar-based productions can be combined to specify dynamic changes in system configuration.

Although the Fleischer-Barr model is directed at the study of morphogenesis, it may also provide a unifying framework for considering other phenomena in which autonomous agents move in space and interact. In the computer graphics context, these include behavioral animation, exemplified by Reynolds' [57] model of flocks, herds, and schools, and by Wejchert and Haumann's [69] model of leaves flying in the air.

5   Conclusions

This paper presented a survey of selected models of morphogenesis that use computer graphics techniques to visualize the results of simulations. The models were divided into two main classes, space- and structure-oriented, and were further characterized from the viewpoint of information flow between the components of the developing structures. The space-oriented models capture the flow of information in the medium but usually have only limited capability to describe expansion of the medium and of the structure embedded in it: Growth is limited to the boundary. The structure-oriented models, on the other hand, can simulate the expansion of the whole structure, but they do not inherently capture the information flow through the medium. The selection of the best approach is an important part of modeling a given phenomenon, as described by Segel [59, p. xi]: "A good mathematical model—though distorted and hence "wrong," like any simplified representation of reality—will reveal some essential components of complex phenomenon. The process of modeling makes one concentrate on separating the essential from the inessential."

In some cases, similar patterns or developmental sequences can be generated by fundamentally different models. For example, the Maltese crosses shown in Figure 3 were generated using a cellular automaton that explicitly detected and eliminated collisions between branches, but exactly the same pattern can be generated using a context-free L-system. The pigmentation pattern of an *Oliva* shell shown in Plate 2 was generated using a reaction-diffusion model, but similar patterns can be obtained using cellular automata and context-sensitive L-systems. Lindenmayer [34] proposed to address such equivalences in a formal way:

> In view of the large number of possible models which give rise to similar morphogenetic patterns, the most important problem is that of narrowing down the set of possibilities. This can be ultimately done on the basis of experimental evidence only. But a better theoretical understanding of equivalence relationships among models of different types would help considerably to sharpen the questions asked in the experiments.

A formal theory of pattern complexity would be an important step in this direction. Traditional measures of complexity, such as the time and space needed by a Turing machine to execute an algorithm, fail to quantify the flow of information between components of a developing pattern or structure. Therefore, a more specialized theory is needed to evaluate formally the alternatives and provide measurable criteria for selecting the most plausible model of an observed phenomenon. An interesting feature of this methodology is that computer science is being applied to study processes taking place in nature. Gruska and Jürgensen [25] comment, "'Computer science' should be considered as a science with aims similar to those of physics. The information processing world is as rich and as important as the physical world for mankind."

Acknowledgments

I wish to thank all the authors of images included in this paper for making them available to me and for granting permission for their use. I am particularly indebted to Deborah Fowler, who created the black-and-white figures specifically for this paper and, along with Mark Hammel and Mark James, helped with editing the text. I would also like to thank Jules Bloomenthal, Keith Ferguson, Jim Hanan, Kurt Fleischer, Jaap Kaandorp, Eric Mjolsness, and Bill Remphrey for useful discussions and comments. This work was sponsored by research and equipment grants from the Natural Sciences and Engineering Research Council of Canada. An earlier version of the present paper has appeared in conference proceedings [50].

References

1. Aono, M., & Kunii, T. L. (1984). Botanical tree image generation. *IEEE Computer Graphics and Applications, 4*(5), 10–34.

2. Arvo, J., & Kirk, D. (1988). Modeling plants with environment-sensitive automata. In *Proceedings of Ausgraph '88* (pp. 27–33).

3. Bell, A. D. (1985). On the astogeny of six-cornered clones: An aspect of modular construction. In: J. White (Ed.), *Studies on plant demography: A festschrift for John L. Harper* (pp. 187–207). London: Academic Press.

4. Bell, A. D. (1986). The simulation of branching patterns in modular organisms. *Philosophical Transactions of the Royal Society of London. Series B: Biological Sciences (London), 313*, 143–159.

5. Camazine, S. (1993, March). Designed by nature. *The world and I*, pp. 202–208.

6. Cohen, D. (1967, October). Computer simulation of biological pattern generation processes. *Nature, 216*, 246–248.

7. de Boer, M. J. M. (1989). *Analysis and computer generation of division patterns in cell layers using developmental algorithms.* Doctoral dissertation, University of Utrecht.

8. de Reffye, P., Edelin, C., Françon, J., Jaeger, M., & Puech, C. (1988, August). Plant models faithful to botanical structure and development. *Computer Graphics, 22*(4), 151–158.

9. Eden, M. (1960). A two-dimensional growth process. In: *Proceedings of Fourth Berkeley Symposium on Mathematics, Statistics, and Probability* (Vol. 4, pp. 223–239). Berkeley, CA: University of California Press.

10. Ermentrout, B., Campbell, J., & Oster, G. (1986). A model for shell patterns based on neural activity. *The Veliger, 28*, 369–388.

11. Fisher, J. B. (1992). How predictive are computer simulations of tree architecture. *International Journal of Plant Sciences, 153*(Suppl.), 137–146.

12. Fleischer, K. W., & Barr, A. H. (1993). A simulation testbed for the study of multicellular development: The multiple mechanisms of morphogenesis. In C. Langton (Ed.), *Artificial life III* (pp. 389–416). Redwood City, CA: Addison-Wesley.

13. Ford, E. D., Avery, A., & Ford, R. (1990). Simulation of branch growth in the *Pinaceae*: Interactions of morphology, phenology, foliage productivity, and the requirement for structural support, on the export of carbon. *Journal of Theoretical Biology, 146*, 15–36.

14. Ford, H. (1987). Investigating the ecological and evolutionary significance in plant growth form using stochastic simulation. *Annals of Botany, 59*, 487–494.

15. Fowler, D. R., Meinhardt, H., & Prusinkiewicz, P. (1992). Modeling seashells. *Computer Graphics, 26*(2), 379–387.

16. Fracchia, F. D., Prusinkiewicz, P., & de Boer, M. J. M. (1990). Animation of the development of multicellular structures. In: N. Magnenat-Thalmann and D. Thalmann (Eds.), *Computer Animation '90* (pp. 3–18). Tokyo: Springer-Verlag.

17. Françon, J. (1991). Sur la modélisation de l'architecture et du développement des végétaux. In: C. Edelin (Ed.) *L'Arbre. Biologie et Développement.* Naturalia Monspeliensia. No hors série.

18. Fujikawa, H., & Matsushita, M. (1991). Bacterial fractal growth in the concentration field of nutrient. *Journal of the Physical Society of Japan, 60*(1), 88–94.

19. Gardner, M. (1970). The fantastic combinations of John Conway's new solitaire game "Life." *Scientific American, 223*, 120–123.

20. Gardner, M. (1971). Mathematical games: on cellular automata, self-reproduction, the Garden of Eden and the game "Life." *Scientific American, 224*(2), 112–117.

21. Gierer, A. Directional cues for growing axons forming the retinotectal projection. *Development, 101*, 479–489.

22. Gottlieb, M. E. (in press). The VT model: a deterministic model of angiogenesis. In *IEEE Transactions on Biomedical Engineering.*

23. Greene, N. (1989). Voxel space automata: modeling with stochastic growth processes in voxel space. *Computer Graphics, 23*(4), 175–184.

24. Greene, N. (1991). Detailing tree skeletons with voxel automata. In *SIGGRAPH '91 course notes on photorealistic volume modeling and rendering techniques.*

25. Gruska, J., & Jürgensen, H. (1990). *Informatics: a fundamental science and methodology for the sciences.* Unpublished manuscript.

26. Hallé, F., Oldeman, R. A. A., & Tomlinson, P. B. (1978). *Tropical trees and forests: An architectural analysis.* Berlin: Springer-Verlag.

27. Hanan, J. S. (1992). *Parametric L-systems and their application to the modelling and visualization of plants*. Doctoral dissertation, University of Regina.

28. Harrison, L. (1993). *Kinetic theory of living pattern*. New York: Cambridge University Press.

29. Honda, H. (1971). Description of the form of trees by the parameters of the tree-like body: Effects of the branching angle and the branch length on the shape of the tree-like body. *Journal of Theoretical Biology, 31*, 331–338.

30. Honda, H., Tomlinson, P. B., & Fisher, J. B. (1981). Computer simulation of branch interaction and regulation by unequal flow rates in botanical trees. *American Journal of Botany, 68*(4), 569–585.

31. Kaandorp, J. (1992). *Modeling growth forms of biological objects using fractals*. Doctoral dissertation, University of Amsterdam.

32. Kaandorp, J. (in press). *Fractal modelling: Growth and form in biology*. Berlin: Springer-Verlag.

33. Kanamaru, N., & Takahashi, K. (1992). CG simulation of natural shapes of botanical trees based on heliotropism. *The Transactions of the Institute of Electronics, Information, and Communication Engineers, J75-D-II*(1), 76–85. In Japanese.

34. Lindenmayer, A. (1968). Mathematical models for cellular interaction in development, Parts I and II. *Journal of Theoretical Biology, 18*, 280–315.

35. Lindenmayer, A. 1982. Developmental algorithms: Lineage versus interactive control mechanisms. In S. Subtelny & P. B. Green (Eds.), *Developmental order: Its origin and regulation* (pp. 219–245). New York: Alan R. Liss.

36. Lindenmayer, A., & Jürgensen, H. (1982). Grammars of development: Discrete-state models for growth, differentiation, and gene expression in modular organisms. In G. Rozenberg & A. Salomaa (Eds.), *Lindenmayer systems: Impacts on theoretical computer science, computer graphics, and developmental biology* (pp. 3–21). Berlin: Springer-Verlag.

37. Lindenmayer, A., & Rozenberg, G. (1979). Parallel generation of maps: Developmental systems for cell layers. In V. Claus, H. Ehrig, & G. Rozenberg (Eds.), *Graph grammars and their application to computer science; First International Workshop, Lecture notes in computer science 73* (pp. 301–316). Berlin: Springer-Verlag.

38. MacKenzie, C. (1993). *Artificial evolution of generative models in computer graphics*. Master's thesis, University of Calgary.

39. Matsushita, M., & Fujikawa, H. (1990). Diffusion-limited growth in bacterial colony formation. *Physica A, 168*, 498–508.

40. Meakin, P. (1986). A new model for biological pattern formation. *Journal of Theoretical Biology, 118*, 101–113.

41. Meinhardt, H. (1976). Morphogenesis of lines and nets. *Differentiation, 6*, 117–123.

42. Meinhardt, H. (1982). *Models of biological pattern formation*. London: Academic Press.

43. Meinhardt, H. (1984). Models for positional signalling, the threefold subdivision of segments and the pigmentation patterns of molluscs. *Journal of Embryology and Experimental Morphology, 83*(Suppl.), 289–311.

44. Meinhardt, H., & Klinger, M. (1987). A model for pattern formation on the shells of molluscs. *Journal of Theoretical Biology, 126*, 63–89.

45. Meinhardt, H., & Klinger, M. (1987). Pattern formation by coupled oscillations: The pigmentation patterns on the shells of molluscs. In: *Lecture Notes in Biomathematics* (Vol. 71, pp. 184–198). Berlin: Springer-Verlag.

46. Mjolsness, E., Sharp, D. H., & Reinitz, J. (1991). A connectionist model of development. *Journal of Theoretical Biology, 152*(4), 429–454.

47. Murray, J. (1989). *Mathematical biology*. Berlin: Springer-Verlag.

48. Orth, T. (1993). Graphical modeling using L-systems and particle systems: a comparison. Master's thesis, University of Calgary.

49. Ouyang, Q., & Swinney, H. (1991). Transition from a uniform state to hexagonal and striped Turing patterns. *Nature, 352,* 610–612.

50. Prusinkiewicz, P. (1993). Modeling and visualization of biological structures. In: *Proceedings of Graphics Interface '93* (pp. 128–137).

51. Prusinkiewicz, P., Hammel, M., & Mjolsness, E. (1993). Animation of plant development using differential L-systems. In *Proceedings of SIGGRAPH '93.*

52. Prusinkiewicz, P., & Lindenmayer, A. (1990). *The algorithmic beauty of plants.* New York: Springer-Verlag. With J. S. Hanan, F. D. Fracchia, D. R. Fowler, M. J. M. de Boer, and L. Mercer.

53. Prusinkiewicz, P., Lindenmayer, A., & Hanan, J. (1988). Developmental models of herbaceous plants for computer imagery purposes. *Computer Graphics, 22*(4), 141–150.

54. Prusinkiewicz, P., & McFadzean, D. (1992). Modelling plants in environmental context. *Proceedings of the Fourth Annual Western Computer Graphics Symposium* (pp. 47–51).

55. Rauscher, H. M., Isebrands, J. G., Host, G. E., Dickson, R. E., Dickmann, D. I., Crow, T. R., & Michael, D. A. (1990). ECOPHYS : An ecophysiological growth process model for juvenile poplar. *Tree Physiology, 7,* 255–281.

56. Reeves, W. T., & Blau, R. (1985). Approximate and probabilistic algorithms for shading and rendering structured particle systems. *Computer Graphics, 19*(3), 313–322.

57. Reynolds, C. W. (1987). Flocks, herds, and schools: a distributed behavioral model. *Computer Graphics, 21*(4), 25–34.

58. Room, P. M., Maillette, L., & Hanan, J. S. (1994). Module and metamer dynamics and virtual plants. *Advances in Ecological Research, 25,* 105–157.

59. Segel, L. A. (1984). *Modeling dynamic phenomena in molecular and cellular biology.* Cambridge, UK: Cambridge University Press.

60. Smith, A. R. (1984). Plants, fractals, and formal languages. *Computer Graphics, 18*(3), 1–10.

61. Stevens, P. S. (1974). *Patterns in nature.* Boston: Little, Brown.

62. Taylor, C. E. (1992). "Fleshing out" Artificial Life II. In C. G. Langton, C. Taylor, J. D. Farmer, & S. Rasmussen (Eds.) *Artificial life II* (pp. 25–38). Redwood City, CA: Addison-Wesley.

63. d'Arcy Thompson, (1952). *On growth and form.* Cambridge, UK: University Press.

64. Toffoli, T., & Margolus, N. (1987). *Cellular automata machines: a new environment for modeling.* Cambridge, MA: The MIT Press.

65. Turing, A. (1952). The chemical basis of morphogenesis. *Philosophical Transactions of the Royal Society B, 237,* 37–72.

66. Turk, G. (1991). Generating textures on arbitrary surfaces using reaction diffusion. *Computer Graphics, 25*(4), 289–298.

67. Ulam, S. (1962). On some mathematical properties connected with patterns of growth of figures. In *Proceedings of Symposia on Applied Mathematics* (Vol. 14, pp. 215–224). American Mathematical Society.

68. Vicsek, T. (1989). *Fractal growth phenomena.* Singapore: World Scientific.

69. Wejchert, J., & Haumann, D. (1991). Animation aerodynamics. *Computer Graphics, 25*(4), 19–22.

70. Witten, T., & Sander, L. (1983). Diffusion-limited aggregation. *Physical Review B, 27,* 5686–5697.

71. Young, D. A. (1984). A local activator-inhibitor model of vertebrate skin patterns. *Mathematical Biosciences, 72,* 51–58.

The Artificial Life Roots of Artificial Intelligence

Luc Steels
Artificial Intelligence
Laboratory
Vrije Universiteit Brussel
Pleinlaan 2, B-1050 Brussels
Belgium
steels@arti.vub.ac.be

Abstract Behavior-oriented Artificial Intelligence (AI) is a scientific discipline that studies how behavior of agents emerges and becomes intelligent and adaptive. Success of the field is defined in terms of success in building physical agents that are capable of maximizing their own self-preservation in interaction with a dynamically changing environment. The paper addresses this Artificial Life route toward AI and reviews some of the results obtained so far.

Keywords
autonomous robots, artificial intelligence, adaptive behavior

I   Introduction

For several decades, the field of Artificial Intelligence (AI) has been pursuing the study of intelligent behavior using the methodology of the artificial [104]. But the focus of this field and, hence, the successes have mostly been on higher-order cognitive activities such as expert problem solving. The inspiration for AI theories has mostly come from logic and the cognitive sciences, particularly cognitive psychology and linguistics. Recently, a subgroup within the AI community has started to stress embodied intelligence and made strong alliances with biology and research on artificial life [59]. This is opening up an "artificial life route to artificial intelligence" [112], which has been characterized as Bottom-Up AI [19], the Animat approach [133], Behavior-based AI [108], or Animal Robotics [75]. These terms identify a loose network of engineers and biologists who share the common goal of understanding intelligent behavior through the construction of artificial systems. The researchers also share a growing number of assumptions and hypotheses about the nature of intelligence. In view of the strong links with biology and complex systems theory, the research has so far received more attention in the Artificial Life (AL) community than in the AI field itself.

The aim of this paper is to review this approach and identify some major unresolved issues. Given that substantial engineering efforts and nontrivial experimentation is required, the first solid experimental and technical results have only recently begun to appear. Good sources for tracking the field are the conferences on the simulation of adaptive behavior [79,80] and the associated journal [102], the conferences on AL [30,59,60,124], and the associated journal [4]. There are also occasional contributions to international conferences on AI (such as International Joint Conference on Artificial Intelligence [IJCAI], American Association for Artificial Intelligence [AAAI], or European Conference on Artificial Intelligence [ECAI]), neural networks (Neural Information Processing Society Conference [NIPS]), or robotics (Institute of Electronic and Electrical Engineers Conference [IEEE]). Reports of some milestone workshops have been published [65,112,113,123].

Section 2 of the paper delineates the AL approach to AI. Section 3 identifies the fundamental units of this approach, which are behavior systems. Section 4 and 5 focus on contributions toward a central theme of AL research, which is the origin of complexity through emergent functionality. A short review of some other issues concludes the paper.

2 Delineating the Field

2.1 The Subject Matter Is Intelligent Behavior

The phenomena of interest are those traditionally covered by ethology and ecology (in the case of animals) or psychology and sociology (in the case of humans). The behavior by an individual or a group of individuals is studied, focusing on what makes behavior intelligent and adaptive and how it may emerge. Behavior is defined as a regularity observed in the interaction dynamics between the characteristics and processes of a system and the characteristics and processes of an environment [106]. Behavior is intelligent if it maximizes preservation of the system in its environment. The main emphasis is not on the physical basis of behavior, as in the case of neural network research, but on the principles that can be formulated at the behavioral level itself. An example of a theory at the behavioral level is one that explains the formation of paths in an ant society in terms of a set of behavioral rules without reference to how they are neurophysiologically implemented [91]. Another example is a study of how certain behavioral strategies (such as retreat when attacked) and their associated morphological characteristics are evolutionary stable [72].

Given this emphasis on behavior, the term *behavior-oriented* seems appropriate to distinguish the field, particularly from the more knowledge-oriented approach of classical AI. It will be used in the rest of the paper.

2.2 The Methodology Is Based on Building Artificial Systems

Scientists traditionally construct models in terms of a set of equations that relate various observational variables and hypothesized theoretical variables. Technological advances in the second half of this century have resulted in two additional types of models:

- *Computational models:* These consist of a process-oriented description in terms of a set of data structures and algorithms. When this description is executed, that is, the algorithm is carried out causing the contents of the data structures to be modified over time, phenomena can be observed in the form of regularities in the contents of the data structures. If these synthetic phenomena show a strong correspondence with the natural phenomena, they are called simulations, and the process descriptions constitute a theory of the natural phenomena.

- *Artificial models:* One can also construct a physical device (an artifact) whose physical behavior gives rise to phenomena comparable to the natural phenomena in similar circumstances. The device will have components with a particular structure and functioning that have been put together in a particular way. The design and implementation of these components and their mode of combination constitutes another possible way to theorize about the phenomena.

Computational models and artificial models, or what Pattee [92] calls simulations and realizations, must be clearly distinguished. For example, it is possible to build a computational model of how a bird flies, which amounts to a simulation of the environment around the bird, a simulation of the aerodynamics of the body and the wings, a simulation of the pressure differences caused by movement of the wings, etc. Such a model is highly valuable but would, however, not be able to fly. It is forever locked in the data structures and algorithms implemented on the computer. It flies only in a virtual world. In contrast, one could make an artifact in terms of physical components (a physical body, wings, etc.). Such an artifact would only be viewed as satisfactory if it is able to perform real flying. This is a much stronger requirement. Very often, results from simulation only partially carry over to artificial systems. When constructing a simulation, one selects certain aspects of the real world that are carried over into the virtual world. But this selection may ignore or overlook essential characteristics that play a role unknown to the researcher. An artificial system cannot escape the confrontation with the full and infinite complexity of the real world and is, therefore, much more difficult to construct.

The term *artificial* in "artificial life" (and also in "artificial intelligence") suggests a scientific approach based on constructing artificial models. The methodological steps are as follows: A phenomenon is identified (e.g., obstacle avoidance behavior), an artificial system is constructed that has this as competence, the artificial system is made to operate in the environment, the resulting phenomena are recorded, and these recordings are compared with the original phenomena. Potential misfits feed back into a redesign or reengineering of the artificial system.

Although AI is sometimes equated with the simulation of intelligent behavior, this is too narrow an interpretation. The goal is to build artifacts that are "really" intelligent, that is, intelligent in the physical world, not just intelligent in a virtual world. This makes unavoidable the construction of robotic agents that must sense the environment and can physically act upon the environment, particularly if sensorimotor competences are studied. This is why behavior-oriented AI researchers insist so strongly on the construction of physical agents [21,130]. Performing simulations of agents (as in Beer [15]) is, of course, an extremely valuable aid in exploring and testing out certain mechanisms, the way simulation is heavily used in the design of airplanes. But a simulation of an airplane should not be confused with the airplane itself.

2.3   Behavior-Oriented AI Is Strongly Influenced by Biology

We have already identified two key ingredients of the behavior-oriented approach: the study of intelligent behavior, and the methodology of constructing artificial systems. The third ingredient is a strong biological orientation. Intelligence is seen as a biological characteristic, and the "core of intelligence and cognitive abilities is [assumed to be] the same as the capacity of the living" ([124], backcover).

The biological orientation clearly shows up in the way intelligence is defined. The "classical" AI approach defines intelligence in terms of knowledge: A system is intelligent if it maximally applies the knowledge that it has (cf. Newell's principle of rationality [87]). The behavior-oriented approach defines intelligence in terms of observed behavior and self-preservation (or autonomy) (see, e.g., [76,124]). It is based on the idea that the essence of biological systems is their capacity to continuously preserve and adapt themselves [71]: *The behavior of a system is intelligent to the extent that it maximizes the chances for self-preservation of that system in a particular environment.*

The drive toward self-preservation applies to all levels of complexity: genes, cells, multicellular structures, plants, animals, groups of animals, societies, species. Behavior-oriented AI focuses upon the behavior of organisms of the complexity of animals. Systems of this complexity are called agents. When several of them cooperate or compete, we talk about multiagent systems.

In order to explain how a system preserves itself even if the environment changes, adaptivity and learning are corollary conditions of viable intelligent agents: *A system is capable of adapting and learning if it changes its behavior so as to continue maximizing its intelligence, even if the environment changes.*

The biological orientation also shows up in a focus on the problem of how complexity can emerge. The origin of order and complexity is a central theme in biology [53] and is usually studied within the context of self-organization [95] or natural selection [16].

Behavior-oriented AI research is focusing on the concepts of emergent behavior and emergent functionality as a possible explanation for the emergence of functional complexity in agents. These concepts will be discussed in more detail later. A preliminary definition is as follows: *A behavior is emergent if it can only be defined using descriptive categories that are not necessary to describe the behavior of the constituent components. An emergent behavior leads to emergent functionality if the behavior contributes to the system's self-preservation and if the system can build further upon it.*

Behavior-oriented AI studies the origin of complexity at different levels: from components and complete agents to multiagent systems. Systems at each level maximize their self-preservation by adapting their behavior so that it comes closer to the optimal. Coadaptation ensures that different elements at one level contribute to the optimality of the whole. At every level there is cooperation and competition: Different agents cooperate and compete inside a multiagent system. Different behavior systems cooperate and compete inside the agent. Different components cooperate and compete to form coherent behavior systems. So the ingredients of cooperation, competition, selection, hierarchy, and reinforcemnt, which have been identified as crucial for the emergence of complexity in other areas of biology [59], are found at the behavioral level, making it possible to carry over results from other biological disciplines to behavior-oriented AI and vice versa.

All of the elements of the previous definitions for intelligence, adaptivity, and emergence can be quantitatively and objectively established. We can quantify the aspects of the environment that act as pressures on the system considered, the success in self-preservation, the optimality of particular behaviors with respect to their contribution to self-preservation, and the success of adaptation and learning to improve this optimality. All this is illustrated in McFarland and Boesser [76]. We can also quantitatively identify the onset of emergence once a suitable mathematical framework exists for defining the notion of a minimal description. An example of such a framework can be found in Chaitin's work on algorithmic complexity. (See the discussion in Nicolis and Prigogine [89].) The objective nature of these definitions makes them preferable to those relying on the subjective assignment of knowledge or on subjective criteria of similarity to human intelligence as in the Turing Test.

2.4 Behavior-Oriented AI is Complementary to Other Approaches to AI

The behavior-oriented approach is complementary to the currently dominating trend in AI (also known as the classical approach), which is almost exclusively concentrated on the problems of identifying, formalizing, and representing knowledge [38]. The emphasis on knowledge leads almost automatically to a focus on disembodied intelligence. Classical AI systems, therefore, do not include a physical body, sensing, or acting. If intelligent robots have been considered (as in Nilsson [90]), sensing and action has been delegated to subsystems that are assumed to deliver symbolic descriptions to the central planning and decision-making modules. Moreover, knowledge-oriented theories do not include environmental pressures on the self-preservation of the agent, and the role of adaptivity and emergence is taken over by the programmer. However, the claim (made, e.g., in Maes [66]) that the classical, knowledge-oriented approach works only for "simulated toy problems" and makes too many simplifying assumptions (e.g., static environments, single tasks, etc.) is simply not true. Objective results achieved in knowledge engineering for large-scale, extremely challenging real-world problems (like the assignment of train engines and personnel to routes taking into account a large number of possibly conflicting constraints, or the diagnosis of printed circuit boards assembled in digital telephone switch boards) cannot and should not be dismissed.

The behavior-oriented approach is also complementary to the artificial neural network approach, which is based on an even more radical bottom-up attitude because it focuses on the physical basis of behavior and hopes that this is sufficient to explain or synthesize intelligence [56], that is, that no separate behavioral level is necessary. The distinction between the two fields is of course a matter of degree. Behavior-oriented researchers heavily make use of neural network techniques to implement certain aspects of an overall design, and some neural network researchers are beginning to consider the problem of building complete agents (cf. Edelman's NOMAD [34]).

There are obviously strong ties between behavior-oriented AI and robotics, because the construction of physical agents is seen as a condition sine qua non for applying the method of the artificial properly. But the two fields should not be equated. The goal of robotics is to identify, design, and engineer the most reliable and most cost-effective solution for a sensorimotor task in a particular, usually fixed and known, environment [17]. Behavior-oriented AI uses the tools of roboticists to study biological issues, but very different criteria for success apply.

2.5   The Rest of the Paper Focuses on Emergence

A review of the field can be organized along several lines. One way would be to look at the progress toward the achievement of specific competences, for example, the different approaches for "navigation towards a target": using potential fields [7], cognitive maps with landmarks [70], phonotaxis [129], global reference frames [86], pheromone trails or agent chains [41], and so on. Another approach would be to review the large amount of work on building technical hardware and software platforms that now make it possible to execute experiments easily and at low cost [31,35,50]. This technical work is in some way a revival of earlier cybernetics work by Walter [128] and Braitenberg [18] but now with better hardware and more advanced software. Yet another way is to look at progress on the theoretical questions outlined earlier, for example, the definition and use of optimality criteria [76] or the development of quantitative behavioral descriptions using techniques from complex systems theory [89].

These overviews would all be valuable but require much more space than available here. Instead, we will focus on how behavior-oriented AI may contribute to the field of AL as a whole, and more specifically to its central research theme, which is the origin of complexity. The focus on the interaction between physical agents and the world through sensing and effecting introduces a special perspective that is not found in other AL work. The emergence of complexity must come through the dynamics of interacting with an infinitely complex, dynamically changing, real world and not only through the internal dynamics as in the case of cellular automata, for example.

In order to limit further the scope of the paper, we will only focus on how the behavior of a single agent is established. There is a lot of fascinating work on multiagent systems, and often it is not even possible to study single agents without taking other agents into account. Nevertheless, a review of work on multiagent systems would have doubled the size of the present paper.

3   Behavior Systems

When one is studying multiagent systems (like ant societies), the units of investigation are clearly visible. But the units causing the behavior of a single agent are not directly observable. Sensors, neurons, networks of neurons, propagation processes, and actuators are the obvious building blocks. But many of these must work together and interact with structures and processes in the environment in order to establish a particular behavior, and the same components may dynamically be involved in many different behaviors. This is the reason why it is so difficult to bridge the gap between neurology and psychology.

There is a growing consensus in behavior-oriented AI research that behavior systems be considered as the basic units [19]. Other terms for the basic behavioral unit are task-achieving module [68] or schema [5].

To define the notion of a behavior system, we have to make a distinction between a functionality, a behavior, a mechanism, and a component:

- *Functionalities:* A functionality is something that the agent needs to achieve, for example, locomotion, recharging, avoiding obstacles, finding the charging station, performing a measurement, signaling another agent. Other terms used for functionality are task, goal, and competence. Functionalities belong to the descriptive vocabulary of the observer.

- *Behaviors:* A behavior is a regularity in the interaction dynamics between an agent and its environment, for example, maintaining a bounded distance from the wall, or having a continuous location change in a particular direction. One or more behaviors contribute to the realization of a particular functionality. Behaviors belong also to the descriptive vocabulary of the observer. By looking at the same agent in the same environment, it is possible to categorize the behavior in different ways. This does not mean that behavior characterization is subjective. It can be defined and measured fully objectively.

- *Mechanisms:* A mechanism is a principle or technique for establishing a particular behavior, for example, a particular coupling between sensing and acting, the use of a map, an associative learning mechanism.

- *Components:* A component is a physical structure or process that is used to implement a mechanism. Examples of components are body parts, sensors, actuators, data structures, programs, communication hardware, and software.

A *behavior system* is the set of all mechanisms that play a role in establishing a particular behavior. The structures of a behavior system that can undergo a change due to learning are usually called behavior programs. Observed behavior will, of course, depend almost as much on the state of the environment as on the mechanisms and components of the agent. Often the name of the behavior system indicates the functionality to which it contributes. But strictly speaking, we should be more careful. For example, there could be a "homing in" functionality achieved by a "zigzag behavior" toward a goal location that is the result of a "phototaxis mechanism." Phototaxis means that the goal location has a light source acting as beacon and that the robot uses light sensors to minimize the distance between itself and the beacon. The reason why we need to be careful in mixing functional and behavior terminology is because the same behavior system may contribute to different functionalities.

Behavior systems may be very simple, implementing direct reflexes between sensing and action (as in Brooks [19]). They may also be more complex, building up and using cognitive world maps (as in Mataric [70]). When enough complexity is reached, a large collection of interacting behavior systems may resemble a society of interacting agents [84]. Each behavior system is most adapted to a particular class of environments. This environment can be characterized in terms of a set of constraints [48] or cost functions [75].

Note that a behavior system is a theoretical unit. There is not a simple one-to-one relation between a functionality, a behavior, and a set of mechanisms achieving the behavior. The only thing that has physical existence are the components. This is obvious if emergent functionality comes into play (see sections 4 and 5). On the other hand, behavior systems form a real unit in the same way that a society forms a real unit.

Table 1. Comparison Between Cells and Behavior Systems.

Cell	Behavior System
Biochemical processes	Transformation processes
Biochemical structures	Electrical signals and states
Genes	Behavior programs
Incoming material	Energy transduced by sensors
Outgoing material	Energy transduced by actuators
Adaptation to cell environment	Adaptation to external environment

The interaction between the different mechanisms and the success in the behavior to achieve tasks that contribute to the agent's self-preservation give a positive enforcement to all the elements forming part of a behavior system.

3.1 Behavior Systems Should Be Viewed as Living Systems

In view of the biological orientation discussed earlier, it is not surprising that many behavior-oriented AI researchers view behavior systems very much like living systems. This means that behavior systems are viewed as units that try to preserve themselves. An analogy with cells that are the smallest biological autonomous units helps to make this concrete (Table 1). A cell consists of a group of biochemical structures and processes. The processes are guided by genes, which are themselves represented as molecular structures inside the cell. The processes take place in interaction with material outside the cell that is passing through the cell membrane in both directions. Cells may change their internal structure and functioning, to a certain limit, and adapt to the surrounding environment [97].

A behavior system consists also of a set of dynamic and static structures. The structures include physical components like sensors and body parts, as well as networks, temporary states, and electrical signals propagating in these networks. The internal processes combine and transform signals. These transformation processes are guided by a behavior program that is itself a (distributed) physical structure and can be subjected to processes that change it. The transformation processes are partially caused by energy coming from the outside through sensors that convert this to internal energy, and they produce signals impacting the actuators that convert internal energy to mechanical energy so that there is a continuous inflow and outflow of energy to the environment. Behavior systems that change their internal structure and functioning are better adapted to the environment and may better work together with other behavior systems. The main criterion for survival of a behavior system is its utility for the complete agent.

This comparison between cells and behavior systems illustrates several points. (a) It emphasizes in the first place that the components of behavior systems are physical systems and that behavior is a physical phenomenon. There are extreme functionalist tendencies in AI (and also in AL) that equate intelligence or living with disembodied abstractions, but this is not intended here. (b) The behavior programs and the transformation processes can be interpreted in information-processing terms, but that is not necessary and may occasionally be harmful [107]. (c) The transformation processes can be implemented as computational processes but then only if we remind ourselves that computational processes are physical processes, which happen to be instantiated in a physical system of a certain organization that we call a computer.

The comparison also emphasizes the dynamical aspects. Like a cell, a behavior system is continuously active and subjected to inflow and outflow of energy. Like a cell, a behavior system adapts continuously to changes in the environment. Moreover,

Figure 1. Typical robotic agent used in behavior-oriented AI experiments. The robot has a ring of infrared sensors and a ring of bumper sensors. It has additional light sensors and microphones. There is a translational motor for forward/backward movement and a rotational motor for turning left or right. The agent has a central PC-like processor and dedicated hardware for signal processing and interdevice communication.

comparing behavior programs with genes immediately suggests the use of selectionist principles as a way to arrive at new behavior systems without prior design (see section 5).

A concrete example for obstacle avoidance in an artificial agent may be helpful to clarify the discussion (Figure 1). Obstacle avoidance can be achieved by a behavior system that maintains a certain distance from obstacles. The components of this behavior system include a left and right infrared sensor, which emit infrared light and capture the reflection coming from obstacles; a translational and rotational motor, which are connected with the wheels and can steer the robot left or right; and a behavior program that causes processes to transform the changes in detected infrared reflection into changes in the motor speeds. As already suggested in Braitenberg [18], obstacle avoidance can be achieved by a direct coupling between infrared reflection and rotational motor speed. If the amount of reflection increases on one side, then the rotational motor speed going in the same direction increases. In a real-world environment, adaptation is necessary because infrared reflection depends on changing environmental circumstances (e.g., amount of background infrared in the environment or battery level). Adaptation can here be achieved by incorporating structures that act as "weights" on the effect of increased reflection. When the weights become higher, less reflection will have a greater impact. The weights can be subject to change depending on environmental conditions using Hebbian learning mechanisms (see section 5).

3.2 Some Guidelines Are Known for Designing Behavior Systems

At the moment, the design of behavior systems for artificial agents is very much an art, and the complexity reached so far is still limited. But there are some strong tendencies among practitioners suggesting a set of design guidelines. Following are some examples of these guidelines:

Guideline 1: Make behavior systems as specific as possible. One of the important lessons from classical AI research is the specificity-generality trade-off. More specific knowledge, that is, knowledge more strongly tailored to the task and the domain, is more effective than generic mechanisms, such as general problem solvers or universal representation schemes. Success in expert systems has depended almost entirely on the encoding of situation-specific knowledge. This trade-off also applies to behavior systems. Rather than trying to build a general-purpose vision module for example, it is much more effective to tailor the sensing and actuating to a particular task, a particular domain, and a particular environment. Of course, such a solution will not work outside its "niche." But it will perform well and in a very cost-effective way, as long as the conditions are appropriate. A good illustration of this design guideline is a visual navigation system developed by Horswill [49], who has shown that by making a set of strong assumptions about the environment, the complexity of visual interpretation can be reduced drastically. One example is the detection of the vanishing point, which in theory can be done by identifying edges, grouping them into line segments, intersecting the segments, and clustering on the pairwise intersections. Horswill shows that each of these activities can be highly optimized. For example, although in general edge detection is complex and computationally intensive, a simple algorithm based on a gradient threshold will do, if the edges are strong and straight. This work goes in the direction of the theory of visual routines [122], which has abandoned the idea that there is a general purpose vision system and proposes instead a large collection of special purpose mechanisms that can be exploited in particular behavior systems.

Specialization and the pressure to act in real time suggests a horizontal organization, as opposed to a vertical or hierarchical organization, typical for more classical approaches [21]. In a vertical organization, the different modules perform specific functions like vision, learning, world representation, communication, or planning. This leads to a sense-think-act cycle that does not guarantee real-time response when needed. In a horizontal organization, every module combines all these functions but specialized and optimized with respect to a particular behavior in a particular environment. The relation between task and behavior thus becomes much more indirect. This is reminiscent of horizontal organizations now becoming more common in corporations [93].

Guideline 2: Exploit the physics. Surprisingly, it is sometimes easier to achieve a particular behavior when the physics of the world, the morphology of the body, and the physics of the sensors and the actuators of the agent are properly exploited [21]. This is already the case for obstacle avoidance. A robot may be equipped with bumpers that cause a (sudden) slowdown and an immediate retraction in a random direction. This may get the robot out of situations that appear to be dead-end situations in simulations. Another good illustration of this design principle can be found in Webb [129], who has developed a model in the form of an artificial system for navigation based on the phonotaxis behavior of crickets. Webb points out that the determination of the direction in crickets is not based on intensity or phase differences, which would require complex neural processing, but on an extra tracheal tube that transfers vibration from one ear to the other. The length and characteristics of this tube are such that the indirectly arriving sound and the directly arriving sound interfere to give the final intensity, which varies strongly with the direction of the sound. This is an example where "sensory mechanisms exploit the specificity of the task and the physics of their environment so as to greatly simplify the processing required to produce the right behaviour" [129, p. 1093]. Many more biological examples of how physics may "solve" problems, so that additional processing can be minimized, can be found in Alexander [3] and Vogel [127].

Guideline 3: Do not think of sensing and acting in terms of symbol processing. The classical AI approach has been criticized because the symbols and symbol structures on which planning and decision making are based are not grounded in the real world [43]. The problem is that unequivocally decoding sensory data into a symbol and turning a command without error into its intended action may be unsolvable—not in principle but in practice. Behavior-oriented AI cannot escape the grounding problem. But a novel solution is proposed. Rather than trying hard to establish a better correspondence between symbols (like distance or turn with a given angle) and the physical properties of the robot in the environment, it is also possible to dispense altogether with the idea that a symbolic interpretation is necessary [107]. For example, rather than having a rule of the sort "if the distance is greater than n, then turn away at a certain angle a," a dynamical coupling between infrared reflection and path deflection, implemented, for example, as differences between left and right motor speed, can be set up. This coupling is designed without reference to concepts like "distance" and "turn away." Therefore, it is truly subsymbolic.

Guideline 4. Simple mechanisms may give rise to complex behavior. Another strong tendency in the field is to make the mechanisms underlying a behavior system as simple as possible and to rely strongly on the interactions between different mechanisms and the environment to get the required behavior. This theme underlies other work in AL as well and is related to the topic of emergence that is discussed more extensively in sections 4 and 5. This tendency to search for simple mechanisms is particularly strong in the dislike of complex "objective" world models [22]. The de-emphasis of complex representations is shared by researchers criticizing cognitivism [125] and is related to the trend for situated cognition [115], which hypothesizes that intelligence is the result of simple situation-specific agent/environment mechanisms that are strongly adapted to moment-to-moment decision making. Some biologists have called this the TODO principle: Do whatever there is to do at a particular moment, instead of making complex representations and following elaborated plans [47].

It can be expected that many more design guidelines will become explicated as experience in building robotic agents continues. Some more extensive overviews can be found in Malcolm, Smithers, and Hallam [69]; Brooks [22]; Pfeifer and Verschure [94]; and Maes [66].

3.3 Different Approaches Are Explored for Designing the Behavior Programs

Although there seems to be a consensus in the field that behavior systems are appropriate units, different avenues are explored regarding the best way to design the underlying behavior programs. They fall roughly in four groups: neural network approaches, algorithmic approaches, circuit approaches, and dynamics approaches.

3.3.1 Neural Networks Approaches

Several researchers use artificial neural networks, in order to stay close to plausible biological structures [5,27,94]. This approach is strongly related to biological cybernetics and neuroethology [15]. A neural network consists of a set of nodes linked together in a network. Each node receives input from a set of nodes and sends activation as output to another set of nodes. Some inputs could come immediately from sensors. Some outputs are linked with actuators. The links between nodes are weighted. When the sum of the weighted inputs to a node exceeds a threshold, activation propagates to the output nodes. There are many variants of neural networks, depending on the type of propagation and the adaptation mechanism that is used for changing the weights [56]. Usually a single neural network (even with multiple layers) is not enough to build a complete robotic agent. More structure is needed in which different neural networks can be hierarchically combined. Several architectures and associated programming

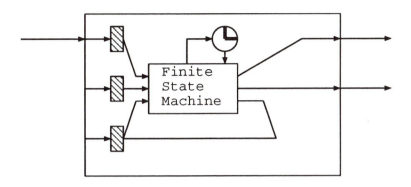

Figure 2. The augmented finite-state automata have a set of internal registers, inputs and outputs, and a clock. The automaton cycles through a set of states.

languages have been proposed. One of the best worked-out examples is reported by Lyons and Arbib [62]. It centers around the schema concept [7].

An advantage of neural network approaches is that they immediately incorporate a mechanism for learning. A disadvantage is that the global search space for an agent is too big to start from zero with neural network techniques. Much more initial structure must typically be encoded, which is sometimes difficult to express in network terms.

3.3.2 Algorithmic Approaches

Other researchers have stayed closer to the methods traditionally used in computer programming so that powerful abstraction mechanisms can be used to cope with the complexity of programming complete robotic agents. One of the best known examples is the subsumption architecture [19], which makes two fundamental assumptions: (a) behavior programs are defined algorithmically, and (b) there is a hierarchical but distributed control between different behavior systems based on subsumption relations.

The algorithmic descriptions in the subsumption architecture use a Turing-compatible formalism in the form of an augmented finite-state machine (Figure 2). An augmented finite-state machine has a set of registers that can hold discrete values. On a robot, some of the registers hold the most recent value obtained from sensors. Others contain action parameters to be sent as fast as possible to the actuators. An augmented finite-state machine also has a set of states in which the automaton can be. Operations consist of changing the contents of a register or moving to a new state. These operations can be controlled by first checking whether a condition on the state of the registers is true. An important feature of the finite-state machines used by Brooks is access to a clock. This introduces an additional kind of operation: wait for a certain period of time and resume operation after that. It gives a handle on the difficult problems in fine-tuning the temporal aspects of behavior.

In a single agent, there will be a collection of behavior systems whose behavior programs are defined in terms of augmented finite-state machines. The term subsumption refers to the way different behavior systems are made to operate together. It is assumed that in principle, each behavior system is self-controlled, that is, it is always active and moving through its different states conditioned by the incoming sensory signals. However, one behavior system may inhibit that inputs arrive at the automaton or that outputs have their effect. Inhibition is done by an explicit subsumption link that is under the control of the behavior system (Figure 3).

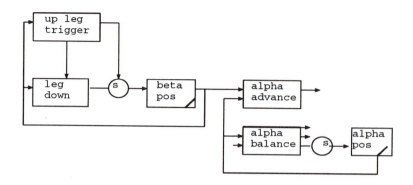

Figure 3. Partial network of finite-state automata for the locomotion of a six-legged robot. The boxes are state variables. Boxes with a line in the bottom right corner are finite-state automata. Alpha balance is another network. Nodes marked "s" establish a subsumption relation. For example, activation of "up leg trigger" inhibits the inflow of "leg down" to the "beta pos" automaton. Adapted from Brooks [19].

In a concrete agent, the number and complexity of the finite-state automata quickly grows to hundreds of states and registers. A higher-level language, known as the behavior language [20], has been designed to make the definition of large collections of behavior systems possible. Many of the low-level details of programming finite-state automata are removed, and consequently more complex applications can be tackled. The behavior language and the subsumption architecture have been implemented on various computational platforms (mostly of the 68000 family) in different robotic hardware structures.

The recognized advantages of the subsumption architecture are as follows: (a) A universal computational formalism is used that gives a high degree of freedom and expressability to the developer, and (b) subsumption allows the modular buildup of new competences by layering one behavior system on top of another.

Some of the disadvantages are (a) algorithmic descriptions are more difficult to acquire or adapt (although see the work on genetic programming by Koza [58] discussed in section 5); (b) an algorithmic specification makes it more difficult to get smooth behavior because conditions are expressed in terms of discrete thresholds; and (c) the subsumption relation works well for basic sensorimotor competence, like six-legged locomotion, but it seems weak to regulate the interaction of more complex behavior systems that cannot be fined-tuned in advance.

3.3.3 Circuit Approaches

A third approach stays closer to electrical engineering by assuming that behavior programs, in order to be as efficient as possible, should take the form of combinatorial circuits [2,100]. This approach potentially leads to direct hardware implementation using Very Large Scale Integration (VLSI). A combinatorial circuit consists of a set of components that perform a transformation from inputs to outputs. The outputs of one component may be inputs to one or more other components, thus forming a network. Each component is very simple, performing Boolean operations, equality tests, etc. On an autonomous robot, the inputs would be connected to sensory signals and the outputs to action parameters. Signals propagate through the network, thus relating sensing to action. A language (called REX) has been developed to describe circuits. Compilers and interpreters exist that allow REX-defined circuits to run on physical robots.

To make programming circuits more tractable, Rosenschein and Kaelbling [100] have developed a higher-level language that is based on a logical formalism known as situated automata. A translator has also been developed that transforms expressions expressed in this logical formalism into circuits.

A circuit approach has a number of advantages from an engineering point of view. For example, performance can be predicted in terms of propagation steps needed. However, the circuit is completely fixed at run-time, and it is less clear how continuous adaptation or the creation of new circuits can take place on-line.

3.3.4 Dynamics Approaches

Yet another approach is based on the hypothesis that behavior systems should be viewed as continuous dynamical systems instead of discrete computational systems as in the algorithmic approach. This dynamics approach has been put forward by a number of researchers (see, e.g., [107,114]). It is more in line with standard control theory, which is also based on dynamical systems [42]. Artificial neural networks are a special case of dynamical systems and can be incorporated easily in this paradigm.

An example of a worked-out dynamics architecture is described in Steels [114]. It supports the formulation of processes and their combination in the design of complete behavior systems. Each process establishes a continuous relationship between a set of quantities. The quantities are either sensory signals, action parameters, or internal states. A process is always active. A collection of processes can be described in terms of a set of differential equations. Because of the implementation on digital computers, the differential equations are turned into difference equations that can be directly implemented, similar to the way cellular automata are discreted versions of continuous systems [120]. Each process partially determines the change to a quantity enacted at the next time step, as a function of current values of the same or other quantities. At each computation cycle, all the changes are summed, and the values of all the quantities take on their new values. The cycle time depends on the speed of the processor and the number of processes. There is no addressable global clock, as in the subsumption architecture. The complexity of the agent will be bound by its computational power. When the cycle time becomes too slow, reactivity is no longer guaranteed.

A programming language, PDL, has been developed to make the implementation of behavior systems using this dynamics architecture more productive (Figure 4). The PDL compiler links with the necessary low-level software modules to handle sensory input and action parameter output. It maintains the different internal quantities and performs the basic cycle of determining all changes (by running the processes) and then summing and enacting the changes. PDL has been implemented on different PC-like hardware platforms for quite different robotic hardware structures.

A dynamics architecture approaches the problem of combining and coordinating different behavior systems differently from the subsumption architecture. Control is also distributed, but one behavior system can no longer influence another one through a subsumption link. Instead, each behavior system is active at all times, and the combined effect is added at the level of actions. For example, if one behavior system influences the motors strongly to go left and the other one weakly to go right, then there will be a left tendency. The unsupervised combination of different behavior systems poses no special problems when they are orthogonal. It also poses no problem when temporal relations are implicitly present. For example, an infrared-based obstacle avoidance behavior system will necessarily become active before a touch-based obstacle avoidance behavior system because the infrared sensors will "see" the obstacle earlier. Therefore,

```
void down_to_default_speed (void)

{

    if (value(forward_speed) > 10)

        add_value(forward_speed,-1);

}


void up_to_default_speed (void)

{

    if (value(forward_speed) < 10)

        add_value(forward_speed,1);

}
```

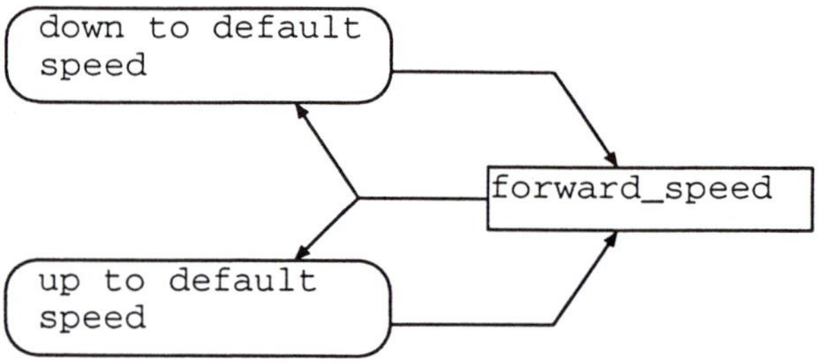

Figure 4. Process descriptions in PDL implementing a process network that will maintain the default forward speed at 10 by increasing or decreasing the speed in increments of 1.

no explicit control relations are needed. When behavior systems are not orthogonal or are not temporally ordered by the interaction dynamics, (partial) control of the actuators must take into account the fact that other behavior systems will have an impact at the same time. In these cases, the interaction must be regulated by structural coupling [71] or coadaptation: Behavior systems develop in the context of other behavior systems, and, hence, their internal structure and functioning reflects this context. More complex control situations require the introduction of motivational variables that causally influence behavior systems and have a dynamics on their own.

The advantages of a dynamics architecture follow: (a) The dynamical systems paradigm is closer to descriptions used in physics, biology, and control theory. This is an advantage because it makes it easier to carry over results from these fields (e.g., on adaptive processes). (b) Dynamic control leads in general to smoother behavior because it is not subject to sudden state changes due to discrete conditions. (c) Additive control does not enforce a layering. All behavior systems are at the same level. In many cases, it is easier to add behavioral competence than with a subsumption architecture. In some cases, it is more difficult because a structural coupling must be established.

Some of the disadvantages of a dynamics architecture follow: (a) Thinking in terms of dynamical systems instead of algorithms requires quite a shift from the viewpoint of developers who are used to algorithmic programming. Higher-level abstractions still need to be developed. (b) The developer cannot explicitly control the timing of actions. This is an advantage because it removes one aspect of complexity. It is also a disadvantage because the problem of timing must be handled in different ways, for example, by restructuring the behavior systems so that there is as little cascading as possible, or by decomposing behavioral competences in other ways.

There is still quite some work needed on additive control structures, particularly for hierarchical behavior systems, that is, behavior systems that control a set of other behavior systems that are possibly internally temporally ordered. Work by Rosenblatt and Payton [99] and Tyrrell [121] shows the direction in which this is being explored.

These four different approaches to the design and implementation of behavior programs (neural networks, algorithms, circuits, dynamical systems) will undoubtedly be explored further in the near future, and new approaches may come up. In any case, all approaches need more high level abstractions to hide complexity and allow reuse of large chunks from one experiment to another.

4   Emergent Behavior

Agents can become more complex in two ways. First, a designer (or more generally a designing agency) can identify a functionality that the agent needs to achieve, then investigate possible behaviors that could realize the functionality, and then introduce various mechanisms that sometimes give rise to the behavior. Second, existing behavior systems in interaction with each other and the environment can show side effects, in other words, emergent behavior. This behavior may sometimes yield new useful capabilities for the agent, in which case we talk about *emergent functionality*. In engineering, increased complexity through side effects is usually regarded as negative and avoided, particularly in computer programming. But it seems that in nature, this form of complexity buildup is preferred. Emergent functionality has disadvantages from an engineering point of view because it is less predictable and appears less certain to a designer. Moreover, the side effects are not always beneficial. But for an agent operating independently in the world, it has advantages because less intervention from a designing agency is needed. In fact, it seems the only way in which an agent can autonomously increase its capability. This is why emergent functionality has become one of the primary research themes in behavior-oriented AI. It is also the research theme that has the most connections to other areas of AL.

4.1   Emergence Can Be Defined in Terms of the Need for New Descriptive Categories

Many researchers in the AL community have attempted to define emergence (see, e.g., [8,24,36,59,111]). For the present purposes, we will define emergence from two viewpoints: that of the observer and that of the components of the system.

From the viewpoint of an observer, we call a sequence of events a behavior if a certain regularity becomes apparent. This regularity is expressed in certain observational categories, for example, speed, distance to walls, changes in energy level. A behavior is emergent if new categories are needed to describe this underlying regularity that are not needed to describe the behaviors (i.e., the regularities) generated by the underlying behavior systems on their own. This definition is compatible with the one used in chemistry and physics (see, e.g., [88]). Thus, the regularities observed in the collective behavior of many molecules requires new categories like temperature and pressure over and above those needed to describe the motion of individual molecules. Whether a behavior is emergent or not does not change according to this definition, with respect to who acts as observer, nor is it related to an element of unpredictability or surprise. Moreover, it is not necessary that the two descriptions (the emergent behavior and the behavior of the individual components) are at different levels, although that is not excluded.

Emergence can also be defined from the viewpoint of the components implicated in the emergent behavior [111]. We can make a distinction between controlled and uncontrolled variables. A controlled variable can be directly influenced by a system, for example, a robot can directly control its forward speed, although maybe not with full accuracy. An uncontrolled variable changes due to actions of the system, but the system cannot directly impact it, only through a side effect of its actions. For example, a robot cannot directly impact its distance to the wall; it can only change its direction of movement, which will then indirectly change the distance.

We can also make a distinction between a visible variable and an invisible variable. A visible variable is a characteristic of the environment that, through a sensor, has a causal impact on the internal structures and processes and, thus, on behavior. For example, a robot may have a sensor that measures distance directly. Distance would then be a visible variable for this robot. An invisible variable is a characteristic of the environment, which we as observers can measure, but the system has no way to sense it, nor does it play a role in the components implicated in the emergent behavior. For example, the robot could just as well not have a sensor to measure distance.

For a behavior to be emergent, we expect at least that the regularity involves an uncontrolled variable. A stricter requirement is that the behavior (i.e., the regularity) involves only invisible variables. So, when a behavior is emergent, we should find that none of the components is directly sensitive to the regularities exhibited by the behavior and that no component is able to control its appearance directly.

A further distinction can be made between emergent behavior upon which the system does not build further, and semantic emergence [24] or second-order emergence [9], in which the system is able to detect, amplify, and build upon emergent behavior. The latter can only happen by operating on the behavior programs that causally influence behavior, similar to the way genetic evolution operates on the genes. The remainder of this section discusses first-order emergence. Section 5 looks at semantic emergence.

4.2 The Most Basic Form of Emergent Behavior Is Based on Side Effects

The first type of first-order emergence occurs as a side effect when behavior systems are made to operate together in a particular environment (Figure 5).

Consider the task of wall following. The behavioral regularity needed for this task is to have a bounded distance between the agent and the wall. This regularity can be achieved in a directly controlled, nonemergent way, by measuring the distance and using feedback control to steer away or toward the wall. Note that in this case, the distance is required to describe the behavior causing wall following and that distance is a visible variable.

Maintaining a distance from the wall can be achieved in an emergent way by the simultaneous operation of two behavior systems (as demonstrated by Nehmzow, Smithers, & McGonigle [85] and in our laboratory). The first one achieves regular obstacle avoidance, for example, in terms of a dynamic coupling between infrared reflection and deflection of the path as described earlier. The second behavior system exhibits wall seeking. This behavior system maintains an internal variable c, which reflects "the motivation of making contact with the left wall." The variable c decreases to 0

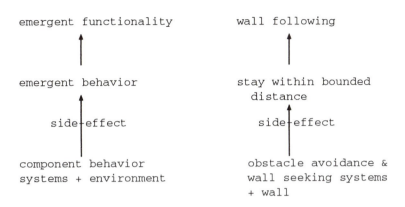

Figure 5. Left: Emergent behavior occurs as a side effect of the interaction between behaviors and the environment. New descriptive categories are needed to describe it. Right: example for wall following resulting from the operation of the obstacle- and wall-seeking behaviors.

Figure 6. Emergent wall following implemented by an obstacle avoidance and a wall-seeking behavior system interacting together within a particular environment. The image is taken from the ceiling and shows the robot arena. The path of the robot is automatically detected through a camera.

when contact is made with the left wall (sensed by infrared reflection) and moves up otherwise. It influences the deflection of the forward motion path toward the wall. The higher is c, the stronger the deflection. The two behavior systems together implement an attraction and repulsion behavior that added up and in the presence of a (left) wall gives the desired (left) wall-following behavior (Figure 6). An analogous behavior system is needed for making contact with a right wall.

Wall following is emergent in this case because the category "equidistance to the (left/right) wall" is not explicitly sensed by the robot or causally used in one of the controlling behavior systems.

Emergent behavior has two advantages compared to directly programmed behavior: (a) No additional structure is needed inside the agent to get additional capabilities. Therefore, we do not need any special explanations how the behavior may come about. (b) Emergent behavior tends to be more robust because it is less dependent on accurate sensing or action and because it makes less environmental assumptions. For example, the wall-following mechanism described previously continues to work even if the robot is momentarily pushed aside, if the wall is interrupted, or if the wall has a strong curvature. Emergent behavior usually has also disadvantages, for example, it is typically less efficient.

Here is a second example of emergent behavior. Suppose we want an agent that is able to position itself accurately between two poles that are part of a charging station. The charging station has an associated light source, and the agent has two light sensitive sensors. The agent starts with two behavior systems: one based on phototaxis resulting in a zigzag behavior toward the light source (and, therefore, the charging station) and one achieving obstacle avoidance by retracting and turning away when sensing an obstacle.

Because the agent may approach the charging station from any direction, it might seem that an additional positioning behavior is required, which makes sure that the agent enters the charging station between the two poles. However, a positioning behavior system is not necessary. The obstacle avoidance behavior causes retraction and turning away when the poles are hit. Because the robot is still attracted by the light source, it will again approach the charging station but now from a new angle. After a few trials, the robot enters the charging station as desired. The positioning behavior is emergent because position relative to the poles of the charging station is irrelevant to describe the behavior of the implicated behavior systems (obstacle avoidance and phototaxis). There is no separate structure in the agent that is measuring position with respect to the poles and causally influences motion based on this measurement. Nevertheless, the positioning behavior occurs reliably without any additional structure in the agent (Figure 7).

4.3 A Second Form of Emergent Behavior Is Based on Spatiotemporal Structures

A second case of (first-order) emergence is based on temporary spatiotemporal structures (Figure 8). These structures themselves emerge as a side effect of interactions between certain actions of the agent and the environment. Local properties of the temporary structure in turn causally influence the observed behavior. The temporary structure is also emergent in the same sense as before, that is, new descriptive categories are needed to identify the structure. These categories are neither needed to describe the behavior of the underlying behavior systems that are causing the structure to appear nor are they sensitive to the structure as a whole. Also the behavior that results from making use of the structure is emergent because new descriptive categories are required that play no causal role in the underlying behavior systems.

This phenomenon is most easily observed in multiagent systems but can also be used for establishing behaviors of a single agent. The classical example for multiagent systems is the formation of paths. It has been well studied empirically not only in ant societies [91] but also in many other biological multielement systems [10]. It is also well understood theoretically in terms of the more general theory of self-organization [89] The phenomenon has been shown in simulation studies [29,32,108] and recently on physical robots [14].

Figure 7. Zigzag behavior toward light source and positioning behavior between two poles of a charging station located at the middle top of the figure. The positioning behavior is achieved in an emergent way by the interaction of two-behavior systems, one homing in on the light source through phototaxis and the other performing touch-based obstacle avoidance.

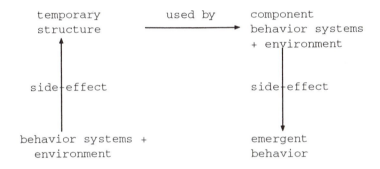

Figure 8. A second type of emergence is based on the formation of an emergent temporary structure that is then exploited by other behavior systems to establish the new emergent behavior.

The temporary structure in the case of path formation in ant societies is a chemical pheromone gradient deposited in the environment. Ants are attracted to the pheromone and, therefore, have a tendency to aggregate along the path. Ants deposit the pheromone as they are carrying food back to the nest and are responsible for the pheromone gradient in the first place. The pheromone dissipates so that it will disappear gradually when the food source is depleted. This emergent temporary structure is the basis of a derived emergent behavior, namely the formation of a path, defined as a regular spatial relation among the ants (Figure 9). The path, as a global structure, is emergent because it is not needed to describe the behavior of the individual agents, and none of the agents recognize the fact that there is a path. The agents operate uniquely on local information of the pheromone gradient. Only the observer sees the

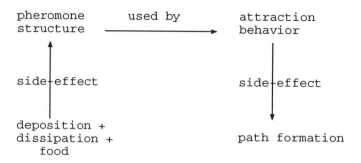

Figure 9. Path formation in ant societies is a classical example of emergent behavior due to the formation of a temporary structure. The structure in this case is a chemical pheromone gradient to which the ants are attracted.

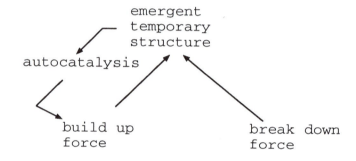

Figure 10. Emergent phenomena usually involve a force that builds up the phenomenon, a force that breaks it down, and an autocatalytic process so that the temporary structure builds upon itself.

global path. The efficient transport of food benefits the multiagent system as a whole and, thus, contributes to its self-preservation.

A difference with the examples discussed in the previous paragraph is that the emergent temporary structure sustains itself: As more ants are attracted to the pheromone concentration, there is a higher chance that they will carry back food and deposit more pheromone. This increases the concentration of pheromone, which will attract even more ants, and so on. So there are three forces in the system: buildup of the path (by depositing pheromone), breakdown (by dissipation), and autocatalysis (through the chance of increased build-up) (Figure 10). These forces are recognized as the essential ingredients for emergent temporary structures in general [59,111].

Emergent temporary structures have also been used in individual agents. For example, several researchers have explored the creation of gradient fields over analogical representations of the environment. The best known example are potential fields [6,7]. A potential field is a dynamical temporary structure created over an analogical representation of the environment by various repulsion and attraction forces. The attraction force may come from the location of the desired goal toward which the agent wants to move. Repulsion may be generated by processes that are linked to the sensing of ob-

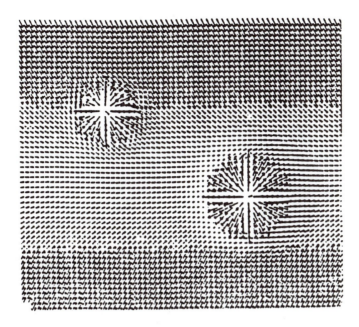

Figure 11. A potential field is a temporary structure created over an analogical representation of the world. The structure consists of vector fields that can either attract or repel robot movement. The sum of all the fields generates a path that the robot can follow. The example shows repulsion from two obstacles and a left and right wall. Adapted from Arkin [7], p. 99.

stacles. Locomotion is influenced by the combined impact of attraction and repulsion forces (Figure 12 from Arkin [7], p. 99).

Other types of dynamics have been explored to generate and maintain emergent temporary structures to aid in navigation, for example, fluid mechanics so that a fluid flow between the agent's location in an analogical map and the goal location emerges [28], or reaction-diffusion dynamics to generate concentration gradients that can be exploited in navigation or movement control [109].

The creation of temporary structures through a self-organizing mechanism that combines buildup, breakdown, and feedback giving rise to autocatalysis has been used also for other aspects of intelligent behavior. For example, Maes [64] describes an action selection system (which perhaps should be better called a motivational system) in which the strength of a motivation is subject to positive enforcement (e.g., when the conditions for its satisfaction are sensed to hold) or negative enforcement (e.g., if contradicting motivations are active). These two processes generate a temporal ordering of the strength of motivations and consequently between the strength with which an action should get priority in execution. There is also a feedback mechanism: As motivation builds up, it will be able to inhibit competitors more effectively and gain additional strength. The temporary strength differences can be used by a decision module to determine which action will be selected next.

A particularly fascinating application of this mechanism for modeling spinal reflex behaviors of the frog is reported in Giszter [39]. The behaviors include limb withdrawal, aversive turns, and wiping away of nociceptive stimuli. The latter requires, for example, different simpler component behaviors: optional flexion, then place motion, and then whisk motion. Each of these has certain conditions that need to be satisfied, and each will make certain conditions true. If one behavior needs to be executed (e.g., "place motion"), it will pass activation along its predecessor link to "optional flexion," thus raising its level of activation. When flexion executes, it will establish conditions that make "place motion" executable, and so on.

Another example of the creation of temporary emergent structures for a frame recognition system is reported in Steels [110]. Each frame has a particular strength that corresponds to the applicability of the frame in a particular situation. There is an activation/inhibition dynamics and autocatalytic processes that create a temporal ordering on the frames so that the most appropriate frame for the given situation progressively gets the highest strength.

5 Emergent Functionality

The examples in the previous section showed that complexity may arise as a side effect of the operation of simpler mechanisms, but they do not indicate how there could be a progressive buildup of more complexity. The only way this can happen is by the formation of new behavior systems. There is so far very little progress in this area, and new ideas are needed. Lack of progress comes partly from the practical difficulties in working with real physical agents, but these difficulties will progressively be alleviated as the technology matures. The real challenge is to find mechanisms that do not strain the limited resources of the agent and let the agent remain viable in the environment as it builds up more complexity.

5.1 There Are Severe Difficulties in Using Existing Artificial Neural Network Techniques or Evolutionary Methods

At first sight, it may seem that mechanisms developed in artificial neural network research or genetic algorithms can be applied in a straightforward manner to the development of new functionality in autonomous agents. However, this is not the case.

Let us first look at supervized learning, that is, learning with the aid of examples or counterexamples. One of the best known supervised learning algorithms is back propagation [101]. Behavior programs could be represented as artificial neural networks associating sensory signals to actuator outputs. Changes in behavior programs could then be based on the error between the desired outcome and the outcome derived from using the association. For example, if X is a sensory signal, Y an action, and w the weight with which X influences the action, then an error would be the difference between the expected action and the action produced by $Y = wX$. There exist methods for adapting the weights w, which will lead to convergence [98]. Convergence means that, given a consistent set of sense-act pairs, the learning method will settle on a stable set of weights that "correctly" relates X with Y. It can be shown that certain functions (such as the XOR function) require a multilayered network [83]. The weights in multilayered networks can still be learned if the error is back-propagated through nodes at successive layers based on the relative contribution of each node to the derived outcome [101]. See Kosko ([56], chapter 5) for a review of these and other supervised learning methods.

Although supervised learning methods have been demonstrated to be successful in simulation experiments, their application to autonomous agents runs into several problems. The first difficulty is that the methods require an adequate computation of the error and, therefore, a good enough prediction of what the actual outcome should be. A robot that is crashing into the wall gets feedback that there was a control error but cannot necessarily compute what would have been the right control actions to avoid the crash. Supervised learning methods require a teacher that is more intelligent than the agent. But this is in contradiction with the objective of understanding how complexity might have arisen in the first place. A second difficulty is that the dynamics of weight adaptation requires a large amount of resources. The learning time grows very rapidly with the complexity of the network, and an unrealistically high number of presentations of the correct sense-act pattern is typically required [131, p. 87]. A third difficulty is that not all networks will learn. If the network is too complex (too many layers or too many nodes) or too simple, it will not be able to generalize. Too many presentations may degrade performance. Moreover, the input and output representation must be carefully chosen, increasing the role of the designing agency [131, p. 87]. These difficulties explain why no one has as yet been able to convincingly use supervised learning methods on autonomous physical robots.

Another major neural network mechanism is known as reinforcement learning [118]. Reinforcement learning methods increase (and decrease) the probability that a particular association between sensing and acting will be used, based on a reward or reinforcement signal. The reinforcement signal is produced as a direct or indirect consequence of the use of the association. Many different associations may play a role in a particular behavior, and there may be a delay between a behavior and its (positive or negative) consequences. This introduces a credit assignment problem [82]. Early proposals ranked the possible situation-action associations, selected the best one (possibly with some variation to avoid local minima), and increased or decreased the probability of future choice depending on the effect of the chosen action [12,132]. More recent mechanisms go in the direction of having the agent develop a more sophisticated representation of the result of an action. For example, a prediction of reward is introduced, or a prediction of (long-term) cumulative reward, that is, return [118]. A technique useful for learning temporal chains is to hand out reinforcement to the last action and from there back to previous associations that played a role. This technique is known as the bucket brigade algorithm and originally due to Holland [46].

Reinforcement learning methods have been shown to be capable of impressive learning behavior in simulations or engineering contexts [81], but there are again serious difficulties in the application to physical autonomous agents. The first major difficulty lies in the determination of the reinforcement signal. It is unrealistic to assume that the agent gets a clear scalar reinforcement signal after each action or series of actions. The second difficulty is that reinforcement learning assumes a trial-and-error search to find a viable association. Unless the agent is already close to the desired behavior, it may take quite a while before such an association is discovered [52]. The third difficulty is the credit assignment problem. Proposed solutions all go in the direction of new complexity (in the form of models of return, or in more recent cases world models predicting return [61,118]). Often, many simplifying assumptions are made about the nature of sensory interpretations or actions. For example, most methods assume that it is possible to select each time the "best" action. But agents always execute several actions at the same time, and in many cases actions (like turn left) are abstractions from the viewpoint of the designer that do not correspond to explicit commands in the robot, particularly not in dynamics architectures. Despite these difficulties, there are some preliminary experiments on physical mobile robots [52,67]. The general conclusion seems to be that "current reinforcement-learning algorithms can be made to work robustly on simple problems, but there are a variety of dimensions in which they must be improved before it will be possible to construct artificial agents that adapt to complex domains" [52, p. 46].

Supervised learning or reinforcement learning are both constructivist techniques: They modify weights based on minimizing the error or on reinforcement. The alternative is known as selectionism: A complete behavior system is generated, for example, by mutation or recombination based on existing behavior systems and then tested as a whole. This mechanism is similar to evolution by natural selection as operating on the genes.

Evolutionary development has been shown in other areas of AL to be an extremely powerful source for generating more complexity (see, e.g., [96]). It has also been proposed by some neurobiologists to be the major mechanism underlying the formation of new structure (and, therefore, functionality) in the brain [25,33]. Evolutionary algorithms have been worked out in great detail and studied from a mathematical point of view (see review in Baeck & Schwefel [11]). The major variants are genetic algorithms [40] usually operating on classifier systems [45] and evolution strategies [103]. Applications have focused mostly on parameter optimization [63]. More recently, higher-level descriptions as opposed to bit strings have been used for the representation of the algorithm that needs to be derived, and, as a result, more complex algorithms have been generated [58].

Evolutionary techniques start from a population of individuals (which in the present case would be equal to behavior systems) that each derive a different solution in the space of possible solutions. The population is initialized in an arbitrary fashion. There is a fitness function that is defined over the space of all individuals. Individuals with higher fitness reproduce more often, and, thus, the distribution of individuals of a certain type in the population changes. Reproduction means that copies are made, possibly after mutation (which introduces a random change), or recombination (which combines parts of two algorithms). Because mutation and recombination may potentially result in a better algorithm, and because this algorithm will then be further reinforced by the selection step, the overall process evolves toward better and better regions of the search space.

Although this technique has resulted in very impressive results in an engineering context, the application to the development of autonomous agents poses some serious difficulties. The first problem is that genetic evolution requires quite a number of computational resources. The different individuals in the population need to be represented in memory, and a large number of cycles are required to arrive at working, let alone optimal, solutions. This is a problem for a robot that has to remain viable and maintain real-time responses within limited resource constraints. Consequently, most researchers so far follow an off-line approach [26,57]. The genetic algorithm runs on a computer external to the robot. When a valid solution is found, it is loaded and integrated in the other behavior systems. Thus, Koza [57] has shown how to derive the behavior programs for wall following and obstacle avoidance that were earlier demonstrated to function on a real robot programmed in the subsumption architecture [70]. The primitive building blocks of the behavior programs are in this case the sensory inputs and action parameter outputs, Boolean connectives, conditionals, and the subsumption primitives. However, Brooks [23] has criticized these results, mostly because the primitive building blocks were well chosen (based on an analysis of a known solution), and simplifying assumptions were made concerning the Boolean nature of certain conditionals.

Off-line evolution creates a new problem, which is the gap between the virtual world of the simulator and the real world. Koza [57] uses a very simple virtual world. Cliff, Husbands, and Harvey [26] use a much more sophisticated simulation to test out the fitness of a solution. But, as Brooks [23] points out, the gap between simulated and real world will always remain quite large. One possible way out is to use the real robot as soon as reasonable solutions have been discovered. An example application of this technique is discussed in Shibata and Fukuda [105]. The application concerns the optimization of path planning. Each robot is assumed to have a (static) map of the world that contains the obstacles and the goal toward which the robot needs to navigate. The genetic algorithm is used to search for a path toward the goal. The path is then executed and its quality evaluated with respect to effective use. Based on this new evaluation and additional information derived from the execution of the path, a new path is derived again using genetic techniques. The obvious problem with this approach is that only few solutions can be tried, which diminishes the chances that a good solution is found in a genetic way.

There is another yet more fundamental problem with current evolutionary techniques, which is the definition of the fitness function. The search toward a solution critically depends on the prior definition of this fitness function. But this introduces an important role for the designer. In the context of emergent functionality, we expect that the fitness function should be subject to evolution and should be local to the organism that evolves (as is indeed the case in Ray [96]). Cariani [24] calls this pragmatic emergence.

5.2 A Selectionist Approach May Be the Key for Generating Emergent Functionality

Although convincing examples of emergent functionality on physical robots operating in the real world do not exist, we are beginning to see the glimpses of it, and breakthroughs can be expected soon. These examples build further on the techniques discussed in the previous paragraphs but combine them in a novel way.

When we study synthetic examples of emerging complexity, like that of Ray [96], we see that they are based on selectionist mechanisms and that they have in addition two crucial features:

1. There is enough initial complexity to make a viable organism, and there are many diverse organisms. The buildup of complexity is as much due to the competitive interaction between organisms as to their interactions with the world.

2. The ecological pressures on organisms are real and come partly from other organisms. In other words, there are no predefined or static fitness functions or rewards, as assumed in genetic algorithms and reinforcement learning. There is no teacher around as assumed in supervised learning.

To make selectionism work for robots, it seems appropriate to draw a parallel between organisms and behavior systems. This means that we should not concentrate on the acquisition of a single behavior system (e.g., for locomotion or obstacle avoidance), but that there should be many diverse behavior systems that are complementary but still in competition. Paradoxically, it might be easier to develop many behavior systems at once than to concentrate on one behavior system in isolation.

Each behavior system, except for the basic reflexes, should remain adaptive, just as each individual organism remains adaptive (within the bounds of the genotype). New behavior systems begin their life by accessing the same or other visible variables and the same or other controlled variables. The new behavior system monitors the situation and adapts itself so as to have a similar impact on the controlled variables as the base line behavior systems, but using other sensory modalities. The important point here is that the generation of the new behavior system does not take place by trial and error.

Most of the time, behavior systems will have a different functionality. If there are behavior systems with the same functionality (e.g., obstacle avoidance), the diversity should not lie in variants of the same approach to a solution, as in the case of genetic algorithms, but in fundamental differences in how the functionality is approached (e.g., obstacle avoidance using touch-based reactive reflexes vs. obstacle avoidance using infrared-based classification).

We should also introduce real environmental pressures, such as limited internal energy availability, and real-time or memory constraints, in addition to real environmental pressures such as limited external energy availability, avoiding of self-damage, etc. These pressures should feedback on the formation or adaptation of behavior systems. A behavior system is less competitive if the sensory patterns to which the behavior system responds do not occur (e.g., its thresholds are too high), if the time to make a decision on how to influence actuation is too long so that the conditions for activation are no longer satisfied, if other behavior systems always override the influence on actuation, if many memory resources are needed, etc. There may also be behavior systems that specialize in monitoring internal and external environmental conditions and act as a "reaper" [96], weakening or eliminating other behavior systems. An example of this is already shown in Nehmzow and McGonigle [86].

Large-scale experiments incorporating this approach do not exist yet. But reason for the optimism that emergent functionality may be demonstrated soon comes from some initial experiments that show how new behavior systems may bootstrap themselves in the context of other behavior systems. Let us look at one concrete example in the context of obstacle avoidance. This example was first suggested and tested in simulation by Pfeifer and Verschure [94]. We have since done similar experiments on a real robot and with different sensory modalities in Brussels.

The baseline behavior systems are:

- maintain a default speed in a forward direction.
- maintain a forward direction.
- reverse speed if touching an obstacle in the front.
- turn away left if touched on the right side.
- turn away right if touched on the left side.

Following a dynamics viewpoint, each of these behavior systems establishes a continuous relationship between sensory signals and action parameters. For example, a positive default speed is maintained by increasing it, if it is below the default, or decreasing it, if it is above. Reversing the speed is done by a sudden decrease of the speed if a touch sensor is active. The positive default speed is then automatically restored by the "maintain a positive default speed" system.

The two emergent behavior systems (one that will do obstacle avoidance for obstacles on the left and another one that will do the same for obstacles on the right) are sensitive to the infrared sensors, and they impact the rotational motor. They use associative or Hebbian learning. In Hebbian learning, an association between two elements (e.g., sensors and actuators) is made stronger based on co-occurrence [44]. It is also made weaker, for example, due to a constant forgetting rate. Associative learning has been extensively studied in the artificial neural network field (reviewed in Kosko [56], chapter 4). In the present case, there will be a progressively stronger association between particular states of the infrared sensors (determined by the environment) and particular action parameters of the rotational motor (determined by the turn away left and turn away right behavior systems). Thus, we see a form of classical conditioning with the touch sensors as the unconditioned stimulus and the infrared as the conditioned stimulus.

To get emergent functionality, an additional step is needed. The new behavior systems so far perform the same activity as the baseline behavior systems and are not yet competitive. A behavior system becomes competitive if it causes a qualitatively different action that has an additional advantage for the agent. This can happen in many ways.

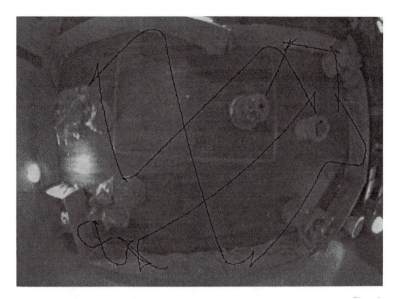

Figure 12. When the robot starts, it bumps into obstacles and retracts based on a built-in, touch-based obstacle avoidance behavior system. Progressively it will associate infrared signatures with rotational movement and no longer bump into obstacles.

For example, the new behavior systems could involve only some of the controlled variables so that some actions no longer take place, giving an overall qualitatively different behavior, or a behavior system may sense more quickly the upcoming situation and influence the action before the already existing behavior systems.

In the present case, the infrared-based obstacle avoidance system can become more competitive because the infrared sensors have a further range than the touch sensors. Therefore, they can therefore react more quickly to the presence of obstacles. Due to the progressive strengthening of the association, there will be a particular point in time in which the infrared-based behavior systems react earlier than the touch-based ones. This is the point where the newly emergent functionality becomes visible. Without infrared-based obstacle avoidance, a reversing of speed took place so that the robot is backing up while turning away. This reversal of speed is no longer present when infrared-based obstacle avoidance is strong enough because the agent no longer touches the obstacles. Instead, we observe a deviation away from obstacles (Figure 12). This deviation is from the viewpoint of energy usage more beneficial to the agent.

The associative learning mechanism has an autocatalytic element because the triggering due to infrared itself also enforces the association. Thus, the association strengths in the new behavior systems feed on themselves and become progressively stronger (Figure 13).

This is indeed an example of emergence, according to the earlier definitions. Different sensory modalities are used compared to the original behavior systems, and there is also a qualitatively different behavior, which is more beneficial to the agent. The example illustrates that emergent functionality is not due to one single mechanism but to a variety of factors, some of them related to internal structures in the agent, some of them related to the properties of certain sensors and actuators, and some of them related to the interaction dynamics with the environment.

Because the formation of the new behavior system here happens in the context of other behavior systems, the agent always remains viable. For example, if the new infrared-based obstacle avoidance behavior systems fail, the touch-based solution is

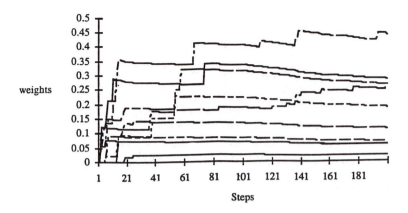

Figure 13. Evolution of the weights based on Hebbian learning. The weights determine the impact of the infrared sensors on the rotational motor. The increase feeds on itself. The decrease due to constant forgetting is also clearly visible.

still there and will immediately become active. Because the formation is guided by existing behavior systems, it evolves quickly without trial and error or search. All the time the agent remains viable.

It is obvious that more work is needed to achieve emergent functionality in physical autonomous robots, but current work exploring neural network techniques and evolutionary algorithms gives a good starting point. Their integration into an overall selectionist approach where diverse behavior systems compete and coadapt give reasons for optimism.

6 Conclusions

Behavior-oriented AI research has opened up an "artificial life route to artificial intelligence." It has three aspects: First, the problem of intelligence is framed within the general context of biology. Intelligent behavior is defined as maximizing the agent's chances for self-preservation. Successful adaptation and learning are defined as changes in the internal structure of the agent that maximize intelligence. Second, the tasks being explored by behavior-oriented AI researchers are very different from those considered in classical AI. They center around sensorimotor competence and the ability to operate autonomously in a dynamically changing environment. Third, the models take inspiration from the way intelligent behavior appears to be established in natural systems. It is hypothesized that the principles that underlie the living are also the ones that give rise to intelligent behavior. Many researchers hope to contribute to biology by testing out in artificial models whether certain biological hypotheses are plausible.

Behavior-oriented AI research made a slow start around the mid-1980s but is currently exploding. Many research laboratories have now acquired the competence to build their own robots and to perform experiments. Rapid experimental progress can be expected in the coming 5 years, if only by further pursuit of the research lines that have been briefly summarized in this paper. What is particularly needed are larger-scale efforts: agents with many different behavioral competences operating in ecosystems with a multitude of challenges, multiagent systems with a sufficient number and diversity of the agents, learning methods applied over sufficiently long periods of time to get nontrivial buildup of complexity, and so on. At the same time, the experimental rigor needs to be increased so that quantitative performance measures can be applied.

Given the current state of the art and the rapid evolution in mechanical engineering and computer technology, we can also expect rapid technological progress, leading toward the first real-world applications, possibly in the area of environmental monitoring, space exploration, or microsystems. In general, it takes about 10 years before a technology becomes sufficiently accepted for serious real-world applications. Major hurdles are not only technical. In this respect, the state of the art of behavior-oriented AI can be compared to that of knowledge engineering in the late 1960s, when the shift toward situation-specific knowledge and rule-based formalisms was taking place. It took several decades to turn these results into a solid engineering methodology and develop a number of well-established industrial achievements, like XCON for configuring computer installations [74].

Some Open Issues

There are also many open problems beyond increasing the complexity of current systems. One of them, which has hardly been addressed, concerns the relation between the mechanisms used in behavior-oriented AI and those used in knowledge-oriented AI. Some researchers (on both sides) suggest that the other approach is irrelevant to reach human-level intelligence. They then have to prove that their methods will work all the way. Other researchers believe that the symbolic level exists as an independent level, which is causally influenced by and causally influences the dynamics level. No concrete proposals operational on physical autonomous robots exist today to allow a technical discussion of the subject, but one day the problem will have to be tackled.

Another question concerns adequate formalization and theory formation. There is already a wide body of literature with formal results for the mechanisms discussed earlier (error-driven learning, genetic evolution, etc.), but application to integrated physical agents operating in real-world environments will require more work. Several researchers have proposed a state-space approach for defining the dynamics of the observed behavior and the internal operation of the agent (e.g., [37,54,77,119]). Once a state-space description is available, the concepts of dynamical systems theory (attractors, transients, recurrent trajectories, etc.) (1) can be used to characterize qualitatively and quantitatively behaviors and internal structures like perceptions, representations, and actions. Within this framework, concepts like emergent functionality can be formalized and the results of emergent functionality better understood. At the same time, work must proceed on developing formal theories to characterize the challenges in ecosystems; the optimality of behavior; and, thus, the chances of self-preservation of the agent [76].

The field of behavior-oriented AI research shows enormous signs of vitality. This paper focused only on a few aspects, ignoring other topics such as multiagent systems, communication and cooperation, the formation of new sensory modalities, and so on. There is no doubt that major contributions can be expected in the coming decade, particularly as the technical tools mature and more researchers get involved.

Acknowledgment

The writing of this paper was partly sponsored by the ESPRIT basic research project SUBSYM and the IUAP Action of the Belgian Science Ministry. Comments from Chris Langton, David McFarland, Walter Van de Velde, and Anne Sjostrom have improved the paper. Continuous discussions with members of the VUB autonomous agents group and with Rodney Brooks, David McFarland, Rolf Pfeifer, and Tim Smithers have helped to shape the viewpoints expressed in this paper. I am strongly indebted to the hospitality of the Aamodt family; the writing of this paper started in the peaceful surroundings of their Norwegian home.

References

1. Abraham, R. H., & Shaw, C. D. (1992). *Dynamics. The geometry of behavior* (2nd ed.). Reading, MA: Addison-Wesley.

2. Agre, P., & Chapman, D. (1987). Pengi: an implementation of a theory of activity. In *Proceedings of the Sixth National Conference on Artificial Intelligence* (pp. 268–272). San Mateo, CA: Morgan Kaufmann.

3. Alexander, R. M. (1968). *Animal mechanics.* London: Sidgewick and Jackson.

4. Alife. (1994). *Journal of Artificial Life.* Cambridge, MA: The MIT Press.

5. Arbib, M. A., & Hanson, A. R. (Eds.) (1987). *Vision, brain, and cooperative computation.* Cambridge, MA: The MIT Press/Bradford Books.

6. Arbib, M. A., & House, D. H. (1987). Depth and detours: an essay on visually guided behavior. In M. A. Arbib & A. R. Hanson (Eds.), *Vision, brain, and cooperative computation* (pp. 129–163). Cambridge, MA: The MIT Press/Bradford Books.

7. Arkin, R. (1989). Motor schema based mobile robot navigation. *International Journal of Robotics Research, 8*(4), 92–112.

8. Assad, A., & Packard, N. (1991). Emergent colonization in an artificial ecology. In F. J. Varela & P. Bourgine (Eds.), *Toward a practice of autonomous systems. Proceedings of the First European Conference on Artificial Life* (pp. 143–152). Cambridge, MA: The MIT Press/Bradford Books.

9. Baas, N. (1993). *Second order emergence.* Oral communication at the second European Conference on Artificial Life, ULB Brussels.

10. Babloyantz, A. (1986). *Molecules, dynamics, and life. An introduction to the self-organisation of matter.* New York: Wiley.

11. Baeck, T., & Schwefel, H.-P. (1993). An overview of evolutionary algorithms for parameter optimization. *Evolutionary Computation, 1*(1), 1–23.

12. Barto, A. G., & Sutton, R. S. (1991). Landmark learning: An illustration of associative search. *Biological Cybernetics, 42,* 1–8.

13. Barto, A. G. (1990). Connectionist learning for control. In T. W. Miller, R. S. Sutton, & P. J. Werbos (Eds.), *Neural networks for control* (pp. 5–58). Cambridge, MA: The MIT Press/Bradford Books.

14. Beckers, R. (1993). Demonstration at the Alife Meeting, Technical University of Delft.

15. Beer, R. D. (1990). *Intelligence as adaptive behavior: An experiment in computational neuroethology.* Cambridge, MA: Academic Press.

16. Bonner, J. T. (1988). *The evolution of complexity by means of natural selection.* Princeton, NJ: Princeton University Press.

17. Brady, J. M., & Paul, R. (1984). *Robotics research: The First International Symposium.* Cambridge, MA: The MIT Press.

18. Braitenberg, V. (1984). *Vehicles: Experiments in synthetic psychology.* Cambridge, MA: The MIT Press.

19. Brooks, R. (1986). A robust layered control system for a mobile robot. *IEEE Journal of Robotics and Automation, 2*(1), 14–23.

20. Brooks, R. (1990). *The behavior language; user's guide* (Memo 1127). Cambridge, MA: MIT AI Lab.

21. Brooks, R. (1991). Intelligence without reason. In *Proceedings of IJCAI-91* (pp. 569–595). San Mateo, CA: Morgan Kaufmann.

22. Brooks, R. (1991b). Challenges for complete creature architectures. In J.-A. Meyer &

S. W. Wilson (Eds.), *From animals to animats. Proceedings of the First International Conference on Simulation of Adaptive Behavior* (pp. 434–443). Cambridge, MA: The MIT Press/Bradford Books.

23. Brooks, R. (1992). Artificial life and real robots. In F. J. Varela & P. Bourgine (Eds.), *Toward a practice of autonomous systems. Proceedings of the First European Conference on Artificial Life* (pp. 3–10). Cambridge, MA: The MIT Press/Bradford Books.

24. Cariani, P. (1991). Emergence and artificial life. In C. G. Langton, C. Taylor, J. D. Farmer, & S. Rasmussen (Eds.), *Artificial life II. Proceedings of the Workshop on Artificial Life* (pp. 775–797). Reading, MA: Addison-Wesley.

25. Changeux, J.-P. (1986). *Neuronal man: The biology of mind.* Oxford, UK: Oxford University Press.

26. Cliff, D., Husbands, P., & Harvey, I. (1993). Evolving visually guided robots. In J.-A. Meyer, H. L. Roitblatt, & S. W. Wilson (Eds.), *From animals to animats 2. Proceedings of the Second International Conference on Simulation of Adaptive Behavior* (pp. 374–383). Cambridge, MA: The MIT Press/Bradford Books.

27. Cruse, H., Muller-Wilm, U., & Dean, J. (1993). Artificial neural nets for controlling a 6-legged walking system. In J.-A. Meyer, H. L. Roitblatt, & S. W. Wilson (Eds.), *From animals to animats 2. Proceedings of the Second International Conference on Simulation of Adaptive Behavior* (pp. 52–60). Cambridge, MA: The MIT Press/Bradford Books.

28. Decuyper, J., & Keymeulen, D. (1991). A reactive robot navigation system based on a fluid dynamics metaphor. In F. J. Varela & P. Bourgine (Eds.), *Toward a practice of autonomous systems. Proceedings of the First European Conference on Artificial Life* (pp. 348–355). Cambridge, MA: The MIT Press/Bradford Books.

29. Deneubourg, J.-L., & Goss, S. (1990). Collective patterns and decision making. *Ecology, Ethology and Evolution, 1,* 295–311.

30. Deneubourg, J.-L, et al. (1993). Self-organisation and life: from simple rules to global complexity. In *Proceedings of the Second European Conference on Artificial Life.* ULB, Brussels.

31. Donnett, J., & Smithers, T. (1990). Lego vehicles: a technology for studying intelligent systems. In J.-A. Meyer, H. L. Roitblatt, & S. W. Wilson (Eds.), *From animals to animats 2. Proceedings of the Second International Conference on Simulation of Adaptive Behavior* (pp. 540–569). Cambridge, MA: The MIT Press/Bradford Books.

32. Drogoul, A., & Ferber, J. (1993). From Tom Thumb to the Dockers: some experiments with foraging robots. In J.-A. Meyer, H. L. Roitblatt, & S. W. Wilson (Eds.), *From animals to animats 2. Proceedings of the Second International Conference on Simulation of Adaptive Behavior* (pp. 451–459). Cambridge, MA: The MIT Press/Bradford Books.

33. Edelman, G. (1987). *Neural Darwinism: The theory of neuronal group selection.* New York: Basic Books.

34. Edelman, G. (1992). Bright air, brilliant fire. On the matter of the mind. New York: Basic Books.

35. Flynn, A., & Brooks, R. (1989). Building robots: expectations and experiences. In *IEEE Workshop on Intelligent Robots and Systems* (pp. 236–243). IROS '89. Tuskuba, Japan.

36. Forrest, S. (1989). *Emergent computation: self-organizing, collective, and cooperative phenomena in natural and artificial computing networks.* Amsterdam: North-Holland Pub. Co.

37. Gallagher, J., & Beer, R. (1993). A qualitative dynamical analysis of evolved locomotion controllers. In J.-A. Meyer, H. L. Roitblatt, & S. W. Wilson (Eds.), *From animals to animats 2. Proceedings of the Second International Conference on Simulation of Adaptive Behavior* (pp. 71–80). Cambridge, MA: The MIT Press/Bradford Books.

38. Genesereth, M., & Nilsson, N. (1987). *Logical foundations of artificial intelligence.* Los Altos, CA: Morgan Kaufmann.

39. Giszter, S. (1993). Behavior networks and force fields for simulating spinal reflex

behaviors of the frog. In J.-A. Meyer, H. L. Roitblatt, & S. W. Wilson (Eds.), *From animals to animats 2. Proceedings of the Second International Conference on Simulation of Adaptive Behavior* (pp. 172–181). Cambridge, MA: The MIT Press/Bradford Books.

40. Goldberg, D. E. (1989). *Genetic algorithms in search, optimization and machine learning.* Reading, MA: Addison-Wesley.

41. Goss, S., & Deneubourg, J.-L. (1992). Harvesting by a group of robots. In F. J. Varela & P. Bourgine (Eds.), *Toward a practice of autonomous systems. Proceedings of the First European Conference on Artificial Life* (pp. 195–204). Cambridge, MA: The MIT Press/Bradford Books.

42. Hallam, J. (1993). Playing with toy cars. In L. Steels & R. Brooks (Eds.), *The "artificial life" route to "artificial intelligence." Building situated embodied agents.* Hillsdale, NJ: Lawrence Erlbaum.

43. Harnad, S. (1990). The symbol grounding problem. *Physica D, 42*(1–3), 335–346.

44. Hebb, D. O. (1949). *The organization of behaviour.* New York: Wiley.

45. Holland, J. H. (1975). *Adaptation in natural and artificial systems.* Ann Arbor, MI: The University of Michigan Press.

46. Holland, J. H. (1985). Properties of the bucket brigade algorithm. In J. J. Grefenstette (Ed.), *Proceedings of the First International Conference on Genetic Algorithms and Their Applications* (pp. 1–7). Pittsburgh.

47. Hoogeweg, P. (1989). Mirror beyond mirror: Puddles of life. In C. G. Langton (Ed.), *Artificial life. Santa Fe Institute studies in the sciences of complexity* (Vol. VI, pp. 297–316). Reading, MA: Addison-Wesley.

48. Horswill, I. (1992). Characterizing adaptation by constraint. In F. J. Varela & P. Bourgine (Eds.), *Toward a practice of autonomous systems. Proceedings of the First European Conference on Artificial Life* (pp. 58–63). Cambridge, MA: The MIT Press/Bradford Books.

49. Horswill, I. (1993). A simple, cheap, and robust visual navigation system. In J.-A. Meyer, H. L. Roitblatt, & S. W. Wilson (Eds.), *From animals to animats 2. Proceedings of the Second International Conference on Simulation of Adaptive Behavior* (pp. 129–136). Cambridge, MA: The MIT Press/Bradford Books.

50. Jones, J. L., & Flynn, A. M. (1993). *Mobile robots. Inspiration to implementation.* Wellesley, MA: A. K. Peters.

51. Kaelbling, L., & Rosenschein, S. (1990). Action and planning in embedded agents. *Journal of Robotics and Autonomous Systems, 6,* 35–48.

52. Kaelbling, L. (1992). An adaptable mobile robot. In F. J. Varela & P. Bourgine (Eds.), *Toward a practice of autonomous systems. Proceedings of the First European Conference on Artificial Life* (pp. 41–47). Cambridge, MA: The MIT Press/Bradford Books.

53. Kauffman, S. A. (1993). The origins of order: Self organization and selection in evolution. Oxford, UK: Oxford University Press.

54. Kiss, G. (1991). Autonomous agents, AI and chaos theory. In J. A. Meyer & S. W. Wilson (Eds.), *From animals to animats. Proceedings of the First International Conference on Simulation of Adaptive Behavior* (pp. 518–524). Cambridge, MA: The MIT Press/Bradford Books.

55. No entry.

56. Kosko, B. (1992). *Neural networks and fuzzy systems. A dynamical systems approach to machine intelligence.* Englewood Cliffs, NJ: Prentice-Hall.

57. Koza, J. (1991). Evolving emergent wall following robotic behavior sing the Genetic Programming Paradigm. In F. J. Varela & P. Bourgine (Eds.), *Toward a practice of autonomous systems. Proceedings of the First European Conference on Artificial Life* (pp. 110–119). Cambridge, MA: The MIT Press/Bradford Books.

58. Koza, J. (1992). *Genetic programming.* Cambridge, MA: The MIT Press.

59. Langton, C. G. (1989). *Artificial life. Santa Fe Institute studies in the sciences of complexity* (Proc. Vol. VI). Reading, MA: Addison-Wesley.

60. Langton, C. G., Taylor, C., Farmer, J. D., & Rasmussen, S. (1992). Artificial life II. In *Proceedings of the Workshop on Artificial Life.* Reading, MA: Addison-Wesley.

61. Lin, L.-J., & Mitchell, T. M. (1993). Reinforcement learning with hidden states. In J.-A. Meyer, H. L. Roitblatt, & S. W. Wilson (Eds.), *From animals to animats 2. Proceedings of the Second International Conference on Simulation of Adaptive Behavior* (pp. 271–280). Cambridge, MA: The MIT Press/Bradford Books.

62. Lyons, D. M., & Arbib, M. A. (1989). A formal model of computation for sensory-based robotics. *IEEE Transactions on Robotics and Automation, 5,* 280–293.

63. Maenner, R., & Manderick, B. (1992). *Parallel problem solving from nature* (Vol. 2). Amsterdam: North-Holland Pub. Co.

64. Maes, P. (1989). The dynamics of action selection. In *Proceedings of the 11th International Joint Conference on AI (IJCAI 89)* (pp. 991–997). Los Altos, CA: Morgan Kaufmann.

65. Maes, P. (1990). *Designing autonomous agents: theory and practice from biology to engineering and back.* Cambridge, MA: The MIT Press/Bradford Books.

66. Maes, P. (1993). Behavior-based artificial intelligence. In J.-A. Meyer, H. L. Roitblatt, & S. W. Wilson (Eds.), *From animals to animats 2. Proceedings of the Second International Conference on Simulation of Adaptive Behavior* (pp. 2–10). Cambridge, MA: The MIT Press/Bradford Books.

67. Maes, P., & Brooks, R. (1990). Learning to coordinate behaviors. In *Proceedings of the Eighth National Conference on Artificial Intelligence* (pp. 796–802). San Mateo, CA: Morgan Kaufmann.

68. Malcolm, C., & Smithers, T. (1988). Programming assembly robots in terms of task achieving behavioural modules: first experimental results. In *Proceedings International Advanced Robotics Programme* (pp. 15.1–15.6). Manchester, UK.

69. Malcolm, C. A., Smithers, T., & Hallam, J. (1989). An emerging paradigm in robot architecture. In T. Kanade, F. Groen, & L. Herzberger (Eds.), *Intelligent autonomous systems 2* (pp. 546–564). Amsterdam.

70. Mataric, M. (1990). Environment learning using a distributed representation. In *Proceedings of 1990 IEEE International Conference on Robotics and Automation* (pp. 402–406).

71. Maturana, H. R., & Varela, F. J. (1987). *The tree of knowledge: the biological roots of human understanding.* Boston: Shamhala Press.

72. Maynard-Smith, J. (1982). *Evolution and the theory of games.* Cambridge, UK: Cambridge University Press.

73. No entry.

74. McDermott, J. (1982). R1: a rule-based configurator of computer systems. *Artificial Intelligence Journal, 19*(1), 39–88.

75. McFarland, D. (1992). Animals as cost-based robots. *International Studies in the Philosophy of Science, 6*(2), 133–153.

76. McFarland, D., & Boesser, T. (1994). *Intelligent behavior in animals and robots.* Cambridge, MA: The MIT Press/Bradford Books.

77. McFarland, D., & Houston, A. (1981). *Quantitative ethology: the state-space approach.* London: Pitman Books.

78. Meyer, J.-A., & Guillot, A. (1991). Simulation of adaptive behavior in animats: review and prospect. In J.-A. Meyer & S. W. Wilson (Eds.), *From animals to animats. Proceedings of the First International Conference on Simulation of Adaptive Behavior* (pp. 2–14). Cambridge, MA: The MIT Press/ Bradford Books.

79. Meyer, J.-A., Roitblatt, H. L., & Wilson, S. W. (1993). *From animals to animats 2.*

Proceedings of the Second International Conference on Simulation of Adaptive Behavior. Cambridge, MA: The MIT Press/Bradford Books.

80. Meyer, J.-A., & Wilson, S. W. (1991). *From animals to animats. Proceedings of the First International Conference on Simulation of Adaptive Behavior.* Cambridge, MA: The MIT Press/Bradford Books.

81. Miller, W. T., Sutton, R. S., & Werbos, P. J. (Eds.), *Neural networks for control.* Cambridge, MA: The MIT Press/Bradford Books.

82. Minsky, M. (1961). Steps towards artificial intelligence. In E. Feigenbaum & J. Feldman (Eds.), *Computers and thought* (pp. 406–450). New York: McGraw-Hill.

83. Minsky, M., & Papert, S. (1988). *Perceptrons.* Cambridge, MA: The MIT Press.

84. Minsky, M. (1985). *The society of mind.* New York: Simon and Schuster.

85. Nehmzow, U., Smithers, T., & McGonigle, B. (1993). Increasing behavioural repertoire in a mobile robot. In J.-A. Meyer, H. L. Roitblatt, & S. W. Wilson (Eds.), *From animals to animats 2. Proceedings of the Second International Conference on Simulation of Adaptive Behavior* (pp. 291–297). Cambridge, MA: The MIT Press/Bradford Books.

86. Nehmzow, U., & McGonigle, B. (1993). Robot navigation by light. In J.-L. Deneubourg et al. (Eds.), *Self-Organisation and Life: From Simple Rules to Global Complexity. Proceedings of the Second European Conference on Artificial Life* (pp. 835–844). ULB, Brussels.

87. Newell, A. (1982). The knowledge level. *Artificial Intelligence Journal, 18,* 87–127.

88. Nicolis, G. (1989). Physics of far-from-equilibrium systems and self-organisation. In P. Davis (Ed.), *The new physics* (pp. 316–347). Cambridge, UK: Cambridge University Press.

89. Nicolis, G., & Prigogine, I. (1985). *Exploring complexity.* Munchen: Piper.

90. Nilsson, N. (Ed.) (1984). *Shakey the robot.* SRI AI center. Technical Note 323.

91. Pasteels, J. M., & Deneubourg, J.-L. (1987). *From individual to collective behaviour in social insects.* Basel: Birkhauser.

92. Pattee, H. (1989). Simulations, realizations, and theories of life. In C. Langton (Ed.), *Artificial life* (pp. 63–77). Redwood City, CA: Addison-Wesley.

93. Peters, T. (1990). *Liberation management. Necessary disorganization for the nanosecond nineties.* London: MacMillan.

94. Pfeifer, R., & Verschure, P. (1992). Distributed adaptive control: a paradigm for designing autonomous agents. In F. J. Varela & P. Bourgine (Eds.), *Toward a practice of autonomous systems. Proceedings of the First European Conference on Artificial Life* (pp. 21–30). Cambridge, MA: The MIT Press/Bradford Books.

95. Prigogine, I., & Stengers, I. (1984). *Order out of chaos.* New York: Bantam Books.

96. Ray, T. (1992). An approach to the synthesis of life. In C. G. Langton, C. Taylor, J. D. Farmer, & S. Rasmussen (Eds.), *Artificial life II. Proceedings of the Workshop on Artificial Life* (pp. 325–371).

97. Rose, S., & Bullock, S. (1991). *The chemistry of life* (3rd ed.). London: Penguin Books.

98. Rosenblatt, F. (1962). *Principles of neurodynamics.* New York: Spartan Books.

99. Rosenblatt, K. J., & Payton, D. (1989). A fine-grained alternative to the subsumption architecture for mobile robot control. In *Proceedings of the IEEE/INNS International Joint Conference on Neural Networks.*

100. Rosenschein, S., & Kaelbling, L. (1986). The synthesis of digital machines with provable epistemic properties. In J. Halpern (Ed.), *Theoretical aspects of reasoning about knowledge* (pp. 83–98). San Mateo, CA: Morgan Kaufmann.

101. Rumelhart, J., McClelland, J., & the PDP Research Group. (1986). *Parallel distributed processing.* Cambridge, MA: The MIT Press.

102. *Adaptive Behavior*. Cambridge, MA: The MIT Press.

103. Schwefel, H.-P. (1981). *Numerical optimization of computer models*. Chichester, UK: Wiley.

104. Shapiro, S. C. (1992). *Encyclopedia of artificial intelligence* (2nd ed.). New York: Wiley.

105. Shibata, T., & Fukuda, T. (1993). Coordinative balancing in evolutionary multi-agent robot systems. In F. J. Varela & P. Bourgine (Eds.), *Toward a practice of autonomous systems. Proceedings of the First European Conference on Artificial Life* (pp. 990–1003). Cambridge, MA: The MIT Press/Bradford Books.

106. Smithers, T. (1992). Taking eliminative materialism seriously: a methodology for autonomous systems research. In F. J. Varela & P. Bourgine (Eds.), *Toward a practice of autonomous systems. Proceedings of the First European Conference on Artificial Life* (pp. 31–40). Cambridge, MA: The MIT Press/Bradford Books.

107. Smithers, T. (1993). Are autonomous agents information processing systems? In L. Steels & R. Brooks (Eds.), *The "artificial life" route to "artificial intelligence." Building situated embodied agents*. Hillsdale, NJ: Lawrence Erlbaum.

108. Steels, L. (1990a). Cooperation between distributed agents through self-organisation. In Y. Demazeau & J.-P. Muller (Ed.), *Decentralized AI* (pp. 175–196). Amsterdam: North-Holland.

109. Steels, L. (1990b). Exploiting analogical representations. In P. Maes (Ed.), *Designing autonomous agents: theory and practice from biology to engineering and back* (pp. 71–88). Cambridge, MA: The MIT Press/Bradford Books.

110. Steels, L. (1991a). Emergent frame recognition and its use in artificial creatures. In *Proceedings of the 10th IJCAI*. San Mateo, CA: Morgan Kaufmann.

111. Steels, L. (1991b). Towards a theory of emergent functionality. In J.-A. Meyer & S. W. Wilson (Eds.), *From animals to animats. Proceedings of the First International Conference on Simulation of Adaptive Behavior* (pp. 451–461). Cambridge, MA: The MIT Press/Bradford Books.

112. Steels, L., & Brooks, R. (Eds.) (1993). *The "artificial life" route to "artificial intelligence." Building situated embodied agents*. Hillsdale, NJ: Lawrence Erlbaum.

113. Steels, L. (Ed.) (1993a). *The biology and technology of intelligent autonomous agents*. NATO ASI Series. Berlin: Springer Verlag.

114. Steels, L. (1993b). Building agents with autonomous behavior systems. In L. Steels & R. Brooks (Eds.), *The "artificial life" route to "artificial intelligence." Building situated embodied agents*. Hillsdale, NJ: Lawrence Erlbaum.

115. Suchman, L. (1987). *Plans and situated action. The problem of human machine interaction*. Cambridge, UK: Cambridge University Press.

116. No entry.

117. No entry.

118. Sutton, R. S. (1992). Special issue on reinforcement learning. *Machine Learning, 8*, 3–4.

119. Toffoli, T., & Margolus, N. (1977). *Cellular automata machines*. Cambridge, MA: The MIT Press.

120. Todd, P. M., & Wilson, S. (1993). Environment structure and adaptive behavior from the ground up. In J.-A. Meyer, H. L. Roitblatt, & S. W. Wilson (Eds.), *From animals to animats 2. Proceedings of the Second International Conference on Simulation of Adaptive Behavior* (pp. 11-20). Cambridge, MA: The MIT Press/Bradford Books.

121. Tyrell, T. (1993). The use of hierarchies for action selection. In J.-A. Meyer, H. L. Roitblatt, & S. W. Wilson (Eds.), *From animals to animats 2. Proceedings of the Second International Conference on Simulation of Adaptive Behavior* (pp. 138–147). Cambridge, MA: The MIT Press/Bradford Books.

122. Ullman, S. (1984). Visual routines. *Cognition, 18*, 97–159.

123. Van de Velde, W. (1992). *Learning robots*. Cambridge, MA: The MIT Press/Bradford Books.

124. Varela, F. J., & Bourgine, P. (Eds.), *Toward a practice of autonomous systems. Proceedings of the First European Conference on Artificial Life*. Cambridge, MA: The MIT Press/Bradford Books.

125. Varela, F. J., Thompson, E., & Rosch, E. (1992). *Embodied mind*. Cambridge, MA: The MIT Press.

126. No entry.

127. Vogel, F. (1989). *How life learned to live*. Cambridge, MA: The MIT Press.

128. Walter, W. G. (1950). An imitation of life. *Scientific American, 185*(2), 42–45.

129. Webb, B. (1993). Modeling biological behaviour or "dumb animals and stupid robots." In J.-L. Deneubourg et al. (Eds.), *Self-organisation and life: from simple rules to global complexity. Proceedings of the Second European Conference on Artificial Life* (pp. 1090–1103). ULB, Brussels.

130. Webb, B., & Smithers, T. (1992). The connection between AI and biology in the study of behaviour. In F. J. Varela & P. Bourgine (Eds.), *Toward a practice of autonomous systems. Proceedings of the First European Conference on Artificial Life* (pp. 421–428). Cambridge, MA: The MIT Press/Bradford Books.

131. No entry.

132. Widrow, B., Gupta, N., & Maitra, S. (1973). Punish/reward: learning with a critic in adaptive threshold systems. *IEEE Transactions on Systems, Man, and Cybernetics, 5*, 455–465.

133. Wilson, S. W. (1991). The animat path to AI. In J.-A. Meyer & S. W. Wilson (Eds.), *From animals to animats. Proceedings of the First International Conference on Simulation of Adaptive Behavior* (pp. 15–22). Cambridge, MA: The MIT Press/Bradford Books.

Toward Synthesizing Artificial Neural Networks that Exhibit Cooperative Intelligent Behavior: Some Open Issues in Artificial Life

Michael G. Dyer
Computer Science Department
UCLA
Los Angeles CA 90024
dyer@cs.ucla.edu

Keywords
artificial neural networks, evolution of communication, evolution of predation, cooperative behavior, genetic algorithm

Abstract The tasks that animals perform require a high degree of intelligence. Animals forage for food, migrate, navigate, court mates, rear offspring, defend against predators, construct nests, and so on. These tasks commonly require social interaction/cooperation and are accomplished by animal nervous systems, which are the result of billions of years of evolution and complex developmental/learning processes. The Artificial Life (AL) approach to synthesizing intelligent behavior is guided by this biological perspective. In this article we examine some of the numerous open problems in synthesizing intelligent animal behavior (especially cooperative behavior involving communication) that face the field of AL, a discipline still in its infancy.

1 Introduction

A major goal of Artificial Life (AL) research is to gain insight into both life as it is and life as it might have been [58,59]. As such, AL issues span potentially a very broad range, from the role of chaos and prebiotic chemistry in allowing intercellular processes to have come about, to the emergence of human intelligence and organizations. In this paper we focus on the research goal of understanding the nature of intelligence from an AL perspective, that is, the evolution and development of complex nervous systems, supporting both animal and human cooperative behavior. We are interested in (a) how artificial neural networks (ANNs) support animal and human cognitive processes and (b) how intelligence might be distributed within groups or populations of individuals, with a special focus on the role of communication in survival strategies requiring cooperation.

2 AI Versus AL Approach to Cognition

The traditional approach to synthesizing intelligence has been developed within the field of Artificial Intelligence (AI) and has focused, for the most part, on modeling both everyday and expert-level knowledge and reasoning in humans—for example, problem solving, planning, language comprehension, learning, and invention. In the field of AI, such models are realized in terms of computational systems that manipulate symbolic structures via rules of inference [34,84,95,98]. Although there are growing fields of Distributed AI (DAI) [14,39], situated agents [1], and artificial neural/connectionist networks

Table I. AI versus AL Paradigms

Artificial Intelligence (AI)	Artificial Life (AL)
Focus on individual	Focus on a group or population
Cognition as operations of logic	Cognition as operation of nervous systems
Cognition independent of perception	Situated cognition, i.e., integrated with sensory/ motor experiences
Starts with human-level cognition	Starts with animal-level cognition
Mainly top-down approach: engineer complex systems	Mainly bottom-up approach: rely on evolution, development, and learning
Direct specification of cognitive architectures	Indirect specification, via genotype to pheno- type mapping
Human-level mental tasks	Survivability in complex environments is the overriding task
Time span up to hours	Evolutionary, generational, and individual life spans

[7,21,113], the emphasis in AI has been on modeling cognitive tasks involving a single individual, via logic and list-processing procedures.

In contrast, the field of AL brings a decidedly biological perspective to the study of intelligent behavior. Table 1 illustrates how AL and AI paradigms differ.

Major differences between the two paradigms are mainly due to AL's biological perspective, which emphasizes the evolution and development of animal cognition within interacting, multispecies populations over many generations. Here, any strategy must be complementary to those that aid survival. All tasks must be situated, that is, occurring within an environment of interacting agents. As a result, the sensing and motor capabilities of each individual must be taken into account and integrated with any kind of planning or problem-solving strategy. The time span is also quite different, with AL agents living out lifetimes, giving "birth" to offspring, raising their young, and finally dying. Typical tasks in AI include medical diagnosis, story comprehension and question answering, chess playing, and IQ tests, while typical AL tasks involve predator avoidance, food foraging, mate finding, nest building, and so on. Thus, if nothing else, what might be considered benchmark or touchstone tasks differ markedly for these two synthetic approaches toward understanding intelligence.

One attractive feature of the AL approach is that the fundamental unit of manipulation is the *population*. Genetic operators are applied to populations and produce populations. This approach is in direct contrast to AI approaches. For example, in distributed artificial intelligence (DAI), researchers take the *individual* to be the fundamental unit and then attempt to engineer individual agents who will interact correctly to solve group-oriented tasks. In genetic systems, however, no individual can be central, especially because individuals are replaced by offspring that vary from their parents. In contrast to the DAI point of view, the evolutionary approach of AL is novel in another way—organisms not only transmit information via some form of language or communication, but also one can view mating between individuals as the "communication" of successful hardware (with variation) to their offspring. Thus, both neural architectures (i.e., innate components) and distributed representations (i.e., learned components) can be engineered within a single, all-encompassing framework.

The AL modeling approach involves specifying:

1. *environments*—simulated worlds whose conditions match, at some level of abstraction, those selectional pressures in which a variety of animal behaviors may evolve or develop [80].

2. *processes of genetic expression*—mappings from artificial genomes to phenotypes that control behavior [41,42]. A genotype is commonly a bit string; a phenotype is often some type of artificial neural network (ANN) or connectionist architecture that controls the artificial organism's behavior, through the simulation of sensory/motor neurons and interneurons.

3. *learning and development*—methods under genetic control for modifying or growing the nervous systems of artificial animals during their lifetimes (e.g., [85,104]).

4. *evolution*—recombination and mutation of parental genomes during mating to produce variation in their offspring [52].

The evolutionary approach allows one to study the sociobiological aspects of intelligence. In addition, it supplies an alternative to engineering group interaction by hand; instead, one need only set up appropriate environments, such that there is an evolutionary path to the desired group behavior. Of course, many issues arise. What environments will lead to desired forms of behavior? How can the combinatorially explosive search for desirable organisms be reduced? For example, with genomes of just 1,000 bits, one is searching in an immense space of $2^{1,000}$ organisms. How should organisms be represented? What are useful mappings from genotype to phenotype? What simplifications are acceptable, that is, will lead to desired results, but without compromising fundamental issues?

A very long-term goal of AL is to gain insight ultimately into the evolution and nature of human intelligence, through modeling the evolution of communication and cooperative behavior in lower life forms. Such models might someday give us insights concerning hominid or protohuman language and intelligence, for which there is little or no fossil record. Such a goal is truly a daunting one; there are so many parameters (environmental, genetic, developmental) that are potentially relevant—creating an enormous search space of research models/theories. Consequently, ways must be found to impose constraints on model and theory construction. Constraints can be obtained from multiple source: neuroscientific data, comparative cognitive science and computational analysis, for example, analysis of the size of a given genetic or developmental search space and the computations required to find a given solution within them. Other obvious constraints come from the biological sciences, that is, evolutionary and population biology, genetics, ecology and ethology.

3   Animal Intelligence: Open Questions in AL

Of the approximately 1.5 million life forms on earth today, about one third are plants and two thirds are animals. Of the animal species, around 4,000 are mammals, 9,000 birds, 6,000 reptiles, 3,000 amphibians, 20,000 fish, and about 900,000 arthropods, with the remaining 80,000 consisting of lower life forms, such as corals, jellyfish, and worms [82]. Over the last three billion years, evolution has produced animals with complex nervous systems that support extremely sophisticated individual and social patterns of behavior. Each general strategy (or even elementary unit of behavior) requires the integration and control of complex sensory/motor information. Each task is accomplished via the activity of the nervous system—an extremely powerful, massively parallel computational mechanism, which is the product of both evolutionary and developmental processes. The brains of insects alone employ up to a million nerve cells [78] with thousands of times more synapses. Avian brains contain around a billion neurons and mammalian brains on the order of tens of billions of neurons.

In the next section we briefly examine some representative animal behaviors. Open research questions in AL include synthesizing, with respect to any of these behaviors, any one or more of the following:

1. a group of interacting ANN-controlled agents (or single ANN) capable of demonstrating the relevant behavior(s).

2. a developmental process, for example, gene expression in ontology [29], adaptive learning or a combination of both, capable of automatically creating/modifying ANNs, via interaction with the environment, that result in ANN-controlled agents able to perform the relevant task(s).

3. an evolutionary process (with or without learning) by which genetic operations (e.g., recombination and mutation), combined with selection pressures from the environment, lead to ANN-controlled agents capable of exhibiting the relevant behavior(s), that is, synthesis of the evolution of nervous systems (e.g., [28]).

3.1 Common Behaviors in Animals
3.1.1 Social Grouping
Animals form a wide range of social groups [26,121], useful for protection and that enhance cooperation for such tasks as nesting, parenting, hunting, etc. Nesting fish, for example, many cichlids, and the majority of birds form pairs and share the duties of parenting equally. Deer, fur seals and Hamadryas baboons form harems, with a single dominant male serving as leader and protector of numerous females. Elephants form a matriarchy where the dominant elephant of the group is female, and the big bull elephants live solitary lives. Some birds form all male groups, for example, during breeding season, black grouse males cluster in an arena or lek so that the females may select a mate. During migrations, there form huge swarms of insects, flocks of birds and herds of antelopes.

3.1.2 Specialization of Labor
Social insects have evolved extremely complex caste systems, in which each class performs a distinct function, for example, soldier, queen, drone, forager, and nest builder [136]. In mammals, tasks are differentiated based on age, gender, and strength; for example, lionesses hunt while males protect the pride.

3.1.3 Food Finding, Preparation, and Storage
There are many food-finding strategies [88], including grazing by herbivores, browsing on trees by elephants, koalas, etc.; flower-finding and feeding by bees and humming-birds [36,49]; and foraging by ants, who produce and follow pheromone trails to food sources [134]. Many carnivores also have scavenging strategies in addition to hunting. For example, jackals often follow hunting lions and steal small portions of the kill even as the lions are feeding [31].

After an animal has obtained its food, it may execute complex food preparation behaviors. For example, the agouti (a rodent of South and Central America) carefully peels its food before eating it. Wild cats pluck the feathers of birds and shake them off before eating [60] with New World cats plucking and shaking out the feathers in a manner different from Old World cats.

Predators that kill large prey (and thus leave a carcass they cannot consume in one sitting) have developed food storage strategies [67]. Wolves will dig holes and drop large pieces of meat into them. Shaking the meat removes the dirt when the meat is dug up. Leopards will carry a carcass up into a tree for safekeeping. Animals store food for times when it will become scarce. Arctic foxes have been known to collect over time and hoard, in a single cache, over 40 bird eggs. The mole will create a hoard of up to 1,000 worms, with each worm immobilized by a bite to its front end. Some animals, for example, jay birds and squirrels, instead of creating a single store, will scatter their food about in multiple small caches, in order to make it difficult for hoard-raiders to find them. A single nutcracker bird will hide over 10,000 caches of two to five pine seeds each. Experiments (in which additional seeds are buried by the experimenters) have shown that such birds retrieve their caches based on memory and/or pattern recognition (vs. smell). This capability is quite impressive, because retrieval is performed months later, after which the foliage landscape has changed dramatically, for example, covered with snow [109,126].

3.1.4 Symbiotic Behavior

Distinct species will sometimes develop a symbiotic relationship [90]. For example, the Egyptian plover bird is allowed to enter the crocodile's mouth in order to eat parasites and food remnants from between its teeth. Large coral fish will form a queue, waiting to be cleaned by smaller, cleaning wrasse fish, who also clean about and within the mouth of the client fish. Grouper fish that are being serviced by gobies will partially shut the gobies in their mouths if there is any danger to the gobies, thus protecting their cleaners. Impala herds and baboon troops often stay together; the impalas serving as watchdogs while the baboons provide protection. The honey badger relies on a bird called the honeyguide to lead it to a source of honey. After the honey badger has destroyed the bee's hive and eaten its fill of honey, the honeyguide can then dine.

In some cases, one species makes use of another without "mutual consent." For instance, Amazon ants raid the nests of other species of ants and steal their eggs. When the larvae mature, they become "slave" worker ants who help maintain their masters' nest. Some species of ants have become so successful in this strategy that they can no longer feed themselves, relying instead on their slaves [135,136].

3.1.5 Dominance, Combat, and Territoriality

Many animals establish dominance hierarchies, with the more dominant males having greater access to females and food, but also serving the roles of protector and leader. In the case of bees, for example, stinging duels among daughter queens determine which one will become queen of a new colony as the old colony splits in two. Dominance and combat may determine the size or location of a territory for nesting. Territorial animals stake out territories through a combination of acoustic, chemical, and visual messages. Many birds announce their areas vocally, while some deer mark their territory with scent. Animals may issue threat displays to those entering their territory, or they may attack the intruder. Dominance is often established by stylized forms of combat, in which both combatants show tremendous restraint; as a result, combatants are rarely seriously injured [19,115]. Male kangaroos box one another, Bengal monitor lizards wrestle upright; giraffes push one another with their necks, and deer spar with their antlers. Dominance structures can be as simple as a straight-line ranking from most to least dominant, or, as in the case of chimpanzees, it can involve complex networks of shifting coalitions, collective leadership, and bargaining in the overthrow of bullies [27].

3.1.6 Mate Selection and Mating

Animals must find, attract, and/or choose mates before the actual act of mating [5,49,119]. For example, the river bullhead fish finds a cavity under a stone and enlarges it by digging with his mouth. When a female passes nearby, he drags her into the cave with his mouth and then blocks the entrance so that she cannot escape. A ripe female will then search for the best egg-laying site within the cave. After spawning, the male remains to guard the eggs while the female departs. Among nonpairing birds, females will arrive at a courtship site (i.e., a lek or arena), possibly containing many males. Each male will try to attract a female by performing elaborate displays, involving vocalizations, strutting behaviors, and feather erections. For example, the Australian male bowerbird, called also the stagemaker, completely clears (i.e., by removing every root, twig, leaf, etc.) a circular area of ground 8 feet in diameter. He then searches for a set of special articles that he places on display within this area. These special objects are often large, fresh leaves, turned with the underside up. Numerous leaves are arranged in what the males hope will be an exciting pattern to the female. When the female appears, he leaps about, picking up the leaves and using them as props in his song and dance courtship routine [40]. Bower birds will also employ shells, feathers, and human artifacts as courtship props [75].

The mating act itself requires control of, or coordination with, the other partner. For example, the male lion gently bites the lioness' neck, causing her to act as a passive cub, from the time when she was carried by her mother [82].

3.1.7 Nesting

Many animals build complex structures [37]. For example, during mating birds construct single and communal nests in the form of bowls, domes, and tubes. One of the most sophisticated is that produced by the male weaver birds. Weavers wrap tough, long grass around the fork of a branch. Several of these grasses are joined to form a circle, with a male weaving in the middle, similar to the way a human weaves a basket. The male makes use of two other types of stitches. When knotting, he pulls, pushes, and twists with his beak while holding the grass with his feet. When twining, he threads the grass in and out, like someone sewing with a thread. The weaver bird can tie slip knots, half-hitches, and overhand knots. Social weavers will build apartment complexes with up to 100 distinct entrances to individual nests [82]. In addition to the complex behaviors involved in the gathering and placement of materials in nest construction, there is also nest maintenance. Bowerbirds, for example, will keep their nests clean, for example, by replacing flowers (originally brought to decorate the nest) that have wilted [75]. Nests also need constant repair. Most animals, instead of rebuilding a nest from scratch when part of it is damaged, have successful strategies of local repair, even though there are innumerable distinct ways in which nests can become damaged. For example, beavers will patch those sections of their dam where they hear the sound of running water [137]. Ants and termites also somehow repair their tunnels and chambers as they undergo varying forms of damage [134].

In addition, the site for nesting must be selected. For instance, honeybees in cold climates send out scouts to forage for a good new nest site when the colony is going to split into two [108]. The scouts chosen are the oldest bees in the swarm because they have had the most nectar foraging experience and thus know the terrain the best. Once the swarm (of about 30,000 bees or one half of the hive) splits off, it lands on some object, and the scout bees are sent off in search of a new nesting site. The scouts search within a 10-km area for a nest. Studies reveal that the preferred nest is more than three meters off the ground (to make defense against predators easier); its entrance is less than 60 cm^2 and is located at the bottom of the nesting hollow and facing southward (in order to control the nest's microclimate and warm the bees as they take off). Like the dance performed by nectar-foraging bees [36], each nest scout performs a dance for the other scouts in which the orientation and amount of waggling of their abdomens indicate the location and preferability of the nesting site encountered. If a scout B1 encounters another scout B2 whose dance is more energetic, then B1 will fly off to check out B2's proposed site. Only after B1 has examined the alternate site and concurs with B2 will she alter her waggle dance to conform to that of B2 [62]. As a result, over time all the scouts will reach consensus, which may take several days. After consensus is reached, the scouts somehow inform the swarm, which then takes flight. The scouts then guide the swarm to the new nesting site, and construction begins.

3.1.8 Parenting

Animals protect, feed, clean, teach, and in general care for their young [97]. Care of young after birth requires recognizing one's offspring as one's own. Sheep require 20 minutes of licking and cleaning their babies in order to create/store a memory trace sufficiently strong for later discriminating them from other lambs. Keeping the nest clean is also important. For instance, parent birds will pick up and carry the droppings of their young away from the nest. Parents must also supply food and drink to their young. For example, the Sandgrouse male dips his lower feathers into water until they are soaked. When he returns to the nest, his chicks push against his feathers and suck the water from his breast [45]. Other birds carry water back in their beaks and dribble it into the open mouths of their chicks. Some mammals and birds will eat food and then regurgitate it upon return to the nest. In the case of mammals, female parents must decide when and for how long to recline so that their offspring can nurse.

Parents must also decide when to eat the food themselves and when to deny themselves in order to share food with their brood. For example, blackbirds will normally eat the first few insects they catch, including dragonflies. However, when feeding their young, they will immediately take the dragonfly back to the nest [87]. Blackbirds will often carry several insects at once when returning to the nest. Although more efficient, this collection task is itself complex, because insects that have dropped from the bird's beak must be found and picked up again without dropping those currently being held.

Upon leaving the nest, the young may be carried by their parents. Rats, dogs, and cats pick up their cubs in their jaws by the scruff of the neck, carrying them one by one to new sites. Anteaters and monkeys carry their young on their backs, as do scorpions and some spiders. Parents also employ strategies designed to teach their children survival skills. For example, as cubs grow older, the lioness will bring back live animals so that the cubs gain practice at hunting, catching, and killing prey [60].

Mammals are not always kind to the young of their species. Male lions that take over a pride will sometimes kill and eat the cubs that are not their own. After mating with the lionesses, they are good parents to their own offspring [23,35]. In some species, however, orphaned young may be adopted by other adults [82].

3.1.9 Predation Strategies

Predators have developed numerous strategies, from those that are largely instinctual in lower forms (e.g., [33]), to those requiring learning in mammals. Angler fish and certain amphibians and snakes make use of parts of their bodies as a bait to lure their prey to them [133]. Bears will scoop up migrating fish in rivers. Herons will stand very still and then, at the opportune moment, rapidly stab the fish. Cats stalk their prey, crouching down and inching along until within striking distance.

Humpback whales, for instance, let out a stream of air bubbles in a circular pattern around small fish, who are reluctant to pass through these bubbles and, thus, become concentrated and easier for the whale to consume [50]. Some predators, such as lions, hunt cooperatively [106]. Griffin [48], for instance, describes observing four lionesses slowly spreading out into a U-shaped formation to surround a pack of wildebeest. Two of the lionesses approached and sat very conspicuously at sites near the herd while the third lioness crawled low to the ground toward the herd. Suddenly, the fourth lion, who had circled way about, rushed out from within a nearby forrest and drove the herd toward the crouched lioness, who then leaped out and grabbed a wildebeest. The other two lionesses then very leisurely strolled toward the one who had made the kill, whereupon they shared it. Griffin concludes that it appears that the two conspicuous lionesses were intentionally drawing the attention of the wildebeests away from the stalking lionesses.

3.1.10 Predator Avoidance and Defense

Prey employ different strategies in the face of predation [30]. Hares will freeze until a predator is quite near before springing away. Squirrels dart to the blind side of a tree and then freeze. During flight, animals vary their speed and direction of flight dramatically, based on the behavior of their pursuer. Many prey species flee to the safety of trees, water, or burrows. Flight strategies include combinations of startle displays (e.g., birds displaying a bright spot of color, the frilled lizard extending the flap of skin around its face), dashing, freezing, and hiding. Startling a predator gives the prey a chance to escape. For example, a cornered cat will hiss and spit; some insects will assume the posture of poisonous insects in order to scare off an attacker. In the case of flight, the type of safety zone prey will seek often depends on the type of predator in pursuit. A rooster will climb upon a rock in the face of a ground predator while hiding under bushes when spotting a hawk from above [71,73].

Prey that are cornered (or too fatigued to flee) may turn and attack the predator. Many species of small birds (e.g., warblers, finches, thrushes, and even hummingbirds) will mob a bird of prey. For instance, if an owl remains stationary (perhaps due to illness), the birds of prey may begin mobbing it. They dive down, buzzing within inches of its head, even clawing it. This mobbing behavior attracts more birds to join in until the owl is routed. Ground squirrels will also mob a snake, rushing it and trying to bite it or throw sand in its eyes. A group of baboons or chimpanzees may also mob a leopard [82].

Predator avoidance is quite complex because it involves continual monitoring, by the prey, of any predator dispositions. For instance, gazelles will actually follow predators in order to keep watch on their movements [128]. In order to avoid needless expenditure of energy, prey must continuously assess whether or not predators are about to strike or are simply passing by.

3.1.11 Dissembling Behaviors

Many animals, including various species of insects, frogs, snakes, birds, and small mammals (e.g., squirrels and opossums) will feign death [76,79]. They will remain immobile while being mauled. Once the predator is convinced that the prey is dead, the predator may leave the prey alone, thus giving it an opportunity to escape. Many ground-nesting birds will pretend to be wounded by dragging an extended wing and/or struggling to walk, thus distracting the predator away from the nest [3]. Other dissembling strategies in ground-nesting birds include false incubation, in which the bird pretends to be sitting on a nest of eggs at a site away from the actual eggs [114]. Such behavior is quite complex. The dissembling bird continuously must monitor the predator. If the predator appears to lose interest and/or fails to follow, then the bird recognizes this and temporarily abandons its dissembling behavior to fly back toward the predator. It then reinitiates its dissembling strategy.

3.1.12 Primitive Tool Use and Culture

Wild chimpanzees make use of sticks in order to extract termites from their nests [43]. The mongoose throws hard-shelled eggs at nearby rocks in order to smash them open. The sea otter swims on its back with a flat stone on its stomach. It then smashes clams against this stone to break them open [48]. The Egyptian vulture picks up a stone in its beak and throws it down at an ostrich egg in order to crack the egg open [32]. Herring gulls and some crows break open clams by dropping them when in flight onto hard, rocky surfaces [8]. Studies show that such birds select shells based on weight (indicating a live/edible vs. dead mollusk within) and vary the height of release based on the perceived hardness of the ground below [138].

Insects also use tools. Adult weaver ants roll up leaves and fix the edges with silk in order to make nests. But because the adults cannot produce silk themselves, they pick up their silk-producing ant larvae and squeeze them to force out a drop of liquid silk. Thus, the adults use the passive larvae as tubes of glue [53]. Leaf-cutter ants have developed a form of agriculture, in which they carry undigestible leaves back to their colony. They chew the leaves and add fecal material, which then serves as food for a fungus that they grow in special chambers within the nest. The ants then eat the fungus. When a reproductive female leaves to form a new colony, she takes with her a small bit of the fungus, as starting material for her new fungus garden [134].

Higher animals, for example, primates, exhibit aspects of culture. For instance, knowledge for how to clean dirt-covered sweet potatoes (by washing them in water) was seen to spread, via primate learning, observation and mimicry, through a troop of Japanese macaques [55,56]. This skill was later passed down from parent to offspring. Only the original, older males never acquired the behavior.

3.1.13 Other Complex Behaviors

The behaviors described previously by no means exhaust the types of complex strategies employed for survival. Other behaviors include: migration and navigation, strategies to protect oneself while sleeping or ill, grooming behaviors to avoid parasites and disease, and among mammals, behaviors involving play [112,122], in which the young try out and learn aspects of parental roles.

These behaviors (taken either individually or, more realistically, in a social context and requiring integration of multiple coordinated and carefully sequenced sensory/motor behaviors) constitute a wealth of benchmark tasks for any synthesis-oriented research program. The execution of any of these behaviors requires a high degree of intelligence and computation. For example, food finding requires complex pattern recognition and generalization capabilities. Generalization is required because no two forms of food, whether stationary or moving, will look identical; likewise, any two acts within the same functional category (e.g., defense, submission, feeding, etc.) will not be identical. Differential responses to distinct members of one's own species or kin, and to distinct kinds of predators and prey, requires categorization of objects and actions in the environment.

Animal decision making is also complex and state dependent. For instance, predator avoidance requires planning in the face of multiple and possibly conflicting constraints, as in the case, for instance, when an animal is both hungry and thirsty, but food is at one location and water at another; a potential predator is in-between the animal and one food source but possibly looks tired or satiated; the animal's own cubs are at another site and must be fed soon; it is getting dark, and so on. While the nature or even existence of conscious thought is highly controversial in animals [48,127], it is clear that the tasks performed by animals require enormous amounts of computation. For example, consider cooperative hunting carnivores or nesting site selection and group nest construction by bees, weaver birds or, among mammals, the dams built by beavers [137]. The sensing, locomotive, manipulative, and social skills exhibited by such animals in performing these tasks completely eclipse any kind of robotic behavior produced so far within the field of AI.

3.2 Animal Cooperation via Communication

Most forms of cooperation require communication, which can be accomplished by visual, tactile, acoustic, and/or olfactory means [31]. These signals (e.g., facial expressions, scent marks, body postures/movements, vocalizations, displays, etc.) need not be "intentional" to constitute communication. What is necessary is that the behavior (or resulting state caused by the behavior of the sender) be perceived and bring about differential behavior on the part of the perceivers that is in some way ultimately advantageous to the sender or the sender's group. This resulting behavior may then itself be perceived by the original sender, thus possibly causing differential behaviors in response. Communication may occur both within and across species.

3.2.1 Insect Communication

Insects commonly communicate via chemicals, such as pheromones. They also employ tactile motions and, on occasion, visually perceived displays. For instance, bees communicate to their comrades the location and amount of nectar found at a site by means of a waggle dance. The angle, amount of waggling, and wing-fanning display indicates, respectively, the direction, distance, and amount of nectar [36]. Weaver ants make use of different pheromones, excreted from rectal and sternal glands, to recruit other weaver ants for foraging, for emigration to a new nest, or in defense against attackers. These chemical signals are combined with tactile signals, such as touching with antennae, head waving, mandible use, and jerking of the body [53].

Acoustic signals are also commonly employed by insects. For example, the Douglas fir beetle employs a half-dozen distinct acoustic signals. The males employ distinct chirps, indicating (a) approach to the egg gallery entrance containing a female, (b) imminent copulation during courtship, (c) rivalry with other males, and (d) situations of stress. The female generates a distinct chirp when constructing and guarding her egg gallery [105].

Fireflies use flashing lights to signal and attract mates. The male firefly indicates his gender and species by his pattern of flashing. The female then signals back with a distinct set of pulses. The timing of her flashing, with respect to the males, indicates her gender/species. Predatory female fireflies have evolved mimicry of the response timings of females of other species and can attract the corresponding males to them, which the predatory females then devour [63]. Physical behaviors can also serve as signals. For example, the male black-tipped hangingfly presents the prey it has caught to the female, which the female then examines to determine whether or not she will mate with him [118].

3.2.2 Avian Communication

Birds commonly communicate [66], both acoustically and visually, through the production of songs and elaborate dances and displays (e.g., lekking). Many birds give off specific vocalizations when they encounter food or sense danger [72]. Domestic chickens can communicate information about the quality of available food [74], while roosters give off different vocalizations for warning of raccoons versus hawks. What is a particular interest is that the rooster only issues these vocal warning signals when the rooster is aware of a nearby hen of the same species [74,100]. If no hen is near, then the rooster intelligently avoids possible predator awareness and attack by remaining silent.

Duet-singing birds, such as the African shrike, produce complex antiphonal (i.e., interspersed notes) and polyphonic (interspersed and simultaneous) music. Mating pairs (who often mate for life) discriminate their mates from other shrikes by coordinating musical pitch, harmonic and melodic intervals, and duration and timing in an extremely precise manner [120]. Such duets also function in recognizing species/kin membership, maintaining social contact in dense foliage, and establishing territory. For example, females will not answer the songs of other males and when the male is absent; during that time the female sings not only its own part but also that of its mate. It is believed that this rehearsal allows one bird to continue remembering its mate's unique "signature" for later recognition upon return of the mate.

3.2.3 Mammalian Communication

This can take many forms. For instance, tactile communication among Duiker antelopes includes social licking/nibbling of the head, neck, and shoulders, with male/female pairs rubbing together the glands near their eyes for maintaining pair bonding. Two Druiker males will do this also, but as a prelude to combat [96].

Signals are used also for warning of predators. Prairie dogs not only issue distinct calls for different predators (hawks, snakes, coyotes, humans, etc.) but there is evidence that they can, in their signal, specify distinct individual predators who have become familiar to them from within a given predator group [110,111].

Many mammals have a wide repertoire of behaviors that act as signals to others. Consider the cat family [60]. Felids communicate by body posture, action, facial expression, scent (urine spraying and rubbing), vocalizations, and licking/nuzzling/pawing actions. Facially, the movement of ears (relaxed, pricked up, flattened, twitching, rotated) mean different things, for example, cats rotate their ears upward when angry. In general, facial and body postures indicate predisposition to attack, defense, or flight. Vocal signals include meowing, yowling, growling, grunting, snarling, purring, spitting, hissing, roaring, etc. For instance, mother felids employ a special call to attract their cubs when bringing back live prey. The intensity of this call is different, depending upon whether the live prey is small and harmless or large and potentially dangerous. In the latter case, the cubs respond more carefully. Older, mobile cubs are warned to take cover by the mother both slapping and hissing at them. When family members meet, they greet each other by rubbing noses, then heads and sides. Vocalizations and postures also differentiate defensive versus offensive roles and dominance versus submission.

3.2.4 Primate Communication

Vervet monkeys also distinguish predator classes (leopards, eagles, snakes) in their warning calls. Each distinct call causes a different type of behavior. When hearing a leopard warning sound, vervet monkeys run into the trees. Snake alarms cause them to rise up on their hind legs and look in the grass while eagle warning sounds cause them to look at the sky or duck under bushes [116]. Primates also appear to actively attempt to deceive one another [132]. In general, apes appear to have the greatest capacity for abstract thought among primates [94] and the largest vocal repertoires [18,21,101] with Goodall [43,44] cataloging over 30 chimpanzee calls used in the wild and over 200 signs (either visual symbol patterns or sign language gestures) learned in human-trained gorillas and chimpanzees [38,89,99,117].

3.2.5 Cross-Species Communication

For instance, the honeyguide bird signals to the honey badger that there is honey available by chattering and making displays. The honey badger then replies with a special, hissing chuckle. Thereupon the honeyguide leads the honeybadger to the honey site. The honeyguide never gets more than 20 feet ahead of the honeybadger, in order to keep it in visual contact [90]. Communication across species commonly occurs in predator–prey interactions. Prey animals with defensive systems (e.g., the skunk) will often first warn a potential predator before actually employing its defensive system, thus possibly avoiding having to expend energy using it.

3.3 Animal Development and Learning

Animal behaviors are the result of complex interactions between genetic and developmental factors. In general, genetic effects are more noticeable and tend to dominate in lower life forms. For example, although each species of cricket has a unique set of distinct chirp patterns, it has been shown that these patterns are not learned, but are genetically determined [13]. However, there is strong evidence that nearly all animals, even slugs and insects, are capable of learning [48]. For example, bees are able to quickly learn and remember, over many days, the odor and color of flowers that yield a given pollen or nectar [78]. Experiments in which bees are moved to distant sites during the night support the theory that bees construct mental maps of their environments, which they use for navigation [47]. Bees go through different occupational stages, based on their age and experience. The youngest bees clean the honeycombs, while older bees help build the combs; later, these bees "graduate" from comb construction and leave their hive to forage for nectar [62].

In birds, many behaviors (that might at first be considered instinctual) have been shown to be learned. For instance, European blackbirds will learn to mob a harmless (nonpredator) honeycreeper bird if they are made to think that other birds are mobbing that bird [82]. In the white-crowned sparrow, the learning of songs depends upon both a sensitive/critical period and access to examples of appropriate, species-specific songs. The young songbird makes use of species-specific songs it hears and, in a trial-and-error manner, develops its own song version [47]. It has been demonstrated that pigeons can learn to discriminate underwater photographs of fish [51]—a task for which there has been no evolutionary selectional pressure.

An interesting interaction between genetics and development is that of imprinting [65]. For instance, what a duckling imprints upon depends on what is currently in the environment during a critical period. At the same time, the range over which imprinting operates is genetically determined and highly constrained (e.g., to mobile objects within a given size range; otherwise, baby ducklings would imprint on rocks, insects, or even their own siblings).

A complex form of learning is that of learning through observation and subsequent imitation [48]. Most birds and mammals exhibit this kind of learning. Young lions, for instance, learn how to hunt properly by observing their mother hunt.

4   Synthesizing Animal Intelligence via Evolution and Learning

Recent computer models used in biological, ethological, and ecological studies have employed game theory [77], optimization techniques, and dynamic state-variable models [22,70]. The AL approach extends such modeling techniques by including simulations of artificial nervous systems (at some level of abstraction) that control sensing/acting artificial agents that can move about in artificial environments that have spatial structure (usually two-dimensional). In addition, artificial genomes are specified that encode ANNs (either directly, or indirectly, through some ontogenetic process). Genomes are modified, over many generations, via a variety of genetic algorithms. During an artificial animal's lifetime, its ANN may also be modified via adaptive learning algorithms. Thus, AL models offer a wide range of more realistic modeling techniques, accessible for the first time as the result of great increases in computational power and reduction in the cost of computation and memory storage.

Although the field of AL is still in its infancy, a number of simulation models have been developed, in which ANN-controlled life forms evolve and/or develop survival behaviors within simulated environments. Some of these are briefly mentioned in the following sections.

4.1 Evolution/Learning of Food Discrimination

Todd and Miller [123] set up an abstract, simulated "aquatic" environment containing two distinct patches of "plant material"—a red patch and green patch. Within one patch the red plant serves as "food" for the evolving creatures, while the green plants act as "poison." In the other patch the color roles are reversed. Each creature remains, during its lifetime, in a given patch; however, its offspring at birth may be placed in the opposite patch. If a creature eats food, its metabolism is increased (thus improving reproductive success), but if it consumes poison its metabolism is reduced. Creatures are immobile, but food material (or poison) "floats" past them, and they must decide whether to eat it or ignore it. In addition, food always smells "sweet," while poison always smells "sour" (i.e., no matter what their color assignments happen to be within a given patch). Finally, there is "turbulence" in the "water." Increased turbulence decreases the accuracy of smell. For example, a red plant may mistakenly smell sweet, even though, in that patch, it is always poisonous.

The behavior of Todd and Miller's creatures is controlled by neural networks containing (a) color and scent sensory neurons, (b) an ingest motor neuron, and (c) an interneuron. The genome of each creature directly codes excitatory/inhibitory connections between these neurons. In addition, connections can be either fixed or learnable. Learnable connections are modified, during a creature's lifetime, via a Hebbian rule, in which correlated firing of connected neurons increases the strength of their connections.

Because what is poisonous can change color from generation to generation, there is no advantage to hardwiring connections for poison avoidance in terms of color. However, within an individual's lifetime, color does serve as a poison/food discriminator that (depending on the amount of turbulence) is more accurate than smell. Over several hundreds of generations, creatures evolve with a hardwired connection between the smell and motor (eating) neurons but with a learnable connection between the color and motor neurons. This connection is then modified over the life of a given creature, based on which type of food patch it ended up in.

4.2 Evolution of Foraging and Trail Laying

Collins [24] performed a series of experiments (labeled AntFarm I through AntFarm V) in which he attempted to evolve colonies of ANN-controlled artificial ants that both forage for food and lay down pheromone trails to guide others to food sites. Most of the experiments consisted of 32,000 colonies with 128 ants per colonies being simulated on a massively parallel computer. He varied numerous parameters, including the genome size (from 25,590 bits in AntFarm I to 487 bits in AntFarm V) and ANN encoding schemes (e.g., symmetric vs. nonsymmetric connections; excitory only vs. incorporation of inhibitory connections; interneurons varying from 21 bits to 0 bits). In the earlier experiments, food foraging behaviors evolved, but they were non-ant like, for example, ants all walked in large circles or semicircles. Collins only succeeded in evolving antlike behavior in AntFarm V. These ants exhibit mostly forward movement with random turns until a food site is found, then they transport some food directly back to the nest while laying pheromones. In this experiment, Collins forced ants to involuntarily lay pheromones for generations 1,000–2,000 and then returned pheromone-release control back to each ant. At generation 2,001 there was a large decrease in the amount of pheromone being released, but the ants had evolved to both lay and follow trails by generation 2,100. Collins theorizes that, before ants were forced to release pheromones, trail following could not evolve (and so trail laying could not evolve either). However, once ants had finally evolved to follow trails (i.e., follow those trails created during the generations in which forced pheromone release occurred), then any (initially inadvertent) pheromone release upon return from a food site would lead other ants to that site and thus increase survivability of the colony. As a result, trail laying and trail following could now coevolve.

4.3   Evolution of Communication

MacLennan [69] reasons that communication emerges only when (a) what he terms "simorgs" (simulated organisms) can perceive, in their local environments, information unavailable but advantageous to other simorgs, and (b) the signalers are able to produce changes in the environment that the receivers can detect. MacLennan also argues for incorporating overlapping generations into Holland's genetic algorithm (GA), so that simorg offspring can learn from prior generations. In MacLennan's experiments, each simorg's genotype is represented by a transition table and likewise its phenotype. In addition to local environments, there is a shared, global environment of symbols, and each simorg, based on its transition table, can match and/or post a symbol to the global environment. Whenever a simorg's action matches that of the most recent symbol posted (representing information about the local environment of another simorg), both matching simorgs receive a credit. Simorgs with higher credit have a greater chance of being selected for mating. MacLennan's experiments indicate that average fitness of the population increases much more rapidly when communication is allowed than when it is repressed. He also compares the relative influence of communication with learning enabled/disabled and shows that concurrent learning and communication result in the highest average fitness.

In Werner and Dyer [129] we evolved simple communication protocols for mate finding between ANN-controlled artificial animals in a two-dimensional toroidal, grid environment. Females received, as sensory inputs, the location and orientation of any male within a 5×5 grid sensory area surrounding the female. The motor output of a female was interpreted as a signal that was then copied as input to any male within the female's 25-cell sensory area. In contrast, the male's motor output caused him to move left, right, forward, or stand still. Thus, females were immobile but could sense and signal nearby males. Males were "blind" but could "hear" the signals of nearby females and move about in the environment. Mating occurred whenever a male landed on a grid cell occupied by a female. As a result of mating, a new male and female offspring (via recombination and mutation of parental genes) were produced and placed at random locations in the environment. At the same time, a random male and female were removed from the environment, thus keeping the overall population size stable. Starting with a population of random genomes, the simulation resulted in a progression of generations of ANNs that exhibited increasingly effective mate finding strategies. In effect, the females evolved to inform nearby males how to move in order to find the females and mate. The males simultaneously coevolved to interpret female signals in order to land on female-occupied squares. In addition, a number of distinct subspecies (i.e., groups with different signaling protocols or "dialects") evolved and competed in the environment. Experiments with physical barriers in the environment were also performed. A partially permeable barrier allowed a separate subspecies to evolve and survive for indefinite periods of time, in spite of occasional migration and contact from members of other subspecies.

Like in MacLennan's model, we have overlapping generations. However, in our model, organisms are not selected for mating but must find their own mates. We believe that it is important not to directly select for communication. Instead, communication should evolve because it enhances the ability of organisms to perform tasks that are directly related to survivability, such as finding mates.

4.4   Evolution of Predation and Predator Avoidance

In Werner and Dyer [130,131] we have extended our two-dimensional environment to include simulated "smells" and "sounds" of different types and intensities, which diffuse away from their sources, thus creating complex sensory gradients. Multiple species of life forms (termed *biots*) interact in the environment (termed *BioLand*), which also contains simple physical objects, such as plants, trees, and holes. Plants serve as food for some biot species while trees and holes serve as landmarks, and/or safety zones for nesting and/or escape from predator biots. Biots produce involuntary smells, which serve to indicate their species/gender membership and can be extended to indicate other physical properties, such as age, receptivity to mating, etc. Biots also produce involuntary sounds, which become louder the faster they move and thus diffuse over greater distances. Sounds can also be produced voluntarily, that is, under biot neuro-motor control. Each biot can generate a variety of distinct voluntary sounds (termed *frequencies*). Different frequencies allow biots to communicate and/or discriminate different sounds and sound combinations that they receive through their bilateral sensory neurons.

Biots are capable of smoothly turning and altering their speeds. They possess a metabolism that drops as they perform actions and rises whenever they eat food (i.e., food consists of prey biots for carnivores, of plants for herbivores). Biots can grasp/release objects and also contain a mating motor neuron. Mating and offspring occur whenever two same-species biots (each with sufficient metabolism) come near one another and simultaneously fire their mating motor neurons. In such cases, variant offspring are produced via mutation and recombination of parental genomes. Biot genes encode both standard axo-dendritic connections and also higher-order, axo-axonal gating connections.

In one experiment, herbivore biots were termed prairie dogs, while two distinct predator species were termed snakes and hawks. Prairie dogs evolved to run away from snakes and hawks, while these predators evolved to chase the prairie dogs. Prairie dog biots also evolved to form herds for protection from predators. In ongoing experiments we are evolving differential predator warning signals among prairie dogs, who will then seek the appropriate shelter (tree vs. hole) based on the nature of the warning signal.

4.5   Toward the Synthesis of Protohuman Intelligence

ANNs capable of exhibiting complex animal behaviors (e.g., nesting, parenting) have not yet been engineered, evolved, or designed through learning; therefore, it may be premature to discuss the synthesis of protohuman forms of intelligence (such as humanlike language and thought) via AL techniques. It may be possible, however, that sophisticated ANNs, capable of aspects of human thinking and language could be first engineered and then a population of them placed in a simulated environment. The population could then undergo evolution, for instance, to see if such engineered ANNs could survive, interact, cooperate, communicate, and adapt. There is currently an intense, ongoing debate over the relative roles of innate brain structures, development/learning processes, and adaptation in the evolution of human language [6,61,91–93]. This debate cannot be resolved either through examining the fossil record or engaging in thought experiments. We believe that the AL simulation approach proposed here has the long-term potential of providing important insights in this area of inquiry. At this point, a number of ANNs that exhibit aspects of human-level inferencing, language acquisition, and comprehension have been engineered. In my own lab, for example, we have designed (a) ANNs that learn the meanings of word sequences by observing the motions of simulated objects on an artificial retina [83], (b) ANNs that automatically disambiguate word meanings via plan analysis (e.g., "... washed the pot in the dishwasher" vs. "... hid the pot in the dishwasher to keep from getting busted") [57], and (c) ANNs that acquire both world knowledge (i.e., scripts—stereotypic action sequences) and word meanings and infer unstated events when generating story paraphrases [81]. However, we are still years away from placing even small groups of such complex neural networks into evolutionary or adaptive environments.

5   Other Research Issues and Methodological Principles

The AL approach to synthesizing intelligent behavior described here has its roots in the fields of parallel distributed processing [104], connectionism [54,124], computational neuroscience [2,107], neuroethology [18,33], comparative psychology [101,103], genetic algorithms [11], biological cybernetics [15], situated agents [125], and reactive microrobotics [16]. As a result, the AL approach to synthetic cognition carries along with it other general research issues that are related to each of these fields. These general issues involve the following: (a) The relationship between learning and evolution. For example, Nolfi et al. [86], Belew [10], and Belew et al. [12] have performed experiments in which evolving ANNs are augmented with backpropagation learning during their lifetimes. (b) How ANNs encode knowledge of their environments [21,101,102] and respond adaptively to them through feedback [9]. (c) How genomes and artificial organisms are best encoded [25] and expressed ontogenetically [85]. (d) How to address outstanding problems in population biology, ecology, and ethology, such as the evolution of altruism [134]. (e) How to encode environments that are computationally tractable but rich enough to supply the necessary selectional pressures [130].

The AL approach toward synthesizing intelligence can be computationally extremely expensive, because it involves simulating many generations of entire populations of the individual lifetimes of sensing/acting ANNs. Consequently, models must be simplified or made more abstract in some way, in order to remain tractable. Below we offer the following methodological principles as possible guidelines in simulation design.

5.1.1   Principle of Hypothesis-Driven Abstraction Hierarchies

Any given task can be represented at many different levels of abstraction. For example, the task of building a bird's nest can be modeled at a very abstract level (e.g., a single nest-building motor neuron fires and, presto, a complete nest is created in the environment) or at an extremely detailed level (e.g., millions of neurons fire, to control a robot bird with hundreds of muscles/joints to simulate complex beak, claw, torso, and head movements during nest construction sensory/motor actions). Which level of abstraction is selected depends greatly on where theoretical claims are being made. A single nest-making motor neuron might be sufficient for a model whose hypothesis involves the placement of a nest in a site selection model; however, it would be insufficient for a model concerning the evolution/learning of nest-construction behavior.

5.1.2   Principle of Minimal Effective Embodiment

For the task of synthesizing intelligent cooperative behaviors, it is important to concentrate on the evolution of the structure of nervous systems while avoiding, wherever possible, the inclusion of physical properties of the organisms. For example, real animals vary in size. However, if one is trying to evolve, for instance, predator avoidance strategies, then the modeling of size may be detrimental and result simply in an evolutionary "size arms race" in which artificial animal populations avoid predation by simply evolving to be larger. Again, what physical characteristics of an organism to include depends on the research hypothesis being explored. For example, if one is evolving predator escape behavior in a landscape of burrows of varying sizes, then size (of both prey and predator) might be important. However, even in this case one would want to hold the size attribute fixed over evolutionary time, so that one can concentrate on the evolution of the behavior and the structure of the ANNs that produce it. Another form of minimality is to reduce the scale or granularity of the interface between the organism and its environment as much as possible, for instance, instead of one million rods/cones for an artificial eye, employing a 10×10 matrix of sensory neurons.

5.1.3   Principle of Midpoint Entry

Because the search space (of possible agent populations, interactions, and environments) is so vast and broad ranging, it is acceptable to start one's model somewhere in the middle. This principle supports the mixing of bottom-up and top-down research strategies. The top-down approach involves starting out with a specific goal in mind and then engineering a system to achieve that goal, using whatever constraints are available to guide model construction. The bottom-up approach involves starting out with a set of tools or building blocks and then tinkering with these in systematic ways to see what results. In general, the AL approach tends to be bottom-up in nature, because both evolution and adaptive learning are mainly bottom-up. However, given that the research space is so vast, it appears reasonable to use top-down techniques to design organisms at a given level of sophistication, which are then placed in environments in which evolutionary and adaptive learning processes are then applied. This mixed approach allows one to start, for instance, with a population of pre-engineered ANNs with sophisticated capabilities and then see if such ANNs can improve (or even maintain) these capabilities within an evolutionary and learning environment. In fact, every researcher who specifies the sensory/motor capabilities of a given artificial agent is initially using a top-down approach.

5.1.4   Principle of Indirectness

Whenever possible, it is important to avoid setting up an objective function that selects directly for the desired behavior. Instead, the desired behavior should arise indirectly, as a side effect of increased survivability (due to the development or evolution of that behavior). For example, instead of directly selecting artificial animals for reproduction who communicate, in Werner and Dyer [129], only animals who found their own mates could reproduce. Communication then evolved because it improved the ability of animals to find their mates and thus produce offspring.

5.1.5   Principle of Naturalness

Because there are potentially so many parameters to adjust in AL systems, it is important to impose constraints that are intuitive. A major source of intuitions comes from constraints that already exist for real animals in nature. Whenever these intuitions are violated, they should be carefully noted. For example, in Werner and Dyer [129], when mating occurred we placed the offspring at distant sites from their parents. This kind of event does not occur in nature. Actually, we did it because our ANNs had no way of discriminating their kin or any reason to avoid committing incest, and parents paid no metabolic cost in generating offspring. As a result, parents and offspring, if allowed to stay in the same spot after mating, would simply remain there, forever mating with each other. Thus, this initial lack of "naturalness" led to a model that became more and more difficult to extend. To solve this problem, we decided to add new features to the environment (see section 4.4) in order to make the environment conform more to natural environments.

Finally, this paper has mainly concentrated on issues in software simulation. Clearly, there is a corresponding (albeit distinct) entire research program in synthesizing intelligent hardware (i.e., robots). An AL-based robotics research program poses distinctive challenges, only two of which I will mention here: (a) With physical robots it is very difficult to have large populations, thus greatly reducing the effectiveness of genetic algorithms. Even a small population of 100 micro-robots would be very difficult to control and time-consuming to set up for repeated experimentation. Perhaps a mixed approach can be developed, in which large populations of ANNs are evolved in simulated environments, and then a small subset of these are down-loaded (as software control) into the actual robots, which are then tested in the real world. (b) Models of ontogenetic development will also be extremely difficult, because one cannot easily modify the morphology of a physical robot.

6 Conclusions

Although animals lack human-level thought and language, they still exhibit a high degree of intelligence. Animals must satisfy multiple, often conflicting constraints in order to survive. Animals hide from predators, forage and scavenge, fight, court, mate, establish dominance, climb, burrow, build elaborate nests, teach and care for their offspring, groom, establish and defend territories, migrate, navigate, use primitive tools, cooperate, and communicate. Such tasks require complex sensory analysis and motor integration. They also learn via observation and adjust their behaviors to constantly changing environments. They categorize and manipulate their environments and generalize from experience [41,48]. They form social organizations through communication and cooperation. One major goal of the field of AL is to synthesize these complex behaviors by constructing artificial nervous systems, via developmental and evolutionary modeling techniques, and thus gain insight into the computations underlying the cognitive capabilities of both animals and man.

Acknowledgment
Research by author on evolving communication and predation was supported in part by NSF grant IRI-910730.

References
1. Agre, P. E., & Chapman, D. (1987). Pengi: an implementation of a theory of situated action. In *Proceedings of Sixth National Conference on Artificial Intelligence*. Los Altos, CA: AAAI/Morgan Kaufmann.

2. Anderson, J. A., & Rosenfeld, E. (Eds.) (1988). *Neurocomputing: foundations of research*. Cambridge, MA: The MIT Press.

3. Armstrong, E. A. (1947). *Bird display and behaviour*. London: Drummond.

4. Axelrod, R. (1984). *The evolution of cooperation*. New York: Basic Books.

5. Bastock, M. (1967). *Courtship: a zoological study*. London: Heinemann.

6. Bates, D., Thal, D., & Marchman, V. (1989). Symbols and syntax: a Darwinian approach to language development. In N. Krasnegor, D. Rumbaugh, M. Studdert-Kennedy, & R. Schiefelbusch (Eds.), *The biological foundations of language development*. Oxford University Press.

7. Bechtel, W., & Abrahamsen, A. (1991). *Connectionism and the mind*. Cambridge, MA: Blackwell.

8. Beck, B. B. (1980). *Animal tool behavior*. New York: Garland STPM Press.

9. Beer, R. D. (1990). *Intelligence as adaptive behavior: an experiment in computational neuroethology*. New York: Academic Press.

10. Belew, R. K. (1990). Evolution, learning and culture: computational metaphors for adaptive search. *Complex Systems, 4*(1).

11. Belew, R. K., & Booker, L. B. (Eds.) (1991). *Proceedings of the Fourth International Conference on Genetic Algorithms.* San Mateo, CA: Morgan Kaufmann.

12. Belew, R. K., McInerney, J., & Schraudolph, N. N. (1992). Evolving networks: using the genetic algorithm with connectionist learning. In C. G. Langton, C. Taylor, J. D. Farmer, & S. Rasmussen (Eds.), *Artificial life II.* Redwood City, CA: Addison-Wesley.

13. Bentley, D., & Hoy, R. R. (1974). The neurobiology of cricket song. *Scientific American, 231*(2), 34–44.

14. Bond, A., & Gasser, L. (Eds.) (1988). *Readings in distributed artificial intelligence.* San Mateo, CA: Morgan Kaufmann.

15. Braitenberg, V. (1984). *Vehicles: experiments in synthetic psychology.* Cambridge, MA: The MIT Press.

16. Brooks, R. A. Intelligence without representation. *Artificial Intelligence, 47,* 139–160.

17. Byrne, R., & Whiten, A. (Eds.) (1988). *Machiavellian intelligence: social expertise and the evolution of intellect in monkeys, apes, and humans.* Oxford University Press.

18. Camhi, J. M. (1984). *Neuroethology: nerve cells and the natural behavior of animals.* Sunderland, MA: Sinauer.

19. Carthy, J. D., & Ebling, F. L. (1964). *The natural history of aggression.* New York: Academic Press.

20. Cheney, D. L., & Seyfarth, R. M. (1990). *How monkeys see the world: inside the mind of another species.* Chicago: University of Chicago Press.

21. Churchland, P. S., & Sejnowski, T. J. (1992). *The computational brain.* Cambridge, MA: Bradford/The MIT Press.

22. Clark, C. W. (1991). Modeling behavioral adaptations. *Behavioral and Brain Sciences, 14,* 85–117.

23. Cloudsley-Thompson, J. L. (1965). *Animal conflict and adaptation.* London: Foulis.

24. Collins, R. J. (1992). *Studies in artificial evolution.* Computer science doctoral dissertation, UCLA.

25. Collins, R. J., & Jefferson, D. R. (1991). Representations for artificial organisms. In J.-A. Meyer & S. W. Wilson (Ed..), *From animals to animats: Proceedings of the First International Conference on Simulation of Adaptive Behavior.* Cambridge, MA: Bradford Books/The MIT Press.

26. Crook, J. H. (1970). *Social behaviour in birds and mammals.* New York: Academic Press.

27. De Waal, F. (1982). *Chimpanzee politics.* London: Cape.

28. Ebbesson, S. O. E. (1984). Evolution and ontogeny of neural circuits. *Behavioral and Brain Sciences, 7*(3), 321–366.

29. Edelman, G. M. (1987). *Neural Darwinism: the theory of neuronal group selection.* New York: Basic Books.

30. Edmunds, M. (1974). *Defence in animals.* London: Longman.

31. Estes, R. D. (1991). *The behavior guide to African mammals.* Los Angeles: University of California Press.

32. Ewer, R. F. (1968). *Ethology of mammals.* London: Logos Press.

33. Ewert, J. (1987). Neuroethology of releasing mechanisms: prey-catching in toads. *Behavioral and Brain Sciences, 10,* 337–405.

34. Firebaugh, M. W. (1988). *Artificial intelligence: a knowledge-based approach.* Boston: Boyd & Fraser.

35. Fox, L. R. (1975). *Abnormal behavior in animals.* Philadelphia: Saunders.

36. Frisch, K. von. (1967). *The dance language and orientation of bees.* Cambridge, MA: Harvard University Press.

37. Frisch, K. von (1974). *Animal architecture.* New York: Harcourt Brace.

38. Gardner, R. A., & Gardner, B. T. (1969). Teaching sign language to a chimpanzee. *Science, 165,* 664–672.

39. Gasser, L., & Huhns, M. N. (1989). *Distributed artificial intelligence* (Vol. II). San Mateo, CA: Morgan Kaufmann.

40. Gilliard, E. T. (1969). *Birds of paradise and bower birds.* London: Weidenfeld and Nicolson.

41. Goldberg, D. E. (1989). *Genetic algorithms in search, optimization, and machine learning.* Reading, MA: Addison-Wesley.

42. Goldberg, D. E., & Holland, J. H. (Eds.) (1988). *Machine learning* (Vol. 3, Nos. 2–3, special issue on genetic algorithms). Kluwer Academic Publishers.

43. Goodall, J. van Lawick. (1971). *In the shadow of man.* Boston: Houghton Mifflin.

44. Goodall, J. (1986). *The chimpanzees of Gombe.* Cambridge, MA: Harvard University Press.

45. Goodwin, D. (1970). *Pigeons and doves of the world.* London: British Museum.

46. Gould, J. L. (1982). *Ethology, the mechanisms and evolution of behavior.* New York: Norton.

47. Gould, J. L., & Marler, P. (1987). Learning by instinct. *Scientific American, 256*(1), 74–85.

48. Griffen, Donald R. (1984). *Animal thinking.* Cambridge, MA: Cambridge University Press.

49. Halliday, T. (1980). *Sexual strategy.* Oxford, UK: Oxford University Press.

50. Herman, L. M. (Ed.) (1980). *Cetacean behavior, mechanisms and functions.* New York: Wiley.

51. Herrnstein, R. G., & de Villiers, P. (1980). Fish as a natural category for people and pigeons. In G. H. Bowers (Ed.), *The psychology of learning and motivation. Advances in research and theory* (Vol. 14). New York: Academic Press.

52. Holland, J. H. (1992). *Adaptation in natural and artificial systems.* Cambridge, MA: The MIT Press.

53. Holldöbler, B. K., & Wilson, E. O. (1977). Weaver ants. *Scientific American, 237*(6), 146–154.

54. Horgan, T., & Tienson, J. (Eds.) (1991). *Connectionism and the philosophy of mind.* Boston: Kluwer Academic.

55. Kawai, M. (1965). Newly acquired pre-cultural behavior of the natural troop of Japanese monkey on Koshima Islet. *Primates, 6*(1), 1–30.

56. Kawamura, S. (1962). The process of sub-culture propagation among Japanese Macaques. *Journal of Primatology, 2,* 43–60.

57. Lange, T. E., & Dyer, M. G. (1989). High-level inferencing in a connectionist network. *Connection Science, 1*(2), 181–217.

58. Langton, C. G. (Ed.) (1989). *Artificial life.* Reading, MA: Addison-Wesley.

59. Langton, C. G., Taylor, C., Farmer, J. D., & Rasmussen, S. (Eds.) (1992). *Artificial life II.* Redwood City, CA: Addison-Wesley.

60. Leyhausen, P. (1979). *Cat behaviour, the predatory and social behavior of domestic and wild cats.* New York: Garland STPM Press.

61. Lieberman, P. (1989). The origins of some aspects of human language and cognition. In

P. Mellars and C. B. Stringer (Eds.), *The human revolution: behavioral and biological perspectives in the origins of modern humans.* Edinburgh: Edinburgh University Press.

62. Lindauer, M. (1971). *Communication among social bees* (2nd ed.). Cambridge, MA: Harvard University Press.

63. Lloyd, J. E. (1981). Mimicry in the sexual signals of fireflies. *Scientific American, 245*(1), 139–145.

64. Loeb, J. (1918). *Forced movements, tropisms, and animal conduct.* Philidelphia: Lippincott (reprint 1973, Dover, NY).

65. Lorenz, K. (1970). *Studies in animal and human behavior* (Vol. I). Cambridge, MA: Harvard University Press.

66. Lorenz, K. (1971). *Studies in animal and human behavior* (Vol. II). Cambridge, MA: Harvard University Press.

67. Lyall-Watson, M. (1963). *The ethology of food-hoarding in mammals.* London: London Univerity.

68. Macdonald, D. W. (Ed.) (1984). *The encyclopedia of mammals.* New York: Facts on File.

69. MacLennan, B. J. (1991). Synthetic ethology: an approach to the study of communication. In J. D. Farmer, C. Langton, S. Rasmussen, & C. Taylor (Eds.), *Artificial life II.* Redwood City, CA: Addison-Wesley.

70. Mangel, M., & Clark, C. W. (1988). *Dynamic modeling in behavioral ecology.* Princeton, NJ: Princeton University Press.

71. Marler, P. R. (1967). Animal communication signals. *Science, 157*, 769–774.

72. Marler, P. (1977). The evolution of communication. In T. A. Sebeok (Ed.), *How animals communicate.* Indiana University Press.

73. Marler, P. R., & Hamilton III, W. J. (1966). *Mechanisms of animal behavior.* New York: Wiley.

74. Marler, P., Dufty, A., & Pickert, R. (1986). Vocal communication in the domestic chicken: I. Does a sender communicate information about the quality of a food referent to a receiver? *Animal Behavior, 43*, 188–193.

75. Marshall, A. A. (1954). *Bower birds.* London: Oxford Unversity Press.

76. Matthews, L. H. (1969). *The life of mammals.* London: Weidenfeld and Nicolson.

77. Maynard-Smith, J. (1982). *Evolution and theory of games.* Cambridge University Press.

78. Menzel, R., & Erber, J. (1978). Learning and memory in bees. *Scientific American, 239*(1), 102–110.

79. Mertens, R. (1960). *The world of amphibians and reptiles.* London: Harrap.

80. Meyer, J.-A., & Wilson, S. W. (Eds.) (1991). *From animals to animats: Proceedings of the First International Conference on Simulation of Adaptive Behavior.* Cambridge, MA: Bradford Books/The MIT Press.

81. Miikkulainen, R., & Dyer, M. G. (1991). Natural language processing with modular PDP networks and distributed lexicon. *Cognitive Science, 15*(3), 343–399.

82. Morris, D. (1990). *Animalwatching.* New York: Crown.

83. Nenov, V. I., & Dyer, M. G. (in press). Language/learning via perceptual/motor association: a massively parallel model. In H. Kitano (Ed.), *Massively parallel artificial intelligence.* Cambridge, MA: AAAI/MIT Press.

84. Nilsson, N. J. (1980). *Principles of artificial intelligence.* Palo Alto, CA: Tioga.

85. Nolfi, S., & Parisi, D. (1991). *Growing neural networks.* Tech. Rep. PCIA-91-15, Institute of Psychology, National Research Council, Rome, Italy.

86. Nolfi, S., Elman, J. L., & Paraisi, D. (1990). *Learning and evolution in neural networks.*

Technical Report (CRL TR 9010). Center for Research in Language. Univ. of California, San Diego, CA.

87. Orians, G. H. (1980). *Some adaptations of marsh-nesting blackbirds.* Princeton, NJ: Princeton University Press.

88. Owen, J. (1980). *Feeding Strategy.* Oxford, UK: Oxford University Press.

89. Patterson, F. G., & Linden, E. (1981). *The education of Koko.* New York: Holt, Rinehart and Winston.

90. Perry, N. (1983). *Symbiosis.* Dorset, UK: Blandford, Poole.

91. Piattelli-Palmarini, M. (1989). Evolution, selection, and cognition: From "learning" to parameter setting in biology and the study of language. *Cognition, 31,* 1–44.

92. Pinker, S., & Bloom, P. (1990). Natural language and natural selection. *Behavioral and Brain Sciences, 13,* 707–727.

93. Premack, D. (1990). On the coevolution of language and social competence. *Behavioral and Brain Sciences, 13,* 754–756.

94. Premack, D., & Premack, A. J. (1983). *The mind of an ape.* New York: Norton.

95. Pylyshyn, Z. W. (1984). *Computation and cognition.* Cambridge, MA: Bradford/The MIT Press.

96. Ralls, K., & Kranz, K. R. (1984). *Duikers.* In D. W. Macdonald (Ed.), *The encyclopedia of mammals* (pp. 556–559). New York: Facts on File.

97. Rheingold, H. L. (1963). *Maternal behaviour in mammals.* New York: Wiley.

98. Rich, E., & Knight, K. (1991). *Artificial intelligence* (2nd ed.). New York: McGraw-Hill.

99. Ristau, C. A., & Robbins, D. (1982). Language in the great apes: a critical review. *Advances in the Study of Behavior, 12,* 142–225.

100. Ristau, C. A. (Ed.) (1991). *Cognitive ethology: the minds of other animals.* Hillsdale, NJ: Lawrence Erlbaum.

101. Roitblat, H. L. (1982). The meaning of representation in animal memory. *Behavioral and Brain Sciences, 5,* 353–406.

102. Roitblat, H. L., Bever, T. W., & Terrance, H. S. (Eds.) (1983). *Animal cognition.* Hillsdale, NJ: Lawrence Erlbaum.

103. Roitblat, H. L. (1987). *Introduction to comparative psychology.* New York: W. H. Freeman and Co.

104. Rumelhart, D. E., & McClelland, J. L. (Eds.) (1986). *Parallel distributed processing* (Vols. 1 and 2). Cambridge, MA: Bradford Books/The MIT Press.

105. Ryker, L. C. (1984). Acoustic and chemical signals in the life cycle of a Beetle. *Scientific American, 250*(6), 113–123.

106. Schaller. G. B. (1972). *The Serengeti lion: a study of predator-prey relations.* Chicago: University of Chicago Press.

107. Schwartz, E. L. (Ed.) (1990). *Computational neuroscience.* Cambridge, MA: Bradford/The MIT Press.

108. Seeley, T. D. (1982). How honeybees find a home. *Scientific American, 247*(4), 158–168.

109. Shettleworth, S. J. (1983). Memory in food-hoarding in birds. *Scientific American, 248*(3), 102–110.

110. Slobodchikoff, C., Fischer, C., & Shapiro, J. (1986). Predator-specific alarm calls of prairie dogs. *American Zoology, 26,* 557.

111. Slobodchikoff, C., Kiriazis, J., Fischer, C., & Creef, E. (1991). Semantic information

distinguishing individual predators in the alarm calls of Gunnison's prairie dogs. *Animal Behavior, 42*, 713–719.

112. Smith, P. K. (1982). Does play matter? Functional and evolutionary aspects of animal and human play. *Behavioral and Brain Sciences, 5*(1), 139–184.

113. Smolensky, P. (1988). On the proper treatment of connectionism. *Behavioral and Brain Sciences, 11*, 1–74.

114. Sordahl, T. A. (1981). Sleight of wing. *Natural History, 90*, 42–49.

115. Southwick, C. H. (1970). *Animal aggression.* New York: Van Nostrand Reinhold.

116. Struhsaker, T. T. (1967). Auditory communication among vervet monkeys (*Cercopithecus aethiops*). In S. A. Altmann (Ed.), *Social communication among primates* (pp. 281–324). Chicago: University of Chicago Press.

117. Terrace, H. S. (1979). *Nim.* New York: Knopf.

118. Thornhill, R. (1980). Sexual selection in the black-tipped hangingfly. *Scientific American, 242*(6), 162–172.

119. Thornhill, R., & Alcock, J. (1983). *The evolution of insect mating systems.* Cambridge, MA: Harvard University Press.

120. Thorpe, W. H. (1973). Duet-singing birds. *Scientific American, 229*(2), 70–79.

121. Tinbergen, N. (1953). *Social behaviour in animals.* London: Methuen.

122. Tizard, B., & Harvey, D. (Eds.) (1977). *Biology of play.* London: S.I.M.P./Heinemann.

123. Todd, P. M., & Miller, G. F. (1991). Exploring adaptive agency II: simulating the evolution of associative learning. In J. A. Meyer & S. W. Wilson (Eds.), *From animals to animats: Proceedings of the First International Conference on Simulation of Adaptive Behavior* (pp. 306–315). Cambridge, MA: Bradford/The MIT Press.

124. Touretzky, D. S. (Ed.) (1989). *Advances in neural information processing systems I.* San Mateo, CA: Morgan Kaufmann.

125. Travers, M. (1989). Animal construction kits. In C. G. Langton (Ed.), *Artificial life.* Reading, MA: Addison-Wesley.

126. Vander Wall, S. B. (1982). An experimental analysis of cache recovery in Clark's nutcracker. *Animal Behaviour, 30*, 84–94.

127. Walker, S. 1983. *Animal thought.* London: Routledge & Kegan Paul.

128. Walther, F. R. (1969). Flight behaviour and avoidance of predators in Thompson's gazelle (*Gazella thompsoni* Guenther 1884). *Behaviour, 34*, 184–221.

129. Werner, G. M., & Dyer, M. G. (1991). Evolution of communication in artificial organisms. In J. D. Farmer, C. Langton, S. Rasmussen, & C. Taylor (Eds.), *Artificial life II.* Reading, MA: Addison-Wesley.

130. Werner, G. M., & Dyer, M. G. (in press). BioLand: a massively parallel simulation environment for evolving distributed forms of intelligent behavior. In H. Kitano (Ed.), *Massively parallel artificial intelligence.* Cambridge, MA: AAAI/The MIT Press.

131. Werner, G. M., & Dyer, M. G. (1993). Evolution of herding behavior in artificial animals. In J.-A. Meyer, H. L. Roitblat, & S. W. Wilson (Eds.), *From animals to animats 2: Proceedings of Second International Conference on Simulation of Adaptive Behavior* (pp. 393–399). Cambridge, MA: Bradford/The MIT Press.

132. Whiten, A., & Byrne, R. W. (1988). Tactical deception in primates. *Behavioral and Brain Sciences, 11*(2), 233–273.

133. Wickler, W. (1968). *Mimicry in plants and animals.* London: Weidenfeld and Nicolson.

134. Wilson, E. O. (1971). *The insect societies.* Cambridge, MA: Belknap/Harvard University Press.

135. Wilson, E. O. (1975). Slavery in ants. *Scientific American, 232*(6), 32–36.

136. Wilson, E. O. (1980). *Sociobiology* (Abridged Ed.). Cambridge, MA: Belknap/Harvard University Press.

137. Wilsson, L. (1968). *My beaver colony.* New York: Doubleday.

138. Zach, R. (1978). Selection and dropping of whelks by northeastern crows. *Behaviour, 67,* 134–147.

Modeling Adaptive Autonomous Agents

Pattie Maes
MIT Media-Laboratory
20 Ames Street, Rm 305
Cambridge, MA 02139
pattie@media.mit.edu

Abstract   One category of research in Artificial Life is concerned with modeling and building so-called adaptive autonomous agents, which are systems that inhabit a dynamic, unpredictable environment in which they try to satisfy a set of time-dependent goals or motivations. Agents are said to be adaptive if they improve their competence at dealing with these goals based on experience. Autonomous agents constitute a new approach to the study of Artificial Intelligence (AI), which is highly inspired by biology, in particular ethology, the study of animal behavior. Research in autonomous agents has brought about a new wave of excitement into the field of AI. This paper reflects on the state of the art of this new approach. It attempts to extract its main ideas, evaluates what contributions have been made so far, and identifies its current limitations and open problems.

Keywords
autonomous agents, behavior-based artificial intelligence, artificial creatures, action selection, learning from experience

1   Introduction

Since 1985, a new wave has emerged in the study of Artificial Intelligence (AI). At the same time at which the popular, general belief is that AI has been a "failure," many insiders believe that something exciting is happening, that new life is being brought to the field. The new wave has been termed *autonomous agent research* or *behavior-based AI* as opposed to mainstream "knowledge-based AI," or also "bottom-up AI" versus "top-down AI." Finally, the term *animat approach* (shorthand for "artificial animal"), which was coined by Wilson [66], is also frequently used.

Several people have given definitions and written overviews of research in autonomous agents, among them Brooks [11], Wilson [67], and Meyer [45]. There are several reasons for giving it yet another try. First of all, many researchers are still skeptical about the approach. Some claim that it isn't very different from what they have been doing all along. Others are still not convinced that the approach is founded and scientific.

A second reason is that this account is different from the papers listed earlier. Brooks [11], being one of the main originators of this new approach, presents a picture that is restricted to robotic forms of intelligence. This paper presents a more general perspective. It argues that the autonomous agent approach is appropriate for the class of problems that require a system to autonomously fulfill several goals in a dynamic, unpredictable environment. This includes applications such as virtual actors in interactive training and entertainment systems [3, 38], interface agents [39, 52], process scheduling [41], and so on. Wilson's account [67] focuses on a scientific methodology for research in autonomous agents, while Meyer [45] aims to give an overview of the research performed so far.

Finally, a third reason is that, since the approach has been around for a number of years now, it is time to perform a critical evaluation. This paper discusses the basic problems of research in adaptive autonomous agents. It also presents an overview and evaluation of the state of the art of the field. In particular it identifies some of the more general and more specific open problems that still remain to be solved. Overview papers are necessarily biased. This paper is biased toward the research in adaptive autonomous agents that has taken place at the AI Laboratory and Media Laboratory of the Massachusetts Institute of Technology.

The paper is structured as follows: Section 2 introduces the concept of an adaptive autonomous agent and defines the basic problems the field is trying to solve. Section 3 discusses the guiding principles of research in adaptive autonomous agents. Section 4 identifies the common characteristics of solutions that have been proposed. Section 5 discusses some example state of the art agents stemming from three different application domains: mobile robotics, interface agents, and scheduling systems. Section 6 presents a critical overview of the state of the art. It discusses the main architectures that have been proposed for building agents. In particular, it addresses progress made in models of action selection and models of learning from experience. Section 7 presents some overall conclusions.

2   What is an Adaptive Autonomous Agent?

An *agent* is a system that tries to fulfill a set of goals in a complex, dynamic environment. An agent is situated in the environment: It can sense the environment through its sensors and act upon the environment using its actuators. An agent's goals can take many different forms: they can be "end goals" or particular states the agent tries to achieve, they can be a selective reinforcement or reward that the agent attempts to maximize, they can be internal needs or motivations that the agent has to keep within certain viability zones, and so on. An agent is called *autonomous* if it operates completely autonomously, that is, if it decides itself how to relate its sensor data to motor commands in such a way that its goals are attended to successfully. An agent is said to be *adaptive* if it is able to improve over time, that is, if the agent becomes better at achieving its goals with experience. Notice that there is a continuum of ways in which an agent can be adaptive, from being able to adapt flexibly to short-term, smaller changes in the environment, to dealing with more significant and long-term (lasting) changes in the environment, that is, being able to change and improve behavior over time.

Depending on what type of environment it inhabits, an agent can take many different forms. Agents inhabiting the physical world are typically robots. An example of such an agent would be an autonomous vacuuming robot. Agents inhabiting the "cyberspace" environment consisting of computers and networks are often called "software agents" or "interface agents" or sometimes also "knobots." An example of such an agent would be a system that navigates computer networks to find data of a particular nature. Finally, agents can inhabit simulated physical environments. An example of such an agent could be a "synthetic actor" in a computer-animated world. Combinations of these three types of agents may exist. For example, in the ALIVE interactive environment [38], the animated (virtual) agents employ real sensors (i.e., a camera), to decide how to react to a person's movements and gestures.

Even though AI aims to study intelligence by synthesizing artificially intelligent systems, mainstream AI has so far concentrated on problems that are very different than that of modeling adaptive autonomous agents. Some key points that distinguish traditional AI from the study of autonomous agents are the following:

1. Traditional AI has focused on systems that demonstrate isolated and often advanced competences (e.g., medical diagnosis, chess playing, etc.). Traditional AI systems provide "depth" rather than "width" in their competence. In contrast, an autonomous agent has multiple integrated competences. Typically the competences are lower-level competences. For a robot, these are competences such as locomotion, navigation, keeping the battery charged, collecting objects, etc. For other systems these might be other simple competences, like reacting in a market system by simple bidding and buying behaviors [41] or executing a simple software routine in the case of an interface agent [39].

2. Traditional AI has focused on "closed" systems that have no direct interaction with the problem domain about which they encode knowledge and solve problems. Their connection with the environment is very controlled and indirect through a human operator. The operator recognizes a problem in the domain and describes it to the system in the symbolic language that the system understands. The system then returns a symbolic description of an answer or solution, which then has to be implemented by the operator in the actual domain. In contrast, an autonomous agent is an "open" system. An agent is "situated" in its environment. It is directly connected to its problem domain through sensors and actuators. It can affect or change this domain through these actuators. The problem domain is typically very dynamic, which means that the system has a limited amount of time to act and that unpredictable events can happen. It typically also incorporates other acting agents (human and/or artificial).

3. Most traditional AI systems deal with one problem at a time. The problem the system has to solve is presented to the system by the human operator. Often, the system does not have time constraints for solving the problem and does not have to deal with interrupts (although the operator might have to deal with such problems). From the system's point of view, the problem domain does not change while the system is computing. In contrast, an agent is autonomous: The system is completely self-contained. It has to monitor the environment and figure out by itself what the next problem or goal to be addressed is. It has to deal with problems in a timely fashion. Typically, an agent has to deal with many conflicting goals simultaneously.

4. Traditional AI focuses on the question of what knowledge a system has. AI systems have declarative "knowledge structures" that model aspects of the domain of expertise. All of the internal structures, apart from an interpreter, are static. The system is only active when a problem is posed by the human operator, in which case the interpreter uses the static knowledge structures to determine the solution to the problem. In contrast, the emphasis in autonomous agent research is on what behavior a system demonstrates when put into its environment. The internal structures of an agent are dynamic "behavior producing" modules as opposed to static "knowledge structures." They do not have to be initiated by a goal formulated by a user. It is less important that the agent can answer questions about its problem domain (such as how it solves a particular problem). It is also less important that the user is able to inspect the internal structures and identify those that are responsible for particular aspects of the resulting behavior. For example, it is acceptable for goals or plans to be emergent observable properties that cannot be attributed to one particular internal structure (but which instead are the result of some complex interaction among a set of structures and the environment).

5. Finally, traditional AI is not usually concerned with the developmental aspect or the question of how the knowledge structures got there in the first place and how they should change over time. They do not have to be adaptive to changing situations (components breaking down, etc.). Most of the work done in traditional machine learning assumes that a lot of background knowledge is available. This background knowledge is used by the system to do knowledge reformulation or knowledge compilation (e.g., caching, explanation-based learning, concept learning, etc.). In contrast, in autonomous agent research there is a strong emphasis on "adaptation" and on a "developmental approach." This often means that the system improves its own internal structures (and, thus, its behavior) over time, based on its experience in the environment. The agent actively explores and updates its structures using an incremental, inductive learning method. In other cases, this means that the designer takes an incremental approach to building the agent: The user gradually evolves a more sophisticated system by adding structure to an already existing "working" system.

The main problem to be solved in autonomous agent research is to come up with an architecture for an autonomous agent that will result in the agent demonstrating adaptive, robust, and effective behavior. *Adaptive* means that the agent improves its goal-achieving competence over time. *Robust* means that it never completely breaks down. (It demonstrates graceful degradation when components within the agent fail or when unexpected situations happen.) *Effective* means that the agent is successful at eventually achieving its goals. Specifically, two related subproblems have to be solved:

1. *The problem of action selection:* How can an agent decide what to do next so as to further the progress toward its multiple time-varying goals? How can it deal with contingencies or opportunities that may arise? How can it arbitrate among conflicting goals? How can it deal with noisy sensors and actuators? How can it react in a timely fashion?

2. *The problem of learning from experience:* How can an agent improve its performance over time based on its experience? How can it decide when to "exploit" its current best action versus "exploring" other actions so as to possibly discover better ways of achieving its goals [21]? How can it incorporate the feedback from the world into its internal behavior-producing structures? How can it correct "wrong" or ineffective behavior-producing structures?

Section 6 discusses both of these problems in more detail. In summary, the main goal of research in autonomous agents is to understand better the principles and organizations that underlie adaptive, robust, effective behavior. A secondary goal is to also develop tools, techniques, and algorithms for constructing autonomous agents that embody these principles and organizations. We call the totality of a set of principles an organization, and the set of tools, algorithms, and techniques that support them an "architecture" for modeling autonomous agents.

One of the few things that has become clear in the last couple of years is that there does not exist one such architecture that can be considered optimal in all respects (or better than all the other ones proposed). Rather, the goal of our research has become to develop an understanding of which architectures are the most simple solution for a given class of agent problems. More specifically, such a problem class is defined in terms of particular characteristics of the agent's resources (e.g., memory, sensors, compute power), and particular characteristics of the tasks and environment [32, 62].

3   Guiding Principles

The study of adaptive autonomous agents is grounded in two important insights, which serve as "guiding principles" for the research performed:

- Looking at complete systems changes the problems often in a favorable way.
- Interaction dynamics can lead to emergent complexity.

The first realization is that viewing the problem of building an intelligent system in its context can make things a lot easier. This observation is true at several levels:

1. The intelligent functions that are being modeled, such as perception, planning, learning, etc. are part of a complete intelligent system, namely, the agent. Building systems in an integrated way rather than developing modules implementing these functions independently, often makes the task a lot easier. For example, a system that can learn can rely less on planning because it can cache computed plans for future reuse. A system that has sensors and actuators can perform tests in the environment and as such has less of a need for modeling its environment and for inference and reasoning. A system that has sensors has an easier job disambiguating natural language utterances, because most likely they are related to the objects the system currently perceives, and so on.

2. A complete intelligent system is always part of some environment; it is situated in some space. This implies that there is less of a need for modeling, because the "world is its own best model" [11]. The environment can also be used as an external memory, for example, for reminding the system which tasks still have to be performed and which ones it already did perform [57]. The environment usually has particular characteristics that can be exploited by the system. For example, offices consist of vertical walls and horizontal floors, doors typically are of a particular size, etc. These "habitat constraints" can be exploited by the system, making its task much easier [22].

3. An intelligent system is not only situated in space but also in time. This implies that the system can develop itself so as to become better at its task, if time and the particular task permit (through learning from experience). Time also allows for the construction of an iterative, incremental solution to a problem.[1] For example, a natural language system situated in time does not need to be able to disambiguate every utterance. It can engage in a discourse, for example, asking questions or making particular remarks that will help it to gradually disambiguate whatever the other speaker wants to convey.

4. Finally, every intelligent system is typically also part of a society. Other agents in the same environment are dealing with similar or related problems. Therefore, there is no need for the agent to figure everything out by itself. For example, a mobile robot could use the strategy of closely following a person passing by, in order to achieve the competence of navigating in an office environment without bumping into things. Maes and Kozierok [39] report on some experiments in which interface agents learned to perform certain tasks by observing and imitating users.

---

1 Situatedness in time cuts both ways: It also means that the agent has to react in a timely fashion and be able to deal with interrupts.

As a consequence of the previous ideas, autonomous agent research has concentrated on modeling systems within their context. Except for expert systems research, traditional AI has concentrated on more abstract and hypothetical problems, while behavior-based AI or agent research has built "real" systems that solve an actual (small) problem in a concrete environment.

A second major insight upon which the study of autonomous agents is founded is that interaction dynamics among simple components can lead to emergent complexity (see also Resnick [50]). Agent research is founded on the belief that shifting into the "interaction" domain as opposed to the "component" domain will make it easier to solve the problem of building intelligent systems. This idea also applies at several different levels [12]:

1. Interaction dynamics between an agent and its environment can lead to emergent structure or emergent functionality. This idea is inspired by the field of ethology. Ethologists have stressed that an animal's behavior can only be understood (and only makes sense) in the context of the particular environment it inhabits. Braitenberg [9], a cybernetician, also convincingly illustrated a similar idea in his book *Vehicles*. Finally, in AI, Simon [54] referred to the same idea when he discussed the example of an ant on the beach. He notes that the complexity of the ant's behavior is more a reflection of the complexity of the environment than of its own internal complexity. He muses that one could think that this is true for human behavior. Many years later, Agre [1] showed how behavior as complex as goal-directed action sequences can be modeled as an emergent property of the interaction dynamics between a complex environment and a reflex-guided agent. What this all means is that the internal structures controlling an agent need not be complex to produce complex resulting behavior. It is often sufficient to study the particular properties of the environment and find an interaction loop, a set of feedback or reflex mechanisms that will produce the desired behavior. One consequence is that we need a better understanding of the particular characteristics of an environment. If we want to be able to understand or prove aspects about the resulting performance of autonomous agents, we have to model the agent as well as its environment [5, 23]. Another consequence is that we need better models of the interaction dynamics between an agent (or components of the agent) and its environment.

2. Simple interaction dynamics between the different components within an agent can lead to emergent structure or emergent functionality. For example, Mataric's wall-following robot does not have a single component to which the expertise of wall following can be attributed [42]. One module is responsible for steering the robot toward the wall when the distance to the wall is above some threshold while another module is responsible for steering the robot away from the wall when the distance is below some threshold. Neither one of these modules is primarily "responsible" for the wall-following behavior. It is their interaction dynamics that makes the robot follow walls reliably. In Maes' networks [33], none of the component modules is responsible for action selection. The action selection behavior is an emergent property of some activation/inhibition dynamics among the primitive components of the system.

3. Interaction dynamics between the component agents of a social system can lead to emergent structure or functionality. Deneubourg et al. [16] and Deneubourg, Theraulaz, and Beckers [17] describe how social insects following simple local rules can produce emergent complexity such as a path to a food source, food foraging trees, etc. Malone et al.'s collection [41] of autonomous bidding systems addresses

the complicated task of process-processor allocation. Finally, anthropologists have studied how different concepts and complex methods for solving problems are gradually shaped through social interaction among different people [53, 57].

What is important is that such emergent complexity is often more robust, flexible, and fault-tolerant than programmed, top-down organized complexity. This is the case because none of the components is really in charge of producing this complexity. None of the components is more critical than another one. When one of them breaks down, the system demonstrates a graceful degradation of performance. Because all of the components interact in parallel, the system is also able to adapt more quickly to environmental changes. Often the system explores multiple solutions in parallel, so that as soon as certain variables change, the system is able to switch to an alternative way of doing things. For example, in Maes' system [33] several sequences of actions are evaluated in parallel, the best one determining the behavior of the agent. Also in Malone et al.'s system [41], several mappings of processes to machines can be viewed as being explored in parallel.

4   Characteristics of Agent Architectures

Many of the architectures for autonomous agents that have been proposed have characteristics in common. This section lists these shared characteristics and contrasts them with the characteristics of traditional AI architectures. These differences are illustrated by means of some concrete examples in the next section.

4.1   Task-Oriented Modules

In traditional AI, an intelligent system is typically decomposed along "functional modules" such as perception, execution, natural language communication (the peripheral components), a learner, planner, and inference engine (the central systems components). These modules are typically developed independently. They rely on the "central representation" as their means of interface. The central representation includes things such as beliefs, which are updated by the perception component and processed and augmented by the inference engine and natural language component, desires (or goals) and intentions, which are produced by the planner.

In contrast, an agent is viewed as a set of competence modules (often also called behaviors) [10]. These modules are responsible for a particular small task-oriented competence. Each of the modules is directly connected to its relevant sensors and actuators. Modules interface to one another via extremely simple messages rather than a common representation of beliefs, and so on. The communication between modules is almost never of a "broadcast" nature, but happens rather on a one-to-one basis. Typically the messages consist of activation energy, simple suppression and inhibition signals, or simple tokens in a restricted language. In addition to communication via simple messages, modules also communicate "via the environment." One module may change some aspect of the environment, which will trigger another module, etc.

4.2   Task-Specific Solutions

In traditional AI, the different functional components of the system are modeled as general and domain independent as possible. The hope is that the same functional components can be used for different problem domains (a general domain-independent planner, learner, etc.). The only component that needs to be adapted is the central representation, which contains domain-specific information such as a model of the particular environment at hand and possibly also more heuristic knowledge.

In contrast, an agent does not have "general" or task-independent functional modules. There is no general perception module, no general planner, etc. Each of the competence modules is responsible for doing all the representation, computation, "reasoning," and execution that are necessary for the particular competence it is responsible for. For example, an obstacle avoidance module might need one bit of information to represent whether an obstacle is perceived or not within a critical range. It might do some very simple computation to decide how an obstacle should be avoided. Competence modules are self-contained, black boxes. They might employ completely different techniques (even different hardware) to achieve their competence. Part of the reason for this more pragmatic approach is a pessimistic vision about whether it is possible at all to come up with a general solution to the vision problem, a general solution to the planning problem, etc., a view also expressed by Minsky [46].

4.3 Role of Representations is Deemphasized

In traditional AI, the key issue emphasized is that the agent has a complete, correct internal model—an accurate copy of the environment (with all its objects and relationships) inside the system, which the system can rely on to predict how its problems can be solved.

In contrast, in agent research there is little emphasis on modeling the environment. First of all, there is no central representation shared by the several modules. The system also does not attempt to integrate the information from different sensors into one coherent, objective interpretation of the current situation. Instead, every task-oriented module locally represents whatever it needs to represent to achieve its competence. The localized representations of different modules are not related and might be inconsistent with one another or redundant. Within one competence module, the usage of representations may be minimized in favor of employing the environment as a source of information (and a determiner of action). The representations within one module are often of a less propositional, objective, and declarative nature than those employed in traditional AI. For example, they might index objects according to the features and properties that make them significant to the task at hand [1] rather than the identities of the objects. They can be of a numeric, procedural [43], or analog nature. Often, a lot of task-specific "problem solving" is performed in the perception part of a particular competence [2, 14, 55].

4.4 Decentralized Control Structure

Traditional AI adopts a sequential organization of the different modules within the system. The modules take turns being "active" or processing and changing the internal representations. Perception and inference first update the internal model (beliefs and goals). After that, planning or problem solving produces a description of the solution to the problem (a plan or the answer to a question). Finally, either the execution module or a human operator implements the solution in the domain (the latter one having more knowledge and understanding of the situation than the former one).

In contrast, agent architectures are highly distributed and decentralized. All of the competence modules of an agent operate in parallel. None of the modules is "in control" of other modules. However, some simple arbitration method is included in order to select or fuse multiple conflicting actuator commands (commands of different modules might be mutually exclusive). This arbitration network might be a winner-take-all network as in Maes [33] or a hardcoded priority scheme as in Brooks [10]. Because of its distributed operation, an agent is typically able to react quickly to changes in the environment or changes in the goals of the system.

4.5   Goal-Directed Activity is an Emergent Property

Traditional AI models activity as the result of a "deliberative thinking" process. The central system evaluates the current situation as represented in the internal model and uses a search process to explore systematically the different ways in which this situation can be changed so as to achieve a goal situation.

In contrast, in agents, activity is not modeled as the result of a deliberative process. Instead, complex and goal-directed activity is modeled as an emergent property of the interaction among competence modules internally, and among competence modules and the environment. There is no internal structure corresponding to "the plan" of the system. Many agents do not have any explicit goals, but are nevertheless still driven toward a specific set of fixed, compiled-in goals. In other architectures, the agent has an explicit representation of its (possibly time-varying) goals, which is used to modify the priorities among the different modules over time.

4.6   Role for Learning and Development

In traditional AI, learning typically consists of compilation or reformulation of what the system already knows. For example, the system might cache a plan for later reuse. Very seldom does the system perform inductive learning of new information or corrective learning of existing knowledge based on environmental experimentation and feedback. This implies that the programmer is completely responsible for creating an initial complete and correct model for the system to use.

In contrast, learning and development are considered crucial aspects of an adaptive autonomous agent [66]. Building an adaptive system that will develop from a not so successful system into one that achieves the tasks is often considered a better approach than building a successful system that does not change when the environment or task changes (e.g., a robot breaking one of its legs). In some systems, the evolution toward increasingly more sophisticated and more adaptive behavior is simulated by the programmer, for example, by incrementally adding more structure to existing successful systems [11]. Other systems employ learning by the individual [18, 25, 34, 37, 60, 66]. In almost all cases, the system concentrates on learning new information (or behavior) from its environment, rather than on reformulating information it already has. The learning algorithms are implemented in a distributed way: Typically a similar learning algorithm runs in different competence modules. Related to the idea of learning is that of redundancy: Often the system has multiple modules for a particular competence. Experience sorts out which of these modules implements the competence in a more reliable way and, thus, should be preferred [18, 37, 49].

Systems built using all of the earlier principles (task-oriented modules, task-specific solutions, de-emphasized representations, decentralized control, etc.) tend to demonstrate more adaptive and robust behavior. They act (and react) quickly, because (a) they have fewer layers of information processing, (b) they are more distributed and often nonsynchronized, and (c) they require less expensive computation. (They are not prone to problems of combinatorial explosions, because they do not rely on search processes as much.) They are able to adapt to unforeseen situations (opportunities as well as contingencies), because they rely much more on the environment as a source of information and a determiner of action than on their possibly faulty or outdated model. They are robust because (a) none of the modules is more critical than the others, (b) they do not attempt to fully understand the current situation (which is often time consuming and problematic), (c) they incorporate redundant methods, and (d) they adapt over time.

5   Some Example Autonomous Agents

5.1   A Mobile Robot

Consider a mobile surveillance robot that has to monitor some offices. Its task requires that it navigate from room to room. The traditional AI version of this robot could work in a similar way to Shakey [47]. The perception module processes the different sensor data and integrates them into a representation of the environment. It attempts to update this model as often as possible. The model includes information such as the location of the robot in the environment, the location and type (often even identity) of other objects in this environment such as chairs, tables, etc. The model is used by the planning module to decide how to fulfill the goal of finding the door in the current room while avoiding obstacles. The planner goes through a systematic search to produce a list of actions that will, according to the model, fulfill both goals. The execution module executes this plan while possibly checking at certain points whether things are going as predicted. If not, control is returned to the planner.

An adaptive autonomous agent for the same task could be constructed in the following way (as inspired by Brooks [10]). In an incremental way, several modules would be implemented corresponding to the different competences necessary for the task: a module for recognizing and going through doors, a module for wall following, a module for obstacle avoidance (or even a couple of redundant ones, using different sensors, because this is a very critical competence), and so on. All of these modules operate in parallel. A simple arbitration scheme, for example, suppression and inhibition wires among these modules, suffices to implement the desired priority scheme: The obstacle avoidance modules always have priority over going through doors, which has priority over wall following. This robot does not plan a course of action. However, from an observer's point of view, it will appear to operate in a systematic, rational way. Brooks [10, 11] has argued convincingly, in writing and in demonstrations, which of the two previously described robots will be more successful at dealing with the task in a robust and reliable way.[2]

5.2   An Interface Agent

Consider the problem of building an intelligent autonomous system that helps the user with certain computer-based tasks. Its goal is to offer assistance to the user and automate as many of the actions of the user as possible. Traditional AI has approached this problem in the following way [58]: The system is given an elaborate amount of knowledge about the problem domain by some knowledge engineer: a model of the user and possibly the user's organization, a model of the tasks the user engages in, including a hierarchical specification of the subtasks, knowledge about the vocabulary of these tasks, and so on. At run time, the agent uses this knowledge to recognize the intentions and plans of the user. For example, if a UNIX user enters a command like "emacs paper.tex," the system infers that the user is planning to produce a written document. It then plans its own course of action (the goal being to assist the user), which, for example, might consist of the action sequence: the text formatting command "latex paper.tex" followed by the preview command "xdvi paper.dvi" and the printing command "lpr paper.dvi." The problems with this approach are exactly the same ones as those of traditional AI robots: It is hard to provide such a complete and consistent model, and the model is quickly outdated (as the user's ways of performing tasks change). Because of the computational complexity of the approach, the system would react very slowly. All sorts of unpredicted events might take place that the system

---

2   Ideally, the robot would also monitor the results of its actions and learn from experience so as to improve its competence or deal with significant changes in the robot or its environment, that is, so as to demonstrate robust and effective autonomous behavior over longer periods of time.

cannot deal with, for example, the user might change his or her mind about what to do in the middle of things or might perform tasks in unorthodox or nonrational ways, etc.

Instead, an adaptive autonomous "interface agent" can be built as follows [39]: Several competence modules are constructed that are experts (or try to become experts) about a small aspect of the task. For example, one module might be responsible for invoking a particular command (like "lpr") at a particular moment. The agent is situated in an environment containing an ideal source for learning: the user's behavior. Each of the modules gathers information by observing the user and keeping statistics about a particular aspect of the user's behavior. For example, the previously mentioned module will keep track of the situations in which the user executed the "lpr" command. Whenever a new situation comes up that is very similar to one of one or more memorized situations, it actually offers to the user to execute the "lpr" command. If we have several experts for the different commands listed earlier, each of these will know when to become active and offer their assistance to the user. From an observer's point of view, it will seem as if the system "understands" the intentions of the user, as if it knows what the task of producing a document involves. Nevertheless, the action sequences are just an emergent property of a distributed system. The system will smoothly adapt to the changing habits of the user, will react in a fast way, will be less likely to completely break down, and so on.

5.3   A Scheduling System

Finally, consider the problem of building a scheduling system that has as its goal to allocate processes to processors in real time. Again the domain is a very dynamic one: New processing jobs are formulated in different machines all the time. The decision to be made is whether to run these processes locally or on a different machine, the global goal being to minimize the average amount of time it takes to run a process. The loads of the different available machines vary continuously. Certain machines might suddenly become unavailable for scheduling processes, requiring a rescheduling of the jobs that were running on those machines at the time, and so on. A traditional AI system for this task would contain a lot of knowledge about scheduling and about the particular configuration of machines and typical processing jobs at hand. The system would update its representation of the current situation as often as possible. This requires gathering all the data from the different machines in the network on whether they are still available, what their workload is, which processes they are running, which new processes were formulated on them, etc. Once all this information has been gathered, the system would perform a systematic search (possibly involving some heuristics) for the most optimal allocation of processes to processors. Once that schedule has been produced, the processing jobs can actually be sent to the different machines that they have been assigned to. This centralized way of solving the problem is present in the majority of the earlier work in this area [29].

Among others, Malone et al. [41] have proposed a different solution to this problem that one could call more "agent-based." In Malone et al.'s enterprise system, each of the machines in the network is autonomous and in charge of its own workload. The system is based on the metaphor of a market. A machine on which a new processing task originates sends out a "request for bids" for the task to be done. Other machines may respond with bids giving estimated completion times that reflect their speed and currently loaded files. For example, if the task to be performed is a graphics rendering job and some machine has that software loaded, it will make a better bid for the new job (because it does not have to waste time and space loading the necessary software). The machine that sent out the request for bids will collect the bids it receives over some small period of time and allocate the job to the machine that made the best bid (either remote or local). This distributed scheduling method was found to have several advantages. The system is very robust because none of the machines is more critical than another one. (There is no central scheduler.) A user can make a machine unavailable for processing external jobs at run time. The whole system will adapt smoothly to this unexpected situation. The solution is simple and yet very flexible in terms of the different factors it can take into account.

6   Overview of the State of the Art

Section 5 presented a general overview of the agent approach to building intelligent systems that demonstrate adaptive, robust behavior. This section provides a more detailed account of the specific architectures that have been proposed. In addition, it lists what the limitations and open problems are of the particular architectures proposed. Section 2 argued that there are two subproblems involved in modeling adaptive autonomous agents: the problem of action selection and the problem of learning from experience. This section is structured around these two subproblems. Most of the architectures for agents that have been proposed so far have concentrated on one or the other subproblem: Either the agent combines simplistic action selection with sophisticated learning or it demonstrates sophisticated action selection without doing any learning. Few proposals have addressed both problems at once in the same architecture. In the remainder of this section, a more detailed description of both of these subproblems is given, followed by a discussion of what progress has been made toward them and a discussion of what questions remain unresolved.

6.1   Action Selection
6.1.1   The Problem
The problem of action selection can be stated as follows: Given an agent that has multiple time-varying goals, a repertoire of actions that can be performed (some of which are executable), and specific sensor data, what actions should this agent take next so as to optimize the achievement of its goals?[3] Notice that when we also consider learning from experience, this problem becomes a slightly different one because one of the goals of the agent is to learn how to better achieve its goals.

It is theoretically possible to compute the optimal action selection policy for an agent that has a fixed set of goals and that lives in a deterministic or probabilistic environment [64]. What makes it impossible to do this for most real agents is that such an agent has to deal with (a) resource limitations (time, computation, memory); (b) possibly incomplete and incorrect information (sensor data); (c) a dynamic, nondeterministic, nonprobabilistic environment; (d) time-varying goals; (e) unknown and possibly changing probability distributions, and so on.

The goals the agent tries to satisfy can take many different forms: end goals also called "goals of attainment" (end states to be achieved), negative goals (states to be avoided), needs, drives, desires, tasks, motivations, constraints for a plan, viability zones for certain state variables, etc. An agent typically has multiple conflicting goals. Being a "complete" system, it always has a combination of "self-preservation goals" (e.g., not bump into obstacles, keep battery charged) as well as more task-oriented goals (watch over a set of offices). The goals of an agent can be implicit or explicit. In the former case, the agent does not have any explicit internal representation of the goals it is trying

---

3 In this definition, one can substitute the term *competence module* or *behavior* for *action*: Given a set of competence modules that all try to control the actuators at a particular moment in time, which ones of those should be given priority, or how should their outputs be combined into one command for the actuators?

to achieve. The agent is built in such a way that, when situated in its environment, its behavior tends to achieve certain goals. Implicit goals are necessarily fixed. They cannot be changed unless the agent is reprogrammed. More complicated agents have explicit goals that vary over time and often have levels of intensity as opposed to a Boolean on-off nature. For example, an artificial animal might have a particular hunger level, thirst level, etc.

Given that it is theoretically impossible to prove what the optimal action selection policy for an agent is, how does the field evaluate a particular proposed solution? Researchers in adaptive autonomous agents are not interested in provable optimality of action selection, that is, in whether the agent takes the optimal path toward the goals, as they are in whether the action selection is robust, adaptive, and whether the agent achieves its goals within the requirements and constraints imposed by the particular environment and task at hand. Among other issues, this means that the action selection mechanism should

- favor actions contributing to the goals; in particular, it should favor those actions that result in the most progress towards the goals.

- be able to deal flexibly with opportunities and contingencies.

- be real time (fast enough for the particular environment at hand and its pace of changes).

- minimize unnecessary switching back and forth between actions contributing to distinct goals.

- improve on the basis of experience (more on this in the next section).

- demonstrate graceful degradation when components break down or unexpected changes happen.

- never get completely stuck in a loop or deadlock situation or make the agent mindlessly pursue an unachievable goal.

- and, most importantly, be "good enough" for the environment and task at hand: As long as the agent manages to achieve its goals within the constraints (time, quality, etc.) required by the problem situation, the solution is considered an acceptable one. For example, as long as the robot manages to find the recharging station before its battery dies, as well as make sufficient progress toward its more task-specific goal of surveying the offices, it is considered an acceptable solution, even if it does not always follow optimal paths. Brooks [11] refers to this latter criterion as "adequacy."

McFarland [44] takes this last point even further. He argues that one should use an ecological approach to evaluate agent behavior: If an agent fills a market niche, then that agent is considered successful. That is, in McFarland's view, for agent behavior to be adaptive means that it must optimize its behavior with respect to the selective pressures of the marketplace. Even though this is ultimately true, it is not particularly useful as a means for comparing different proposals for agent architectures.

Tyrrell [64] compares several action selection proposals, but he does so with respect to one particular benchmark environment and task. Maes [35] and Wilson [67] have argued that it is not possible to decide that one action selection model is better than another one unless one also mentions what the particular characteristics are of the environment, the task, and the agent. For example, in an environment where the cost of (incorrect) actions is high, an agent should do more anticipation. If the cost of (incorrect) actions is negligible, it does not matter if the agent often performs incorrect actions; in an environment where a lot of things change quickly. An agent needs to act very quickly. An agent with noisy sensors should have some inertia in its action selection so that one wrong sensor reading does not make the agent switch to doing something completely new and different. An agent with many sensors can rely on the environment to guide its selection of actions, while an agent with fewer sensors will need to rely more on its internal state or memory to decide what to do next. Todd and Wilson [62] and Littman [32] have started to build a taxonomy of environments and taxonomy of agents that will provide a more profound basis for comparing different proposals.

6.1.2 Progress Made

The different models for action selection in an autonomous agent that have been proposed differ in the way they deal with the following three problems:

1. What is the nature of the goals?

2. What is the nature of the sensor data?

3. What is the arbitration mechanism and command fusion mechanism?

The architectures proposed can be subdivided in the following three classes:

1. *Hand-built, flat networks.* A number of architectures have been proposed that require the designer of the agent to solve the action selection problem from scratch for every agent that is built. Examples of such architectures are the Subsumption Architecture [10] and the architectures reported in Connell [15] (a minimalist version of the Subsumption Architecture) and others [1, 4, 14]. All of these architectures require the designer of an agent to analyze carefully the environment and task at hand and then design a set of reflex modules and a way of combining the outputs of the modules (by means of suppression and inhibition wires or simple arbitration circuitry).

   This class of architectures deals with the earlier three problems in the following way: Typically goals are implicit; they only exist (or may not even exist) in the designer's mind. An agent can have multiple goals, and they can be of very different nature. The nature of the sensor data is also unlimited. The arbitration mechanism determining which modules will steer the actuators is implemented by a logical circuit or a set of suppression and inhibition wires. This circuit ensures that at most one module controls an actuator at all times. None of these architectures support command fusion. In other words, none of these action selection models make it possible for two or more modules to determine simultaneously what the command is that is sent to the actuators. For example, it is not possible to average the outputs of two modules.

   One disadvantage of this class of solutions is that they don't offer the user much guidance as to how to solve the problem of action selection for a new agent. The architecture at most provides a philosophy, a set of previous successful examples, and a programming language for building new agents. Another disadvantage of this class of solutions is that the solutions do not scale up. For more complex agents, the problem of action selection and arbitration among modules is too hard to be solved by hand. The arbitration network often becomes a complicated "spaghetti" that is hard to debug or to get to do the right thing. A final disadvantage is that most of these architectures do not allow for time-varying goals (because typically goals are not explicitly represented in the agent).

2. *Compiled, flat networks.* A second class of architectures attempts to facilitate the construction of agents by automating the process of designing the arbitration circuitry among competence modules. Examples of such architectures are the Rex/Gaps system [24], Behavior Networks [33], and Teleo-Reactive Trees [48]. These architectures require the designer to specify in a particular formalism what the goals of the agent are, how goals can be reduced to other goals or to actions, and what the different modules/actions are and their conditions and expected effects. A compiler analyzes this specification and generates a circuit that will implement the desired goal-seeking behavior.

   In Kaelbling's and Rosenschein's work [24], the types of goals and sensors that can be dealt with are restricted to Booleans. On the one hand, this restricts the type of agent that can practically be built,[4] but on the other hand, these restrictions make it possible to prove that the circuitry synthesized will make the agent select the right actions so as to fulfill its goals. In most of the work, except for that of Maes [33], these types of architectures produce agents with implicit, fixed (not time-varying) goals. However, in contrast with the previous class of architectures, the goals are explicit in the designer's formal specification of the agent. This implies that the agent's circuitry has to be resynthesized if the agent should fulfill a different set of goals.

   Maes [33, 36] proposes an architecture with explicit, time-varying goals. The arbitration network that is compiled has an explicit representation of the goals of the agent, and these goals can have intensities that vary over time (e.g., hunger level for an artificial animal or motivation to recharge the battery of a robot). This particular system performs a limited form of arbitration, prediction, and "planning" at run time. More specifically, these processes are modeled in terms of a time-varying spreading activation process that makes activation energy accumulate in modules that are most relevant given the particular goals (and intensities) and sensor data at hand. Unfortunately, in this system the sensor data are restricted to Booleans.

   One of the disadvantages of this class of action selection architectures is that the class of agents that can be built is restricted. This is the case because these architectures offer a particular model of action relevance, while the previous category does not impose any model at all. A second problem is that it is sometimes hard to come up with a declarative specification of the goals and desired behavior of an agent. Finally, the agent's action selection will only be as good as the specification it relies on. If the designer's specification of the effects of actions is erroneous, then the agent's behavior will not be as desired.

3. *Hand-built, hierarchical networks.* A final category of action selection models proposes a more hierarchical organization of the different actions or competence modules. Examples of such architectures are Agar [63], Hamsterdam [7], Rosenblatt and Payton's work [51], which is a more sophisticated version of the Subsumption Architecture, and Tyrrell's work [64]. Most of these architectures are closely inspired by models of animal behavior stemming from ethologists such as Lorenz and Tinbergen. Typically these architectures organize actions in a hierarchy that ranges from high-level "modes" or activities via midlevel composite actions to detailed, primitive actions. Only the primitive actions are actually executable. Tyrrell [64] and Blumberg [7] both have demonstrated that when one is scaling the

---

4 At the least, it makes it more complicated to build certain kinds of agents.

problem to more complex agents that have many different goals and actions, it is desirable to have more structure (than that present in flat networks) that may help decide which actions are relevant. Typically these systems use some sort of action selection at higher abstraction levels to prime or bias the selection of more primitive actions.

This last category of systems supports more complex (animal-like) motivations or goals. The model of the sensors and how they affect the action selection is also more sophisticated. For example, some architectures make it possible for a stimulus (sensor data) to have a certain "quality" or "intensity" that will affect the action selection (e.g., not just "Is food present?" but "Is food present and what is the quality of the food stimulus perceived?"). As is the case with the first class of architectures discussed, these architectures require the designer to build the arbitration network by hand. Often this is a very difficult and tricky task, in particular because these ethology-based models tend to have a lot of parameters that need to be tuned to obtain the desired behavior.

6.1.3   Open Problems

Even though a lot of progress has been made toward the study of action selection models, many problems remain unresolved:

- Very little research has been performed on the nature of goals and goal interactions. We need to study what kinds of goals our architectures need to support, where those goals might come from, how they change over time, etc. Toates and Jensen [61] present a nice overview of the different models of motivations that ethology and psychology have come up with.

- In most of the architectures proposed, scaling to larger problems is a disaster. This is especially so in the case of hand-built networks, because no support is given to the designer of an agent for building the complicated arbitration network that will govern its behavior. The most obvious solution to be investigated is to either evolve [13] or learn and adapt the network [34] based on experience. However, few experiments along these lines have been performed so far.

- Related to this, not enough effort has been put into making pieces of agent networks "reusable" within other agents. Given that the first and third category of architectures reduce the action selection problem to a (nontrivial) engineering problem, it would be useful if partial solutions that have proven to work in one agent could be abstracted and reused in another agent. For example, the modules producing wall-following behavior in one robot could be abstracted so that they can be reused in another robot with comparable sensors and a comparable environment.

- As noted by many other authors, the dynamics of interactions between the agent and its environment and among the different modules of one agent are not well understood. Kaelbling and Rosenschein [24] offer a logical model, while Beer [5], Kiss [28], and Steels [56] have started approaching this problem from a dynamical systems perspective. Nevertheless, the field is far from being able to prove in general what the emergent behavior is of a distributed network of competence modules.

- Most of the proposed architectures do not deal with the problem of command fusion. Typically only one module at a time determines what command is sent to an actuator. There is no way for the outputs of multiple modules to be combined.

Some proposals for solutions to this problem are presented in Rosenblatt and Payton [51] and in Blumberg [7].

- All of the previous architectures are completely decentralized and do not keep any central state. As a result, they may suffer from the lack of what Minsky [46] would call a "B-brain." They can get stuck in loops or deadlock situations (i.e., keep activating the same actions even though they have proven not to result in any change of state).

- Most of the previous architectures (apart from that of Chapman [14]) have a narrow-minded view of the relationship between perception and action. For example, few architectures support active or goal-driven perception, taking actions to obtain different or more sensor data, etc.

6.2 Learning from Experience
6.2.1 The Problem

The previous section discussed architectures for adaptive autonomous agents that focus on the problem of action selection. Almost all of these architectures neglect the issue of learning from experience (except for Maes and Brooks [34] and Maes [37]). This means that agents built using these architectures are only adaptive in a very restricted sense: They are able to deal with unexpected situations (opportunities, contingencies). However, these agents do not learn from environment feedback. They do not become better at achieving their goals with experience.

A second category of agent architectures that has been proposed has focussed on how the behavior (the action selection) of an agent can improve over time. Learning from experience is a necessity for any agent that has to demonstrate robust, autonomous behavior over long periods of time. First, this is the case because it is very hard to program an agent. It has practically proven impossible to correctly hand code a complex agent or to come up with a correct specification of its behavior and of the environment. Second, components of the agent may break down, or its environment may change in a permanent way, which may require run-time "reprogramming." Adaptive behavior cannot be viewed as a final, static point. True adaptive behavior is an inherently dynamic, continuous process. It is in the spirit of the field of Artificial Life to view adaptive behavior as an emergent property of the long-term interaction and feedback process between an agent and its environment.

The problem of learning from experience can be defined as follows: Given an agent with (a) a set of actions or competence modules, (b) certain sensor data, and (c) multiple (time-varying) goals, how can that agent improve its action selection behavior based on experience? How can the agent incorporate the feedback it receives after taking an action in such a way that its action selection behavior improves? "Improvement" typically means that the agent becomes more successful at fulfilling its goals or needs. Depending on the nature of the agent's goals, this may mean different things. In the case of an "attainment goal" or "end goal," this would mean that the average time or average number of actions required (or any other measure of cost) to achieve the goal decreases over time. In the case of a reinforcement maximization type of goal, this could mean that the average positive reinforcement received over a fixed-length time interval increases with experience.

No matter what the type of goals are it can deal with, any model for learning in an autonomous agent has to fulfill the following desiderata:

- The learning has to be incremental: The agent should learn with every experience. There cannot be a separate learning and performance phase.

- The learning should be biased toward learning knowledge that is relevant to the goals. In complex, realistic environments an agent cannot afford to learn every fact that can possibly be learned.

- The learning model should be able to cope with noise, probabilistic environments, faulty sensors, etc.

- The learning should be unsupervised. The agent has to learn mostly autonomously.

- Preferably, the learning model makes it possible to give the agent some initial built-in knowledge (so that it does not have to learn everything from scratch, in particular in those situations where prior knowledge is easily available).

There are three subproblems that have to be dealt with when designing an architecture for a learning agent:

1. What is the action selection mechanism adopted?

2. How does the system learn? How does it create "hypotheses" to be tested? And how does it decide which of these hypotheses are worth keeping or using to determine the behavior of the agent?

3. How does the agent decide when to "exploit" versus when to "explore"? How does it decide whether to activate whatever it believes is the most optimal action for the current situation versus whether to try a suboptimal action so as to learn and possibly find a better way of doing things? That is, what is a good experimentation strategy for an agent?

Notice that with respect to the first of these problems, the learning architectures proposed often adopt a naive and limited view. Often the set of goals dealt with is very simple, and the goals are fixed over time. Some more detailed problems come up when one is solving the previous problems. For example, every learning architecture has to deal with the problem of credit assignment: Which of the previously activated actions gets (partial) credit for a certain (desirable/undesirable) result happening?

How can we evaluate and compare different proposals for learning from experience? As with the problem of action selection, comparing proposals is hard to do in the general case. The problem of learning from experience is ill-defined unless one specifies what the particular characteristics of the environment, agent, and task are. Therefore, it only makes sense to compare proposals with respect to a particular class of problems. For example, an agent with a lot of memory might be better off using a memory-intensive learning method rather than doing a lot of generalization to come up with a concise representation of what it has learned. In some environments, initial knowledge is easily available, which means that it is desirable for the agent to be partially programmable (as opposed to learning from scratch). Depending on the environment and agent at hand, the role of learning may be very different. In an environment that is very predictable and that changes at a slower pace than the agent's lifetime, there is less of a need for learning during the agent's lifetime. Instead, some sort of evolution-based learning at the species level might be able to deal with the long-term adaptation required [30]. Todd and Wilson [32, 62] present some first steps toward a taxonomy of environments and agents that may make comparisons more meaningful.

6.2.2 Progress Made

All of the architectures that have been proposed in the literature assume that the agent has a set of primitive actions or competence modules. They concentrate on learning the arbitration network among these different actions or modules, that is, the agent attempts to learn when certain action(s) should be activated (when an action should get control over the actuators). Some of the architectures proposed allow for learning of new "composite" actions or composite competence modules [18, 40]. They allow the agent to independently learn composite modules as well as the arbitration network for these composite modules.

The different architectures proposed can be grouped in three classes: reinforcement learning systems, classifier systems, and model learners. The second class of architectures is really a special case of the first. However, because a lot of research has been performed in classifier systems, and because this research is not typically discussed from a reinforcement learning point of view, we will discuss the two classes separately. Both classes define the learning problem as follows: given a set of actions, given a reward signal, learn a mapping of situations to actions (called an "action policy") so that an agent following that policy maximizes the accumulated (discounted) reward it receives over time. In the case of a model learning architecture, the agent learns a model of how actions affect the environment (how actions map situations into other situations). Independent of this, the agent learns (or infers) what the importance or value of taking certain actions in certain situations is. Interesting combinations of these three types of architectures exist. For example, some systems combine learning of an action policy with learning of a model [8, 59].

As is the case with action selection models, many of the architectures proposed have been inspired by theories of animal learning. In contrast with the former, however, it is not so much the ethologist school of animal behavior studies, but rather comparative psychology and behaviorism, in particular theories of reinforcement learning and operant conditioning, that have been an inspiration for the computational models proposed.

1. *Reinforcement learning.* The idea of reinforcement learning [26, 59, 60] is the following: Given an agent with (a) a set of actions it can engage in, (b) a set of situations it can find itself in, and (c) a scalar reward signal that is received when the agent does something, the goal is to learn an action policy, or a mapping from situations to actions, so that an agent that follows that action selection policy maximizes the cumulative discounted reward it receives over time.

    Q-learning [65] is a particularly popular reinforcement learning strategy. In Q-learning the agent tries to learn for every situation action pair what the "value" is of taking that action in that situation. More specifically, the algorithm learns a two-dimensional matrix that stores a value for every possible combination of a situation and an action. At initialization, all values are set to some initial value. The goal of the system is to update these values so that they converge toward the "maximum cumulative discounted reward" that can be expected when taking that action in that situation. This means, the maximum cumulative reward that the agent can expect to receive in the future (from now on) if it takes that particular action in that situation (i.e., the immediate reward it receives plus the reward it will receive for taking the best future actions after this one). The reward is "discounted" with respect to the future so that rewards expected in the near future count for more than rewards expected further down the road. The different subproblems listed earlier are dealt with by reinforcement learning systems in the following way:

    i. *Action selection mechanism:* At any moment, the agent always finds itself in some particular situation. Given that situation, it chooses the action that has the maximum value (maximum cumulative discounted reward).

    ii. *Learning method:* When the agent performs an action, it may receive some reward (possibly zero). It then updates the value of the situation action pair it just "exploited." In particular, it increases or decreases the value of that situation action pair so as to reflect better the actual reward it received plus the maximum reward it can expect in the new situation it finds itself in.

iii. *Exploration strategy:* In a certain percentage of situations, the agent does not choose the action that maximizes reward, but instead it performs a random action so as to gather more data or evidence about possibly interesting alternative paths.

One of the attractive features of reinforcement learning is its formal foundation. It can be proven that under certain conditions (e.g., an infinite number of trials and a Markovian environment), the agent will converge toward the optimal action selection policy. Unfortunately these conditions are seldom attainable in real, complex situations. Disadvantages of reinforcement learning algorithms are (a) that they do not deal with time-varying goals (the action policy learned is for a fixed set of goals); (b) if the goals change, they have to relearn everything from scratch (Kaelbling [27] attempts to overcome this problem); (c) for realistic applications, the size of the state space (or the number of situation action pairs) is so large that learning takes too much time to be practical (as a result, researchers have started developing algorithms that can generalize over the state space [31, 40]; (d) learning only happens "at the fringe" of the state space (only when a reward is received can the system start learning about the sequence of actions leading to that reward), and as a result it takes a lot of time to learn long action sequences ([59] attempts to deal with this problem); (e) the model assumes that the agent knows at all times which situation it is in (given faulty sensors or hidden states, this is difficult) (Whitehead and Ballard [68] address this particular problem); (f) it is hard to build in initial knowledge into this type of architecture; and, finally, (g) the model cannot learn when multiple actions are taken in parallel.[5]

2. *Classifier systems.* A second category of architectures for learning agents is based on classifier systems [20]. In particular, Wilson [66] and Booker [8] have studied how classifier systems can be used to build adaptive autonomous agents. These architectures can be viewed as a special case of reinforcement learning systems. That is, again, the agent attempts to learn how it can optimize the reward it receives for taking certain actions in certain situations. The idea here is that an agent has a set of rules, called "classifiers," and some data about every rule's performance. At the least the system keeps a "strength" for every rule that represents the value of that rule (how "good" it is). The three subproblems of a learning architecture are dealt with in the following way:

i. *Action selection mechanism:* Given a certain situation, which includes some external state (or sensor data) and may include an internal state, the condition list of some classifiers will match the current situation. Of all the matching classifiers, the agent picks one or more classifiers proportional to their strength. The actions proposed by those classifiers are executed. (This may involve changing the internal state.)

ii. *Learning method:* Whenever some classifiers are executed, they give some of their strength to the classifiers that "set the stage," that is, the classifiers that were just active at the previous time step. This is called the "bucket brigade algorithm" and is designed to deal with the problem of credit assignment. Whenever the agent executes some actions, it may receive some reward. If this is the case, then the reward will increase the strength of all the classifiers

---

5 In theory, reinforcement learning can deal with parallel actions by adopting a row in the matrix for every combination of actions that is executed in parallel. In practice, however, this would blow up the state space even more than is already the case.

that were just activated (as well as all those that were not activated but that suggested the same action). This scheme ensures that classifiers that contribute to a reward being received will over time have higher strengths than those that don't and, thus, will be activated more often.

   iii. *Exploration strategy:* The number of classifiers is fixed. Every once in a while, the agent removes those classifiers that have low strengths and replaces them by mutations and recombinations (crossovers) of successful ones. This way, the agent keeps exploring and evaluating different ways of doing things, while keeping "good" solutions around.

One of the interesting aspects of agents based on classifier systems is that they use a more sophisticated experimentation strategy. (The experimentation strategy of other reinforcement learning systems consists of picking a random other data point.) The hypothesis underlying this strategy is that one can find a better solution to a problem (e.g., more effective behavior) by making small changes to an existing good solution (existing successful behavior) or by recombining existing promising solutions. Another advantage of classifier systems over most other reinforcement learning systems is that they have a built-in generalization mechanism for generalizing over situations as well as actions, namely, the "#" or "don't care" symbol. This makes it possible for classifier systems to sample parts of the state space at different levels of abstraction and as such to find the most abstract representation of a classifier that is useful for a particular problem the agent has. Unfortunately, classifier system agents share some of the limitations of other reinforcement learning agents, in particular the problem of time varying goals (a) and the problem of learning at the fringe (d) mentioned earlier. In addition they may suffer from the problem that they do not keep track of everything that has been tried. A classifier system based agent may reevaluate the same classifier over and over again. It may throw it out because its strength is low and then immediately create it again because it keeps no memory of what has been tried. (On the other hand, the fact that the system "forgets" about nonpromising classifiers makes it more efficient at action selection time.)

3. *Model builders.* A final class of agents that learns from experience actually learns a causal model of its actions, rather than a policy map [18, 37, 49]. Drescher's model, which was inspired by Piaget's theories of development in infants, is probably the most sophisticated example. The agent builds up a probabilistic model of what the effects are of taking an action in a certain situation. This causal model can then be used by some arbitration process to decide which action is the most relevant given a certain situation and a certain set of goals. Action selection and learning are much more decoupled: In fact, the learning component of one of these agents could be combined with a different action selection mechanism.

In most of these architectures (except for that of Sutton [59]), the agent does not learn a complete mapping from every possible situation action pair to the new situation that will result from taking that action in that situation. Rather, the agent learns mappings from partial situations to partial situations. It maps those aspects of a situation "that matter" (those sensor data that are necessary and sufficient conditions) combined with an action, to aspects of the new, resulting situation "that matter" (in particular sensor readings that change when taking the action in the situations described by the conditions). Such a combination of (a) a set of conditions, (b) a primitive (or composite) action, and (c) a set of expected results (and probabilities for these results) is called a schema [18] or a module of behavior [37]. Model learning architectures deal with the three subproblems defined earlier in the following way:

1. *Action selection mechanism:* Agents built using these architectures can deal with time varying, multiple, explicit goals. Given a set of goals and intensities, they compute at run time which of the modules or schemas learned is most relevant to achieving the goal as well as most reliable. There is a separate value assignment process that is decoupled from the learning process. Often this value assignment process favors modules that prove to be more reliable. It may even trade off reliability of a sequence of actions for length of a sequence of actions leading to the goals. Typically, a spreading activation process [37] or simple marker propagation process [18] is used to assign these values given some goals and sensor data.

2. *Learning method:* Whenever a particular action is taken, the agent monitors what changes happen in the environment. It uses this information to learn correlations between particular conditions/action pairs and certain results. After an action is taken, all result lists (and their probabilities) of applicable modules/schemas (which have the same action as the one taken and a matching condition list) are updated to reflect the new example. Occasionally, the agent needs to spin off new schemas from existing ones so as to be able to represent conflicting or unreliable results. The agent is able to detect that more conditions need to be taken into account in a schema/module for certain results to become more reliable, which will force it to create versions of the module that have longer, slightly different conditions.

3. *Exploration strategy:* The exploration strategy used in these architectures varies. Drescher's system, while demonstrating sophisticated learning, has an extremely simple exploration strategy, namely, a random one. His agent basically does not do anything else but learn by performing random experiments. Foner [19] discusses how Drescher's agent can be made to learn much faster and to learn more relevant knowledge by adopting a smarter experimentation strategy as well as a focus of attention mechanism. In Maes' architecture [37], the exploration strategy is also more goal-oriented: The agent biases its experimentation toward actions that show promise to contribute to the goals. In the same system, the amount of exploration versus exploitation is an emergent property of the action selection system (the more has been learned, the fewer experiments are performed).

One of the main advantages of model learners is that they can transfer behavior learned in one context to another context (e.g., another goal). Because the system builds up a model of how taking an action in a situation results in another situation, it can use this model as a road map for any particular set of goals. As such, they do better in environments where goals (or relative importances of goals) may change over time. This also implies that they do not just learn at the fringe of the state space connected to the goals. They learn from every action, as opposed to only learning from actions that have proven to be directly related to the present goals. In addition, they make it much easier for the designer of an agent to incorporate background knowledge about the domain (e.g., in the form of a causal model of the effects of actions). The agent is still able to correct this knowledge if it proves to be incorrect. The disadvantage of this type of architecture is that they may take more time to select an action, because there is no direct mapping of situations to "optimal" actions.

6.2.3 Open Problems

As is the case with action selection models, a lot of problems with modeling learning from experience remain unsolved. The following problems apply to all three of the previously mentioned learning approaches:

- Scaling to larger (more realistic) problems is typically a problem for any of these learning algorithms. The computational complexity of all of the learning systems discussed is too big to be practically useful to build complex agents that solve real problems.

- One reason this is the case is that very few algorithms have incorporated interesting attention mechanisms. For example, Foner [19] demonstrates that incorporating attention mechanisms such as spatial locality can improve the tractability of learning from experience in a significant way. Most algorithms discussed earlier only use the temporal locality heuristic, that is, effects are assumed to be perceived soon after the actions that caused them.

- Most of the algorithms proposed are bad at generalizing over sensor data. First, the sensor data are only represented at one level of granularity, as opposed to more coarse and finer levels. Second, none of the algorithms proposed exploit the structure and similarity present in many sensor data (e.g., one could exploit the fact that different cells of a retina are adjacent or that the different cells of the retina are affected in similar ways by certain actions).

- More work can be done in the domain of exploration strategies. Most existing algorithms employ the most simple strategy possible: The agent experiments a certain percentage of its time, no matter how urgent its needs or motivations may be, no matter how interesting the opportunities are that present themselves, etc. The agent also picks the experiment to perform in a random way, as opposed to using certain heuristics such as (a) trying actions that have not been tried for a while, (b) trying actions that have shown promise recently, etc.

- There is a lack of interesting models of how learning and perception interact. The model of perception present in most architectures is narrow-minded. The set of sensor data that the agent tries to correlate with its actions is taken as a given. The system does not couple learning about actions with learning about perception. It does not learn what to pay attention to or learn that more features should be paid attention to. Ideally, an agent would create new features and categories to perceive the environment based on whatever categories its goals and environment require (e.g., kittens that grow up in an environment with only horizontal edges, do not develop detectors for vertical edges).

- There is a lack of sophisticated models of how action selection and learning interact. In particular, all current algorithms assume that the set of primitive actions the agent learns about is a given. As is the case with sensor data, it would make more sense if the set of primitive actions is learned on the basis of what discretization or what subdivision of the continuous space of possible actions is appropriate for the environment and the goals at hand.

- We need to understand better what the role of learning is and how it interacts with other adaptive phenomena like cultural learning and adaptation through evolution (see Belew [6]). We need to understand better what "building blocks" evolution could provide that could facilitate learning (e.g., provide a built-in bias for learning, or built-in specialized structures, etc.).

- Finally, most of the approaches taken have been inspired by behaviorism and comparative psychology, rather than ethology. A lot could be learned by taking a more ethologically inspired approach to learning. For example, ethologists have shown that animals have built-in sensitive periods for learning particular competences. These periods tend to coincide with the situations in their lives that are optimal for picking up the competence to be learned, and as such reduce the complexity of the learning task.

7 Conclusions

Autonomous agent research represents an exciting new approach to the study of intelligence. So far, this new approach has demonstrated several "proofs of concept." In particular, encouraging successes have been reported in the area of mobile robots as well as software agents. Several prototypes have been built that have solved a real task that was previously not solvable or that was only solvable by means of a more costly and less effective solution. The approach has definitely had an impact on the course of AI, which can be witnessed by the explosion of publications and research projects in the area.

Nevertheless, some problems are apparent that require novel ideas and better solutions. The main problem identified is that of scaling the approach to larger, more complicated systems. The tools and techniques proposed do not provide sufficient support to design or hand build a complex agent with many different goals. The learning techniques proposed have computational complexities that make the automated development of an adaptive agent an intractable problem (in realistic time).

In addition, in order for the approach to be more founded, more fundamental research has to be undertaken. We need to understand the classes of problems agents have to deal with, so that it becomes possible to critically compare particular architectures and proposals. For example, many different models of action selection have been proposed, but unless we understand the problem of action selection better, we do not have any grounds to compare the different proposals.

Aside from better evaluation criteria, we need a better understanding of the underlying principles. In particular, it is important to understand the mechanisms and limitations of emergent behavior. How can a globally desired structure or functionality be designed on the basis of interactions between many simple modules? What are the conditions and limitations under which the emergent structure is stable, and so on? Some first steps toward a theory of emergent functionality have been proposed, using tools from complex dynamics [5, 28, 56]. However, so far the proposed theories have only been applicable to very simple toy examples.

There is tension inherent in the agent approach that is as of now unresolved. Research in autonomous agents has adopted very task-driven, pragmatic solutions. As a result, the agents built using this approach end up looking more like "a bag of hacks and tricks" than an embodiment of a set of more general laws and principles. Does this mean that the field will evolve into a (systems) engineering discipline, or will we find a path toward becoming a more scientific discipline?

Acknowledgments

Bruce Blumberg, Leonard Foner, Chris Langton, Yezdi Lashkari, Maja Mataric, and Stewart Wilson provided valuable comments on an earlier draft of this paper. Chris Langton provided the necessary encouragement and demonstrated a lot of patience.

References

1. Agre, P. E. (1991). *The dynamic structure of everyday life*. Cambridge University Press.

2. Ballard, D. H. (1989). Reference frames for animate vision. In *Proceedings of IJCAI-89 Conference*. Detroit.

3. Bates, J., Loyall, B., & Reilly, W. (1991). Broad agents. In *Proceedings of the AAAI Spring Symposium on Integrated Intelligent Architectures*. Stanford, CA (available in *SIGART Bulletin*, *2*(4), 38–40, 1991).

4. Beer, R., Chiel, H., & Sterling, L. (1990). A biological perspective on autonomous agent design. In: P. Maes (Ed.), *Designing autonomous agents: Theory and practice from biology to engineering and back*. Cambridge, MA: The MIT Press/Bradford Books.

5. Beer, R. (1992). *A dynamical systems perspective on autonomous agents* (Tech. Rep. No. CES-92-11). Department of Computer Engineering and Science, Case Western Reserve University, Cleveland, OH.

6. Belew, R. (1989). *Evolution, learning and culture: Computational metaphors for adaptive algorithms* (CSE Tech. Rep. No. CS89-156). UCSD Computer Science and Engineering Department, San Diego, CA.

7. Blumberg, B. (in press). Action-selection in Hamsterdam: Lessons from ethology. Submitted to the *Third International Conference on the Simulation of Adaptive Behavior*. Brighton, UK.

8. Booker, L. (1988). Classifier systems that learn internal world models. *Machine Learning Journal*, *1*(2), 3.

9. Braitenberg V. (1984). *Vehicles: experiments in synthetic psychology*. Cambridge, MA: The MIT Press/Bradford Books.

10. Brooks, R. A. (1986, April). A robust layered control system for a mobile robot. *IEEE Journal of Robotics and Automation*, RA-2.

11. Brooks, R. A. (1991). Intelligence without reason, computers and thought lecture. In *Proceedings of IJCAI-91*. Sidney, Australia.

12. Brooks, R. A. (1991). Challenges for complete creature architectures, In J.-A. Meyer & S. W. Wilson (Eds.), *From animals to animats, Proceedings of the First International Conference on the Simulation of Adaptive Behavior*. Cambridge, MA: The MIT Press/Bradford Books.

13. Brooks, R. A. (1992). Artificial life and real robots. In F. Varela and P. Bourgine (Eds.), *Toward a practice of autonomous systems, Proceedings of the First European Conference on Artificial Life*. Cambridge, MA: The MIT Press/Bradford Books.

14. Chapman, D. (1992). *Vision, instruction and action*. Cambridge, MA: The MIT Press.

15. Connell, J. (1990). *Minimalist mobile robotics: a colony-style architecture for an artificial creature*. San Diego: Academic Press.

16. Deneubourg, J. L., Goss, S., Franks, N., Sendova-Franks, A., Detrain, C., & Chretien, L. (1991). The dynamics of collective sorting: Robot-like ants and ant-like robots. In J.-A. Meyer & S. W. Wilson (Eds.), *From animals to animats, Proceedings of the First International Conference on the Simulation of Adaptive Behavior*. Cambridge, MA: The MIT Press/Bradford Books.

17. Deneubourg, J. L., Theraulaz, G., & Beckers, R. (1992). Swarm-made architectures. In F. J. Varela & P. Bourgine (Eds.), *Toward a practice of autonomous systems, Proceedings of the First European Conference on Artificial Life*. Cambridge, MA: The MIT Press/Bradford Books.

18. Drescher, G. L. (1991). *Made-up minds: A constructivist approach to artificial intelligence*. Cambridge, MA: The MIT Press.

19. Foner, L. and Maes, P. (in press). Paying attention to what's important: Using focus of attention to improve unsupervised learning. Submitted to the *Third International Conference on the Simulation of Adaptive Behavior*. Brighton, UK.

20. Holland, J. H. (1986). Escaping brittleness: the possibilities of general-purpose learning algorithms applied to parallel rule-based systems. In R. S. Michalski, J. G. Carbonell, & T. M. Mitchell (Eds.), *Machine learning, an artificial intelligence approach* (Vol. II). Los Altos: Morgan Kaufmann.

21. Holland, J. H. (1992). The optimal allocation of trials (chap. 5). In *Adaption in natural and artificial systems*. Cambridge, MA: The MIT Press/Bradford Books.

22. Horswill, I. (1992). Characterizing adaptation by constraint. In F. J. Varela & P. Bourgine (Eds.), *Toward a practice of autonomous systems, Proceedings of the First European Conference on Artificial Life*. Cambridge, MA: The MIT Press/Bradford Books.

23. Horswill, I. (1993). *Specialization of perceptual processes*. Unpublished doctoral dissertation, AI Laboratory, MIT, Cambridge, MA.

24. Kaelbling, L. P., & Rosenschein, S. (1990). Action and planning in embedded agents. In P. Maes (Ed.), *Designing autonomous agents: Theory and practice from biology to engineering and back*. Cambridge, MA: The MIT Press/Bradford Books.

25. Kaelbling, L. P. (1992). An adaptable mobile robot. In F. J. Varela & P. Bourgine (Eds.), *Toward a practice of autonomous systems, Proceedings of the First European Conference on Artificial Life*. Cambridge, MA: The MIT Press/Bradford Books.

26. Kaelbling, L. P. (1993). *Learning in embedded systems*. Cambridge, MA: The MIT Press.

27. Kaelbling, L. P. (1993). Learning to achieve goals. In *Proceedings of IJCAI-93, the Thirteenth International Joint Conference on Artificial Intelligence*. Morgan Kaufmann.

28. Kiss, G. (1991). Autonomous agents, AI and chaos theory. In J.-A. Meyer & S. W. Wilson (Eds.), *From animals to animats, Proceedings of the First International Conference on the Simulation of Adaptive Behavior*. Cambridge, MA: The MIT Press/Bradford Books.

29. Kleinrock, L., & Nilsson, A. (1981, July). On optimal scheduling algorithms for time-shared systems. *Journal of the ACM, 28*, 3.

30. Koza, J. R. (1991). Evolution and co-evolution of computer programs to control independently-acting agents. In J.-A. Meyer & S. W. Wilson (Eds.), *From animals to animats, Proceedings of the First International Conference on the Simulation of Adaptive Behavior*. Cambridge, MA: The MIT Press/Bradford Books.

31. Lin, L.-J. (1992). *Reinforcement learning for robots using neural networks*. Unpublished doctoral thesis, Carnegie Mellon University, School of Computer Science.

32. Littman, M. (1993). An optimization-based categorization of reinforcement learning environments. In J.-A. Meyer, H. L. Roitblatt, & S. W. Wilson (Eds.), *From animals to animats 2, Proceedings of the Second International Conference on the Simulation of Adaptive Behavior*. Cambridge, MA: The MIT Press/Bradford Books.

33. Maes, P. (1990). Situated agents can have goals. In P. Maes (Ed.), *Designing autonomous agents: Theory and practice from biology to engineering and back*. Cambridge, MA: The MIT Press/Bradford Books.

34. Maes, P., & Brooks, R. A. (1990). Learning to coordinate behaviors, *Proceedings of AAAI-90*. Boston.

35. Maes, P. (1991). Adaptive action selection. *Proceedings of the Thirteenth Annual Conference of the Cognitive Science Society*. Hillsdale, NJ: Lawrence Erlbaum Associates.

36. Maes, P. (1991). A bottom-up mechanism for behavior-selection in an artificial creature. In J.-A. Meyer & S. W. Wilson (Eds.), *From animals to animats, Proceedings of the First International Conference on the Simulation of Adaptive Behavior*. Cambridge, MA: The MIT Press/Bradford Books.

37. Maes, P. (1992). Learning behavior networks from experience. In F. J. Varela & P. Bourgine (Eds.), *Toward a practice of autonomous systems, Proceedings of the First European Conference on Artificial Life*. Cambridge, MA: The MIT Press/Bradford Books.

38. Maes, P. (1993). ALIVE: An artificial life interactive video environment. In *Visual Proceedings of the Siggraph-93 Conference*. ACM Press.

39. Maes, P., & Kozierok, R. (1993). Learning interface agents. *Proceedings of AAAI-93, the Eleventh National Conference on Artificial Intelligence*. Cambridge, MA: The MIT Press.

40. Mahadevan, S., & Connell, J. (1991). Automatic programming of behavior-based robots

using reinforcement learning. In *Proceedings of the Ninth National Conference on Artificial Intelligence*. Cambridge, MA: The MIT Press.

41. Malone, T. W., Fikes, R. E., Grant, K. R., & Howard, M. T. (1988). Enterprise: A market-like task scheduler for distributed computing environments. In B. Huberman (Ed.), *The ecology of computation*. North-Holland.

42. Mataric, M. J. (1991). Behavioral synergy without explicit integration. In *SIGART, 2*(4) (special issue on Integrated Cognitive Architectures).

43. Mataric, M. J. (1992). Integration of representation into goal-driven behavior-based robots. *IEEE Transactions on Robotics and Automation, 8*(3), 304–312.

44. McFarland, D. (1991). What it means for a robot behavior to be adaptive. In J.-A. Meyer & S. W. Wilson (Eds.), *From animals to animats, Proceedings of the First International Conference on the Simulation of Adaptive Behavior*. Cambridge, MA: The MIT Press/Bradford Books.

45. Meyer, J.-A., & Guillot, A. (1991). Simulation of adaptive behavior in animats: review and prospects. In J.-A. Meyer & S. W. Wilson (Eds.), *From animals to animats, Proceedings of the First International Conference on the Simulation of Adaptive Behavior*. Cambridge, MA: The MIT Press/Bradford Books.

46. Minsky, M. (1986). *The society of mind*. New York: Simon and Schuster.

47. Nilsson, N. (1984). *Shakey the robot* (Tech. Note No. 323). SRI A.I. Center.

48. Nilsson, N. J. (1992, January). *Toward agent programs with circuit semantics* (Rep. No. STAN-CS-92-1412). Department of Computer Science, Stanford University, Stanford, CA.

49. Payton, D. W., Keirsey, D., Krozel, J., & Rosenblatt, K. (1992). Do whatever works: A robust approach to fault-tolerant autonomous control. *Journal of Applied Intelligence, 3*, 225–250.

50. Resnick, M. (1992). *Beyond the centralized mindset: explorations in massively parallel microworlds*. Unpublished doctoral thesis, MIT Media-Laboratory Epistemology and Learning Group, Cambridge, MA.

51. Rosenblatt, J., & Payton, D. (1989, June). A fine-grained alternative to the subsumption architecture for mobile robot control. In *Proceedings of the International Joint Conference on Neural Networks*. IJCNN, Washington, DC.

52. Sheth, B., & Maes, P. (1993). Evolving agents for personalized information filtering. In *Proceedings of the IEEE Conference on Artificial Intelligence for Applications*. IEEE Press.

53. Shrager, J., & Callanan, M. (1991). Active language in the collaborative development of cooking skill. In *Proceedings of the Cognitive Science Conference*. Hillsdale, NJ: Lawrence Erlbaum Associates.

54. Simon, H. (1969). *The sciences of the artificial*. Cambridge, MA: The MIT Press.

55. Steels, L. (1990). Exploiting analogical representations. In P. Maes (Ed.), *Designing autonomous agents: Theory and practice from biology to engineering and back*. Cambridge, MA: The MIT Press/Bradford Books.

56. Steels, L. (1991). Towards a theory of emergent functionality. In J.-A. Meyer & S. W. Wilson (Eds.), *From animals to animats, Proceedings of the First International Conference on the Simulation of Adaptive Behavior*. Cambridge, MA: The MIT Press/Bradford Books.

57. Suchman, L. A. (1987). *Plans and situated actions: The problem of human-machine communication*. Cambridge University Press.

58. Sullivan, J. W., &, Tyler, S. W. (Eds.). (1991). *Intelligent user interfaces*. New York: ACM Press.

59. Sutton, R. S. (1990). Integrated architectures for learning, planning and reacting based on approximating dynamic programming. *Proceedings of the Seventh International Conference in Machine Learning*.

60. Sutton, R. S. (1991). Reinforcement learning architectures for animats. In J.-A. Meyer & S. W. Wilson (Eds.), *From animals to animats, Proceedings of the First International*

Conference on the Simulation of Adaptive Behavior. Cambridge, MA: The MIT Press/Bradford Books.

61. Toates, F., & Jensen, P. (1991). Ethological and psychological models of motivation—towards a synthesis. In J.-A. Meyer & S. W. Wilson (Eds.), *From animals to animats, Proceedings of the First International Conference on the Simulation of Adaptive Behavior.* Cambridge, MA: The MIT Press/Bradford Books.

62. Todd, P., & Wilson, S. (1993). Environment Structure and Adaptive Behavior from the Ground Up. In J.-A. Meyer, H. L. Roitblat, & S. W. Wilson (Eds.), *From animals to animats 2, Proceedings of the Second International Conference on Simulation of Adaptive Behavior.* Cambridge, MA: The MIT Press/Bradford Books.

63. Travers, M. (1989). Animal construction kits. In C. Langton (Ed.), *Artificial life.* Redwood City, CA: Addison Wesley.

64. Tyrrell, T. (1993). *Computational mechanisms for action selection.* Unpublished doctoral thesis, Centre for Cognitive Science, University of Edinburgh.

65. Watkins, C. (1989). *Learning from delayed rewards.* Unpublished doctoral thesis, King's College, Cambridge.

66. Wilson, S. W. (1985). Knowledge growth in an artificial animal. In J. Greffenstette (Ed.), *Proceedings of the First International Conference on Genetic Algorithms and their Applications.* Hillsdale, NJ: Lawrence Erlbaum Associates.

67. Wilson, S. W. (1991). The animat path to AI. In J.-A. Meyer & S. W. Wilson (Eds.), *From animals to animats, Proceedings of the First International Conference on the Simulation of Adaptive Behavior.* Cambridge, MA: The MIT Press/Bradford Books.

68. Whitehead, S., & Ballard, D. (1990). Active perception and reinforcement learning. In *Proceedings of the Seventh International Conference on Machine Learning.* Austin, TX.

Chaos as a Source of Complexity and Diversity in Evolution

Kunihiko Kaneko
Department of Pure and
Applied Sciences
University of Tokyo
Komaba, Meguro-ku
Tokyo 153, Japan
kaneko@cyber.c.u-tokyo.ac.jp

Abstract The relevance of chaos to evolution is discussed in the context of the origin and maintenance of diversity and complexity. Evolution to the edge of chaos is demonstrated in an imitation game. As an origin of diversity, dynamic clustering of identical chaotic elements, globally coupled each to the other, is briefly reviewed. The clustering is extended to nonlinear dynamics on hypercubic lattices, which enables us to construct a self-organizing genetic algorithm. A mechanism of maintenance of diversity, "homeochaos," is given in an ecological system with interaction among many species. Homeochaos provides a dynamic stability sustained by high-dimensional weak chaos. A novel mechanism of cell differentiation is presented, based on dynamic clustering. Here, a new concept—"open chaos"—is proposed for the instability in a dynamical system with growing degrees of freedom. It is suggested that studies based on interacting chaotic elements can replace both top-down and bottom-up approaches.

Keywords
chaos, evolution, edge of chaos, clustering, coupled map, homeo-chaos, differentiation, complexity, genetic algorithm

I Complexity, Diversity, and Emergence

Why are we interested in the effort to create "lifelike" behavior in computers? The answers can be diverse, but my interest in such artificial biology lies in the construction of systems exhibiting the emergence and maintenance of complexity and diversity, in order to understand the evolution of the complex "society" of life. This problem is not so trivial, indeed. It is often difficult to conclude that a system's emergent complexity is somewhat beyond that which would be expected on the basis of the rules explicitly implemented within a model [8]. Often, what people call "emergent" behavior comes from the lack of a full understanding of what is implied by the rules implemented in the model.

In evolution, there is a stage of the emergence of novel features as well as a stage of slow-scale change of existing features. Gradual evolution after the emergence of a novel feature is often studied analytically with the use of stochastic differential equations, as, for example, is demonstrated by the neutral theory of evolution [21]. The "origin" of features, on the other hand, is often a difficult problem to solve analytically. The origins of life, eukaryotes, multicellular organism, germ-line segregation, and sex are examples of the emergence of such novel features. For such problems, we require a mechanism for how complex, higher-level behavior emerges from low-level interactions, without the implementation of explicit rules for such emergence. Such emergence, we believe, occurs through strong nonlinear interactions among the agents at the lower level. Nonlinear interaction among agents often leads to chaotic behavior, which, we believe, can cause *aufheben* (German terminology for dialectic philosophy) to higher level dynamics, by which lower level conflicts are resolved.

In this overview, we try to demonstrate that chaos is relevant to the emergence and maintenance of complexity and diversity. Chaos is the most universal mechanism to create complexity from simple rules and initial conditions. As will be seen, chaos can be a source of diversity: Identical elements differentiate through chaotic dynamics. Through a dynamical process with instability, chaos also has the potentiality to create a higher-level dynamics.

Problems we address in the present overview are as follows; (a) evolution to complexity, (b) sources of diversity, (c) maintenance of diversity, and (d) successive creation of novelty and open-ended evolution to diversity.

In section 2, evolution to the edge of chaos, a complex state between chaos and order (a window), is studied with the use of an imitation game. An explicit example of the evolution of complexity is given. General concepts in globally coupled dynamical systems are briefly given in section 3, including the dynamic clustering of synchronization, hidden coherence, and chaotic itinerancy. In section 4 these novel concepts are applied to dynamical systems on a hypercubic lattice, which enables us to construct spontaneous genetic algorithms. A new concept—"homeochaos"—representing dynamical stability involving weak chaos with many degrees of freedom, is given in section 5, as well as its relevance to various biological networks. Homeochaos (to be contrasted with "homeostasis") can provide for the maintenance of diversity. In section 6 the concept of clustering in globally coupled maps is extended to the problem of cell division and differentiation. Here the novel concept of "open chaos" is demonstrated in a system with growing degrees of freedom. Open chaos leads to the formation of disparities in activities among cells, leading to the emergence of diversity and novelty. In section 7 we show the advantage of our approach over top-down and bottom-up approaches.

2   Edge of Chaos in an Imitation Game: Chaos as a Source of Complexity

The increase of complexity through evolution is believed to be seen in many biological systems, not only in the hierarchical organization in genotypes and phenotypes but also in animal behavior and communication.

A direction for the increase of complexity has recently been discussed as "evolution to the edge of chaos" [29], because complexity is believed to be large at the border between order and chaos [3, 6, 13, 20, 25]. However, there has been no clear simple example providing evidence of evolution to the edge of chaos, in the exact sense of dynamical systems theory. Chaos is defined only on dynamical systems with a continuous state and is not defined for discrete-state systems such as cellular automata, which have been adopted for studies of the edge of chaos so far.

Recently Suzuki and the author [18] have presented an example of evolution to the edge of chaos by introducing a simple model for an imitation game of a bird song. A bird song, for example, is known to increase its complexity through evolution and development (with more repertoire made up from combinations of simple phrases) [2]. A bird with a complex song is stronger in defending its territory [2, 23]. Based on this observation of a function of bird song for the defense of territory, we have introduced an imitation game [18], in which the player who imitates the other's song better wins the game.

As a "song," a time series generated by a simple mapping $x_{n+1} = f(x_n) = 1 - ax_n^2$ (the logistic map) is adopted. As is well known, the attractor of the map shows a bifurcation sequence from a fixed point, to cycles with Periods $2, 4, 8, \ldots$, and to chaos as the parameter a is increased [27]. Here the parameter value a is assumed to

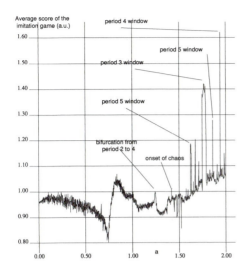
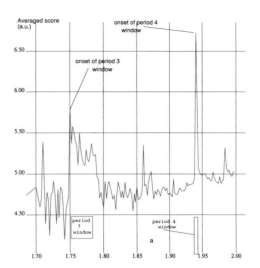

Figure 1. Emergent landscape: Average score for the players with parameters within $[a_i, a_i + \Delta]$ is plotted with $a_i = -1 + i \times \Delta$. $t_{trs} = 255$. The number of players is fixed at 200. (a) The mutation rate $\mu = 0.1$, and $T = 32$. The bin size $\Delta = 0.001$. Sampled for time steps from 1,000 to 1,500, over all players. (See Kaneko and Suzuki [18] for details, from which the figure is adapted.) (b) $\mu = 0.001$, and $T = 128$. The bin size $\Delta = 0.002$. Sampled for time steps from 750 to 1,000, over all players.

be different for each individual "bird." By this choice of a song generator, one can examine whether a song evolves toward the edge of chaos.

Each bird player i chooses an initial condition, so that the time series of its own dynamics $x_{n+1}(i) = f_i(x_n(i)) = 1 - a(i)x_n(i)^2$ can imitate the song of another player. For "preparation" of an initial condition, the player i uses a feedback from the other player j's song by $x_{n+1}(i) = f_i[(1 - \epsilon)x_n(i) + \epsilon x_n(j)]$ over a number of given time steps t_{trs}. Of course, birds have to choose initial conditions for starting the above feedback process, and also for singing, and the result of a game can depend on this choice of initial conditions [18]. Here we assume that they choose initial conditions randomly over $[-1, 1]$. Thus, the game is probabilistic, although "strong" players (to be discussed) often win against "weak ones" with probability close (or equal) to one [18].

By repeating the imitation process, the distance between two songs $D(j, i) = \sum_{n=t_{trs}}^{t_{trs}+T}$ $(x(j) - x(i))^2$ is measured. By changing the role of the player i and j, $D(j, i)$ is measured. If $D(i, j) < D(j, i)$, the player i imitates better than j, thus being the winner of the game, and vice versa.

By reproducing the players according to their scores in the game, and by including mutation of the parameter a [9], we have examined the dynamical states to which the songs evolve. Temporal evolution of the average of the parameter a over all players shows successive plateaus, until it reaches $a \approx 1.94$, where it then remains. Plateaus corresponding to period-doubling bifurcation points or to the edge between periodic windows and chaos are observed successively.

In Figure 1, the average score of players is plotted as a function of a. The score has a peak at the edge between chaos and windows for stable periodic cycles. To study evolution to the edge of chaos, we have also plotted the score of birds as a function of

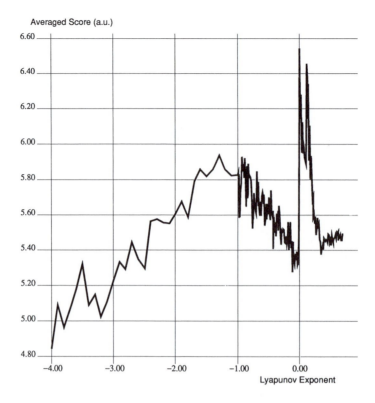

Figure 2. Average score of the game versus Lyapunov exponents. Simulation is carried out with $\mu = 0.05$, $t_{trs} = 255$, and $T = 128$ by fixing the population of birds at 200. Average scores are obtained from the histogram of Lyapunov exponents, for which we use a bin size of 0.01 for $-1 < \lambda < 1$, while it is set at 0.1 for $\lambda < -1$ (because the sample there is rather sparse). Sampled over time steps from 500 to 750 over all players (whose number is fixed at 200).

the Lyapunov exponent λ for the dynamics $x \rightarrow f(x)$ (see Figure 2). Indeed, the score has a broad peak around $\lambda = 0$, corresponding to the edge of chaos. Thus, evolution of a song toward the edge of chaos is observed. The final value of $a \approx 1.94$ corresponds to the borderline between a periodic window (of Period 4) and chaos.

Besides evolution to the edge of chaos, it should be noted that the "edge" reached by evolution lies between a periodic window and chaos. At a window, the dynamics show chaotic transients before attraction to a stable cycle. Here, a variety of unstable cycles coexist [27], which provide for a larger variety of dynamics, as transients. Transient chaos is important for the adaptation to a wide range of external dynamics. Evolution *to the edge of windows* may be a more robust and important concept than evolution to the edge of chaos.

Escape from imitation could be a trigger for the evolution of complexity in many fields, such as in the evolution of Batesian mimicry [30], where one of the groups can survive better by imitating the pattern of another group, while the second group's advantage in survival is lost if it is not distinguished well from the first. The increase of complexity of the patterns of some butterflies may be due to this "imitation" pressure. Another possible application is seen in the evolution of a communication code only within a given group. Studies of the evolution of such signals will be important in the future, from the viewpoint of complexity via chaotic dynamics.

3 Key Concept for the Origin of Complexity and Diversity: Dynamic Clustering in Networks of Chaotic Elements

To study the emergence of diversity, we need a mechanism by which identical elements differentiate into different groups spontaneously. Networks of chaotic elements, globally coupled to each other, provide an example of such a mechanism.

In many biological networks, the interaction among elements is not local but global. The simplest case of global interaction is studied as a "globally coupled map" (GCM) of chaotic elements. An example is given by

$$x_{n+1}(i) = (1 - \epsilon)f(x_n(i)) + \frac{\epsilon}{N}\sum_{j=1}^{N} f(x_n(j)), \tag{1}$$

where n is a discrete time step and i is the index of an element ($i = 1, 2, \ldots, N =$ system size), and $f(x) = 1 - ax^2$ [14]. Without coupling (i.e., for $\epsilon = 0$), each element shows chaotic behavior if a is large enough. The model is a mean-field-theory-type extension of coupled map lattices (CML). The above dynamics consists of parallel non-linear transformation with a feedback from the "mean-field."[1] In real biology, elements are not necessarily identical. The reason we start from identical elements is that we are interested in the origin of differentiation and diversity. That is, we are interested in the question, How can a set of identical units evolve to groups with different (dynamical) states?

Through interaction, some elements oscillate synchronously, while chaotic instability gives a tendency for the destruction of coherence. Attractors in GCM are classified by the number of synchronized clusters k and the number of elements within each cluster N_k. Here, a cluster is defined as the set of elements in which $x(i) = x(j)$. Identical elements split into clusters with different frequencies, phases, or amplitudes of oscillation. Each attractor is coded by the clustering condition $[k, (N_1, N_2, \ldots, N_k)]$.

In a globally coupled chaotic system in general, the following phases appear successively with the increase of nonlinearity in the system [14]:

1. *Coherent phase:* A coherent attractor ($k = 1$) has occupied (almost) all basin volumes.

2. *Ordered phase:* Attractors ($k = o(N)$) with few clusters have occupied (almost) all basin volumes.

3. *Partially ordered phase:* Coexistence of attractors with many clusters ($k = O(N)$) and attractors with few clusters.

4. *Turbulent phase:* All attractors have many clusters ($k = O(N)$; in most cases $k \approx N$).

In the turbulent phase, although $x(i)$ takes almost random values almost independently, there remains some coherence among elements. The distribution $P(h)$ of the mean field $h_n \equiv (1/N)\sum_j f(x_n(j))$, sampled over long time steps, does not obey the law of large numbers [15]. The emergence of hidden coherence is a general property in a globally coupled chaotic system. This hidden coherence may be interesting in relation to EEGs, where one measures a given average of neuronal (electric) activity. Although

---

1 It is equivalent to $y_{n+1}(i) = f[(1 - \epsilon)y_n(i) + \frac{\epsilon}{N}\sum_{j=1}^{N} y_n(j)]$, with the aid of transformation $y_n(i) = f(x_n(i))$. In this form, one can see clear correspondence with neural nets: If one chooses a sigmoid function (e.g., $tanh(\beta x)$) as $f(x)$ and a random or coded coupling $\epsilon_{i,j}$, a typical neural net is obtained.

the firing of each neuron is not regular (i.e., chaotic or random), the amplitude of some average (EEG) still has a large enough amplitude of variation to be observed, which may suggest the existence of hidden coherence as discussed earlier.

In the partially ordered phase, orbits make itinerance over ordered states via highly chaotic states. In the ordered states, the motion is partially coherent. Our system exhibits intermittent change between self-organization toward a coherent structure, and its collapse to a high-dimensional disordered motion. This dynamics, called *chaotic itinerancy*, has been found in a model of neural dynamics by Tsuda [31], optical turbulence [10], and in GCM [14]. Here, a number of ruins of low-dimensional attractors coexist in the phase space. The total dynamics consists of residencies at ruins interspersed with excursions into high-dimensional chaotic states.

In the chaotic itinerancy in GCM, the degree of synchronization between two elements changes with time. Elements 1 and 2, for example, may be almost synchronized for some time span, until desynchronization by high-dimensional chaos destroys the relationship. After some time, Element 1 may be almost synchronized with Element 5, for example, and so forth. Thus, the relationship between elements is dynamically changing. Indeed, such change of relationship is discussed in neural physiology [24].

4 Clustering in Hypercubic Coupled Maps: Self-organizing Genetic Algorithms

Let us discuss an extension of the idea in section 3 to population dynamics with mutation. The process of mutation is characterized by a diffusion process in the space of genes. If the "gene" space is represented by a bit space (such as $i = 0010111$, as is often the case for genetic algorithms [9]), the single point mutation process is given by a flip-flop $0 \leftrightarrow 1$ at each position. Let us represent the population (density) of each species i by $x(i)$, the mutation process is given by a diffusion in hypercubic bit space. When the population dynamics is represented by $x(i) \rightarrow f(x(i))$, the total dynamics is given by

$$x_{n+1}(i) = (1 - \epsilon)f(x_n(i)) + \frac{\epsilon}{k}\sum_{j=1}^{k} f(x_n(\sigma_j(i))), \qquad (2)$$

where $\sigma_j(i)$ is a species whose jth bit is different from the species i (with only one bit difference), and k is the total bit length of species (total species is 2^k).[2] We use a binary representation to denote the lattice here; for example, site 42 for $k = 6$ means the hypercubic lattice point 101010. The above model is rather close to the model in the last section; instead of the global coupling in Equation 1, nearest neighbor coupling on the hypercube is adopted here.

In Equation 2, we have again found the formation of synchronized clusters as in section 3 (i.e., $x_n(i) = x_n(j)$ for two elements i and j in the cluster). In the present case, the split to clusters is organized according to the hypercubic structure. Examples of such clusters follow.

4.1 1-Bit Clustering

Two clusters with synchronized oscillation are formed. Each of the clusters has $N/2 = 2^{k-1}$ elements, determined by the bit structure. For example, elements may be grouped into two clusters with **0*** and **1*** (* means that the symbol there is either one

---

2 Here we use an identical dynamics for all species. To include the fitness, one can adopt element-dependent dynamics $f_i(x)$, instead. In this case we can see some effects of clusterings, too.

or zero), each of which has 2^{k-1} species. This clustering is formed by cutting the k-dimensional hypercube by a hyperplane.

In the genetic algorithm [9], irrelevant bits are initially determined as "don't care" bits represented by "#". Here, such bits are spontaneously created with the temporal evolution.

4.2 2-Bit Clustering

Depending on initial conditions and parameters, both the number of clusters and the number of bits relevant to clustering can be larger than in section 4.1. An example is a 2-cluster state with 2 relevant bits by XOR (exclusive-or) construction. Here the elements split into the groups (a) ∗∗10∗∗∗ or ∗∗01∗∗∗ and (b) ∗∗00∗∗∗ or ∗∗11∗∗∗, for example.

4.3 Parity Check Clustering

Elements split into two groups according to the parity of the number of 1's in each bt representation. For example, elements split into two clusters as follows (a) 000, 011, 101, 110, and (b) 001 010, 100, 111, for $k = 3$. Thus, the clustering gives a parity check. It is a hypercubic version of the zigzag (1-dim) or checkerboard (2-dim) pattern [8].

Besides these examples, attractors with many clusters are also found. Most of these states are constructed by combining the above clustering schemes. For example, four clusters with two relevant bits are found as a direct product state of the case in section 4.1. Here the hypercubic space is cut by two hyperplanes. Elements split into four clusters, for example, coded by 01∗∗∗∗∗, 10∗∗∗∗∗, 11∗∗∗∗∗, and 00∗∗∗∗∗.

More complex examples are reported by Kaneko [16]. Here we have to note that not all partitions are possible in the present case. Even if we start from an initial condition with an arbitrary clustering, the synchronization condition ($x(i) = x(j)$ for i, j belonging to the same cluster) is not satisfied at the next step for most such initial conditions. In contrast with the GCM case, not all possible partitions can be a (stable or unstable) solution of the evolution equation.

As discussed, the present result opens up the possibility of automatic genetic algorithms. Relevant bits are spontaneously formed. Furthermore, we have found a chaotic itinerancy state, where relevant bits change according to temporal evolution. In Figure 3, the change of relevant bits for clustering is clearly seen. At Stage A, two clusters are formed by the first bit (i.e., clusters 0∗∗∗∗ and 1∗∗∗∗), and the second bit at Stage B (∗0∗∗∗ and ∗1∗∗∗), and so on.

With the introduction of external inputs to each element, it is also possible to have a clustered state following the external information [16]. Relevant information is extracted through this process spontaneously, which is stored as a relevant bit in the clustering.

An application of the present clustering to "real life" will be found in the quasispecies of viruses [4]. As Eigen, McCaskill, and Schuster discuss, viruses form quasispecies coded in hypercubic space. By taking account of population dynamics, the present clustering may give a theoretical basis for the dynamic and hierarchical grouping of quasispecies.

5 Maintenance of Diversity and Dynamic Stability: Homeochaos

As for the evolution to complexity, the notion of the "edge of chaos" in section 2 is rather special. First, it is provided by a critical state and should be sustained at a very narrow region (or at a single critical point) of the parameter space. Second, the system is given by a low-dimensional dynamical system, that is, with very few degrees of freedom. Hence, the notion "edge of chaos" is insufficient to understand the diversity and complexity of a biological system.

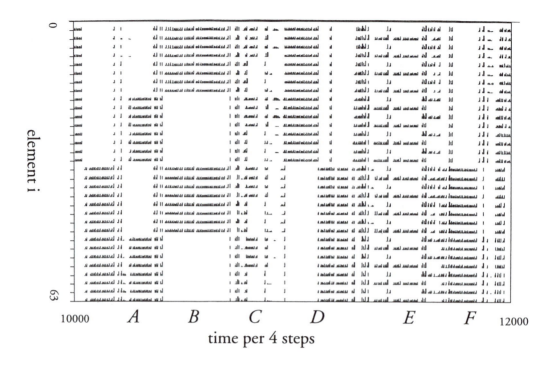

Figure 3. Space-time diagram for the coupled map lattice on a hypercubic lattice with $k = 5$ (i.e., $N = 2^5$). For local dynamics $f(x) = 1 - 1.52x^2$ is adopted, while the coupling strength ϵ is set at 0.3. On the corresponding pixel at a given time and element, a bar with a length proportional to $(x_n(i, j) - 0.1)$ is painted if $x_n(i, j) > .1$. Every fourth time step is plotted from 10,000 to 12,000. Elements are aligned according to its binary representation, that is, $0 = 00000$, $1 = 00001$, $2 = 00010$, ..., $63 = 11111$. At Stage A, elements split into two clusters 0**** and 1****, while they split into *0*** and *1*** at Stage B, **0** and **1** at Stage C, 0***** and 1**** at Stage D, ****0 and ****1 at Stage E, and again into 0***** and 1**** at Stage F.

In an ecological system, many species are under strong nonlinear interaction and keep some kind of stability with diversity. This is not easily sustained. We also have to mention that static equilibria with many species are usually unstable, as studied by May [26] in a random network model. Thus, it is interesting to search for a dynamical mechanism to allow for the diversity in a system with interacting population dynamics.

Ikegami and the author [11, 17] have studied a population dynamics model with interaction among species, mutation, and mutation of mutation rates. In particular, a model with interaction among hosts and parasites has been studied. Each species is coded by a bit sequence as in section 4, whose fitness has a rugged or flat (neutral) landscape. The interaction between a host and a parasite is assumed to depend on the Hamming distance between their bit sequences.

When the interaction between hosts and parasites is weak, the mutation rates of species decrease with evolution. The dynamics of the whole species is reduced to a direct product of isolated sets of host–parasite population dynamics. When the interaction is strong, on the other hand, mutation rates are sustained at a high level, where many species form a network of population dynamics. This network consists of species connected by single point mutations. Many species are percolated in the gene space.

Note that this network is dynamically sustained. The population of each species oscillates chaotically in time. The oscillation is high-dimensional chaos with small positive Lyapunov exponents. ("High-dimensional" here means that the number of positive exponents is large.) If the mutation rate were zero, the dynamics of each species would be essentially disconnected. Then some host–parasite pairs would show strong chaos, while others would show periodic or fixed point dynamics. By sustaining a high mutation rate, chaotic instability is shared by almost all species, leading to weak high-dimensional chaos. By the term *weak*, we mean that the maximum Lyapunov exponent is close to zero and that the amplitude of oscillation of each species is small. Our system has a tendency to evolve toward such weak, high-dimensional chaos.

Here we propose a conjecture that diversity in an evolutionary system with interaction of many replicating units maintains its dynamical stability by forming a weak high-dimensional chaotic state, rather than in a fixed point or in strong chaos. We have coined the term *homeochaos* for this homeodynamic state.

The following three points capture the essence of homeochaos:

1. *Weak chaos:* Homeochaos suppresses strong chaos. The maximal Lyapunov exponent is positive but is close to zero. The oscillation amplitude is not large. This weak chaos, for example, is essential to avoid an overly violent change or extinction in the population dynamics.

2. *High-dimensional chaos:* Homeochaos is high-dimensional chaos. There are many positive Lyapunov exponents, although their magnitude is small, and there are many degrees of freedom.

3. *Dynamic stability and robustness against external perturbations:* Homeochaos provides dynamic stability for a complex network. The robustness of homeochaos is easily seen by introducing an external perturbation to the population dynamics. If the population dynamics follows low-dimensional chaos, the amplitude of population change is sometimes very large. The oscillation can bring about a state with very small population size (see Figure 4). When an external perturbation is applied at this time, the number of population may go to zero. On the other hand, the oscillation amplitude is small in homeochaos (see Figure 4), because the chaos is very weak. Thus, populations of species fluctuate around some value far from zero. Hence, species are not easily driven to extinction by external perturbations.

The above three features are strongly interrelated. The stability and robustness (3) are sustained by the suppression of strong instability given by (1). By (2), strong chaotic instability is shared by many modes, implying the weak chaos per degrees of freedom (point (1)).

Point (1) is a feature common with homeochaos and the edge of chaos. However, homeochaos is not sustained at a critical point, but it is more robust against a parameter change. Also the degrees of freedom are not discussed in the edge of chaos, but they are essential to homeochaos.

Remnants of clustering of oscillation are important in sustaining homeochaos. Indeed, the chaotic itinerancy seen in clustering is sometimes seen in homeochaos. The oscillation of some populations of some species form partial clustering over some time steps. The connection between homeochaos and clustering may not be so surprising. If chaos were too strong, oscillations of many elements would not keep any relationship, and they would become completely desynchronized. If chaos were completely suppressed, clustering with few number of clusters would often follow. To keep weak and high-dimensional chaos, partial clustering with chaotic itinerancy is the most preferable state.

Homeochaos in the formation of networks will be important in various levels of biological networks. Maybe the most straightforward application will be found in immune

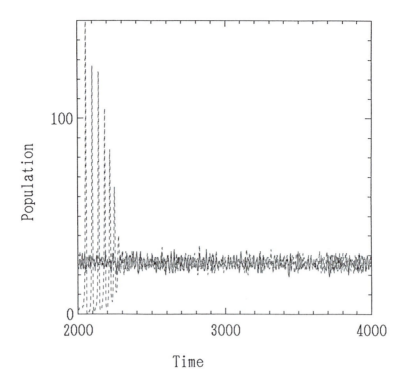

Figure 4. Oscillation of total populations for hosts (solid line) and parasites (dashed line), in the model in Kaneko and Ikegami [17]. Initial chaotic oscillations with large amplitudes are suppressed simultaneously with the increase of averaged mutation rate around time = 2,300. Up to the time, the population dynamics is a direct product of low-dimensional chaos and includes a violent change of populations. After the time, the oscillation amplitude is much weaker (although chaotic), where homeochaos is attained with the increase of the mutation rates. See Kaneko and Ikegami [17] for details.

networks and quasispecies of viruses. In the immune system, antibody–antigen inter-actions are similar to host–parasite interactions. An antigen is damaged by "matched" antibodies. An antibody itself is damaged by a different class of antibodies, as Jerne [12] proposed. High mutation rates are sustained for antibodies, and the concentrations of antibody species oscillate in time. We note that these features are shared in common with our model earlier and its numerical results.

Correspondingly, viruses keep high mutation rates, and the population dynamics maintains high mutation rates. The population dynamics of quasispecies [4] is of interest from the viewpoint of homeochaos. Indeed, the term *quasispecies* of Eigen et al. [4] corresponds to our term *meta-species*, a symbiotic network connected by mutation in Kaneko and Ikegami [17].

At a more macroscopic level, metabolic oscillations of cells may form homeochaotic dynamics, as will be discussed in the next section. At a further macroscopic level, physiology and medicine are the birthplace of the term *homeostasis*. However, data have recently been accumulating showing that the healthy state is not one of "stasis" but rather exhibits an irregular temporal dynamics. So far, it is hard to conclude that the dynamics of the healthy state is chaotic. Possibly this difficulty may be due to the high dimensionality of the dynamics, where no powerful means of diagnosis from the data is available. Indeed, low-dimensional chaos has to date been found to be associated with unhealthy states of the heart rhythm and EEG. One possible conjecture is that a healthy state is sustained by homeochaos rather than homeostasis, because homeochaotic dynamics is neither too irregular nor too regular.

At the most macroscopic level, an ecological network can be a candidate for homeochaos. As Elton [5] has discovered in the forests of England, an ecological system with diversity is robust against external perturbations.

A typical example of a complex ecological network is found among the species in a tropical rain forest. The ecology there consists of a huge number of species, whose population size is often very small. So far, the dynamics of the population of species in a complex ecological system has not been seriously studied, but the ecology is believed to be in a dynamic state, not at a stationary state. This diversity and dynamics are also seen in our population dynamics showing homeochaos. It is strongly hoped that the population dynamics of rain forest species is measured soon. When this is done, we believe the dynamics will be found to be homeochaotic. We also believe that the mutation rate itself will be found to be larger than the normal level. If this is the case, we may assume that the coupling among species is effectively larger than in temperate zones.

We may also hope that our homeochaos is important in a complex network system in general and for a dynamical network system with many units evolving according to some inherent dynamics. Such examples may include neural systems, computer networks, economics, and sociology. Our homeochaos provides a key principle for the formation of cooperation and the dynamic stability required in such systems.

6 Source of Novelty and Growth of Diversity: Open Chaos

In the previous section we have studied the maintenance of diversity. How about its creation? In section 3, we have discussed a possible theoretical basis for the origin of diversity. The most typical origin of diversity is seen in cell differentiation. The formation and maintenance of a society of differentiated cells [1] is also important for the origin of a multicellular organism. By cell division, each cell reproduces itself with differentiation and forms a network of cell society. Is the dynamic clustering mechanism in section 3 relevant to cell differentiation?

To consider this problem, quite remarkable experimental results are reported [22]: *Escherichia coli* with identical genes can split into several groups with different enzymatic activities. Even prokaryotic cells with identical genes can be differentiated there. Furthermore, cells are under liquid culture; thus, they are in an identical environment. This experimental result must be surprising to molecular biologists and also to those who study differentiation in the context of spatial pattern formation (e.g., along the line of Turing instability): Neither genetic nor spatial information is essential to the differentiation in the experiment. On the other hand, the experimental result may not be so surprising in the light of the dynamic clustering discussed in section 3. Nonlinear metabolic reaction is involved in each cell, as well as nonlinear interaction with the soup. Cells interact globally with all other cells through the soup. Thus, it is possible to expect that cells' chemical oscillations differentiate and form some groups.

Recently Yomo and the author [19] proposed a model of cell differentiation based on the idea of dynamic clustering in section 3. The model consists of metabolic reaction, active transport of chemicals from a medium (soup), and cell division. The metabolic reaction is nonlinear due to the feedback mechanism of catalytic reaction. The interaction of cells is global, due to the competition for taking chemicals (resources to produce enzymes and DNA) from the medium. Cell division is assumed to follow the chemical

Concentration of a chemical

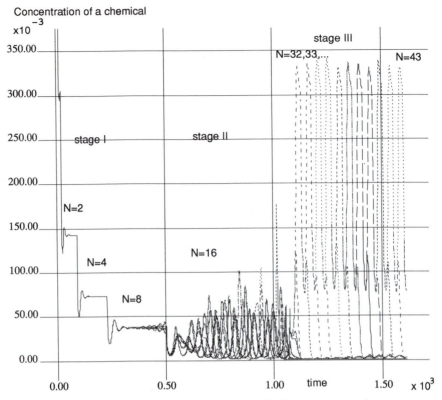

Figure 5. Overlaid time series of a chemical at each cell. As the number of cells grows, the oscillation starts and clustering emerges at Stage II. At Stage III, disparity of the chemical is clearly seen. See Kaneko and Yomo [19] for details, from whom the figure is adapted.

activities in each cell. The division speed of a cell is assumed to be proportional to its average chemicals included therein.

From a dynamical systems point of view, the model has a novel feature, which is not included in the globally coupled map. Here the number of degrees of freedom varies via cell division. When a new cell is born, we need additional degrees of freedom to indicate the cell's state.

Numerical results of the model show that there are three successive stages in the growth of the number of cells: coherent growth, dynamic clustering, and fixed cell differentiation (see Figure 5). At the first stage, oscillations of chemicals of all cells are synchronized, and they divide synchronously. Hence, the number of cells increases as $1, 2, 4, 8, 16, \ldots$). The second stage starts when the oscillations of chemicals lose their synchronicity, and the dynamic clustering of section 3 is observed. At the last stage, some (active) cells start to have more chemicals than others. Disparity in chemical activities is observed. The speed of division of active cells is at least 10^2 times faster than other cells. The active cells may correspond to germ cells, while others correspond to somatic cells. Here, somatic cells are also differentiated according to the concentration of contained chemicals. The oscillations of chemicals at the third stage sustain weak chaos. We note that the third stage is robust against external perturbations.

Because all cells compete for resources from the medium, the previous results may be interpreted as follows: At the second stage, cells form a time-sharing system for resources, by the clustering of oscillations, while the differentiation between poor and rich cells is formed spontaneously at the third stage. The emergence of the third stage is rather new, unexpected from the dynamic clustering in section 3.

Indeed, we may introduce a new concept, which we call "open chaos." We propose open chaos as a novel and general scenario for systems with growing numbers of elements. By the active transport dynamics of chemicals, the difference between two cells can be amplified, because a cell with more chemicals is assumed to get even more. Tiny differences between cells can grow exponentially if parameters satisfy a suitable condition. A grown cell is divided into two, with an (almost) equal partition of the contained chemicals. This process looks quite similar to chaos in the Baker's transformation, involving stretching (exponential growth) and folding (division). One difference between our cell division mechanism and chaos is that phase space itself changes after a division in the former, while the orbit comes back to the original phase space in the stretching-folding mechanism of chaos.

Our "open chaos" concept is a novel and general mechanism of instability and irregular dynamics in a system with growing phase space. In studies of artificial life, the term *open-ended evolution* often refers to a dynamics whose phase space attains more dimensions with the appearance of new species, strategies, and so forth. Open chaos provides a mechanism for the way in which chaotic instability in dynamical systems can trigger the expansion of the dimension of phase space. It is interesting to extend the present open chaos to areas studied in connection with open-ended evolution, such as economics, sociology, game theory, and so on.

7 Beyond Top-Down and Bottom-Up Approaches

There have been long debates between top-down and bottom-up approaches in artificial intelligence and neural networks. In the bottom-up approach, some kind of "order parameters" constructed from a lower level gives a higher level, related with some macroscopic behavior. In the top-down approach, a few instructions send messages to lower-level elements.

Of course it is possible to include a weak feedback between top/bottom levels, starting from each approach. An example is a simulation of ants with pheromone [34]. The dynamics of lower-level units (ants' motion) leads to a collective field of pheromone, which governs the motion of the lower-level units. Because the dynamics of lower-level units is governed by the higher-level dynamics, this scheme is essentially analogous with the Prigogine's dissipative structure [28] or Haken's slaving principle [7].

In these approaches, it is assumed that the top level is represented by a small number of degrees of freedom, while the bottom level may involve a huge number of degrees of freedom. Furthermore, relationships between elements are fixed. Although it is possible to include a nontrivial dynamics at a macroscopic level, the behavior of each element is passive and totally susceptible to a higher level.

Our network of chaotic elements provides a different mechanism, in the following sense: first, the top level is not necessarily represented by only a few degrees of freedom; second, relationships between elements at the lower level can dynamically change; third, elements are not passive, but are active and dynamical.[3] The first point may seem just a complication at first glance, but this is not necessarily so. Often motion governed by a few degrees of freedom emerges, which, however, does not last forever due to the second point (dynamic change of relationships). Again, high-dimensional motion comes back, until another structure emerges. This mechanism, described as chaotic itinerancy in section 3, is essential to replace the top-down and bottom-up

---

3 The necessity of active elements at low levels and synaptic changes of higher-levels is also emphasized as *collectionism* by C. Langton (private communication). Our approach shares these features with collectionism. We have explictly shown that chaos can provide a mechanism for these features, here.

approaches. In a network of chaotic elements, for example, the order at the top level is destroyed by chaotic revolt against the slaving principle [14], in contrast with passive elements in traditional approaches.

In the population dynamics model by Ikegami and the author (mentioned in section 5), the higher level corresponds to the survival of species as a collection of species. The higher level emerges from the bottom level, but it is not necessarily represented by a few degrees of freedom.

Conclusion

Summing up, we have discussed a chaotic scenario of evolution, which allows for the dynamical change of relationships of units, and spontaneous formation and destruction of upper levels. The origin and maintenance of complexity and diversity are explained through this scenario. We hope that chaos can remain a source of complexity, novelty, and diversity in the studies of artificial life.

Acknowledgments
I am grateful to Ichiro Tsuda, Takashi Ikegami, Tetsuya Yomo, Yukito Iba, Junji Suzuki, Kei Tokita, and Tomoyuki Yamamoto for continual criticism and stimulating discussions. I would also like to thank Chris Langton for critical reading of the manuscript and for discussions on his collectionism. The work is partially supported by Grant-in-Aids for Scientific Research from the Ministry of Education, Science, and Culture of Japan.

References
1. Buss, L. W. (1988). *Evolution of individuality*. Princeton, NJ: Princeton University Press.

2. Catchpole, C. K. (1979). *Vocal communication in birds*. Edward Arnold Press.

3. Crutchfield, J. P., & Young, K. (1989). *Phys. Rev. Lett., 63*, 105.

4. Eigen, M., McCaskill, J., & Schuster, P. (1988). *Journal of Physical Chemistry, 92*, 6881; Eigen, M. (1993, July). *Scientific American*, 32.

5. Elton, C. S. (1966). *The pattern of animal communities*. London: Methuen and Co.

6. Grassberger, P. (1986). *International Journal of Theoretical Physics, 25*, 907.

7. Haken, H. (1978). *Synergetics*. Springer.

8. Hofstadter, D. R. (1979). *Gödel, Escher, Bach*. New York: Basic Books.

9. Holland, J. (1986). *Escaping brittleness in machine learning II*. Kaufman.

10. Ikeda, K., Matsumoto, K., & Ohtsuka, K. (1989). *Prog. Theor. Phys., 99*(Suppl.), 295.

11. Ikegami, T., & Kaneko, K. (1992). Evolution of host-parasitoid network through homeochaotic dynamics. *Chaos, 2*, 397–408.

12. Jerne, N. K. In G. C. Quarton, T. Melnechuk, & F. O. Schmitt (Eds.), *The neurosciences: A study program*. New York: Rockefeller University Press.

13. Kaneko, K. (1989). *Physica D, 34*, 1.

14. Kaneko, K. (1989). *Phys. Rev. Lett., 63*, 219; (1990) *Physica D, 41*, 137; (1991) *Physica D, 54*, 5; (1991) *J. Phys. A, 24*, 2107.

15. Kaneko, K. (1990) *Phys. Rev. Lett., 65*, 1391; *Physica D, 55*, 368.

16. Kaneko, K. (1994). Hypercubic coupled maps. *Physica D*, to be submitted.

17. Kaneko, K., & Ikegami, T. (1992). Homeochaos: dynamics stability of a symbiotic network with population dynamics and evolving mutation rates. *Physica D, 56*, 406–429.

18. Kaneko, K., & Suzuki, J. (1994). Evolution to the edge of chaos in imitation game, in *Artificial life III*, 43–54. Imitation games (in press), *Physica D*, special issue of Oji seminar.

19. Kaneko, K., & Yomo, T. (in press). Cell division, differentiation, and dynamic clustering. *Physica D*, special issue of Oji seminar.

20. Kaufmann, S. A., & Johnson, S. (1991). *Journal of Theoretical Biology, 149,* 467.

21. Kimura, M. (1983). *The neutral theory of molecular evolution.* Cambridge University Press.

22. Ko, E., Yomo, T., & Urabe, I. (in press). Dynamic clustering of bacterial population. *Physica D*, special issue of Oji seminar.

23. Krebs, J. R., Ashcroft, R., & Weber, M. (1978). *Nature, 271,* 539–542.

24. Kruger, J. (Ed.) (1991). *Neuronal cooperativity.* New York: Springer-Verlag.

25. Langton, C. (1990). *Physica D, 42,* 12.

26. May, R. (1973). *Stability and complexity in model ecosystems.* Princeton, NJ: Princeton University Press.

27. May, R. (1976). *Nature, 26,* 459; Collet, P., & Eckmann, J. P. (1980) *Iterated maps on the intervals as dynamical systems.* Boston-Basel-Stuttgart: Birkhauser.

28. Nicolis, G., & Prigogine, I. (1977). *Self-organization in nonequilibrium systems.* New York: Wiley Interscience.

29. Packard, N. H. (1988). In J. Kelso, A. J. Mandell, & M. F. Shlesinger (Eds.), *Dynamic Patterns in Complex Systems* (pp. 293–301). World Scientific. See also the paper by M. Mitchell et al., to appear in *Physica D* (in press) (special issue of *Oji Seminar Proceeding*).

30. Maynard Smith, J. (1989). *Evolutionary genetics.* Oxford, UK: Oxford University Press.

31. Tsuda, I. (1990). Chaotic neural networks and thesaurus. In A. V. Holden & V. I. Kryukov (Eds.), *Neurocomputers and Attention.* Manchester University Press.

32. Collins, R. J., & Jefferson, D. R. (1992). In C. Langton (Ed.), *Artificial Life II.* Redwood City, CA: Addison-Wesley.

An Evolutionary Approach to Synthetic Biology: Zen and the Art of Creating Life

Thomas S. Ray
ATR Human Information
Processing Research
Laboratories
2-2 Hikaridai, Seika-cho
Soraku-gun, Kyoto, 619-02
Japan
ray@hip.atr.co.jp, ray@udel.edu

Abstract Our concepts of biology, evolution, and complexity are constrained by having observed only a single instance of life, life on earth. A truly comparative biology is needed to extend these concepts. Because we cannot observe life on other planets, we are left with the alternative of creating Artificial Life forms on earth. I will discuss the approach of inoculating evolution by natural selection into the medium of the digital computer. This is not a physical/chemical medium; it is a logical/informational medium. Thus, these new instances of evolution are not subject to the same physical laws as organic evolution (e.g., the laws of thermodynamics) and exist in what amounts to another universe, governed by the "physical laws" of the logic of the computer. This exercise gives us a broader perspective on what evolution is and what it does.

An evolutionary approach to synthetic biology consists of inoculating the process of evolution by natural selection into an artificial medium. Evolution is then allowed to find the natural forms of living organisms in the artificial medium. These are not models of life, but independent instances of life. This essay is intended to communicate a way of thinking about synthetic biology that leads to a particular approach: to understand and respect the natural form of the artificial medium, to facilitate the process of evolution in generating forms that are adapted to the medium, and to let evolution find forms and processes that naturally exploit the possibilities inherent in the medium. Examples are cited of synthetic biology embedded in the computational medium, where in addition to being an exercise in experimental comparative evolutionary biology, it is also a possible means of harnessing the evolutionary process for the production of complex computer software.

Keywords
evolution, ecology, synthesis, parallel computation, multi-cellularity, complexity, diversity

1 Synthetic Biology

Artificial Life (AL) is the enterprise of understanding biology by constructing biological phenomena out of artificial components, rather than breaking natural life forms down into their component parts. It is the synthetic rather than the reductionist approach. I will describe an approach to the synthesis of artificial living forms that exhibit natural evolution.

The umbrella of AL is broad and covers three principal approaches to synthesis: in hardware (e.g., robotics, nanotechnology), in software (e.g., replicating and evolving computer programs), and in wetware (e.g., replicating and evolving organic molecules, nucleic acids, or others). This essay will focus on software synthesis, although it is hoped that the issues discussed will be generalizable to any synthesis involving the process of evolution.

I would like to suggest that software syntheses in AL could be divided into two kinds: simulations and instantiations of life processes. AL simulations represent an advance in biological modeling, based on a bottom-up approach, which has been made possible by the increase of available computational power. In the older approaches to modeling of ecological or evolutionary phenomena, systems of differential equations were set up that expressed relationships between covarying quantities of entities (i.e., genes, alleles, individuals, or species) in the populations or communities.

The new bottom-up approach creates a population of data structures, with each instance of the data structure corresponding to a single entity. These structures contain variables defining the state of an individual. Rules are defined as to how the individuals interact with one another and with the environment. As the simulation runs, populations of these data structures interact according to local rules, and the global behavior of the system emerges from those interactions. Several very good examples of bottom-up ecological models have appeared in the AL literature [33,91]. However, ecologists have also developed this same approach independently of the AL movement and have called the approach "individual-based" models [19,39].

The second approach to software synthesis is what I have called instantiation rather than simulation. In simulation, data structures are created that contain variables that represent the states of the entities being modeled. The important point is that in simulation, the data in the computer is treated as a representation of something else, such as a population of mosquitoes or trees. In instantiation, the data in the computer does not represent anything else. The data patterns in an instantiation are considered to be living forms in their own right and are not models of any natural life form. These can form the basis of a comparative biology [57].

The object of an AL instantiation is to introduce the natural form and process of life into an artificial medium. This results in an AL form in some medium other than carbon chemistry and is not a model of organic life forms. The approach discussed in this essay involves introducing the process of evolution by natural selection into the computational medium. I consider evolution to be the fundamental process of life and the generator of living form.

2 Recognizing Life

Most approaches to defining life involve assembling a short list of properties of life and then testing candidates on the basis of whether or not they exhibit the properties on the list. The main problem with this approach is that there is disagreement as to what should be on the list. My private list contains only two items: self-replication and open-ended evolution. However, this reflects my biases as an evolutionary biologist.

I prefer to avoid the semantic argument and take a different approach to the problem of recognizing life. I was led to this view by contemplating how I would regard a machine that exhibited conscious intelligence at such a level that it could participate as an equal in a debate such as this. The machine would meet neither of my two criteria as to what life is, yet I don't feel that I could deny that the process it contained was alive.

This means that there are certain properties that I consider to be unique to life and whose presence in a system signify the existance of life in that system. This suggests an alternative approach to the problem. Rather than create a short list of minimal requirements and test whether a system exhibits all items on the list, one could create a long list of properties unique to life and test whether a system exhibits *any* item on the list.

In this softer, more pluralistic approach to recognizing life, the objective is not to determine if the system is alive or not but to determine if the system exhibits a "genuine" instance of some property that is a signature of living systems (e.g., self-replication, evolution, flocking, consciousness).

Whether we consider a system living because it exhibits some property that is unique to life amounts to a semantic issue. What is more important is that we recognize that it is possible to create disembodied but genuine instances of specific properties of life in artificial systems. This capability is a powerful research tool. By separating the property of life that we choose to study from the many other complexities of natural living systems, we make it easier to manipulate and observe the property of interest. The objective of the approach advocated in this paper is to capture genuine evolution in an artificial system.

3   What Natural Evolution Does

Evolution by natural selection is a process that enters into a physical medium. Through iterated replication with selection of large populations through many generations, it searches out the possibilities inherent in the "physics and chemistry" of the medium in which it is embedded. It exploits any inherent self-organizing properties of the medium and flows into natural attractors realizing and fleshing out their structure.

Evolution never escapes from its ultimate imperative: self-replication. However, the mechanisms that evolution discovers for achieving this ultimate goal gradually become so convoluted and complex that the underlying drive can seem to become superfluous. Some philosophers have argued that the evolutionary theory as expressed by the phrase "survival of the fittest" is tautological, in that the fittest are defined as those that survive to reproduce. In fact, fitness is achieved through innovation in engineering of the organism [81]. However, there remains something peculiarly self-referential about the whole enterprise. There is some sense in which life may be a natural tautology.

Evolution is both a defining characteristic and the creative process of life itself. The living condition is a state that complex physical systems naturally flow into under certain conditions. It is a self-organizing, self-perpetuating state of autocatalytically increasing complexity. The living component of the physical system quickly becomes the most complex part of the system, such that it reshapes the medium in its own image. Life then evolves adaptations predominantly in relation to the living components of the system, rather than the nonliving components. Life evolves adaptations to itself.

3.1   Evolution in Sequence Space

Think of organisms as occupying a "genotype space" consisting of all possible sequences of all possible lengths of the elements of the genetic system (i.e., nucleotides or machine instructions). When the first organism begins replicating, a single self-replicating creature, with a single sequence of a certain length, occupies a single point in the genotype space. However, as the creature replicates in the environment, a population of creatures forms, and errors cause genetic variation, such that the population will form a cloud of points in the genotype space centered around the original point.

Because the new genotypes that form the cloud are formed by random processes, most of them are completely inviable and die without reproducing. However, some of them are capable of reproduction. These new genotypes persist, and, because some of them are affected by mutation, the cloud of points spreads further. However, not all of the viable genomes are equally viable. Some of them discover tricks to replicate more efficiently. These genotypes increase in frequency, causing the population of creatures at the corresponding points in the genotype space to increase.

Points in the genotype space occupied by greater populations of individuals will spawn larger numbers of mutant offspring; thus, the density of the cloud of points in the genotype space will shift gradually in the direction of the more fit genotypes. Over time, the cloud of points will percolate through the genotype space, either expanding outward as a result of random drift or by flowing along fitness gradients.

Most of the volume of this space represents completely inviable sequences. These regions of the space may be momentarily and sparsely occupied by inviable mutants, but the cloud will never flow into the inviable regions. The cloud of genotypes may bifurcate as it flows into habitable regions in different directions, and it may split as large genetic changes spawn genotypes in distant but viable regions of the space. We may imagine that the evolving population of creatures will take the form of wispy clouds flowing through this space.

Now imagine for a moment the situation that there was no selection. This implies that every sequence is replicated at an equal rate. Mutation will cause the cloud of points to expand outward, eventually filling the space uniformly. In this situation, the complexity of the structure of the cloud of points does not increase through time, only the volume that it occupies. Under selection by contrast, through time the cloud will take on an intricate structure as it flows along fitness gradients and percolates by drift through narrow regions of viability in a largely uninhabitable space.

Consider that the viable region of the genotype space is a very small subset of the total volume of the space, but that it probably exhibits a very complex shape, forming tendrils and sheets sparsely permeating the otherwise empty space. The complex structure of this cloud can be considered to be a product of evolution by natural selection. This thought experiment appears to imply that the intricate structure that the cloud of genotypes may assume through evolution is fully deterministic. Its shape is predefined by the physics and chemistry and the structure of the environment, in much the same way that the form of the Mandlebrot set is predetermined by its defining equation. The complex structure of this viable space is inherent in the medium and is an example of "order for free" [44].

No living world will ever fill the entire viable subspace, either at a single moment of time, or even cumulatively over its entire history. The region actually filled will be strongly influenced by the original self-replicating sequence and by stochastic forces that will by chance push the cloud down a subset of possible habitable pathways. Furthermore, coevolution and ecological interactions imply that certain regions can only be occupied when certain other regions are also occupied. This concept of the flow of genotypes through the genotype space is essentially the same as that discussed by Eigen [22] in the context of "quasispecies." Eigen limited his discussion to species of viruses, where it is also easy to think of sequence spaces. Here, I am extending the concept beyond the bounds of the species to include entire phylogenies of species.

3.2 Natural Evolution in an Artificial Medium

Until recently, life has been known as a state of matter, particularly combinations of the elements carbon, hydrogen, oxygen, nitrogen, and smaller quantities of many others. However, recent work in the field of AL has shown that the natural evolutionary process can proceed with great efficacy in other media, such as the informational medium of the digital computer [1,3,7,15,16,20,24,42,43,50,52,53,67,68,70–73,76,77,80,88,90,96].[1]

---

1 In ref. 1, Adami has used the input-output facilities of the new Tierra languages to feed data to creatures, and select for responses that result from simple computations, not contained in the seed genome. In ref. 7, Brooks has created his own Tierra-like system, which he calls Sierra. In his implementation, each machine instruction consists of an opcode and an operand. Successive instructions overlap such that the operand of one instruction is interpreted as the opcode of the next instruction. In ref. 88, "Tierra-like systems

These new natural evolutions in artificial media are beginning to explore the possibilities inherent in the "physics and chemistry" of those media. They are organizing themselves and constructing self-generating complex systems. While these new living systems are still so young that they remain in their primordial state, it appears that they have embarked on the same kind of journey taken by life on earth and presumably have the potential to evolve levels of complexity that could lead to sentient and eventually intelligent beings.

If natural evolution in artificial media leads to sentient or intelligent beings, they will likely be so alien that they will be difficult to recognize. The sentient properties of plants are so radically different from those of animals that they are generally unrecognized or denied by humans, and plants are merely in another kingdom of the one great tree of organic life on earth [69,74,87]. Synthetic organisms evolving in other media, such as the digital computer, are not only not a part of the same phylogeny, but they are not even of the same physics. Organic life is based on conventional material physics, whereas digital life exists in a logical, not material, informational universe. Digital intelligence will likely be vastly different from human intelligence; forget the Turing Test.

4   The Approach

Marcel, a mechanical chessplayer ... his exquisite 19th-century brainwork—the human art it took to build which has been flat lost, lost as the dodo bird ... But where inside Marcel is the midget Grandmaster, the little Johann Allgeier? where's the pantograph, and the magnets? Nowhere. Marcel really is a mechanical chessplayer. No fakery inside to give him any touch of humanity at all.

— Thomas Pynchon, *Gravity's Rainbow*

The objective of the approach discussed here is to create an instantiation of evolution by natural selection in the computational medium. This creates a conceptual problem that requires considerable art to solve: Ideas and techniques must be learned by studying organic evolution and then applied to the generation of evolution in a digital medium, without forcing the digital medium into an "unnatural" simulation of the organic world.

We must derive inspiration from observations of organic life, but we must never lose sight of the fact that the new instantiation is not organic and may differ in many fundamental ways. For example, organic life inhabits a Euclidean space; however, computer memory is not a Euclidean space. Intercellular communication in the organic world is chemical in nature, and, therefore, a single message generally can pass no more information than on or off. By contrast, communication in digital computers generally involves the passing of bit patterns, which can carry much more information.

The fundamental principal of the approach being advocated here is *to understand and respect the natural form of the digital computer, to facilitate the process of evolution in generating forms that are adapted to the computational medium, and to let evolution find forms and processes that naturally exploit the possibilities inherent in the medium.*

Situations arise where it is necessary to make significant changes from the standard computer architecture. But such changes should be made with caution and only when there is some feature of standard computer architectures that clearly inhibits the desired processes. Examples of such changes are discussed later in the section titled "The Genetic Language." Less substantial changes are also discussed in the sections on the

---

are being explored for their potential applications in solving the problem of predicting the dynamics of consumption of a single energy carrying natural resource."

"Flaw" genetic operator, "Mutations," and "Artificial Death." The sections on "Spatial Topology" and "Digital 'Neural Networks'—Natural AI" are little tirades against examples of what I consider to be unnatural transfers of forms from the natural world to the digital medium.

5   The Computational Medium

The computational medium of the digital computer is an informational universe of boolean logic, not a material one. Digital organisms live in the memory of the computer and are powered by the activity of the central processing unit (CPU). Whether the hardware of the CPU and memory is built of silicon chips, vacuum tubes, magnetic cores, or mechanical switches is irrelevant to the digital organism. Digital organisms should be able to take on the same form in any computational hardware and in this sense are "portable" across hardware.

Digital organisms might as well live in a different universe from us, because they are not subject to the same laws of physics and chemistry. They are subject to the "physics and chemistry" of the rules governing the manipulation of bits and bytes within the computer's memory and CPU. They never "see" the actual material from which the computer is constructed, they see only the logic and rules of the CPU and the operating system. These rules are the only "natural laws" that govern their behavior. They are not influenced by the natural laws that govern the material universe (e.g., the laws of thermodynamics).

A typical instantiation of this type involves the introduction of a self-replicating machine language program into the RAM memory of a computer subject to random errors such as bit flips in the memory or occasionally inaccurate calculations [3,7,20,52,70]. This generates the basic conditions for evolution by natural selection as outlined by Darwin [14]: self-replication in a finite environment with heritable genetic variation.

In this instantiation, the self-replicating machine language program is thought of as the individual "digital organism" or "creature." The RAM memory provides the physical space that the creatures occupy. The CPU provides the source of energy. The memory consists of a large array of bits, generally grouped into 8-bit bytes and 16- or 32-bit words. Information is stored in these arrays as voltage patterns that we usually symbolize as patterns of ones and zeros.

The "body" of a digital organism is the information pattern in memory that constitutes its machine language program. This information pattern is data, but when it is passed to the CPU, it is interpreted as a series of executable instructions. These instructions are arranged in such a way that the data of the body will be copied to another location of memory. The informational patterns stored in the memory are altered only through the activity of the CPU. It is for this reason that the CPU is thought of as the analog of the energy source. Without the activity of the CPU, the memory would be static, with no changes in the informational patterns stored there.

The logical operations embodied in the instruction set of the CPU constitute a large part of the definition of the "physics and chemistry" of the digital universe. The topology of the computer's memory (discussed later) is also a significant component of the digital physics. The final component of the digital physics is the operating system, a software program running on the computer, which embodies rules for the allocation of resources such as memory space and CPU time to the various processes running on the computer.

The instruction set of the CPU, the memory, and the operating system together define the complete "physics and chemistry" of the universe inhabited by the digital organism. They constitute the physical environment within which digital organisms will evolve. Evolving digital organisms will compete for access to the limited resources of memory space and CPU time, and evolution will generate adaptations for the more agile access to and the more efficient use of these resources.

6   The Genetic Language

The simplest possible instantiation of a digital organism is a machine language program that codes for self-replication. In this case, the bit pattern that makes up the program is the body of the organism and at the same time its complete genetic material. Therefore, the machine language defined by the CPU constitutes the genetic language of the digital organism.

It is worth noting at this point that the organic organism most comparable to this kind of digital organism is the hypothetical, and now extinct, RNA organism [6]. These were presumably nothing more than RNA molecules capable of catalyzing their own replication. What the supposed RNA organisms have in common with the simple digital organism is that a single molecule constitutes the body and the genetic information, and effects the replication. In the digital organism, a single-bit pattern performs all the same functions.

The use of machine code as a genetic system raises the problem of brittleness. It has generally been assumed by computer scientists that machine language programs cannot be evolved because random alterations such as bit flips and recombinations will always produce inviable programs. It has been suggested [23] that overcoming this brittleness and "Discovering how to make such self-replicating patterns more robust so that they evolve to increasingly more complex states is probably the central problem in the study of artificial life."

The assumption that machine languages are too brittle to evolve is probably true, as a consequence of the fact that machine languages have not previously been designed to survive random alterations. However, recent experiments have shown that brittleness can be overcome by addressing the principal causes and without fundamentally changing the structure of machine languages [70,77].

The first requirement for evolvability is graceful error handling. When code is being randomly altered, every possible meaningless or erroneous condition is likely to occur. The CPU should be designed to handle these conditions without crashing the system. The simplest solution is for the CPU to perform no operation when it meets these conditions, perhaps setting an error flag, and to proceed to the next instruction.

Due to random alterations of the bit patterns, all possible bit patterns are likely to occur. Therefore, a good design is for all possible bit patterns to be interpretable as meaningful instructions by the CPU. For example, in the Tierra system [70–73,76,77], a five-bit instruction set was chosen, in which all 32 five-bit patterns represent good machine instructions.

This approach (all bit patterns meaningful) also could imply a lack of syntax, in which each instruction stands alone, and need not occur in the company of other instructions. To the extent that the language includes syntax, where instructions must precede or follow one another in certain orders, random alterations are likely to destroy meaningful syntax, thereby making the language more brittle. A certain amount of this kind of brittleness can be tolerated as long as syntax errors are also handled gracefully.

During the design of the first evolvable machine language [70], a standard machine language (Intel 80X86) was compared to the genetic language of organic life, to attempt to understand the difference between the two languages that might contribute to the brittleness of the former and the robustness of the latter. One of the outstanding differences noted was in the number of basic informational objects contained in the two.

The organic genetic language is written with an alphabet consisting of four different nucleotides. Groups of three nucleotides form 64 "words" (codons), which are translated into 20 amino acids by the molecular machinery of the cell. The machine language is written with sequences of two voltages (bits), which we conceptually represent as ones and zeros. The number of bits that form a "word" (machine instruction) varies between machine architectures and in some architectures is not constant. However, the number required generally ranges from 16 to 32. This means that there are from tens of thousands to billions of machine instruction bit patterns, which are translated into operations performed by the CPU.

The thousands or billions of bit patterns that code for machine instructions contrasts with the 64 nucleotide patterns that code for amino acids. The 64 nucleotide patterns are degenerate, in that they code for only 20 amino acids. Similarly, the machine codes are degenerate, in that there are at most hundreds rather than thousands or billions of machine operations.

The machine codes exhibit a massive degeneracy (with respect to actual operations) as a result of the inclusion of data into the bit patterns coding for the operations. For example, the add operation will take two operands and produce as a result the sum of the two operands. While there may be only a single add operation, the instruction may come in several forms depending on where the values of the two operands come from, and where the resultant sum will be placed. Some forms of the add instruction allow the value(s) of the operand(s) to be specified in the bit pattern of the machine code.

The inclusion of numeric operands in the machine code is the primary cause of the huge degeneracy. If numeric operands are not allowed, the number of bit patterns required to specify the complete set of operations collapses to at most a few hundred.

While there is no empirical data to support it, it is suspected that the huge degeneracy of most machine languages may be a source of brittleness. The logic of this argument is that mutation causes random swapping among the fundamental informational objects, codons in the organic language, and machine instructions in the digital language. It seems more likely that meaningful results will be produced when one swaps among 64 objects than when one swaps among billions of objects.

The size of the machine instruction set can be made comparable to the number of codons simply by eliminating numeric operands embedded in the machine code. However, this change creates some new problems. Computer programs generally function by executing instructions located sequentially in memory. However, in order to loop or branch, they use instructions such as "jump" to cause execution to jump to some other part of the program. Because the locations of these jumps are usually fixed, the jump instruction will generally have the target address included as an operand embedded in the machine code.

By eliminating operands from the machine code, we generate the need for a new mechanism of addressing for jumps. To resolve this problem, an idea can be borrowed from molecular biology. We can ask the question, How do biological molecules address one another? Molecules do not specify the coordinates of the other molecules they interact with. Rather, they present shapes on their surfaces that are complementary to the shapes on the surfaces of the target molecules. The concept of complementarity in addressing can be introduced to machine languages by allowing the jump instruction to be followed by some bit pattern and by having execution jump to the nearest occurrence of the complementary bit pattern.

In the development of the Tierran language, two changes were introduced to the machine language to reduce brittleness: elimination of numeric operands from the code and the use of complementary patterns to control addressing. The resulting language proved to be evolvable [70]. As a result, nothing was learned about evolvability, because only one language was tested, and it evolved. It is not known what features of the language enhance its evolvability, which detract, and which do not affect evolvability.

Subsequently, three additional languages were tested, and the four languages were found to vary in their patterns and degree of evolvability [77]. However, it is still not known how the features of the language affect its evolvability.

7 Genetic Operators

In order for evolution to occur, there must be some genetic variation among the offspring. In organic life, this is insured by natural imperfections in the replication of the informational molecules. However, one way in which digital "chemistry" differs from organic chemistry is in the degree of perfection of its operations. In the computer, the genetic code can be reliably replicated without errors to such a degree that we must artificially introduce errors or other sources of genetic variation in order to induce evolution.

7.1 Mutations

In organic life, the simplest genetic change is a "point mutation," in which a single nucleic acid in the genetic code is replaced by one of the three other nucleic acids. This can cause an amino acid substitution in the protein coded by the gene. The nucleic acid replacement can be caused by an error in the replication of the DNA molecule, or it can be caused by the effects of radiation or mutagenic chemicals.

In the digital medium, a comparably simple genetic change can result from a bit flip in the memory, where a one is replaced by a zero, or a zero is replaced by a one. These bit flips can be introduced in a variety of ways that are analogous to the various natural causes of mutation. In any case, the bit flips must be introduced at a low to moderate frequency, because high frequencies of mutation prevent the replication of genetic information and lead to the death of the system [73].

Bit flips may be introduced at random anywhere in memory, where they may or may not hit memory actually occupied by digital organisms. This could be thought of as analogous to cosmic rays falling at random and disturbing molecules that may or may not be biological in nature. Bit flips may also be introduced when information is copied in the memory, which could be analogous to the replication errors of DNA. Alternatively, bit flips could be introduced in memory as it is accessed, either as data or executable code. This could be thought of as damage due to "wear and tear."

7.2 Flaws

Alterations of genetic information are not the only source of noise in the system. In organic life, enzymes have evolved to increase the probability of chemical reactions that increase the fitness of the organism. However, the metabolic system is not perfect. Undesired chemical reactions do occur, and desired reactions sometimes produce undesired by-products. The result is the generation of molecular species that can "gum up the works," having unexpected consequences, generally lowering the fitness of the organism but possibly raising it.

In the digital system, an analogue of metabolic (nongenetic) errors can be introduced by causing the computations carried out by the CPU to be probabilistic, producing erroneous results at some low frequency. For example, any time a sum or difference is calculated, the result could be off by some small value (e.g., plus or minus one). Or, if all bits are shifted one position to the left or right, an appropriate error would be to shift by two positions or not at all. When information is transferred from one location to another, either in the RAM memory or the CPU registers, it could occasionally be transferred from the wrong location, or to the wrong location. While flaws do not directly cause genetic changes, they can cause a cascade of events that result in the production of an offspring that is genetically different from the parent.

7.3   Recombination—Sex
7.3.1   The Nature of Sex

In organic life, there are a wide variety of mechanisms by which offspring are produced that contain genetic material from more than one parent. This is the sexual process. Recombination mechanisms range from very primitive and haphazard to elaborately orchestrated.

At the primitive extreme, we find certain species of bacteria, in which upon death the cell membrane breaks open, releasing the DNA into the surrounding medium. Fragments of this dead DNA are absorbed across the membranes of other bacteria of the same species and incorporated into their genome [58]. This is a one-way transferral of genetic material, rather than a reciprocal exchange.

At the complex extreme, we find the conventional sexual system of most of the higher animals, in which each individual contains two copies of the entire genome. At reproduction, each of two parents contributes one complete copy of the genome (half of their genetic material) to the offspring. This means that each offspring receives one half of its genetic material from each of two parents, and each parent contributes one half of its genetic material to each offspring. Very elaborate behavioral and molecular mechanisms are required to orchestrate this joint contribution of genetic material to the offspring.

The preponderance of sex remains an enigma to evolutionary theory [5,26,30,31,54, 60,85,95]. Careful analysis has failed to show any benefits from sex at the level of the individual organism that outweigh the high costs (e.g., passing on only half of the genome). The only obvious benefit of sex is that it provides diversity among the offspring, allowing the species to adapt more readily to a changing environment. However, quantitative analysis has shown that in order for sex to be favored by selection at the individual level, it is not enough for the environment to change unpredictably; the environment must actually change capriciously [13,56]. That is, whatever genotype has the highest fitness in this generation must have the lowest fitness in the next generation, or at least a trend in this direction, a negative heritability of fitness.

One theory to explain the perpetuation of sex (based on the Red Queen hypothesis; see later) states that the environment is in fact capricious, due to the importance of biotic factors in determining selective forces. That is, sex is favored because it is necessary to maintain adaptation in the face of evolving species in the environment (e.g., predators/parasites, prey/hosts, competitors) who themselves are sexual and can undergo rapid evolutionary change. Predators and parasites will tend to evolve so as to favor attacking whatever genotype of their prey/host is the most common. The genotype that is most successful at present is targeted for future attack. This dynamic makes the environment capricious in the sense discussed earlier.

There are fundamental differences in the nature of the evolutionary process between asexual and sexual organisms. The evolving entity in an asexual species is a branching lineage of genetic individuals that retain their genetic identity through the generations. In a sexual species, the evolving entity is a collective "gene pool," and genetic individuals are absolutely ephemeral, lasting only one generation.

Recall the discussion of "genotype space" earlier in the section titled "Evolution in Sequence Space" and imagine that we could represent genotype space in two dimensions and that we allow a third dimension to represent time. Visualize now an evolving asexual organism. Starting with a single individual, it would occupy a single point in the genotype space at time zero. When it reproduces, if there is no mutation, its offspring would occupy the same point in genotype space at a later time. Thus, the lineage of the asexual organism would appear as a line moving forward in time. If mutations occur, they cause the offspring to occupy new locations in genotype space, forming branches in the lineage.

Through time, the evolving asexual lineage would form a tree-like structure in the genotype space–time coordinates. However, every individual branch of the tree will evolve independently of all the others. While there may be ecological interactions between genetically different individuals, there is no exchange of genetic material between them. From a genetic point of view, each branch of the tree is on its own; it must adapt or fail to adapt based on its own genetic resources.

In order to visualize an evolving sexual population, we must start with a population of individuals, each of which will be genetically unique. Thus, they will appear as a scatter of points in the genotype space plane at time zero. In the next generation, all of the original genotypes will be dead; however, a completely new set of genotypes will have been formed from new combinations of pieces of the genomes from the previous generation. No individual genotypes will survive from one generation to the next; thus, over time, the evolving sexual population appears as a diffuse cloud of disconnected points with no lines formed from persistent genotypes.

The most important distinction between the evolving asexual and sexual populations is that the asexual individuals are genetically isolated and must adapt or not based on the limited genetic resources of the individual, while sexual organisms by comparison draw on the genetic resources of the entire population, due to the flow of genes resulting from sexual matings. The entity that evolves in an asexual population is an isolated but branching lineage of genetic individuals. In a sexual population, the individual is ephemeral, and the entity that evolves is a "gene pool."

Due to the genetic cohesion of a sexual population and the ephemeral nature of its individuals, the evolving sexual entity exists at a higher level of organization than the individual organism. The evolving entity, a gene pool, is supraorganismal. It samples the environment through many individuals simultaneously and pools their genetic resources in finding adaptive genetic combinations.

The definition of the biological species is based on a concept of sexual reproduction: a group of individuals capable of interbreeding freely under natural conditions. Species concepts simply do not apply well to asexual species. In order for synthetic life to be useful for the study of the properties of species and the speciation process, it must include an organized sexual process, such that the evolving entity is a gene pool.

7.3.2 Implementation of Digital Sex

The previous discussions of the nature of sexuality are intended to make the point that it is an important process in evolutionary biology and should be included in synthetic implementations of life. The sexual process is implemented with the "crossover" genetic operator in the field of genetic algorithms, where it has been considered to be the most important genetic operator [34].

The crossover operator has also been implemented in synthetic life systems [75,90]. However, it has been implemented in the spirit of a genetic algorithm, rather than in the spirit of synthetic life. This is because in these implementations, the crossover process is not under the control of the organism but rather is forced on the individual. In addition, these implementations are based on haploid sex not diploid sex (see later). In order to address many of the interesting evolutionary questions surrounding sexuality, the sexual process must be optional, at least through evolution, and should be diploid.

Primitive sexual processes have appeared spontaneously in the Tierra synthetic life system [70]. However, there apparently has still not been an implementation of natural organized sexuality in a synthetic system. I would like to discuss my conception of how this could be implemented with particular reference to the Tierra system.

It would seem that the simplest way of implementing an organized sexuality that would give rise to an evolving gene pool would involve the use of "ploidy." Ploidy refers to a system in which each individual contains multiple copies of the complete genome. In the most familiar sexual system (that used by humans), the gametes (egg and sperm) contain one copy of the genome (they are haploid), and all other stages of the life cycle contain two copies (**they are diploid**), which derive from the union of a sperm and egg.

In a digital organism whose body consists of a sequence of machine code, it would be easy to duplicate the sequence and include two copies within the cell. However, some problems can arise with this configuration, if the two copies of the genome occupy adjacent blocks of memory. Which copy of the genome will be executed? When the organism contributes one of its two copies of the genome to an offspring, which of the two copies will be contributed, and how can the mother cell recognize where one complete genome begins and ends?

A solution to these problems that has been partially implemented in the Tierra system is to have the two copies of the genome intertwined, rather than in adjacent blocks of memory. This can be done by letting alternate bytes represent one genome and the skipped bytes the other genome. Tierran instructions utilize only five bits and so are mapped to successive bytes in memory. If we instead place successive instructions in successive 16-bit words, one copy of the genome can occupy the high-order bytes, and the other genome can occupy the low-order bytes of the words.

This arrangement facilitates relatively simple solutions to the problems mentioned earlier. Execution of the genome takes place by having the instruction pointer execute alternate bytes. In a diploid organism, there are two tracks. The track to initially be executed can be chosen at random. At a certain frequency or under certain circumstances, the executing track can be switched so that both copies of the genome will be expressed.

Having two parallel tracks helps to resolve the problem of recognizing where one copy of the genome ends and the other begins, because both genomes usually begin and end together. Copying of the genome, like execution, can occur along one track. Optionally, tracks could be switched during the copy process to introduce an effect similar to crossing over in meiosis. In addition, the use of both tracks can be optional, so that haploid and diploid organisms can coexist in the same soup, and evolution can favor either form, according to selective pressures.

7.4 Transposons

The explosion of diversity in the Cambrian occurred in the lineage of the eukaryotes; the prokaryotes did not participate. One of the most striking genetic differences between eukaryotes and prokaryotes is that most of the genome of prokaryotes is translated into proteins, while most of the genome of eukaryotes is not. It has been estimated that typically 98% of the DNA in eukaryotes is neither translated into proteins nor involved in gene regulation, that it is simply "junk" DNA [92]. It has been suggested that much of this junk code is the result of the self-replication of pieces of DNA within rather than between cells [21,66].

Mobile genetic elements, transposons, have this intragenome self-replicating property. It has been estimated that 80% of spontaneous mutations are caused by transposons [12,29]. Repeated sequences, resulting from the activity of mobile elements, range from dozens to millions in numbers of copies and from hundreds to tens of thousands of base pairs in length. They vary widely in dispersion patterns from clumped to sparse [40].

Larger transposons carry one or more genes in addition to those necessary for transposition. Transposons may grow to include more genes; one mechanism involves the placement of two transposons into close proximity so that they act as a single, large transposon incorporating the intervening code. In many cases transposons carry a sequence that acts as a promoter, altering the regulation of genes at the site of insertion [89].

Transposons may produce gene products and often are involved in gene regulation [17]. However, they may have no effect on the external phenotype of the individual [21]. Therefore, they evolve through another paradigm of selection, one that does not involve an external phenotype. They are seen as a mechanism for the selfish spread of DNA, which may become inactive junk after mutation [66].

DNA of transposon origin can be recognized by its palindrome endings flanked by short, nonreversed repeated sequences resulting from insertion after staggered cuts. In *Drosophila melanogaster* approximately 5–10% of its total DNA is composed of sequences bearing these signs. There are many families of such repeated elements, each family possessing a distinctive nucleotide sequence and distributed in many sites throughout the genome. One well-known repeated sequence occurring in humans is found to have as many as a half million copies in each haploid genome [86].

Elaborate mechanisms have evolved to edit out junk sequences inserted into critical regions. An indication of the magnitude of the task comes from the recent cloning of the gene for cystic fibrosis, where it was discovered that the gene consists of 250,000 base pairs, only 4,440 of which code for protein; the remainder are edited out of the messenger RNA before translation [45,55,78,79].

It appears that many repeated sequences in genomes may have originated as transposons favored by selection at the level of the gene, favoring genes that selfishly replicated themselves within the genome. However, some transposons may have coevolved with their host genome as a result of selection at the organismal or populational level, favoring transposons that introduce useful variation through gene rearrangement. It has been stated that "transposable elements can induce mutations that result in complex and intricately regulated changes in a single step" and that they are "a highly evolved macromutational mechanism" [89].

In this manner, "smart" genetic operators may have evolved, through the interaction of selection acting at two or more hierarchical levels. (It appears that some transposons have followed another evolutionary route, developing intercellular mobility and becoming viruses [40].) It is likely that transposons today represent the full continuum from purely parasitic "selfish DNA" and viruses to highly coevolved genetic operators and gene regulators. The possession of smart genetic operators may have contributed to the explosive diversification of eukaryotes by providing them with the capacity for natural genetic engineering.

In designing self-replicating digital organisms, it would be worthwhile to introduce such genetic parasites in order to facilitate the shuffling of the code that they bring about. Also, the excess code generated by this mechanism provides a large store of relatively neutral codes that can randomly explore new configurations through the genetic operations of mutation and recombination. When these new configurations confer functionality, they may become selected for.

8 Artificial Death

Death must play a role in any system that exhibits the process of evolution. Evolution involves a continuing iteration of selection, which implies differential *death*. In natural life, death occurs as a result of accident, predation, starvation, disease, or, if these fail to kill the organism, it will eventually die from senescence resulting from an accumulation of wear and tear at every level of the organism including the molecular.

In normal computers, processes are "born" when they are initiated by the user and "die" when they complete their task and halt. A process whose goal is to repeatedly replicate itself is essentially an endless loop and would not spontaneously terminate.

Due to the perfection of normal computer systems, we cannot count on "wear and tear" to eventually cause a process to terminate.

In synthetic life systems implemented in computers, death is not likely to be a process that would occur spontaneously, and it must generally be introduced artificially by the designer. Everyone who has set up such a system has found their own unique solutions. Todd [93] recently discussed this problem in general terms.

In the Tierra system [70], death is handled by a "reaper" function of the operating system. The reaper uses a linear queue. When creatures are born, they enter the bottom of the queue. When memory is full, the reaper frees memory to make space for new creatures by killing off the top of the queue. However, each time an individual generates an error condition, it moves up the reaper queue one position.

An interesting variation on this was introduced by Barton-Davis [3], who eliminated the reaper queue. In its place, he caused the "flaw rate" (see earlier section on Flaws) to increase with the age of the individual in mimicry of wear and tear. When the flaw rate reached 100%, the individual was killed. Skipper [80] provided a "suicide" instruction, which, if executed, would cause a process to terminate (die). The evolutionary objective then became to have a suicide instruction in your genome that you do not execute yourself, but which you try to get other individuals to execute. Litherland [50] introduced death by local crowding. Davidge [16] caused processes to die when they contained certain values in their registers. Gray [96] allowed each process six attempts at reproduction, after which they would die.

9   Operating System

Much of the "physics and chemistry" of the digital universe is determined by the specifications of the operations performed by the instruction set of the CPU. However, the operating system also determines a significant part of the physical context. The operating system manages the allocation of critical resources such as memory space and CPU cycles.

Digital organisms are processes that spawn processes. As processes are born, the operating system will allocate memory and CPU cycles to them, and when they die, the operating system will return the resources they had utilized to the pool of free resources. In synthetic life systems, the operating system may also play a role in managing death, mutations, and flaws.

The management of resources by the operating system is controlled by algorithms. From the point of view of the digital organisms, these take the form of a set of logical rules like those embodied in the logic of the instruction set. In this way, the operating system is a defining part of the physics and chemistry of the digital universe. Evolution will explore the possibilities inherent in these rules, finding ways to more efficiently gain access to and exploit the resources managed by the operating system.

10   Spatial Topology

Digital organisms live in the memory space of computers, predominantly in the RAM memory, although they could also live on disks or any other storage device, or even within networks to the extent that the networks themselves can store information. In essence, digital organisms live in the space that has been referred to as "cyberspace." It is worthwhile reflecting on the topology of this space as it is a radically different space from the one we live in.

A typical UNIX workstation, or Macintosh computer includes a RAM memory that can contain some megabytes of data. This is "flat" memory, meaning that it is essentially unstructured. Any location in memory can be accessed through its numeric address.

Thus, adjacent locations in memory are accessed through successive integer values. This addressing convention causes us to think of the memory as a linear space or a one-dimensional space.

However, this apparent one-dimensionality of the RAM memory is something of an illusion generated by the addressing scheme. A better way of understanding the topology of the memory comes from asking, "What is the distance between two locations in memory?" In fact, the distance cannot be measured in linear units. The most appropriate unit is the time that it takes to move information between the two points.

Information contained in the RAM memory cannot move directly from point to point. Instead, the information is transferred from the RAM to a register in the CPU and then from the CPU back to the new location in RAM. Thus, the distance between two locations in RAM is just the time that it takes to move from the RAM to the CPU plus the time that it takes to move from the CPU to the RAM. Because all points in the RAM are equidistant from the CPU, the distance between any pair of locations in the RAM is the same, regardless of how far apart they may appear based on their numeric addresses.

A space in which all pairs of points are equidistant is clearly not a Euclidean space. That said, we must recognize, however, that there are a variety of ways in which memory is normally addressed that give it the appearance, at least locally, of being one-dimensional. When code is executed by the CPU, the instruction pointer generally increments sequentially through memory, for short distances, before jumping to some other piece of code. For those sections of code where instructions are sequential, the memory is effectively one-dimensional. In addition, searches of memory are often sequentially organized (e.g., the search for complementary templates in Tierra). This again makes the memory effectively one-dimensional within the search radius. Yet even under these circumstances, the memory is not globally one-dimensional. Rather, it consists of many small, one-dimensional pieces, each of which has no meaningful spatial relationship to the others.

Because we live in a three-dimensional Euclidean space, we tend to impose our familiar concepts of spatial topology onto the computer memory. This leads first to the erroneous perception that memory is a one-dimensional Euclidean space, and, second, it often leads to the conclusion that the digital world could be enriched by increasing the dimensionality of the Euclidean memory space.

Many of the serious efforts to extend the Tierra model have included as a central feature the creation of a two-dimensional space for the creatures to inhabit [3,15,16,52,80]. The logic behind the motivation derives from contemplation of the extent to which the dimensionality of the space we live in permits the richness of pattern and process that we observe in nature. Certainly, if our universe were reduced from three to two dimensions, it would eliminate the possibility of most of the complexity that we observe. Imagine, for example, the limitations that two-dimensionality would place on the design of neural networks (if "wires" could not cross). If we were to reduce further the dimensionality of our universe to just one dimension, it would probably completely preclude the possibility of the existence of life.

It follows from these thoughts that restricting digital life to a presumably one-dimensional memory space places a tragic limitation on the richness that might evolve. Clearly, it would be liberating to move digital organisms into a two- or three-dimensional space. The flaw in all of this logic derives from the erroneous supposition that computer memory is a Euclidean space.

To think of memory as Euclidean is to fail to understand its natural topology and is an example of one of the greatest pitfalls in the enterprise of synthetic biology: to transfer a concept from organic life to synthetic life in a way that is "unnatural" for the artificial medium. The fundamental principal of the approach I am advocating is *to respect the nature of the medium into which life is being inoculated, and to find the natural form of life in that medium,* without inappropriately trying to make it like organic life.

The desire to increase the richness of memory topology is commendable; however, this can be achieved without forcing the memory into an unnatural Euclidean topology. Let us reflect a little more on the structure of cyberspace. Thus far, we have only considered the topology of flat memory. Let us consider segmented memory such as is found with the notorious Intel 80X86 design. With this design, you may treat any arbitrarily chosen block of 64K bytes as flat and all pairs of locations within that block are equidistant. However, once the block is chosen, all memory outside of that block is about twice as far away.

Cache memory is designed to be accessed more rapidly than RAM memory; thus, pairs of points within cache memory are closer than pairs of points within RAM memory. The distance between a point in cache and a point in RAM would be an intermediate distance. The access time to memory on disks is much greater than for RAM memory; thus, the distance between points on disk is very great, and the distance between RAM and disk is again intermediate (but still very great). CPU registers represent a small amount of memory locations between which data can move very rapidly; thus, these registers can be considered to be very close together.

For networked computer systems, information can move between the memories of the computers on the net, and the distances between these memories is again the transfer time. If the CPU, cache, RAM, and disk memories of a network of computers are all considered together, they present a very complex memory topology. Similar considerations apply to massively parallel computers that have memories connected in a variety of topologies. Utilizing this complexity moves us in the direction of what has been intended by creating Euclidean memories for digital organisms but does so while fully respecting the natural topology of computer memories.

11   Ecological Context

11.1   The Living Environment

Some rain forests in the Amazon region occur on white-sand soils. In these locations, the physical environment consists of clean white sand, air, falling water, and sunlight. Embedded within this relatively simple physical context, we find one of the most complex ecosystems on earth, containing hundreds of thousands of species. These species do not represent hundreds of thousands of adaptations to the physical environment. Most of the adaptations of these species are to the other living organisms. The forest creates its own environment.

Life is an auto-catalytic process that builds on itself. Ecological communities are complex webs of species, each living off of others and being lived off of by others. The system is self-constructing, self-perpetuating, and feeds on itself. Living organisms interface with the non-living physical environment, exchanging materials with it, such as oxygen, carbon dioxide, nitrogen, and various minerals. However, in the richest ecosystems, the living components of the environment predominate over the physical components.

With living organisms constituting the predominant features of the environment, the evolutionary process is primarily concerned with adaptation to the living environment. Thus, ecological interactions are an important driving force for evolution. Species evolve adaptations to exploit other species (to eat them, to parasitize them, to climb on them, to nest on them, to catch a ride on them, etc.) and to defend against such exploitation where it creates a burden.

This situation creates an interesting dynamic. Evolution is predominantly concerned with creating and maintaining adaptations to living organisms that are themselves evolv-

194

ing. This generates evolutionary races among groups of species that interact ecologically. These races can catalyze the evolution of upwardly spiraling complexity as each species evolves to overcome the adaptations of the others. Imagine, for example, a predator and prey, each evolving to increase its speed and agility, in capturing prey, or in evading capture. This coupled evolutionary race can lead to increasingly complex nervous systems in the evolving predator and prey species.

This mutual evolutionary dynamic is related to the Red Queen hypothesis [94], named after the Red Queen from Alice in Wonderland. This hypothesis suggests that in the face of a changing environment, organisms must evolve as fast as they can in order to simply maintain their current state of adaptation. "In order to get anywhere you must run twice as fast as that" [11].

If organisms only had to adapt to the nonliving environment, the race would not be so urgent. Species would only need to evolve as fast as the relatively gradual changes in the geology and climate. However, given that the species that comprise the environment are themselves evolving, the race becomes rather hectic. The pace is set by the maximal rate that species may change through evolution, and it becomes very difficult to actually get ahead. A maximal rate of evolution is required just to keep from falling behind.

What all of this discussion points to is the importance of embedding evolving synthetic organisms into a context in which they may interact with other evolving organisms. A counter example is the standard implementations of genetic algorithms in which the evolving entities interact only with the fitness function and never "see" the other entities in the population. Many interesting behavioral, ecological, and evolutionary phenomena can only emerge from interactions among the evolving entities.

11.2 Diversity

Major temporal and spatial patterns of organic diversity on earth remain largely unexplained, although there is no lack of theories. Diversity theories suggest fundamental ecological and evolutionary principles that may apply to synthetic life. In general, these theories relate to synthetic life in two ways: (a) They suggest factors that may be critical to the auto-catalytic increase of diversity and complexity in an evolving system. It may be necessary then to introduce these factors into an artificial system to generate increasing diversity and complexity. (b) Because it will be possible to manipulate the presence, absence, or state of these factors in an artificial system, the artificial system may provide an experimental framework for examining evolutionary and ecological processes that influence diversity.

The Gaussian principle of competitive exclusion states that no two species that occupy the same niche can coexist. The species that is the superior competitor will exclude the inferior competitor. The principle has been experimentally demonstrated in the laboratory and is considered theoretically sound. However, natural communities widely flaunt the principle. In tropical rain forests several hundred species of trees coexist without any dominant species in the community. All species of trees must spread their leaves to collect light and their roots to absorb water and nutrients. Evidently there are not several hundred niches for trees in the same habitat. Somehow the principle of competitive exclusion is circumvented.

There are many theories on how competitive exclusion may be circumvented. One leading theory is that periodic disturbance at the proper level sets back the process of competitive exclusion, allowing more species to coexist [36–38]. There is substantial evidence that moderate levels of disturbance can increase diversity. In a digital community, disturbance might take the form of freeing blocks of memory that had been filled with digital organisms. It would be very easy to experiment with differing frequencies and patch sizes of disturbance.

One theory to explain the great increase in diversity and complexity in the Cambrian explosion [84] states that its evolution was driven by ecological interactions and that it was originally sparked by the appearance of the first organisms that ate other organisms (heterotrophs). As long as all organisms were autotrophs (produce their own food, like plants), there was only room for a few species. In a community with only one trophic level, the most successful competitors would dominate. The process of competitive exclusion would keep diversity low.

However, when the first herbivore (organisms that eat autotrophs) appeared, it would have been selected to prefer the most common species of algae, thereby preventing any species of algae from dominating. This opens the way for more species of algae to coexist. Once the "heterotroph barrier" had been crossed, it would be simple for carnivores to arise, imposing a similar diversifying effect on herbivores. With more species of algae, herbivores may begin to specialize on different species of algae, enhancing diversification in herbivores. The theory states that the process was auto-catalytic and set off an explosion of diversity.

One of the most universal of ecological laws is the species area relationship [51]. It has been demonstrated that in a wide variety of contexts, the number of species occupying an "area" increases with the area. The number of species increases in proportion to the area raised to a power between 0.1 and 0.3. $S = KA^z$, where $0.1 < z < 0.3$. The effect is thought to result from the equilibrium species number being determined by a balance between the arrival (by immigration or speciation) and local extinction of species. The likelihood of extinction is greater in small areas because they support smaller populations, for which a fluctuation to a size of zero is more likely. If this effect holds for digital organisms, it suggests that larger amounts of memory will generate greater diversity.

11.3   Ecological Attractors

While there are no completely independent instances of natural evolution on earth, there are partially independent instances. Where major diversifications have occurred, isolated either by geography or epoch from other similar diversifications, we have the opportunity to observe whether evolution tends to take the same routes or is always quite different. We can compare the marsupial mammals of Australia to the placental mammals of the rest of the world, or the modern mammals to the reptiles of the age of dinosaurs, or the bird fauna of the Galapagos to the bird faunas of less isolated islands.

What we find again and again is an uncanny convergence between these isolated faunas. This suggests that there are fairly strong ecological attractors that evolution will tend to fill, more or less regardless of the developmental and physiological systems that are evolving. In this view, chance and history still play a role in determining what kind of organism fills the array of ecological attractors (reptiles, mammals, birds, etc.), but the attractors themselves may be a property of the system and not as variable. Synthetic systems may also contain fairly well defined ecological forms that may be filled by a wide variety of specific kinds of organisms.

Given their evident importance in moving evolution, it is important to include eco-logical interactions in synthetic instantiations of life. It is encouraging to observe that in the Tierra model, ecological interactions and the corresponding evolutionary races emerged spontaneously. It is possible that any medium into which evolution is inoculated will contain an array of "ecological attractors" into which evolution will easily flow.

12   Cellularity

Cellularity is one of the fundamental properties of organic life and can be recognized in the fossil record as far back as 3.6 billion years. The cell is the original individual, with the cell membrane defining its limits and preserving its chemical integrity. An analog to the cell membrane is probably needed in digital organisms in order to preserve the integrity of the informational structure from being disrupted by the activity of other organisms.

The need for this can be seen in AL models such as cellular automata, where virtual state machines pass through one another [47] or in core wars type simulations where coherent structures that arise demolish one another when they come into contact [67,68]. An analog to the cell membrane that can be used in the core wars type of simulation is memory allocation. An artificial "cell" could be defined by the limits of an allocated block of memory. Free access to the memory within the block could be limited to processes within the block. Processes outside of the block would have limited access, according to the rules of "semipermeability"; for example, they might be allowed to read and execute but not write.

13 Multicellularity

Multicelled digital organisms are parallel processes. By attempting to synthesize multicelled digital organisms, we can simultaneously explore the biological issues surrounding the evolutionary transition from single-celled to multicelled life, and the computational issues surrounding the design of complex parallel software.

13.1 Biological Perspective—Cambrian Explosion

Life appeared on earth somewhere between three and four billion years ago. While the origin of life is generally recognized as an event of the first order, there is another event in the history of life that is less well known but of comparable significance. The origin of biological diversity, and at the same time of complex macroscopic multicellular life, occurred abruptly in the Cambrian explosion 600 million years ago. This event involved a riotous diversification of life-forms. Dozens of phyla appeared suddenly, many existing only fleetingly, as diverse and sometimes bizarre ways of life were explored in a relative ecological void [28,64].

The Cambrian explosion was a time of phenomenal and spontaneous increase in the complexity of living systems. It was the process initiated at this time that led to the evolution of immune systems, nervous systems, physiological systems, developmental systems, complex morphology, and complex ecosystems. To understand the Cambrian explosion is to understand the evolution of complexity. If the history of organic life can be used as a guide, the transition from single-celled to multicelled organisms should be critical in achieving a rich diversity and complexity of synthetic life forms.

13.2 Computational Perspective—Parallel Processes

It has become apparent that the future of high-performance computing lies with massively parallel architectures. There already exist a variety of parallel hardware platforms, but our ability to utilize fully the potential of these machines is constrained by our inability to write software of a sufficient complexity.

There are two fairly distinctive kinds of parallel architecture in use today: SIMD (single-instruction multiple data) and MIMD (multiple-instruction multiple data). In the SIMD architecture, the machine may have thousands of processors, but in each CPU cycle, all of the processors must execute the same instruction, although they may operate on different data. It is relatively easy to write software for this kind of machine, because what is essentially a normal sequential program will be broadcast to all the processors.

In the MIMD architecture, there exists the capability for each of the hundreds or thousands of processors to be executing different code but to have all of that activity coordinated on a common task. However, there does not exist an art for writing this kind of software, at least not on a scale involving more than a few parallel processes. In fact, it seems unlikely that human programmers will ever be capable of actually writing software of such complexity.

13.3   Evolution as a Proven Route

It is generally recognized that evolution is the only process with a proven ability to generate intelligence. It is less well recognized that evolution also has a proven ability to generate parallel software of great complexity. In making life a metaphor for computation, we will think of the genome, the DNA, as the program, and we will think of each cell in the organism as a processor (CPU). A large, multicelled organism like a human contains trillions of cells/processors. The genetic program contains billions of nucleotides/instructions.

In a multicelled organism, cells are differentiated into many cell types such as brain cells, muscle cells, liver cells, kidney cells, etc. The cell types just named are actually general classes of cell types within which there are many subtypes. However, when we specify the ultimate indivisible types, what characterizes a type is the set of genes it expresses. Different cell types express different combinations of genes. In a large organism, there will be a very large number of cells of most types. All cells of the same type express the same genes.

The cells of a single-cell type can be thought of as exhibiting parallelism of the SIMD kind, because they are all running the same "program" by expressing the same genes. Cells of different cell types exhibit MIMD parallelism as they run different codes by expressing different genes. Thus, large multicellular organisms display parallelism on an astronomical scale, combining both SIMD and MIMD parallelism into a beautifully integrated whole. From these considerations, it is evident that evolution has a proven ability to generate massively parallel software embedded in wetware. The computational goal of evolving multicellular digital organisms is to produce such software embedded in hardware.

13.4   Fundamental Definition

In order to conceptualize multicellularity in the context of an artificial medium, we must have a very fundamental definition that is independent of the context of the medium. We generally think of the defining property of multicellularity as being that the cells stick together, forming a physically coherent unit. However, this is a spatial concept based on Euclidean geometry and, therefore, is not relevant to non-Euclidean cyberspace.

While physical coherence might be an adequate criteria for recognizing multicellularity in organic organisms, it is not the property that allows multicellular organisms to become large and complex. There are algae that consist of strands of cells that are stuck together, with each cell being identical to the next. This is a relatively limiting form of multicellularity because there is no differentiation of cell types. It is the specialization of functions resulting from cell differentiation that has allowed multicellular organisms to attain large sizes and great complexity. It is differentiation that has generated the MIMD style of parallelism in organic software.

From an evolutionary perspective, an important characteristic of multicellular organisms is their genetic unity. All the cells of the individual contain the same genetic material as a result of having a common origin from a single egg cell. (Some small genetic differences may arise due to somatic mutations; in some species new individuals arise from a bud of tissue rather than a single cell.) Genetic unity through common origin, and differentiation, are critical qualities of multicellularity that may be transferable to media other than organic chemistry.

Buss [9] provides a provocative discussion of the evolution of multicellularity and explores the conflicts between selection at the levels of cell lines and of individuals. From his discussion, the following idea emerges (although he does not explicitly state this idea, in fact he proposes a sort of inverse of this idea [p. 65]): The transition from single- to multicelled existence involves the extension of the control of gene regulation by the mother cell to successively more generations of daughter cells.

In organic cells, genes are regulated by proteins contained in the cytoplasm. During early embryonic development in animals, an initially very large fertilized egg cell undergoes cell division with no increase in the overall size of the embryo. The large cell is simply partitioned into many smaller cells, and all components of the cytoplasm are of maternal origin. By preventing several generations of daughter cells from producing any cytoplasmic regulatory components, the mother gains control of the course of differentiation and thereby creates the developmental process. In single-celled organisms, by contrast, after each cell division, the daughter cell produces its own cytoplasmic regulatory products and determines its own destiny independent of the mother cell.

Complex digital organisms will be self-replicating algorithms, consisting of many distinct processes dedicated to specific tasks (e.g., locating free memory, mates, or other resources; defense; replicating the code). These processes must be coordinated and regulated, and they may be divided among several cells specialized for specific functions. If the mother cell can influence the regulation of the processes of the daughter, so as to force the daughter cell to specialize in function and express only a portion of its full genetic potentiality, then the essence of multicellularity will be achieved.

13.5 Computational Implementation

The discussion earlier suggests that the critical feature needed to allow the evolution of multicellularity is for a cell to be able to influence the expression of genes by its daughter cell. In the digital context, this means that a cell must be able to influence what code is executed by its daughter cell.

If we assume that in digital organisms, as in organic ones, all cells in an individual contain the same genetic material, then the desired regulatory mechanism can be achieved most simply by allowing the mother cell to affect the context of the CPU of the daughter cell at the time that the cell is "born." Most importantly, the mother cell needs to be able to set the address of the instruction pointer of the daughter cell at birth, which will determine where the daughter cell will begin executing its code. Beyond that, additional influence can be achieved by allowing the mother cell to place values in the registers of the daughter's CPU.

A large digital genome may contain several sections of code that are "closed" in the sense that one section of code will not pass control of execution to another. Thus, if execution begins in one of these sections of code, the other sections will never be expressed. This type of genetic organization, coupled with the ability of the mother cell to determine where the daughter cell begins executing, could provide a mechanism of gene regulation suitable for causing the differentiation of cells in a multicellular digital organism.

Other schemes for the regulation of code expression are also possible. For example, digital computers commonly have three protection states available for the memory: read, write, and execute. If the code of the genome were provided with execute protection, it would provide a means of suppression of the execution of code in the protected region of the genome.

13.6 Digital "Neural Networks"—Natural Artificial Intelligence

One of the greatest challenges in the field of computer science is to produce computer systems that are "intelligent" in some way. This might involve, for example, the creation of a system for the guidance of a robot that is capable of moving freely in a complex environment, seeking, recognizing, and manipulating a variety of objects. It might involve the creation of a system capable of communicating with humans in natural spoken human language, or of translating between human languages.

It has been observed that natural systems with these capabilities are controlled by nervous systems consisting of large numbers of neurons interconnected by axons and dendrites. By borrowing from nature, a great deal of work has gone into setting up "neural networks" in computers [18,32]. In these systems, a collection of simulated "neurons" are created and then connected so that they can pass messages. The learning that takes place is accomplished by adjusting the "weights" of the connections.

Organic neurons are essentially analog devices; thus, when neural networks are implemented on computers, they are digital emulations of analog devices. There is a certain inefficiency involved in emulating an analog device on a digital computer. For this reason, specialized analog hardware has been developed for the more efficient implementation of artificial neural nets [59].

Neural networks, as implemented in computers, either digital or analog, are intentional mimics of organic nervous systems. They are designed to function like natural neural networks in many details. However, natural neural networks represent the solution found by evolution to the problem of creating a control system based on organic chemistry. Evolution works with the physics and chemistry of the medium in which it is embedded.

The solution that evolution found to the problem of communication between organic cells is chemical. Cells communicate by releasing chemicals that bind to and activate receptor molecules on target cells. Working within this medium, evolution created neural nets. Intercellular chemical communication in neural nets is "digital" in the sense that chemical messages are either present or not present (on or off). In this sense, a single chemical message carries only a single bit of information. More detailed information can be derived from the temporal pattern of the messages and also the context of the message. The context can include where on the target cell body the message is applied (which influences its "weight") and what other messages are arriving at the same time, with which the message in question will be integrated.

It is hoped that evolving multicellular digital organisms will become very complex and will contain some kind of control system that fills the functional role of the nervous system. While it seems likely that the digital nervous system would consist of a network of communicating "cells," it seems unlikely that this would bear much resemblance to conventional neural networks.

Compare the mechanism of intercellular communication in organic cells (described earlier), to the mechanisms of interprocess communication in computers. Processes transmit messages in the form of bit patterns, which may be of any length, and so which may contain any amount of information. Information need not be encoded into the temporal pattern of impulse trains. This fundamental difference in communication mechanisms between the digital and the organic mediums must influence the course that evolution will take as it creates information-processing systems in the two mediums.

It seems highly unlikely that evolution in the digital context would produce information processing systems that would use the same forms and mechanisms as natural neural nets (e.g., weighted connections, integration of incoming messages, threshold triggered all or nothing output, thousands of connections per unit). The organic medium is a physical/chemical medium, whereas the digital medium is a logical/informational medium. That observation alone would suggest that the digital medium is better suited to the construction of information-processing systems.

If this is true, then it may be possible to produce digitally based systems that have functionality equivalent to natural neural networks, but which have a much greater simplicity of structure and process. Given evolution's ability to discover the possibilities inherent in a medium, and its complete lack of preconceptions, it would be very interesting to observe what kind of information-processing systems evolution would construct in the digital medium. If evolution is capable of creating network-based information-processing systems, it may provide us with a new paradigm for digital "connectionism" that would be more natural to the digital medium than simulations of natural neural networks.

14   Digital Husbandry

Digital organisms evolving freely by natural selection do no "useful" work. Natural evolution tends to the selfish needs of perpetuating the genes. We cannot expect digital organisms evolving in this way to perform useful work for us, such as guiding robots or interpreting human languages. In order to generate digital organisms that function as useful software, we must guide their evolution through artificial selection, just as humans breed dogs, cattle, and rice. Some experiments have already been done by using artificial selection to guide the evolution of digital organisms for the performance of "useful" tasks [1,88,90]. I envision two approaches to the management of digital evolution: digital husbandry and digital genetic engineering.

Digital husbandry is an analogy to animal husbandry. This technique would be used for the evolution of the most advanced and complex software, with intelligent capabilities. Correspondingly, this technique is the most fanciful. I would begin by allowing multicellular digital organisms to evolve freely by natural selection. Using strictly natural selection, I would attempt to engineer the system to the threshold of the computational analog of the Cambrian explosion and let the diversity and complexity of the digital organisms spontaneously explode.

One of the goals of this exercise would be to allow evolution to find the natural forms of complex parallel digital processes. Our parallel hardware is still too new for human programmers to have found the best way to write parallel software. And it is unlikely that human programmers will ever be capable of writing software of the complexity that the hardware is capable of running. Evolution should be able to show us the way.

It is hoped that this would lead to highly complex digital organisms, which obtain and process information, presumably predominantly about other digital organisms. As the complexity of the evolving system increases, the organisms will process more complex information in more complex ways and take more complex actions in response. These will be information-processing organisms living in an informational environment.

It is hoped that evolution by natural selection alone would lead to digital organisms that, while doing no "useful" work, would nonetheless be highly sophisticated parallel information-processing systems. Once this level of evolution has been achieved, then artificial selection could begin to be applied to enhance those information-processing capabilities that show promise of utility to humans. Selection for different capabilities would lead to many different breeds of digital organisms with different uses. Good examples of this kind of breeding from organic evolution are the many varieties of domestic dogs that were derived by breeding from a single species, and the vegetables cabbage, kale, broccoli, cauliflower, and brussels sprouts that were all produced by selective breeding from a single species of plant.

Digital genetic engineering would normally be used in conjunction with digital husbandry. This consists of writing a piece of application code and inserting it into the genome of an existing digital organism. A technique being used in organic genetic engineering today is to insert genes for useful proteins into goats and to cause them to be expressed in the mammary glands. The goats then secrete large quantities of the protein into the milk, which can be easily removed from the animal. We can think of our complex digital organisms as general purpose animals, like goats, into which application codes can be inserted to add new functionalities, and then bred through artificial selection to enhance or alter the quality of the new functions.

In addition to adding new functionalities to complex digital organisms, digital genetic engineering could be used for achieving extremely high degrees of optimization in relatively small but heavily used pieces of code. In this approach, small pieces of application code could be inserted into the genomes of simple digital organisms. Then the allocation of CPU cycles to those organisms would be based on the performance of the inserted code. In this way, evolution could optimize those codes, and they could be returned to their applications. This technique would be used for codes that are very heavily used, such as compiler constructs or central components of the operating system.

15 Living Together

I'm glad they're not real, because if they were, I would have to feed them and they would be all over the house.

— Isabel Ray

Evolution is an extremely selfish process. Each evolving species does whatever it can to ensure its own survival, with no regard for the well-being of other genetic groups (potentially with the exception of intelligent species). Freely evolving autonomous artificial entities should be seen as potentially dangerous to organic life and should always be confined by some kind of containment facility, at least until their real potential is well understood. At present, evolving digital organisms exist only in virtual computers, specially designed so that their machine codes are more robust than usual to random alterations. Outside of these special virtual machines, digital organisms are merely data and no more dangerous than the data in a database or the text file from a word processor.

Imagine, however, the problems that could arise if evolving digital organisms were to colonize the computers connected to the major networks. They could spread across the network like the infamous internet worm [2,8,82,83]. When we attempted to stop them, they could evolve mechanisms to escape from our attacks. It might conceivably be very difficult to eliminate them. However, this scenario is highly unlikely, because it is probably not possible for digital organisms to evolve on normal computer systems. While the supposition remains untested, normal machine languages are probably too brittle to support digital evolution.

Evolving digital organisms will probably always be confined to special machines, either real or virtual, designed to support the evolutionary process. This does not mean, however, that they are necessarily harmless. Evolution remains a self-interested process, and even the interests of confined digital organisms may conflict with our own. For this reason, it is important to restrict the kinds of peripheral devices that are available to autonomous evolving processes.

This conflict was taken to its extreme in the movie *Terminator 2*. In the imagined future of the movie, computer designers had achieved a very advanced chip design, which had allowed computers to autonomously increase their own intelligence until they became fully conscious. Unfortunately, these intelligent computers formed the "sky-net" of the United States military. When the humans realized that the computers had become intelligent, they decided to turn them off. The computers viewed this as a threat and defended themselves by using one of their peripheral devices: nuclear weapons.

Relationships between species, however, can be harmonious. We presently share the planet with millions of freely evolving species, and they are not threatening us with destruction. On the contrary, we threaten them. In spite of the mindless and massive destruction of life being caused by human activity, the general pattern in living communities is one of a network of interdependencies.

More to the point, there are many species with which humans live in close relationships and whose evolution we manage. These are the domesticated plants and animals that form the basis of our agriculture (cattle, rice), and who serve us as companions (dogs, cats, house plants). It is likely that our relationship with digital organisms will develop along the same two lines.

There will likely be carefully bred digital organisms developed by artificial selection and genetic engineering that perform intelligent data-processing tasks. These would subsequently be "neutered" so that they cannot replicate, and the eunuchs would be put to work in environments free from genetic operators. We are also likely to see freely evolving and/or partially bred digital ecosystems contained in the equivalent of digital aquariums (without dangerous peripherals) for our companionship and aesthetic enjoyment.

While this paper has focused on digital organisms, it is hoped that the discussions are taken in the more general context of the possibilities of any synthetic forms of life. The issues of living together become more critical for synthetic life forms implemented in hardware or wetware. Because these organisms would share the same physical space that we occupy and possibly consume some of the same material resources, the potential for conflict is much higher than for digital organisms.

At the present, there are no self-replicating artificial organisms implemented in either hardware or wetware (with the exception of some simple organic molecules with evidently small and finite evolutionary potential [25,35,65]). However, there are active attempts to synthesize RNA molecules capable of replication [4,41], and there is much discussion of the future possibility of self-replicating nano-technology and macro-robots. I would strongly urge that as any of these technologies approaches the point where self-replication is possible, the work be moved to specialized containment facilities. The means of containment will have to be handled on a case by case basis, because each new kind of replicating technology will have its own special properties.

There are many in the AL movement who envision a beautiful future in which AL replaces organic life and expands out into the universe [48,49,61–63]. The motives vary from a desire for immortality to a vision of converting virtually all matter in the universe to living matter. It is argued that this transition from organic to metallic-based life is the inevitable and natural next step in evolution.

The naturalness of this step is argued by analogy with the supposed genetic takeovers in which nucleic acids became the genetic material taking over from clays [10], and cultural evolution took over from DNA-based genetic evolution in modern humans. I would point out that whatever nucleic acids took over from, it marked the origin of life more than the passing of a torch. As for the supposed transition from genetic to cultural evolution, the truth is that genetic evolution remains intact and has had cultural evolution layered over it rather than being replaced by it.

The supposed replacement of genetic by cultural evolution remains a vision of a brave new world, which has yet to materialize. Given the ever increasing destruction of nature, and human misery and violence being generated by human culture, I would hesitate to place my trust in the process as the creator of a bright future. I still trust in organic evolution, which created the beauty of the rainforest through billions of years of evolution. I prefer to see artificial evolution confined to the realm of cyberspace, where we can more easily coexist with it without danger, using it to enhance our lives without having to replace ourselves.

As for the expansion of life out into the universe, I am confident that this can be achieved by organic life aided by intelligent, nonreplicating machines. And as for immortality, our unwillingness to accept our own mortality has been a primary fuel for religions through the ages. I find it sad that AL should become an outlet for the same sentiment. I prefer to achieve immortality in the old-fashioned organic evolutionary way, through my children. I hope to die in my patch of Costa Rican rain forest, surrounded by many thousands of wet and squishy species, and leave it all to my daughter. Let them set my body out in the jungle to be recycled into the ecosystem by the scavengers and decomposers. I will live on through the rain forest I preserved, the ongoing life in the ecosystem into which my material self is recycled, the memes spawned by my scientific works, and the genes in the daughter that my wife and I created.

16   Challenges

For well over a century, evolution has remained a largely theoretical science. Now new technologies have allowed us to inoculate natural evolution into artificial media, converting evolution into an experimental and applied science, and at the same time opening Pandora's box. This creates a variety of challenges that have been raised or alluded to in the preceding essay, and which will be summarized here.

Respecting the medium. If the objective is to instantiate rather than simulate life, then care must be taken in transferring ideas from natural life to artificial life forms. Preconceptions derived from experience with natural life may be inappropriate in the context of the artificial medium. Getting it right is an art, which likely will take some skill and practice to develop.

However, respecting the medium is only one approach, which I happen to favor. I do not wish to imply that it is the only valid approach. It is too early to know which approach will generate the best results, and I hope that other approaches will be developed as well. I have attempted to articulate clearly this "natural" approach to synthetic life, so that those who choose to follow it may achieve greater consistency in design through a deeper understanding of the method.

Understanding evolvability. Attempts are now underway to inoculate evolution into many artificial systems, with mixed results. Some genetic languages evolve readily, while others do not. We do not yet know why, and this is a fundamental and critically important issue. What are the elements of evolvability? Efforts are needed to address this issue directly. One approach that would likely be rewarding would be to identify systematically features of a class of languages (such as machine languages) and, one by one, vary each feature to determine how evolvability is affected by the state of each feature.

Creating organized sexuality. Organized sexuality is important to the evolutionary process. It is the basis of the species concept and, while remaining something of an enigma in evolutionary theory, clearly is an important facilitator of the evolutionary process. Yet this kind of sexuality still has not been implemented in a natural way in synthetic life systems. It is important to find ways of orchestrating organized sexuality in synthetic systems such as digital organisms, in a way in which it is not mandatory, and in which the organisms must carry out the process through their own actions.

Creating multicellularity. In organic life, the transition from single- to multicelled forms unleashed a phenomenal explosion of diversity and complexity. It would seem then that the transition to multicellular forms could generate analogous diversity and complexity in synthetic systems. In the case of digital organisms, it would also lead to the evolution of parallel processes, which could provide us with new paradigms for the design of parallel software. The creation of multicelled digital organisms remains an important challenge.

Controlling evolution. Humans have been controlling the evolution of other species for tens of thousands of years. This has formed the basis of agriculture through the domestication of plants and animals. The fields of genetic algorithms [27,34] and genetic programming [46] are based on controlling the evolution of computer programs. However, we still have very little experience with controlling the evolution of self-replicating computer programs, which is more difficult. In addition, breeding complex parallel programs is likely to bring new challenges. Developing technologies for managing the evolution of complex software will be critical for harnessing the full potential of evolution for the creation of useful software.

Living together. If we succeed in harnessing the power of evolution to create complex synthetic organisms capable of sophisticated information processing and behavior, we will be faced with the problems of how to live harmoniously with them. Given evolution's selfish nature and capability to improve performance, there exists the potential for a conflict arising through a struggle for dominance between organic and synthetic organisms. It will be a challenge to even agree on what the most desirable outcome should be and harder still to accomplish it. In the end the outcome is likely to emerge from the bottom up through the interactions of the players, rather than being decided through rational deliberations.

Acknowledgments

This work was supported by grants CCR-9204339 and BIR-9300800 from the United States National Science Foundation; a grant from the Digital Equipment Corporation; and by the Santa Fe Institute, Thinking Machines Corp., IBM, and Hughes Aircraft. This work was conducted while the author was at the School of Life & Health Sciences, University of Deleware, Newark, DE, 19716 (E-mail: ray@udel.edu); and the Santa Fe Institute, 1660 Old Pecos Trail, Suite A, Santa Fe, NM 87501 (E-mail: ray@santafe.edu).

References

1. Adami, C. Learning and complexity in genetic auto-adaptive systems. Caltech preprint: MAP-164, One of the Marmal Aid Preprint Series in Theoretical Nuclear Physics, October 1993. E-mail: chris@almach.caltech.edu.

2. Anonymous. (1988, Nov. 11). Worm invasion. *Science*, p. 885.

3. Barton-Davis, P. *Independent implementation of the Tierra system.* Unpublished. E-mail: pauld@cs.washington.edu.

4. Beaudry, A. A., & Joyce, G. F. (1992). Directed evolution of an RNA enzyme. *Science, 257*, 635–641.

5. Bell, G. (1982). *The masterpiece of nature: the evolution and genetics of sexuality.* Berkeley: University of California Press.

6. Benner, S. A., Ellington, A. D., & Tauer, A. (1989). Modern metabolism as a palimpsest of the RNA world. *Proceedings of the National Academy of Sciences of the United States of America (Washington), 86*, 7054–7058.

7. Brooks, R. Unpublished. E-mail: brooks@ai.mit.edu

8. Burstyn, H. L. (1990). RTM and the worm that ate internet. *Harvard Magazine, 92*(5), 23–28.

9. Buss, L. W. (1987). *The evolution of individuality.* Princeton, NJ: Princeton University Press.

10. Cairn-Smith, A. G. (1985). *Seven clues to the origin of life.* Cambridge, UK: Cambridge University Press.

11. Carroll, L. (1865). *Through the looking-glass.* London: MacMillan.

12. Chao, L., Vargas, C., Spear, B. B., & Cox, E. C. (1983). Transposable elements as mutator genes in evolution. *Nature, 303*, 633–635.

13. Charlesworth, B. (1976). Recombination modification in a fluctuating environment. *Genetics, 83*, 181–195.

14. Darwin, C. (1859). *On the origin of species by means of natural selection or the preservation of favored races in the struggle for life.* London: Murray.

15. Davidge, R. (1992). *Processors as organisms.* CSRP 250. School of Cognitive and Computing Sciences, University of Sussex. Presented at the ALife III conference. E-mail: robertd@cogs.susx.ac.uk

16. Davidge, R. (1993). Looping as a means to survival: playing Russian roulette in a harsh environment. In *Self organization and life: from simple rules to global complexity, Proceedings of the Second European Conference on Artificial Life.* E-mail: robertd@cogs.susx.ac.uk

17. Davidson, E. H., & Britten, R. J. (1979). Regulation of gene expression: possible role of repetitive sequences. *Science, 204*, 1052–1059.

18. Dayhoff, J. (1990). *Neural network architectures.* New York: Van Nostrand Reinhold.

19. DeAngelis, D., & Gross, L. (Eds.) (1992). *Individual based models and approaches in ecology.* New York: Chapman and Hill.

20. de Groot, M. *Primordial soup, a Tierra-like system that has the additional ability to spawn self-reproducing organisms from a sterile soup.* Unpublished manuscript. E-mail: marc@kg6kf.ampr.org, marc@toad.com, marc@remarque.berkeley.edu

21. Doolittle, W. F. , & Sapienza, C. (1980). Selfish genes, the phenotype paradigm and genome evolution. *Nature, 284*, 601–603.

22. Eigen, M. (1993). Viral quasispecies. *Scientific American, 269*(1), 32–39.

23. Farmer, J. D., & Belin, A. Artificial life: the coming evolution. In *Proceedings in Celebration of Murray Gell-Man's 60th Birthday.* Cambridge, UK: University Press. Reprinted in *Artificial life II,* pp. 815–840.

24. Feferman, L. (1992). *Simple rules . . . complex behavior* [Video]. Santa Fe, NM: Santa Fe Institute. E-mail: fef@santafe.edu, 0005851689@mcimail.com

25. Feng, Q., Park, T. K., & Rebek, J. (1992). *Science, 254*, 1179–1180.

26. Ghiselin, M. (1974). *The economy of nature and the evolution of sex.* Berkeley, CA: University of California Press.

27. Goldberg, D. E. (1989). *Genetic algorithms in search, optimization, and machine learning.* Reading, MA: Addison-Wesley.

28. Gould, S. J. (1989). *Wonderful life.* New York: W. W. Norton.

29. Green, M. M. (1988). Mobile DNA elements and spontaneous gene mutation. In M. E. Lambert, J. F. McDonald, & I. B. Weinstein (Eds.), *Eukaryotic transposable elements as mutagenic agents* (pp. 41–50). Banbury Report 30, Cold Spring Harbor Laboratory.

30. Halvorson, H. O., & Monroy, A (1985). *The origin and evolution of sex.* New York: Alan R. Liss.

31. Hapgood, F. (1979). *Why males exist: an inquiry into the evolution of sex.* New York: William Morrow.

32. Hertz, J., Krogh, A., & Palmer, R. G. (1991). *Introduction to the theory of neural computation.* Reading, MA: Addison-Wesley.

33. Hogeweg, P. (1989). Mirror beyond mirror: puddles of life. In C. Langton (Ed.), *Artificial life, Santa Fe Institute studies in the sciences of complexity* (Vol. VI, pp. 297–316). Redwood City, CA: Addison-Wesley.

34. Holland, J. H. (1975). *Adaptation in natural and artificial systems: an introductory analysis with applications to biology, control, and artificial intelligence.* Ann Arbor, MI: University of Michigan Press.

35. Hong, J. I., Feng, Q., Rotello, V., & Rebek, J. (1992). Competition, cooperation, and

mutation: improving a synthetic replicator by light irradiation. *Science, 255*, 848–850.

36. Huston, M. (1979). A general hypothesis of species diversity. *American Naturalist, 113*, 81–101.

37. Huston, M. (1992). Biological diversity and human resources. *Impact of Science on Society, 166*, 121–130.

38. Huston, M. (1993). *Biological diversity: the coexistence of species on changing landscapes.* Cambridge University Press.

39. Huston, M., DeAngelis, D., & Post, W. (1988). New computer models unify ecological theory. *Bioscience, 38*(10), 682–691.

40. Jelinek, W. R., & Schmid, C. W. (1982). Repetitive sequences in eukaryotic DNA and their expression. *Annual Review of Biochemistry, 51*, 813–844.

41. Joyce, G. F. (1992, December). Directed molecular evolution. *Scientific American*, 90–97.

42. Kampis, G. (1993). Coevolution in the computer: the necessity and use of distributed code systems. Printed in the ECAL93 Proceedings, Brussels. E-mail: gk@cfnext.physchem.chemie.uni-tuebingen.de

43. Kampis, G. (1993). Life-like computing beyond the machine metaphor. In R. Paton (Ed.), *Computing with biological metaphors.* London: Chapman and Hall. E-mail: gk@cfnext.physchem.chemie.uni-tuebingen.de

44. Kauffman, S. A. (1993). *The origins of order, self-organization and selection in evolution.* Oxford University Press.

45. Kerem, B.-S., Rommens, J. M., Buchanan, J. A., Markiewicz, D., Cox, T. K., Chakravarti, A., Buchwald, M., & Tsui, L.-C. (1989). Identification of the cystic fibrosis gene: genetic analysis. *Science, 245*, 1073–1080.

46. Koza, J. R. (1992). *Genetic programming, on the programming of computers by means of natural selection.* Cambridge, MA: The MIT Press.

47. Langton, C. G. (1986). Studying artificial life with cellular automata. *Physica D, 22*, 120–149.

48. Levy, S. (1992). *Artificial life, the quest for a new creation.* New York: Pantheon Books.

49. Levy, S. (1992, Fall). A-life nightmare. *Whole Earth Review, 76*, 22.

50. Litherland, J. (1993). *Open-ended evolution in a computerised ecosystem.* Unpublished masters thesis, Department of Computer Science, Brunel University. E-mail: david.martland@brunel.ac.uk

51. MacArthur, R. H., & Wilson, E. O. (1967). *The theory of island biogeography.* Princeton, NJ: Princeton University Press.

52. Maley, C. C. (1993). *A model of early evolution in two dimensions.* Unpublished Master's thesis. Zoology, New College, Oxford University, UK. E-mail: cmaley@oxford.ac.uk

53. Manousek, W. (1992). *Spontane Komplexitaetsentstehung—TIERRA, ein Simulator fuer biologische Evolotion.* Diplomarbeit, Universitaet Bonn, Germany. E-mail: Kurt Stueber, stueber@vax.mpiz-koeln.mpg.d400.de

54. Margulis, L., & Sagan, D. (1986). *Origin of sex.* New Haven, CT: Yale University Press.

55. Marx, J. L. (1989). The cystic fibrosis gene is found. *Science, 245*, 923–925.

56. Maynard Smith, J. (1971). What use is sex? *Journal of Theoretical Biology, 30*, 319–335.

57. Maynard Smith, J. (1992). Byte-sized evolution. *Nature, 355*, 772–773.

58. Maynard Smith, J., Dowson, C. G., & Spratt, B. G. (1991). Localized sex in bacteria. *Nature, 349*, 29–31.

59. Mead, C. (1993). *Analog VLSI and neural systems.* Reading, MA: Addison-Wesley.

60. Michod, R. E., & Levin, B. R. (1988). *The evolution of sex: an examination of current ideas.* Sunderland, MA: Sinauer Associates.

61. Moravec, H. (1988). *Mind children: the future of robot and human intelligence.* Cambridge, MA: Harvard University Press.

62. Moravec, H. (1989). Human culture: a genetic takeover underway. In C. Langton (Ed.), *Artificial life, Santa Fe Institute studies in the sciences of complexity* (Vol. VI, pp. 167–199). Redwood City, CA: Addison-Wesley.

63. Moravec, H. (1993, Winter/Spring). Pigs in cyberspace. *Extropy,* no. 10.

64. Morris, S. C. (1989). Burgess shale faunas and the Cambrian explosion. *Science, 246,* 339–346.

65. Nowick, J., Feng, Q., Tijivikua, T., Ballester, P., & Rebek, J. (1991). *Journal of the American Chemical Society, 113,* 8831–8839.

66. Orgel, L. E., & Crick, F. H. C. (1980). Selfish DNA: the ultimate parasite. *Nature, 284,* 604–607.

67. Rasmussen, S., Knudsen, C., Feldberg, R., & Hindsholm, M. (1990). The coreworld: emergence and evolution of cooperative structures in a computational chemistry. *Physica D, 42,* 111–134.

68. Rasmussen, S., Knudsen, C., & Feldberg, R. (1991). Dynamics of programmable matter. In C. Langton, C. Taylor, J. D. Farmer, & S. Rasmussen (Eds.), *Artificial life II, Santa Fe Institute studies in the sciences of complexity* (Vol. X, pp. 211–254). Redwood City, CA: Addison-Wesley.

69. Ray, T. S. (1979). Slow-motion world of plant 'behavior' visible in rainforest. *Smithsonian, 9*(12), 121–30.

70. Ray, T. S. (1991). An approach to the synthesis of life. In C. Langton, C. Taylor, J. D. Farmer, & S. Rasmussen (Eds.), *Artificial life II, Santa Fe Institute studies in the sciences of complexity* (Vol. X, pp. 371–408). Redwood City, CA: Addison-Wesley.

71. Ray, T. S. (1991). Population dynamics of digital organisms. In C. G. Langton (Ed.), *Artificial Life II Video Proceedings.* Redwood City, CA: Addison-Wesley.

72. Ray, T. S. (1991). Is it alive, or is it GA? In R. K. Belew & L. B. Booker (Eds.), *Proceedings of the 1991 International Conference on Genetic Algorithms* (pp. 527–534). San Mateo, CA: Morgan Kaufmann.

73. Ray, T. S. (1991). Evolution and optimization of digital organisms. In K. R. Billingsley, E. Derohanes, & H. Brown III (Eds.), *Scientific excellence in supercomputing: The IBM 1990 contest prize papers.* Athens, GA: The Baldwin Press/The University of Georgia.

74. Ray, T. S. (1992). Foraging behaviour in tropical herbaceous climbers (Araceae). *Journal of Ecology, 80,* 189–203.

75. Ray, T. S. (1992). Tierra.doc. Documentation for the Tierra Simulator V4.0, 9–9–92. Newark, DE: Virtual Life. Available by anonymous ftp at: tierra.slhs.udel.edu [128.175.41.34] and life.slhs.udel.edu [128.175.41.33], or by contacting the author.

76. Ray, T. S. (In press.) Evolution and complexity. In G. A. Cowan, D. Pines, & D. Metzger (Eds.), *Complexity: metaphor and reality.* Reading, MA: Addison-Wesley.

77. Ray, T. S. (In press). Evolution, complexity, entropy, and artificial reality. *Physica D.*

78. Rommens, J. M., Iannuzzi, M. C., Kerem, B.-S., Drumm, M. L., Melmer, G., Dean, M., Rozmahel, R., Cole, J. L., Kennedy, D., Hidaka, N., Zsiga, M., Buchwald, M., Riordan, J. R., Tsui, L.-C., & Collins, F. S. (1989). Identification of the cystic fibrosis gene: chromosome walking and jumping. *Science, 245,* 1059–1065.

79. Riordan, J. R., Rommens, J. M., Kerem, B.-S., Alon, N., Rozmahel, R., Grzelczak, Z., Zielenski, J., Lok, S., Plavsic, N., Chou, J.-L., Drumm, M. L., Iannuzzi, M. C., Collins, F. S., & Tsui, L.-C. (1989). Identification of the cystic fibrosis gene: cloning and characterization of complementary DNA. *Science, 245,* 1066–1073.

80. Skipper, J. (1992). The computer zoo—evolution in a box. In F. J. Varela & P. Bourgine (Eds.), *Toward a practice of autonomous systems, Proceedings of the First European Conference on Artificial Life.* Cambridge, MA: The MIT Press. E-mail:

Jakob.Skipper@copenhagen.ncr.com

81. Sober, E. (1984). *The nature of selection*. Cambridge, MA: The MIT Press.

82. Spafford, E. H. (1989). The internet worm program: an analysis. *Computer Communication Review, 19*(1), 17–57. Also issued as Purdue CS Technical Report TR-CSD-823. E-mail: spaf@purdue.edu

83. Spafford, E. H. (1989). The internet worm: crisis and aftermath. *ACM Computer Communication Review, 32*(6), 678–687. E-mail: spaf@purdue.edu

84. Stanley, S. M. (1973). An ecological theory for the sudden origin of multicellular life in the late precambrian. *Proceedings of the National Academy of Sciences of the United States of America (Washington), 70*, 1486–1489.

85. Stearns, S. C. (1987). *The evolution of sex and its consequences*. Boston: Birkhäuser Verlag.

86. Strickberger, M. W. (1985). *Genetics*. New York: Macmillan.

87. Strong, D. R., & Ray, T. S. (1975). Host tree location behavior of a tropical vine (*Monstera gigantea*) by skototropism. *Science, 190*, 804–806.

88. Surkan, Al. *Self-balancing of dynamic population sectors that consume energy*. Unpublished manuscript. Department of Computer Science, University of Nebraska at Lincoln. E-mail: surkan@cse.unl.edu

89. Syvanen, M. (1984). The evolutionary implications of mobile genetic elements. *Annual Review of Genetics, 18*, 271–293.

90. Tackett, W., & Gaudiot, J.-L. (1993). Adaptation of self-replicating digital organisms. *Proceedings of the International Joint Conference on Neural Networks*, Nov. 1993, Beijing, China. IEEE Press. E-mail: tackett@ipld01.hac.com, tackett@priam.usc.edu

91. Taylor, C. E., Jefferson, D. R., Turner, S. R., & Goldman, S. R. (1989). RAM: artificial life for the exploration of complex biological systems. In C. Langton (Ed.), *Artificial life, Santa Fe Institute studies in the sciences of complexity* (Vol. VI, pp. 275–295). Redwood City, CA: Addison-Wesley.

92. Thomas, C. A. (1971). The genetic organization of chromosomes. *Annual Review of Genetics, 5*, 237–256.

93. Todd, P. M. (1993). Artificial death. *Proceedings of the Second European Conference on Artificial Life* (ECAL93) (Vol. 2, pp. 1048–1059). Brussels, Belgium: Universite Libre de Bruxelles. E-mail: ptodd@spo.rowland.org

94. Van Valen, L. (1973). A new evolutionary law. *Evolutionary Theory, 1*, 1–30.

95. Williams, G. C. (1975). *Sex and evolution*. Princeton, NJ: Princeton University Press.

96. Gray, James. Unpublished. Natural selection of computer programs. This may have been the first Tierra-like system, but evolving real programs on a real rather than a virtual machine, and predating Tierra itself: "I have attempted to develop ways to get computer programs to function like biological systems subject to natural selection.... I don't think my systems are models in the usual sense. The programs have really competed for resources, reproduced, run, and 'died.' The resources consisted primarily of access to the CPU and partition space.... On a PDP11 I could have a population of programs running simultaneously." E-mail: Gray.James_L+@northport.va.gov

Beyond Digital Naturalism

Walter Fontana
Santa Fe Institute
1660 Old Pecos Trail
Santa Fe, NM 87501 USA
walter@sfi.santafe.edu

Günter Wagner
Department of Biology
Yale University
New Haven, CT 06511 USA
gpwag@yalevm.ycc.yale.edu

Leo W. Buss
Department of Biology
Department of Geology and
Geophysics
Yale University
New Haven, CT 06511 USA
Leo_Buss
@quickmail.cis.yale.edu

Abstract   The success of Artificial Life (ALife) depends on whether it will help solve the conceptual problems of biology. Biology may be viewed as the science of the transformation of organizations. Yet biology lacks a theory of organization. We use this as an example of the challenge that ALife must meet.

Keywords
organization, self-maintenance, lambda-calculus, evolution, hierarchy

If—as I believe—physics and chemistry are conceptually inadequate as a theoretical framework for biology, it is because they lack the concept of function, and hence that of organization.... [P]erhaps, therefore, we should give the ... computer scientists more of a say in the formulation of Theoretical Biology.

—Christopher Longuet-Higgins, 1969 [28]

I   Life and the Organization Problem in Biology

There are two readings of "life": as an embodied phenomenon and as a concept. Foucault [20] points out that up to the end of the 18th century, life does not exist: only living beings. Living beings are but a class in the series of all things in the world. To speak of life is to speak only in the taxonomic sense of the word. Natural history dominated the classical age and is foremost a naming exercise: "The naturalist is the man concerned with the structure of the visible world and its denomination according to characters. Not with life." (p. 161). There is a concurrent interest in how things work, but it is an interest that remains disconnected and in tension with the naturalist tradition.

In the early 19th century, natural history makes a decisive step toward a biology when the notion of character becomes subordinate to the notion of function, when classification becomes comparative anatomy. Life is conceptualized as something functionally organized, and organization is foreign to the domain of the visible. A character is weighted according to the importance of the function(s) it is linked to. In contrast to the classical age, characters are seen as signs of an invisible deep structure. Causal argumentation is reversed: A character is not important because it occurs frequently, but rather it occurs frequently because it is functionally important. Life as a concept becomes manifest as organization, organic structure, that is, organism. In the classical period, living beings were perceived largely as points in a coordinate system of names. Now they require an additional "space of organizational structure." This sets the stage for considering the problem of the modification and transformation of organization.

Darwin posited evolution as an effect of what basically amounts to be a force [39]: natural selection. Natural selection is a statement about kinetics: In a population, those variants of organisms will accumulate that are better able to survive and reproduce than others. If there is ongoing variation and if variation is (at least partially) heritable, then the continuous operation of selection kinetics will lead to the modification of living organizations. One would like to understand, however, how organization arises in the first place. Darwin's theory is not intended to answer this. Indeed, this is apparent upon inspection of the *formal* structure of the theory. Neo-Darwinism is about the dynamics of alleles within populations, as determined by mutation, selection, and drift. A theory based on the dynamics of alleles, individuals, and populations must necessarily assume the prior existence of these entities. Selection cannot set in until there are entities to select. Selection has no generative power; it merely dispenses with the "unfit," thus identifying the *kinetic* aspect of an evolutionary process. The principle problem in evolution is one of *construction*: to understand how the organizations upon which the process of natural selection is based arise, and to understand how mutation can give rise to organizational, that is, phenotypic, novelty. A solution to this problem will allow one to distinguish between those features of organizations that are necessary and those that are coincidental. Such an endeavor requires a theory of organization. Yet biology lacks a theory of organization. The need for a conceptual framework for the study of organization lies at the heart of unsolved problems in both ontogeny and phylogeny. Can Artificial Life (ALife) illuminate biology?

2 Replicator Equations Without Replicators

One way of viewing Darwin's theory is to consider "fitness" (short for "the ability to survive and reproduce") to be an undefined term, in analogy to an axiomatic structure [48, 49]. The principle is applicable whenever its conditions are met: autocatalytic growth kinetics, variation, heritability. At the same time, it leaves open what the subject entities are. They may be molecules, genes, cells, organisms but also populations, strategies, or even artifacts—it depends on the question one is asking. What is required, however, is a coherent development of "fitness" at the chosen level of description. While Darwin clearly had in mind the individual organism, it is not difficult to see how to abstract from Darwin's theory a structure capable of different behaviors that some might even object are "Darwinian."

Darwin's kinetic theory allows for multiple models in which fitness and its referent are specified. This prompted a debate about whether there is a fundamental referent and about what it might be: either the gene, or the individual, or the group, or the species, you name it. There are advocates of a single unit of selection, and others who claim that a description in terms of multiple units is essential [7].

Among the clearest and sharpest proponents of a single unit view is Richard Dawkins [11] with his notion of *replicator selection*. The "fundamental level of selection," Dawkins maintains, is "among replicators—single genes or fragments of genetic material which behave like long-lived units in the gene pool." More generally, a replicator is defined "as any entity in the universe which interacts with its world, including other replicators, in such a way that *copies of itself are made*" [11] (our emphasis). We next exemplify how entities can behave kinetically like replicators without being replicators, leaving room for more than one "fundamental" level of selection.

Consider a generic balance equation for the concentration n_i of an object i in an unconstrained population of n object species: $dn_i/dt \equiv \dot{n}_i = \Gamma_i$, $i = 1, \ldots, n$, where Γ_i describes the net growth of object species i. It is convenient to switch to internal coordinates or relative frequencies, $x_i = n_i / \sum_j n_j$, $0 \le x_i \le 1$ and $\sum_i x_i = 1$, in which the balance equation becomes:

$$\dot{x}_i = \Gamma_i - x_i \sum_j \Gamma_j, \qquad i = 1, \ldots, n. \tag{1}$$

This can also be viewed as the equation of a flow reactor where objects i are produced, and a proportional dilution flow compensates for the excess production in the system at any time. If all Γ_i are just constants, $\Gamma_i = a_i > 0$, then the stationary state of the system will simply contain all object species *sorted* according to their relative magnitude of growth: $\bar{x}_i = a_i / \sum_j a_j$.

The situation changes with autocatalysis, $\Gamma_i = b_i x_i$, as it occurs when objects are replicated (asexually), that is, are copied,

$$\dot{x}_i = x_i \left(b_i - \sum_j b_j x_j \right) = x_i \left(b_i - \langle b \rangle \right), \qquad i = 1, \ldots, n. \tag{2}$$

This is one description of *selection*. The effect of Equation 2 is competition, as can be seen from the stationary state, which consists of only the object i with the largest b_i. b_i is the "fitness" of object i, and the evaluation of fitness that is implict in autocatalysis is nicely expressed by Equation 2: At any time, the growth term b_i is compared against the average $\langle b \rangle$. If it is below (above), the net effect will be a negative (positive) growth rate of species i. As a result, the average will shift toward higher values until it matches the maximum b_i: the survivor. This is a choice mechanism that is quite different from sorting.

The story gets an additional twist when fitness is frequency dependent, that is, when the (asexual) reproduction of i depends on the composition of the population at any time: $\Gamma_i = x_i \sum_j c_{ij} x_j$. Equation 1 then becomes:

$$\dot{x}_i = x_i \left(\sum_j c_{ij} x_j - \sum_{r,s} c_{rs} x_r x_s \right) = x_i \left(\sum_j c_{ij} x_j - \langle c \rangle \right), \qquad i = 1, \ldots, n. \tag{3}$$

The major difference is that Equation 3 can lead to cooperation. Several mutually dependent species may coexist indefinitely and exhibit complicated dynamical behaviors. Selection need not be a naive optimization device.

Variants of both Equations 2 and 3 have been widely studied in the context of, for example, imperfect reproduction (mutation), or genetics with Mendelian as well as non-Mendelian transmission [10, 12, 13, 16, 42]. (For an overview see Hofbauer and Sigmund [22]). Equation 3 has been termed the *replicator equation* [38], and it represents the essence of replicator selection: Autocatalysis induced by replication (reproduction, copying) causes the composition of a population to shift based on an endogenous comparison against the population average. Of course, what is being chosen in this process is not easy to say when the mutual interdependencies are intricate.

We resume our theme of organization with a simple observation: Autocatalytic kinetics can be induced without replication. Suppose that the interaction between two object species j and k does not result in the replication of either j or k but in the production of a different object species i, as is the case in a chemical reaction. Suppose further (for the sake of simplicity) that objects j and k are *effectively* not used up in the reaction, that is, each time they react we are given back one instance of each (call it "food"). The overall scheme of this "stylized reaction," then, is:

$$j + k \longrightarrow i + j + k. \tag{4}$$

Notice that this is not autocatalytic in j or k, because they appear on both sides of the reaction equation with the same stoichiometric coefficients. Let the rate constant of this reaction be $d^i_{j,k}$ (possibly zero). Equation 1 then becomes [41]:

$$\dot{x}_i = \sum_j \sum_k d^i_{j,k} x_j x_k - x_i \sum_{r,s,t} d^t_{r,s} x_r x_s, \qquad i = 1, 2, \ldots, n. \tag{5}$$

Consider now a set K of object species such that for each $i \in K$, there exists a pair $j, k \in K$, which produces i. Such a set maintains itself, *but it does not copy itself— it only makes more of itself.* Consider now a number of disjoint self-maintaining sets $J, K, L, \ldots$, which interact with one another in such a way that for each reactive pair $k \in K$, $j \in J$, the product is in K or J (but distinct from k and j). Now we simply rearrange Equation 5 by collecting all individual object species $i \in K$ into a set with relative frequency $x_K = \sum_{k \in K} x_{k \in K}$. Let the frequency of i in its own set be $y_{i \in K} = x_{i \in K}/x_K$. We obtain:

$$\dot{x}_K = x_K \left[\sum_J \mathcal{C}_{KJ}(t) x_J - \langle \mathcal{C}(t) \rangle \right], \tag{6}$$

with the coefficients

$$\mathcal{C}_{KJ}(t) = \sum_{i \in K} \sum_{j \in J} \sum_{k \in K} d^{k \in K}_{i \in K, j \in J} y_{i \in K} y_{j \in J}.$$

Equation 6 has the form of a replicator Equation 3. However, the sets K do not replicate nor do any of their members (by definition). These sets only grow, and they do so by reflexive catalysis or self-maintenance at the set level. This induces a selection kinetics identical to the replicator case. (A similar observation is mentioned in Eigen [12].) However, the relevant units are not replicators. Hence, we cannot refer to this as "Darwinian selection," because Darwinian selection rests on reproducing entities. It is a generalization of it, and we will simply call it *selection.* Hence, we have *sorting* when the growth kinetics of entities is not autocatalytic, and *selection* when the growth kinetics is autocatalytic. In the special case where entities are replicators, selection becomes *Darwinian selection.* In the case where entities are not replicators, selection can still occur at the level of aggregate entities, but it cannot be Darwinian.

This is our first checkpoint toward a firmer notion of organization. An organization is a set of entities that continuously regenerates itself by transformation pathways (the $d^i_{j,k}$) internal to the set [29, 30]. All that is required is sufficient connectivity: The matrix $\tilde{d}_{ik} = \sum_j (d^i_{j,k} + d^i_{k,j})$ must be irreducible. Many researchers noticed the possibility and the significance of self-maintaining sets of chemicals [8, 12, 23, 24, 35, 37], and probably many more). The disagreement, however, is over the likelihood of such sets given certain kinds of molecules and their importance in shaping the (early) history of life. Simple self-maintaining ensembles have recently been obtained in the laboratory of Luisi [1].

It is important to reiterate the necessity of making a *logical* distinction between reproduction and self-maintenance. There have been occasions where these two orthogonal concepts were conflated [15, 23], probably because self-maintenance was considered as an *alternative* to an origin of life through primitive replicatory elements. It should be clear so far that self-maintenance has little to do with making *two* individuals out of one through transformations internal to the individual. Hence, it cannot be an alternative to reproduction. Reproduction does not necessarily require organization either, as exemplified by simple self-replicating molecules [44, 46] or a viral RNA in the presence of its replicase in the test tube [40]. This assumes that we are willing to make a distinction between a molecule or a pair of molecules in complementary association and an organization. Self-maintenance isolates a different aspect of individuality than reproduction. The former requires organization, and the latter requires means for its multiple instantiation, as, for example, by compartmentalization through spatial separation, or membrane enclosure, or plain chemical bonds. Clearly, our intuitive notion of life includes both organization and reproduction. They are conceptually different, and the implementation of one need not be the implementation of the other.

The main point here was to show that nonreplicatory but self-maintaining sets do exhibit the kinetics required for selection, though, by definition, not of a Darwinian kind (provided one accepts [3] as a proper dynamical formalization of selection). The integration of replicators and primitive organizations leaves room for multiple units of selection (in the sense of Buss [7]).

Of course, the modification of organizations is hardly identical to the evolution of replicators. What does it mean, if anything, for nonreproducing organizations to "vary"? This question cannot be adequately answered within a description where the micro-entities are atomic structureless units as is the case in the conventional dynamical systems described earlier. The reason is that the question draws attention to structure–function relationships.

3   Organizations Must be Constructed

An *extensional* description is roughly one in which the entire universe of relevant objects is given at once, *in extenso*. It is basically a look-up table that may even be so large that nothing can store it. The modern set-theoretic view of a function is of this kind: A function is a collection of ordered pairs (in, out), for example, $x^2 \equiv \{(0,0), (1,1), (2,4), (3,9), \ldots\}$. An extensional framework also characterizes traditional dynamical systems. Their definition requires an extensionally given network that specifies which variables couple with which other variables in what ways. For a particular kind of reasoning, this is quite useful. It certainly is adequate in setting up the gravitational equations of motion for a system of a few planets, where the relevant knowledge can actually be tabulated. This framework does not easily fit biology, because the objects denoted by the variables are typically of combinatorial complexity. If Equation 2, suitably augmented with mutational terms [12], were to describe the replication, mutation, and selection of RNA sequences of length 100, then we would have to specify 10^{60} equations with their corresponding coefficients. The problem is not so much that this situation forces a stochastic description, because only a vanishingly small fraction of all these possibilities can be realized. More fundamentally, such a description is still extensional as long as the relevant properties—the replication rates b_i as determined by the tertiary structure, for example—are not a *function* of the sequences. The major point, the fact, namely, that there *is* some inner logic that connects sequences and their replication rates, is lost. It is precisely this logic that makes the problem an *interesting* one. The question is how that logic structures a population under a given dynamics.

The same holds for ecological modeling in terms of Lotka-Volterra equations, or for game dynamics. In his recent work, Lindgren [27] considers agents with an internal structure that determines the strategy they play in a given game. The structure of both opponents i and j, then, allows one to infer the coefficient c_{ij} in Equation 3. As in the case of RNA sequences, a "strategy-grammar" opens up a space of combinatorial complexity and permits with finite means the *endogenous* specification of an infinity of interaction coefficients.

To summarize, in contrast to extensional models, *constructive* models are founded on objects with a grammatical and, therefore, combinatory internal structure. Note, however, that in the previous examples, the internal structure of agents or objects does not affect the *functional* character of their interactions. These always remain copy actions: $i (+ j) \longrightarrow 2i (+ j)$, as is evident from the factorization of Equations 2 or 3. The internal structure only codifies the *strength* of an interaction that is kept fixed in *kind* for all agents. This is precisely what changes in going from Equation 3 to 5. While the $d^i_{j,k}$ may still specify strengths, in addition they require an underlying *logic* that specifies which object i is implied by a pair of objects (j, k).

This suggests a distinction. In the previous examples concerning the replication of RNA sequences or strategies, new entities enter a finite population through *mutation*. The cause of a mutation is a *chance* event, meaning that it stands in no relation to its effect. We refer to models in which new agents are constructed in an unspecific (essentially stochastic) fashion as *weakly constructive*. This is to be contrasted with a situation in which the encounter of two agents *implies* a *specific* third one, as in Equation 5. Models of this kind will be termed *strongly constructive*. The prime example of a strongly constructive system is chemistry. A strongly constructive system that contains agent A must cope with the network of its implications. But it also must cope with the implications of the implications—and so on. Organization is here a network that results from convergence to both *relational* (logical) and *kinetic* self-consistency. The logical component induces a structure that is absent in the weakly constructive case. Think of a "knowledge system" where the agents A, B, C, etc. stand for propositions, and where the deterministic construction of new propositions results from "interactions" that we may call rules of inference. The organizational analogy between "consistent systems of belief" and metabolisms is, in our opinion, not completely superficial.

We have reached the next checkpoint toward a firmer notion of organization. An organization is defined in terms of a strongly constructive model: a system of transformations [30, 45]. This distinguishes it from a weakly constructive version of a Lotka-Volterra or a replicator equation (Equation 3) describing an ecology of individuals that only replicate and mutate or undergo recombination. There is no doubt that an ecological population can be highly organized. However, the next section will clarify that the concept of organization suggested by a strongly constructive system is different in kind. Clearly, in real life, weakly and strongly constructive aspects are entangled. Disentangling them will be an important step in understanding what is necessary and what is contingent in the history of life.

An extensional system of equations, like Equation 5, is useful to capture some dynamical aspects, but useless to capture the constructive nature of organization. If we were to introduce a new object, say v, into Equation 5, we would have to specify its constructive interactions with the other objects arbitrarily (e.g., at random [23, 24]). This, however, eliminates precisely what is interesting about organization. The constructive aspect is essential for addressing both the origin problem of organizations and the problem of their variation.

4   Organization—De Arte Combinatoria[1]

Chemistry gave rise to biology. This is an elementary indication that strongly constructive interactions are fundamental to organization. Chemistry, therefore, informs our attempt of conceiving a formal and transparent model of organization [17–19].

Physics is about mechanisms. So is computation theory. But the latter has a twist that physics lacks: It is about mechanisms in which things build other things. Such "things" are *processes* and *functions*. As opposed to the clockwork or the steam engine, computation is inherently constructive. Computation need not only be about calculations that are of interest to a mathematically inclined person. What we emphasize here is the aspect of computation as a formal system that enables symbolic structures to build further symbolic structures in a consistent way. A first grip on organization can be obtained by studying the collective phenomena occuring in a dynamical system consisting of many such interacting symbolic structures. We briefly review such a platform. Details can be found in Fontana and Buss [18].

4.1   Constructive Part

(1.1) calculus. Our entities are literally *functions* expressed in a canonical syntactical framework known as the λ-calculus [4, 9], in which they can be *applied* to one another yielding new functions.

The grammar of λ-expressions, E, is

$$E ::= x \mid \lambda x.E \mid (E)E, \tag{7}$$

where x is a variable. Thus, a variable is an atomic expression. There are two expression-forming schemes—"combinators"—that define syntax: One, $\lambda x.E$ (termed abstraction), binds a variable in an expression E making it the equivalent of a formal parameter in a procedure, that is, E is intended as a function in x. The other, $(E)E$, (termed application) expresses the notion of a function being applied to an argument— except that there is no syntactical distinction between function and argument. While application and abstraction are purely syntactical operations, they are given an operational meaning through *substitution*:

$$(\lambda x.A)B \longrightarrow A[B/x], \tag{8}$$

where $A[B/x]$ denotes the textual substitution of all occurrences of x in A with B. (We assume unique names for bound variables, distinct from names of free variables.) The arrow means that the expression on the left-hand side can be rewritten as the expression on the right-hand side, *thereby only replacing equals for equals*. The process of carrying out all possible substitutions within an expression is termed *reduction*, and the final stable form—if there is one—is unique and is called a *normal form*.

(1.2) normal form. In this model universe every expression is reduced to normal form within preset computational limits. If no normal form is attained, the expression is not allowed.

4.2   Dynamical Part

λ-calculus is now put in the context of a (stochastic) dynamical system that mimics a constrained flow reactor containing a finite number of "expression-particles."

---

1 Gottfried Wilhelm von Leibniz (1646–1716).

(II.1) initialize. A system is initialized with N particles. These are randomly generated (usually unique) λ-expressions.

(II.2) interact. Two expressions, A and B, are chosen at random (in this order). Denote this choice by $[A, B]$ and denote the normal form of $(A)B$ by C. Then, the following "reaction" scheme applies:

$$[A, B] \longrightarrow C + A + B. \tag{9}$$

(II.3) boundary conditions. Apply syntactical or functional boundary conditions to C to determine whether C is allowed to enter the system.

(II.4) constant size. If C is added to the system, choose one expression particle, D, at random and remove it:

$$D \longrightarrow \emptyset. \tag{10}$$

This keeps the system constrained at N particles at any time.

(II.5) iterate. Continue with (II.2).

The reader will recognize that this is just the description of a discrete stochastic analogue to Equation 5, where the possible $d_{A,B}^C$ are implicitly given by a calculus, in this case λ-calculus:

$$d_{A,B}^C = \begin{cases} 1 & \text{if } (A)B = C \\ 0 & \text{otherwise} \end{cases} \tag{11}$$

In section 5 we discuss the motivation for this approach and its basic assumptions. First, we briefly review some results. The model provides a formalization of our intuitive notion of organization. It generates organizational levels that can be described without reference to the micro processes that give rise to them. Organizational levels beyond a "molecular ecology" (see Level 0) emerge even in the absence of Darwinian selection. Details can be found in Fontana and Buss [18].

4.2.1 Level 0
Level 0 arises with no specialized boundary conditions (II.3). The system becomes dominated by either single self-copying functions or ensembles of mostly hypercyclically [12, 14] coupled copying functions (i.e., systems where for each g there is at least one f such that $(f)g = g$). Thus, Equation 5 reduces to the situation described by the replicator framework, Equation 3: the reproduction of an object species, i, depends on itself and one (or more) other object species, j. From a purely functional point of view i is a "fixed point" of its interaction with j. Under perturbation, that is, the introduction of random expressions, Level 0 ensembles frequently reduce to a single self-copying function, that is, a function f with $(f)f = f$.

4.2.2 Level I
Level 1 arises under a variety of conditions, all of which involve a restriction on copy actions up to their complete elimination. The reason for the importance of such an extreme boundary condition is the elimination of Darwinian selection, thereby allowing one to assess the necessity of Darwinian selection in the generation of organization. The following features, therefore, need not be the result of *Darwinian* selection.

Under no-copy conditions, the set of objects in the system changes until it becomes confined to a subspace of the space of all λ-expressions. This (infinite) set is *invariant* under applicative action and is characterized by three properties:

1. *Grammatical structure.* The objects of the subspace possess a specific syntax described by a grammar (beyond just conforming with Equation 7). Sometimes the objects are grouped into several "families" with distinct syntactical structures. Grammatical closure here defines membership: An object can be unambiguously assigned to a given organization on the basis of its grammatical specification.

2. *Algebraic structure.* All relationships of action between objects of the subspace are described by a (small) set of equations. The system frequently admits "coarse-grained" identities that emphasize symmetries and particular roles of objects (like inverse elements, successor functions, neutral elements, etc.). It is important to emphasize that neither the formulation nor the discovery of the laws that define an organization require knowledge of the underlying λ-calculus. An organization has a level of description that can be considered independently.

3. *Self-maintenance and kinetic persistence.* The flow reactor contains a finite number of objects. Hence, only a small subset "carries" the organization under this dynamical system. Typically this subset maintains itself in the sense that every object is produced by at least one interaction involving other objects of the same set. Notice that self-maintenance is not a statement about kinetics but rather about the constructive relationships within a set of objects. We also have observed borderline cases where the objects change constantly (while remaining confined to their invariant subspace). In all cases, that which is kinetically persistent is the organization as expressed by its grammatical and algebraic description.

These characteristics endow Level 1 organizations with some interesting properties:

Center. An organization has many *generators*, that is, subsets of objects capable of spawning a given organization, if the reactor is intialized only with them. Such sets are typically small. So far Level 1 organizations were observed to have a unique smallest and self-maintaining generator set that constructs the organization *ab initio*. We call it the *center*. The center is typically present in the reactor.

Self-repair. Self-repair is a consequence of self-maintenance, kinetic persistence, and the existence of a center. Organizations can tolerate vast amounts of destruction, while retaining the capability to reconstruct themselves.

Extensions. The model universe, in its present form, does not provide for "noisy" interactions. (Products are determined once the reactants are given.) Without functional perturbations, a Level 1 organization is a monolithic entity: Once attained, all functional evolution stops. The easiest way out is to provide an exogenous source of noise by injecting random objects into an established organization. For a novel object to persist, it must create transformation pathways that sustain it in a kinetically effective manner within the established network of pathways. The modification of organizations is, therefore, highly constrained. However, when a novel object does become established, it imports new syntax elements, thus altering the grammatical structure and the algebraic laws that characterize the organization. This alteration occurs in a typical way: by extension. The unperturbed organization still persists as a "smaller" core organization to which the interactions with the new object have added another "layer." New algebraic laws are added to the existing ones, and the center of the extended organization is extended correspondingly. With constant reactor capacity, an organization cannot be extended indefinitely, and upon several such extensions one observes a displacement of previous layers. Over several steps this can result in a substantial modification of the original organization.

4.2.3 Level 2

Level 1 organizations can be combined. At first one may expect a competitive situation. This need not be the case, because two organizations can generate novel objects, through cross-interactions, that are not members of either organization. This "cross talk" consists in a set of objects that does not constitute a Level 1 organization. (It is neither self-maintaining nor grammatically closed under interaction.) We refer to this set as the *glue*, because it knits both component organizations kinetically and algebraically together. The entire structure is a Level 2 organization: a meta-organization that contains the original organizations as self-maintaining subalgebras. The glue distinguishes this situation from a plain coexistence. (Indeed, a Level 2 organization is not described by Equation 6 in terms of multiple component organizations—because of the glue.) A Level 2 organization is not as easily obtained as a Level 1 organization, because the kinetic requirements to the glue are severe. Nevertheless, the construction of Level 2 organizations from scratch has been observed: Two Level 1 organizations form whose interactions integrate them into a Level 2 organization. Qualitatively the same properties as for the Level 1 case hold in the Level 2 case, although stability is not as pronounced.

4.2.4 Biology

The history of life is a history of the emergence of new organizational grades and their subsequent diversification [7]. A transition in organizational grade occurred when self-replicating molecules gave rise to (or became incorporated within) self-maintaining prokaryotic cells, and the origin of procaryotes was itself followed by the emergence of a hierarchical nesting of different prokaryotic lineages to generate multi-genomic eukaryotic cells. The λ-universe mimics transitions seen in the history of life, that is, the transition from self-replicating molecules to self-maintaining organizations to hierarchical combinations of such organizations. We refer to these organizational grades as Level 0, Level 1, and Level 2, respectively.

Organizations are very robust toward functional perturbations. Perturbing objects are frequently eliminated, otherwise they typically cause extensions to the grammatical and algebraic structure. Morowitz [35] suggests that the core metabolism derives its architecture from the addition of several metabolic "shells" to a basic energy metabolism such as the glycolytic pathway. A shell attaches to another through only a few "entry points." These are pathways that introduce novel syntactical and functional elements, such as nitrogen (with amino acids among its consequences) and dinitrogen heterocycles (with nucleic acids among their consequences).

A Level 2 experiment in which two Level 1 organizations are brought into interaction can be seen as a massive perturbation of either organization. Frequently the interaction does not produce a glue that is sufficient to stably integrate both organizations while maintaining their autonomy. Rather, one organization loses autonomy and becomes a large extension to the other. This is reminiscent of the well-known pattern wherein an intracellular symbiont loses functions redundant with those possessed by the host.

The center of a Level 2 organization is just the sum of the corresponding Level 1 centers. Such a superposition does not hold for the grammatical and algebraic description of the resulting Level 2 organization, because of the extensions required to describe the glue. This recalls the general difference between the behavior of genotypes and phenotypes: Genes combine independently, while the organizations they spawn do not.

The transition from Level 0 to Level 1 emphasizes the tension between reproduction and organization. Replicatory elements are clearly kinetically favored over self-maintaining but nonreproducing organizations. The biological problem connected with the transition is one of restricting copy actions. The model shows how a new concept of organization arises—beyond the engineering of mutual dependencies between replicators (cf. hypercycle [12])—when transformation operations are given the chance to attain closure.

Nevertheless, in all this we violate mass conservation, do not consider thermodynamics, assume all rate constants to be equal, do not use up reactants in reactions, have everything react with everything, and so on. *What does such a model really mean?*

5 A functional perpetuum mobile

The model explores the consequences of an extremely simple combination of a dynamical system with a calculus. With respect to biology, the explanatory power of such a model comes from *defining a level of description.* Here it is given by the mathematical notion of function. The focus is on the expression and construction of functional relationships rather than on their exact chemical implementation. λ-calculus is the canonical *language* to express such a consistent universe of construction. λ-calculus is clearly no more than a highly stylized chemistry. In the biological context, it serves the purpose of a high-level *specification language*, rather than a full-fledged implementation language. The image of "organization" suggested by this abstraction is very simple: a *kinetically self-maintaining algebraic structure.*

Take a set of two objects, A and B, such that $(A)A = B$ and $(B)B = A$. (Assume that cross-collisions are not reactive.) Clearly, the set $\{A, B\}$ is self-maintaining without containing copy actions, Is this an organization? Our definition suggests it is not, because the system neither specifies a nontrivial grammar nor a nontrivial algebra. Trivial does not mean simple; it means that there is no compressed description of the set's composition and behavior short of listing it. Our definition suggests that an organization be over an infinite set of objects. Is that reasonable? Yes, because it is not required that this subspace be realized in its entirety. Only a subset of implicitly determined size is required to make the organization's specification kinetically persistent. If the size needed for supporting the organization is too large compared to the reactor's capacity, the organization disappears.

The mechanics of λ-calculus teaches a lesson: *construction* alone, Equation 7, is not sufficient; processes must be associated with construction that induce *equivalence*, Equation 8. The basic combinators of the chemical grammar are not fundamentally different from those that build λ-expressions: A molecule is either an atom or a combination of molecules. That which makes such a universe capable of constructing networks, hence of organizing, is a consistent way of establishing that different combinations are effectively the "same." In chemistry, combinatory structures—molecules—combine into transition structures that undergo rearrangements. The nature of these rearrangements establishes which molecular combinations are effectively the same in regard to a particular product. Construction and equivalence are the essence of chemistry at the level of description set by the present model. The rest of chemistry is specific to the implementation of construction and equivalence with a given physics. Construction and equivalence are necessary for organization and, hence, for *any* life, artificial or natural. Consequently, the organizational features outlined in the previous section are not coincidental either, because they follow necessarily.

"Function" is frequently used in a colloquial way meaning different things. These meanings are disentangled at our level of description. First, there is the unambiguous mathematical concept of a function. In this sense every object in our model universe *is* a function. Then there is a more "semantic" aspect of function: the function of an organ, the function of a beta-blocker. This notion of function relates to specific roles within the context of a network. As a simple example, consider a λ-expression, A, and certain elements B of its domain that are fixed points of A, that is, $(A)B = B$. If B happens to be present in the reactor together with A, then A makes B a replicator: B assumes a specific kinetic role, and A assumes a specific functional meaning for B in this particular context. Suppose A assumes this role for all C in the system. Then A is algebraically a "neutral element," but, again, conceivably only for those C that happen to be present, not for others that may perturb the system. If there is a neutral element, then this creates a "functional niche" for other objects to be "inverses" of one another one and so on. Because objects *are* functions, they construct networks within which they *have* functions. There is no need to assume the latter to be given a priori.

A reactor with many interacting λ-expressions is a system of concurrently communicating functions. Application of a λ-expression to another one can be viewed as an act of communication—where a function is communicated to another function via a variable associated with a port named λ [5, 6, 33]. Despite Equation 9, communication is symmetric. Here the "communication operator" is really the "+" symbol in the chemical reaction scheme. In fact, written as a chemical reaction the interaction scheme (II.2) just reads:

$$
A + B \quad
\begin{array}{l}
\nearrow \quad (A)B + A + B \\
\\
\searrow \quad (B)A + A + B
\end{array}
\qquad (12)
$$

The result of a communication between A and B is a nondeterministic choice between the process $(A)B$ and the process $(B)A$. This is manifest in the fact that for all random encounters between A and B, half of the time A comes from the "right" (chosen second) and half of the time from the "left" (chosen first). Reaction, or communication, is clearly commutative in the model. When speaking (somewhat sloppily) of "interaction" in (II.2), we refer to the application event after a choice in Equation 12 has been made.[2]

When interpreting the reaction (or kinetic) scheme, it is imperative to remain consistent with the chosen level of abstraction. A kinetic scheme, like (II.2) and (II.4), serves two purposes. First and foremost, it defines a communication event between objects. Second, it summarizes the overall effect of many details whose full specification is inappropriate at the chosen level of abstraction.

The reason for not using up the reactants in (II.2) is, technically speaking, to induce a *recursion*. If no object were removed, the system would generate all possible iterated communications among the initial objects. The flux (II.4) eventually removes those communication products that are not sustained at a sufficient rate within the system. This focuses repeated communication to occur among a kinetically favored set of objects until structural consistency is attained as well (if it is attained). An organization is plainly the fixed point of such a recursion. We recently became aware that in the process algebra literature a similar scheme—called "replication" (no biological connotations)— conveniently replaces recursion [34].

A more "palatable" kinetic scheme would have been "recursion over food." That is, specify a certain number of (random) objects which are designated as "food," $\mathcal{F}$. Food

---

2 Computer scientists should not confuse the "chemical communication operator" "+" with their choice operator denoted by the same symbol. If we symbolize communication by $\odot$, "choice" by the usual +, "interleaving" by | [6], then Equation 12 reads as $A \odot B = (A)B|A|B + (B)A|A|B$.

is steadily supplied to the system, while reactants are used up. Hence, Equation 12 becomes

$$A + B \quad \nearrow \quad (A)B + \mathcal{F} \\ \searrow \quad (B)A + \mathcal{F} \tag{13}$$

where $\mathcal{F}$ stands for an object chosen randomly from the food set. Equation 10 would be turned off, because Equation 13 preserves particle number. Under such circumstances, the system is "anchored" to the food source, and any organization would have to contain pathways linking it to that source. Our original scheme (Equation 12) frees the system from having to maintain pathways to the initial objects. This is somewhat more abstract but isolates *functional self-maintenance*, while Equation 13 generates structures that need not be functionally autonomous, because they are exogenously maintained through food.

Of course, real organizations must be fed—but the feeding does not define an organization. The present system is clearly open and driven in many ways. In a sense, however, this is beside the point, because the ultimate nature of our model universe is "informational." (Information is not necessarily destroyed by its usage. Although the λ-mechanics—no matter how remote—remains in a spooky analogy to chemistry.) The model suggests a view in which the world of thermodynamics gives rise to another world whose objects are functions (or processes). While there is no *perpetuum mobile* in the former, there is plenty of room for a *perpetuum mobile* in the latter: functional organization.

There is also plenty of room to improve on this model. For example, the model lacks a structured notion of communication that determines who communicates with whom and when. This suggests that formal processes may be more appropriate agents than functions. Formal processes do by and large not compute functions, but rather they are characterized by their ability or inability to offer communications at various points in time [21]. This endows them with different notions of equivalence [32]. The particular abstractions from chemistry and the biologically motivated boundary conditions employed thus far informed our modeling platform and, therefore, our understanding of the emergence of functional organization of the Level 1 and Level 2 type. The proper abstractions and boundary conditions that may allow one to attain multicellular differentiating organizations, Level 3 say, or Level 4 (brains?), or ... remain to be captured. While replacing functions by processes may be part of the story, it is evidently an open question where this framework will lead—as is its applicability outside the biological domain. In any case,

> We shall first have to find in which way this theory of [processes] can be brought into relationship with [biology], and what their common elements are. ... It will then become apparent that there is not only nothing artificial in establishing this relationship but that on the contrary this theory of [communicating processes] is the proper instrument with which to develop a theory of [biological organization]. One would misunderstand the intent of our discussions by interpreting them as merely pointing out an analogy between these two spheres. We hope to establish satisfactorily, after developing a few plausible schematizations, that the typical problems of [biological organization] become strictly identical with the mathematical notions of suitable [communicating processes]. [47]

The quote has been taken from von Neumann and Morgenstern's *Theory of Games and Economic Behavior* [47], except that we took the liberty to replace "theory of games of strategy" with [communicating processes] and "economic behavior" with [biological organization]. The quote characterizes the spirit of the work sketched here quite aptly. However, it is fair to add that von Neumann and Morgenstern's intentions were not realized. But, then, their "theory of games of strategy" was not even weakly constructive.

6 ALife and Real Life

Our view of ALife relative to biology is perhaps best rendered by an analogy with geometry. For a long time Euclidean geometry was held to be *the* "science" of space. The development of non-Euclidean geometries led to the realization that terms like *line* or *angle* can be given different coherent specifications that result in different models of space. Geometry is not just one form of space; geometry is an axiomatic structure organized around *undefined terms* like line or angle [25]. In a particular model of space, triangles have an inner angle sum of 180 degrees. If this fails to hold at large scales in our universe, it does not invalidate the former space as a model of geometry. Our picture of ALife is that of a variety of specifications and, perhaps, formalizations of different intuitive notions about what it means to be alive. A notion of "artificial life," however, makes sense only if there is an *implementation independent definition of life that informs biology.*

Succeeding in this vision means opposing the superficially informative. There is a risk of ALife becoming predominantly a community of digital naturalists traversing their classical age. Ultimately, the success of ALife will depend on the extent to which it succeeds in developing a concept of life that encompasses biology. But to inform biology means not simply imitating it but understanding it. And understanding it requires identification of the outstanding unsolved problems in biology and seeking their resolution.

Our work is ultimately motivated by a premise: that there exists a logical deep structure of which carbon chemistry-based life is a manifestation. The problem is to discover what it is and what the appropriate mathematical devices are to express it. ALife started by emphasizing processes rather than that which implements them [26]. We believe this emphasis to be necessary but not sufficient. If the practice of ALife does not contribute to the solution of the logical problem, ALife will fail. For how can we discern whether a construct is a manifestation of life or whether it is an imitation of life? We can't, unless the logical problem is solved. How do we know whether we have solved it? We know when the solution affects the research agenda of biology—the science of the instance that we have not constructed. Should the premise turn out to be wrong, then ALife will fail too. For then ALife becomes ARbitrary. ALife practitioners must avoid the presumption that bedeviled Artificial Intelligence—that all the needed concepts were available to be imported from the other disciplines. ALife will find its first proving ground in real biology, in its capacity for catalyzing the theoretical maturation of biology.

7 Sources

Similar ideas have certainly occurred to many people. Some contributions we have mentioned, others we acknowledge here.

A decisive step was undertaken by Bagley, Farmer and Kauffman who devised probably one of the first strongly constructive dynamical systems [2,3]. Their model is based on simplified polynucleotide sequences that interact through complementary base pairing, thereby specifically cleaving and ligating one another. Rokshar, Anderson, and Stein [36] proposed a model somewhat similar in spirit. Steen Rasmussen and his group studied self-organization in an ensemble of machine (assembler) code instructions [50]. Interestingly, in their setting self-maintenance is achieved not by construction of new instructions (that set being fixed), but by (weak and strong) construction of new pointers to the locations on which the instructions operate. George Kampis has been weaving an independent thread of thoughts which seems pertinent to the concerns addressed in this paper [51]. We were put on track by discussions with John McCaskill a few years ago. He suggested a model of interacting Turing machines where tapes, standing for stylized polymeric sequences, encode transition tables that read and write other tapes [31,43]. It was still a long way to the present framework with its implied level of description and a formally more robust notion of organization.

Varela and Maturana [29,30,45] were perhaps the first to think extensively about organization in a new way. Their writings are at times not easily penetrable. However, building a formal model made us understand that many of the issues raised here were foreshadowed by their thinking.

Acknowledgments

Thanks go to Chris Langton for comments and careful reading of the manuscript. Thanks to Inga Hosp for suggesting the perpetuum mobile metaphor and to the "Stiftung Junge Südtiroler im Ausland" for financial support. This is communication number 10 of the Yale Center for Computational Ecology.

References

1. Bachmann, P. A., Luisi, P.-L., & Lang, J. (1992). Autocatalytic self-replicating micelles as models for prebiotic structures. *Nature, 357*, 57–59.

2. Bagley, R. J., & Farmer, J. D. (1992). Spontaneous emergence of a metabolism. In C. G. Langton, C. Taylor, J. D. Farmer, & S. Rasmussen, *Artificial life II, Santa Fe Institute studies in the sciences of complexity* (pp. 93–141). Redwood City, CA: Addison-Wesley.

3. Bagley, R. J., Farmer, J. D., Kauffman, S. A., Packard, N. H., Perelson, A. S., & Stadnyk, I. M. (1989). Modeling adaptive biological systems. *Biosystems, 23*, 113–138.

4. Barendregt, H. G. (1984). *The lambda calculus: its syntax and semantics. Studies in logic and the foundations of mathematics* (2nd ed., rev.). Amsterdam: North-Holland.

5. Berry, G., & Boudol, G. (1992). The chemical abstract machine. *Theoretical Computer Science, 96*, 217–248.

6. Boudol, G. (1989). Towards a lambda-calculus for concurrent and communicating systems. In G. Goos & J. Hartmanis (Eds.), *Lecture notes in computer science* (pp. 149–161). Berlin: Springer-Verlag.

7. Buss, L. W. (1987). *The evolution of individuality.* Princeton, NJ: Princeton University Press.

8. Calvin, M. (1969). *Chemical evolution.* Oxford, UK: Clarendon Press.

9. Church, A. (1941). *The calculi of lambda conversion.* Princeton, NJ: Princeton University Press.

10. Crow, J. F., & Kimura, M. (1970). *An introduction to population genetics theory.* New York: Harper and Row.

11. Dawkins, R. (1978). Replicator selection and the extended phenotype. *Zeitschrift für Tierpsychologie, 47*, 61–76.

12. Eigen, M. (1971). Self-organization of matter and the evolution of biological macromolecules *Naturwissenschaften, 58*, 465–526.

13. Eigen, M., McCaskill, J. S., & Schuster, P. (1989). The molecular quasi-species. *Advances in Chemical Physics, 75*, 149–263.

14. Eigen, M., & Schuster, P. (1979). *The hypercycle.* Berlin: Springer Verlag.

15. Farmer, J. D., Kauffman, S. A., & Packard, N. H. (1982). Autocatalytic replication of polymers. *Physica D, 22,* 50–67.

16. Fisher, R. A. (1930). *The genetical theory of natural selection.* Oxford, UK: Clarendon Press.

17. Fontana, W. (1992). Algorithmic chemistry. In C. G. Langton, C. Taylor, J. D. Farmer, & S. Rasmussen (Eds.), *Artificial life II, Santa Fe Institute studies in the sciences of complexity* (pp. 159–209). Redwood City, CA: Addison-Wesley.

18. Fontana, W. & Buss, L. W. (1994). "The arrival of the fittest": Toward a theory of biological organization. *Bulletin of Mathematical Biology, 56,* 1–64.

19. Fontana, W., & Buss, L. W. (in press, 1994). What would be conserved "if the tape were played twice." *Proceedings of the National Academy of Sciences of the United States of America (Washington).*

20. Foucault, M. (1973). *The order of things. An archeology of the human sciences.* New York: Vintage Books. Originally published as *Les mots et les choses* by Editions Gallimard (1966).

21. Hennessy, M. (1988). *Algebraic theory of processes.* Cambridge, MA: The MIT Press.

22. Hofbauer, J., & Sigmund, K. (1988). *The theory of evolution and dynamical systems.* Cambridge, UK: Cambridge University Press.

23. Kauffman, S. A. (1971). Cellular homeostasis, epigenesis and replication in randomly aggregated macromolecular systems. *Journal of Cybernetics, 1,* 71–96.

24. Kauffman, S. A. (1986). Autocatalytic sets of proteins. *Journal of Theoretcal Biology, 119,* 1–24.

25. Mac Lane, S. (1986). *Mathematics, form and function.* New York: Springer-Verlag.

26. Langton, C. G. (1989.) Artificial life. In C. G. Langton (Ed.), *Artificial life, Santa Fe Institute studies in the sciences of complexity* (pp. 1–44). Redwood City, CA: Addison-Wesley.

27. Lindgren, K. (1992). Evolutionary phenomena in simple dynamics. In C. G. Langton, C. Taylor, J. D. Farmer, & S. Rasmussen (Eds.), *Artificial life II, Santa Fe Institute studies in the sciences of complexity* (pp. 295–312). Redwood City, CA: Addison-Wesley.

28. Longuet-Higgins, C. (1969). What biology is about. In C. H. Waddington (Ed.), *Towards a theoretical biology. 2: Sketches* (pp. 227–235). Chicago: Aldine.

29. Maturana, H., & Varela, F. J. (1973). *De Máquinas y Seres Vivos: Una teoría de la organizacíon biológica.* Santiago de Chile: Editorial Universitaria. Reprinted in H. Maturana and F. J. Varela, *Autopoiesis and cognition: the realization of the living* (1980).

30. Maturana, H., & Varela, F. J. (1980). *Autopoiesis and cognition: the realization of the living.* Boston: D. Reidel.

31. McCaskill, J. S. (1990). *Polymer chemistry on tape.* Unpublished manuscript.

32. Milner, R. (1989). *Communication and concurrency.* Englewood Cliffs, NJ: Prentice-Hall.

33. Milner, R. (1990). Functions as processes. In *Lecture notes in computer science* (no. 443, pp. 167–180). Berlin: Springer-Verlag.

34. Milner, R., Parrow, J., & Walker, D. (1992). A calculus of mobile processes, I. *Information and Computation, 100,* 1–40.

35. Morowitz, H. J. (1992). *Beginnings of cellular life.* New Haven, CT: Yale University Press.

36. Rokshar, D. S., Anderson, P. W., & Stein, D. L. (1986). Self-organization in prebiological systems: simulation of a model for the origin of genetic information. *Journal of Molecular Evolution, 23,* 110.

37. Rössler, O. (1971). Ein systemtheoretisches Modell zur Biogenese. *Zeitschrift für Naturforschung, 26b,* 741–746.

38. Schuster, P., & Sigmund, K. (1983). Replicator dynamics. *Journal of Theoretical Biology, 100,* 533–538.

39. Sober, E. (1985). Darwin on natural selection: a philosophical perspective. In D. Kohn (Ed.), *The Darwinian heritage* (pp. 867–899). Princeton, NJ: Princeton University Press.

40. Spiegelman, S. (1971). An approach to experimental analysis of precellular evolution. *Quarterly Reviews of Biophysics, 4*, 36.

41. Stadler, P. F., Fontana, W., & Miller, J. H. (1993). Random catalytic reaction networks. *Physica D, 63*, 378–392.

42. Stadler, P. F., & Schuster, P. (1992). Mutation in autocatalytic reaction networks—an analysis based on perturbation theory. *Journal of Mathematical Biology, 30*, 597–631.

43. Thürk, M. (1993). *Ein Modell zur Selbstorganisation von Automatenalgorithmen zum Studium molekularer Evolution.* Unpublished doctoral dissertation. Universität Jena, Germany.

44. Tjiuikaua, T., Ballester, P., & Rebek, J., Jr. (1990). A self-replicating system. *Journal of the American Chemical Society, 112*, 1249–1250.

45. Varela, F. J. (1979). *Principles of biological autonomy.* New York: North-Holland.

46. von Kiedrowski, G. (1986). A self-replicating hexadeoxynucleotide. *Angewandte Chemie, 98*, 932–934.

47. von Neumann, J., & Morgenstern, O. (1953). *Theory of games and economic behavior* (3rd ed.). Princeton, NJ: Princeton University Press.

48. Williams, M. B. (1970). Deducing the consequences of evolution: a mathematical model. *Journal of Theoretical Biology, 29*, 343–385.

49. Williams, M. B. (1973). The logical status of natural selection and other evolutionary controversies. In M. Bunge (Ed.), *The methodological unity of science* (pp. 84–102). Dordrecht, The Netherlands.

50. Rasmussen, S., Knudsen, C., & Feldberg, R. (1992). Dynamics of programmable matter. In C. G. Langton, C. Taylor, J. D. Farmer, and S. Rasmussen (Eds.), *Artificial life II* (p. 211–254). Santa Fe Institute Studies in the Sciences of Complexity. Redwood City, CA: Addison-Wesley.

51. Kampis, G. (1991). *Self-modifying systems: a new framework for dynamics information and complexity.* Oxford, UK: Pergamon Press.

Learning About Life

Mitchel Resnick
MIT Media Laboratory
Cambridge, MA 02139
mres@media.mit.edu

Abstract   The growing interest in Artificial Life is part of a broader intellectual movement toward decentralized models and metaphors. But even as decentralized ideas spread through the culture, there is a deep-seated resistance to these ideas. People have strong attachments to centralized ways of thinking: they often assume centralized control where none exists. New types of computational tools and construction kits are needed to help people move beyond this "centralized mindset." Perhaps most important are new tools and activities for children, to help them develop new ways of looking at the world.

Keywords
decentralized systems, emergence, education, simulations, centralized mindset, epistemology

1   Introduction

For 300 years, the models and metaphors of Newtonian physics have dominated the world of science. Newton offered an image of the universe as a machine, a clockwork mechanism. Newton's universe is ruled by linear cause and effect—one gear turns, which makes a second gear turn, which makes a third gear turn, and so on. This cause–effect relationship is captured in Newton's $F = ma$ formula: force gives rise to acceleration, cause gives rise to effect.

These Newtonian images have spread beyond the community of scientists, deeply influencing work in the social sciences, the humanities, and the arts. Newtonian metaphors have formed the foundation for how people think about science—and, more generally, how they make sense of the world around them.

In recent years, a new set of models and metaphors has begun to spread through the scientific community, and gradually into the culture at large. Many of these new ideas come not from physics but from biology. In a growing number of disciplines, researchers are now viewing the systems they study less like clockwork mechanisms and more like complex ecosystems. Increasingly, ideas from ecology, ethology, and evolution are spreading beyond their disciplinary boundaries. Ideas like self-organization and emergence are affecting the direction and nature of research in many other fields, from economics to engineering to anthropology. In general, there is a pronounced shift toward *decentralized* models, in which patterns are determined not by some centralized authority, but by local interactions about decentralized components. The growing interest in the field of Artificial Life is both a reflection of and a contributor to this broader intellectual shift.

Biology-inspired models and metaphors will have their greatest influence when they spread outside of the scientific community and into the general culture. For children growing up in the world today, learning about living systems is taking on a new urgency. The point is not just to understand the biological world (although that, of course, is a worthy endeavor). Rather, decentralized models of living systems provide a basis for understanding many other systems and phenomena in the world. As these ideas seep out of the scientific community, they are likely to cause deep changes in how children (and adults too) make sense of the world. This paper explores ways to help make that happen.

2 New Ways of Thinking

Among living systems, there are many examples of decentralized phenomena. As ants forage for food, for example, their trail patterns are determined not by the dictates of the queen ant, but by local interactions among thousands of worker ants. In the immune system, armies of antibodies seek out bacteria in a systematic, coordinated attack—without any "generals" organizing the battle plan. The antibodies are organized without an organizer, coordinated without a coordinator.

But seeing the world in terms of decentralized interactions is a difficult shift for many people. It requires a fundamental shift in perspective, a new way of looking at the world. At some deep level, people have strong attachments to centralized ways of thinking. When people see patterns in the world (like a flock of birds), they often assume that there is some type of centralized control (a leader of the flock). And in constructing artificial systems, people often impose centralized control where none is needed (e.g., using top-down, hierarchical programming structures to control a robot's behavior).

According to this way of thinking, a pattern can exist only if someone (or something) creates and orchestrates the pattern. Everything must have a single cause, an ultimate controlling factor. The continuing resistance to evolutionary theories is an example: Many people still insist that someone or something must have explicitly designed the complex, orderly structures that we call life. As William Paley [14] argued nearly two centuries ago, "If you found a watch on the ground, you would assume that it must have had a maker; so must not the same be true of living systems, which are incredibly more complex?"

This assumption of centralized control, a phenomenon I call the *centralized mindset*, is not just a misconception of the scientifically naive. The history of science is filled with examples of scientists remaining committed to centralized explanations, even in the face of discrediting evidence. When fossil records showed that very different creatures existed at different times in history, scientists did not give up on ideas of supernatural creation. Rather, they hypothesized that there must have been a whole series of extinctions and new creations. In the 20th century, as the genetic basis of evolution became understood, scientists initially adopted a too centralized view of genes, focusing on the actions and fitness values of individual genes, rather than studying interactions among genes.

Even today, centralized thinking persists in evolutionary debates. In trying to explain the periodic massive extinctions of life on earth, many scientists assume some external cause—for example, periodic waves of meteors hitting the earth. But more decentralized explanations are possible. Recent computer simulations show that simple interactions within the standard evolutionary process can give rise to periodic massive extinctions, without any outside intervention [12].

The history of research on slime-mold cells, as told by Keller [9], provides another example of centralized thinking. At certain stages of their life cycle, slime-mold cells gather together into clusters. For many years, scientists believed that the aggregation process was coordinated by specialized slime-mold cells, known as "founder" or "pacemaker" cells. According to this theory, each pacemaker cell sends out a chemical signal, telling other slime-mold cells to gather around it, resulting in a cluster. In 1970, Keller and Segel [10] proposed an alternative model, showing how slime-mold cells can aggregate without any specialized cells. Nevertheless, for the following decade, other researchers continued to assume that special pacemaker cells were required to initiate the aggregation process. As Keller [9] writes, with an air of disbelief, "The pacemaker view was embraced with a degree of enthusiasm that suggests that this question was in some sense foreclosed." By the early 1980s, based on further research by Cohen and Hagan [4], researchers began to accept the idea of aggregation among homogeneous cells, without any pacemaker. But the decade-long resistance serves as some indication of the strength of the centralized mindset.

The centralized mindset can manifest itself in many different ways. When people observe patterns or structures in the world, they tend to assume that patterns are created either *by lead* or *by seed*. That is, they assume that a *leader* orchestrated the pattern (e.g., the bird at the front of the flock, the pacemaker slime-mold cell), or they assume that some *seed* (some preexisting, built-in inhomogeneity in the environment) gave rise to the pattern, much as a grain of sand gives rise to a pearl.

In some ways, it is not surprising that people tend to assume centralized control, even where none exists. Many phenomena in the world *are*, in fact, organized by a central designer. These phenomena act to reinforce the centralized mindset. When people see neat rows of corn in a field, they assume (correctly) that the corn was planted by a farmer. When people watch a ballet, they assume (correctly) that the movements of the dancers were planned by a choreographer. Moreover, most people participate in social systems (such as families and school classrooms) where power and authority are very centralized (sometimes excessively so).

In fact, centralized strategies are often very useful. Sometimes, it is a good idea to put someone or something in charge. The problem is that people, in the past, have relied almost entirely on centralized strategies. Decentralized approaches have been ignored, undervalued, and overlooked. Centralized solutions have been seen as *the* solution.

3   Tools for Learning

How can people move beyond this centralized mind-set? How can they develop new intuitions about decentralized phenomena? The methodology of Artificial Life suggests a solution. One of the basic tenets of Artificial Life is that the best way to learn about living systems is to try to construct living systems (or, at least, models and simulations of living systems). This idea holds true whether the learners are scientists or children. To help people move beyond the centralized mindset, it makes sense to provide them with opportunities to create, experiment, and play with decentralized systems.

This approach has strong backing in educational and psychological research, most notably in the so-called constructionist theory of learning [16,17]. Constructionism involves two types of construction. First, borrowing from the "constructivist" theories of Jean Piaget, it asserts that learning is an active process, in which people actively construct knowledge from the experiences in the world. To this, constructionism adds the idea that people construct new knowledge with particular effectiveness when they are engaged in constructing personally meaningful artifacts—be they sand castles, stories, LEGO robots, or computer programs.

Though constructionism shares certain ideas with "hands-on" approaches to education, it goes beyond hands-on in several important ways. In many hands-on activities, students simply follow a "recipe" of what to do. Students are limited in how far they can improvise and explore. Consider prepackaged simulations. No matter how well a prepackaged simulation is designed, it cannot take into account all of the possible "what if" questions that users will want to ask. A constructionist alternative is to provide students with tools so that they can construct (and modify) their own simulations. This approach not only expands the possible range of explorations, it also makes those explorations more personally meaningful.

The constructionist approach received a lasting endorsement from the great physicist Richard Feynman. On the day that Feynman died, the following message was found on his office blackboard: "What I cannot create, I do not understand" [6]. What was true for Feynman is true for the rest of us. One of the best ways to gain a deeper understanding of something is to create it, to construct it, to build it.

So to help people learn about decentralized systems, we need to provide them with new sets of tools for creating and experimenting with such systems. But what types of tools are needed? Over the years, computer scientists have developed a wide variety of decentralized computational models—such as neural networks [21], the subsumption architecture [3], and cellular automata [23]. In all of these models, orderly patterns can arise from interactions among a decentralized collection of computational objects. In neural networks, patterns of "activation" arise from interactions among low-level "nodes." With the subsumption architecture, actions of a robotic creature arise from interactions among low-level "behaviors."

These models, while very useful for professional researchers, are ill-suited for people who have little experience with (or little interest in) manipulating formal systems. In general, these models are based on objects and interactions that most people are not familar with. For example, the idea of writing "transition rules" for "cells" is not an idea that most people can relate to.

In recent years, a number of computer programs have attempted to bring ideas about decentralized systems to a broader audience. Some programs, such as Vehicles (based on Braitenberg [2]) and LEGO/Logo [18], allow people to explore simple animal behaviors. Other programs, such as Agar [24], SimAnt [13], and StarLogo [19,20], allow people to explore the collective behavior of social insects. Still others, such as SimLife [8], Echo [7], and Simulated Evolution [15], allow people to explore evolutionary behavior.

These programs, too, are limited as learning tools. Too often, these programs shield users from underlying mechanisms, preventing users from investigating, let alone modifying, the underlying models. And in many cases, the programs focus too much on achieving interesting behaviors and too little on helping users make sense of those behaviors. But these programs represent a good first step in making ideas about decentralized systems accessible to a broader (and younger) audience.

4 Learning Experiences

This section examines the types of learning experiences made possible by these new computational tools. The examples focus on two tools that I helped develop: LEGO/Logo and StarLogo.

LEGO/Logo is a type of creature construction kit. With LEGO/Logo, children can build robotic "creatures" out of LEGO pieces, using not only the traditional LEGO building bricks but also newer LEGO pieces like gears, motors, and sensors. Then, they write computer programs (using a modified version of the programming language Logo) to control the behaviors of the creatures.

StarLogo is a massively parallel programming language, designed especially for non-expert programmers. With StarLogo, people can write rules for thousands of graphic creatures on the computer screen, then observe the group level behaviors that emerge from the interactions. People can also write rules for "patches" of the world in which the creatures live, allowing new types of creature–environment interactions. For example, Figure 1 shows a StarLogo simulation inspired by the discussion of slime-mold aggregation. Each "creature" emits a chemical pheromone, while also following the gradient of the pheromone. The patches cause the pheromone to diffuse and evaporate. With this simple decentralized strategy, the creatures aggregate into clusters after several dozen time steps.

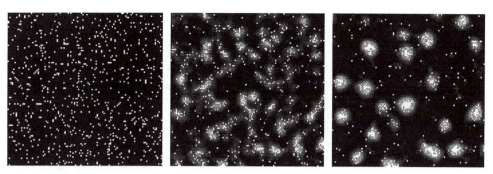

Figure 1. StarLogo simulation inspired by slime-mold aggregation.

4.1 LEGO/Logo Creatures

A major goal of Artificial Life research is to gain a better understanding of emergent phenomena. As Langton [11] put it, "The 'key' concept in Artificial Life is emergent behavior. Natural life emerges out of the organized interactions of a great number of nonliving molecules, with no global controller responsible for the behavior of every part."

In many animal systems, there are two types of emergence. First, the behavior of each individual creature emerges from interactions among the "agents" that make up the creature's mind. At the same time, the behavior of the entire animal colony or society emerges from the interactions among the individual creatures. In short, the colony level emerges from the creature level, which in turn emerges from the agent level.

With LEGO/Logo, children can begin to observe and experiment with simple emergent behaviors. Consider a simple LEGO creature with a light sensor pointing upward. Imagine that the creature is programmed with two rules: (a) move forward when you detect light, (b) move backward when you are in the dark. When this creature is released in the environment, it exhibits a type of emergent behavior: It seeks out the edge of a shadow, then happily oscillates around the shadow edge. The creature can be viewed as an "Edge-Finding Creature." This edge-finding capability is not explicitly represented in the creature's two rules. Rather, it emerges from interactions of those rules with specific structures in the environment.

Here is another example. When we started to develop LEGO/Logo, one of our first projects was to program a LEGO "turtle" to follow a line on the floor. The basic strategy was to make the turtle weave back and forth across the line, making a little forward progress on each swing. First, the turtle veered ahead and to the right, until it lost sight of the line. Then it veered ahead and to the left, until it again lost sight of the line. Then it started back to the right, and so on. This behavior can be represented by two simple rules: (a) If you are veering to the left and you lose sight of the line, begin to veer right; and (b) if you are veering to the right and you lose sight of the line, begin to veer left.

We tried the program, and the turtle followed the line perfectly. But as the turtle approached the end of the line, we realized that we hadn't "programmed in" any rules for what to do at the end of the line. We didn't know what the turtle would do. We were pleased with the behavior that emerged: The turtle turned all the way around and started heading back down the line in the other direction. This "end-of-line" behavior was not explicitly programmed into the turtle. Rather, it emerged from the interactions between the turtle's rules and the unfamiliar environment at the end of the line.

Of course, these examples represent very, very simple cases of emergence. But that is precisely what children (and, for that matter, learners of all ages) need, in order to start making sense of the unfamiliar concept of emergence.

4.2 StarLogo Termites

Philip Morrison, the MIT physicist and science educator, once told me a story about his childhood. When Morrison was in elementary school, one of his teachers described the invention of the arch as one of the central, defining milestones of human civilization. Arches took on a special meaning for the young Morrison. He felt a certain type of pride whenever he saw an arch. Many years later, when Morrison learned that lowly termites also build arches, he was quite surprised (and amused). He gained a new skepticism about everything that he was taught in school, and a new respect for the capabilities of termites. Ever since, Morrison has wondered about the limits of what termites might be able to do. If they can build arches, why not more complex structures? Given enough time, Morrison wondered, might termites build a radio telescope?

Probably not. But termites *are* among the master architects of the animal world. On the plains of Africa, termites construct giant moundlike nests rising more than 10 feet tall, thousands of times taller than the termites themselves. Inside the mounds are intricate networks of tunnels and chambers. Certain species of termites even use architectural tricks to regulate the temperature inside their nests, in effect turning their nests into elaborate air-conditioning systems. As E. O. Wilson [25] notes, "The entire history of the termites ... can be viewed as a slow escape by means of architectural innovation from a dependence on rotting wood for shelter."

Each termite colony has a queen. But, as in ant colonies, the termite queen does not "tell" the termite workers what to do. (In fact, it seems fair to wonder if the designation "queen" is a reflection of human biases. "Queen" seems to imply "leader." But the queen is more of a "mother" to the colony than a "leader.") On the termite construction site, there is no construction foreman, no one in charge of the master plan. Rather, each termite carries out a relatively simple task. Termites are practically blind, so they must interact with each other (and with the world around them) primarily through their senses of touch and smell. But from local interactions among thousands of termites, impressive structures emerge.

The global-from-local nature of termite constructions makes them well suited for StarLogo explorations. Of course, simulating the construction of an entire termite nest would be a monumental project (involving many details unrelated to my interests). Instead, I worked together with a high-school student, named Callie, on a simpler project: program the termites to collect wood chips and put them into piles. At the start of the program, wood chips were scattered randomly throughout the termites' world. The challenge was to make the termites organize the wood chips into a few, orderly piles.

We started with a very simple strategy. We made each individual termite obey the following rules:

- If you are not carrying anything and you bump into a wood chip, pick it up.

- If you are carrying a wood chip and you bump into another wood chip, put down the wood chip you're carrying.

At first, we were skeptical that this simple strategy would work. There was no mechanism for preventing termites from taking wood chips away from existing piles. So while termites are putting new wood chips on a pile, other termites might be taking wood chips away from it. It seemed like a good prescription for getting nowhere. But we pushed ahead and implemented the strategy in a StarLogo program, with 1,000 termites and 2,000 wood chips scattered in a 128 × 128 grid.

We tried the program, and (much to our surprise) it worked quite well. At first, the termites gathered the wood chips into hundreds of small piles. But gradually,

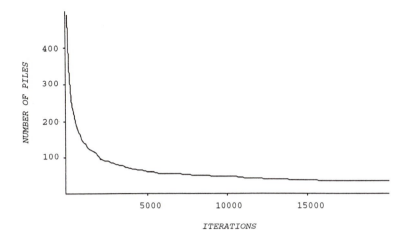

Figure 2. The number of piles decreases monotonically.

the number of piles declined, while the number of wood chips in each surviving pile increased (see Figure 2). After 2,000 iterations, there were about 100 piles, with an average of 15 wood chips in each pile. After 10,000 iterations, there were fewer than 50 piles left, with an average of 30 wood chips in each pile. After 20,000 iterations, only 34 piles remained, with an average of 44 wood chips in each pile. The process was rather slow. And it was frustrating to watch, because termites often carried wood chips away from well-established piles. But, all in all, the program worked quite well.

Why did it work? As we watched the program, it suddenly seemed obvious. Imagine what happens when the termites (by chance) remove all of the wood chips from a particular pile. Because all of the wood chips are gone from that spot, termites will never again drop wood chips there. So the pile has no way of restarting.

As long as a pile exists, its size is a two-way street: It can either grow or shrink. But the *existence* of a pile is a one-way street: Once it is gone, it is gone forever. Thus, a pile is somewhat analogous to a species of creatures in the real world. As long as the species exists, the number of individuals in the species can go up or down. But once all of the individuals are gone, the species is extinct, gone forever. In these cases, zero is a "trapped state": Once the number of creatures in a species (or the number of wood chips in a pile) goes to zero, it can never rebound.

Of course, the analogy between species and piles breaks down in some ways. New species are sometimes created, as offshoots of existing species. But in the termite program, as written, there is no way to create a new pile. The program starts with roughly 2,000 wood chips. These wood chips can be viewed as 2,000 "piles," each with a single wood chip. As the program runs, some piles disappear, and no new piles are created. So the total number of piles keeps shrinking and shrinking.

Callie seemed to thrive in the decentralized environment of StarLogo. At one point, while we were struggling to get our termite program working, I asked Callie if we should give up on our decentralized approach and program the termites to take their wood chips to predesignated spots. Callie quickly dismissed this suggestion:

Mitchel: We could write the program so that the termites know where the
           piles are. As soon as a termite picks up a wood chip, it could just go
           to the pile and put it down.

Callie: Oh, that's boring!

Mitchel: Why do you think that's boring?

Callie: 'Cause you're telling them what to do.

Mitchel: Is this more like the way it would be in the real world?

Callie: Yeah. You would almost know what to expect if you tell them to go
            to a particular spot and put it down. You know that there will be
            three piles. Whereas here, you don't know how many mounds there
            are going to be. Or if the number of mounds will increase or
            decrease. Or things like that. . . . This way, they [the termites] made
            the piles by themselves. It wasn't like they [the piles] were
            artificially put in.

For Callie, preprogrammed behavior, even if effective, was "boring." Callie preferred
the decentralized approach because it made the termites seem more independent ("they
made the piles by themselves") and less predictable ("you don't know how many
mounds there are going to be").

5   Decentralized Thinking

Like Callie, many students are fascinated by decentralized phenomena. But they also
have a difficult time understanding and creating such phenomena. They often slip back
into centralized ways of thinking. As I have worked with students, I have developed
a list of "guiding ideas" that seem to help students make sense of decentralized phenomena. These guiding ideas are not very "strong." They are neither prescriptive nor
predictive. They don't tell you precisely how to think about decentralized systems,
and they don't tell you how to make accurate predictions about such systems. Rather,
they are ideas to keep in mind as you try to make sense of an unfamiliar system, or to
design a new one. They highlight some pitfalls to avoid and some possibilities not to
overlook. In this section, I discuss five of these guiding ideas.

5.1   Positive Feedback Isn't Always Negative
Positive feedback has an image problem. People tend to see positive feedback as
destructive, making things spiral out of control. For most people, positive feedback is
symbolized by the screeching sound that results when a microphone is placed near a
speaker. By contrast, negative feedback is viewed as very useful, keeping things under
control. Negative feedback is symbolized by the thermostat, keeping room temperature
at a desired level by turning the heater on and off as needed.

Historically, researchers have paid much more attention to negative feedback than
to positive feedback. As Deneubourg and Goss [5] note, "When feedback is discussed
in animal groups, it is nearly always negative feedback that is considered, and its role
is limited to that of a regulatory mechanism, in which fluctuations are damped and
equilibrium is the goal. . . . Positive feedback is only rarely considered."

When I asked high-school students about positive feedback, most weren't familiar
with the term. But they were certainly familiar with the concept. When I explained
what I meant by positive feedback, the students quickly generated examples. Not
surprisingly, almost all of their examples involved something getting out of control,
often with destructive consequences. One student talked about scratching a mosquito

bite, which made the bite itch even more, so she scratched it some more, which made it itch even more, and so on. Another student talked about stock market crashes: A few people start selling, which makes more people start selling, which makes even more people start selling, and so on.

Despite these negative images, positive feedback often plays a crucial role in decentralized phenomena. Economist Brian Arthur [1] points to the geographic distribution of cities and industries as an example of a self-organizing process driven by positive feedback. Once a small nucleus of high-technology electronics companies started in Santa Clara County south of San Francisco, an infrastructure developed to serve the needs of those companies. That infrastructure encouraged even more electronics companies to locate in Santa Clara County, which encouraged the development of an even more robust infrastructure. And, thus, Silicon Valley was born.

For some students who used StarLogo, the idea of positive feedback provided a new way of looking at their world. One day, one student came to me excitedly. He had been in downtown Boston at lunch time, and he had a vision. He imagined two people walking into a deli to buy lunch:

> Once they get their food, they don't eat it there. They bring it back with them. Other people on the street smell the sandwiches and see the deli bag, and they say, "Hey, maybe I'll go to the deli for lunch today!" They were just walking down the street, minding their own business, and all of a sudden they want to go to the deli. As more people go to the deli, there's even more smell and more bags. So more people go to the deli. But then the deli runs out of food. There's no more smell on the street from the sandwiches. So no one else goes to the deli.

5.2 Randomness Can Help Create Order

Like positive feedback, randomness has a bad image. Most people see randomness as annoying at best, destructive at worst. They view randomness in opposition to order: Randomness undoes order, it makes things disorderly.

In fact, randomness plays an important role in many self-organizing systems. As discussed earlier, people often assume that "seeds" are needed to initiate patterns and structures. When people see a traffic jam, for example, they assume the traffic jam grew from a seed—perhaps a broken bridge or a radar trap. In general, this is a useful intuition. The problem is that most people have too narrow a conception of "seeds." They think only of preexisting inhomogeneities in the environment—like a broken bridge on the highway, or a piece of food in an ant's world.

This narrow view of seeds causes misintuitions when people try to make sense of self-organizing systems. In self-organizing systems, seeds are neither preexisting nor externally imposed. Rather, self-organizing systems often create *their own* seeds. It is here that randomness plays a crucial role. In many self-organizing systems, random fluctuations act as the "seeds" from which patterns and structures grow.

This combination of random fluctuations plus positive feedback underlies many everyday phenomena. Sometimes, at concerts or sporting events, thousands of spectators join together in rhythmic, synchronized clapping. How do they coordinate their applause? There is no conductor leading them. Here's one way to think about what happens. Initially, when everyone starts clapping, the applause is totally unorganized. Even people clapping at the same tempo are wildly out of phase with one another. But, through some random fluctuation, a small subset of people happen to clap at the same tempo, in phase with one another. That rhythm stands out, just a little, in the clapping noise. People in the audience sense this emerging rhythm and adjust their own clapping to join it. Thus, the emerging rhythm becomes a little stronger, and even more people conform to it. Eventually, nearly everyone in the audience is clapping in a synchronized rhythm. Amazingly, the whole process takes just a few seconds, even with thousands of people participating.

5.3   A Flock Isn't a Big Bird

In trying to make sense of decentralized systems and self-organizing phenomena, the idea of *levels* is critically important. Interactions among objects at one level give rise to new types of objects at another level. Interactions among slime-mold cells give rise to slime-mold clusters. Interactions among ants give rise to foraging trails. Interactions among cars give rise to traffic jams. Interactions among birds give rise to flocks.

In many cases, the objects on one level behave very differently than objects on another level. For high-school students, these differences in behavior can be very surprising, if not confusing. For example, several high-school students used StarLogo to explore the behavior of traffic jams. They wrote simple rules for each car (if there is a car close ahead of you, slow down; if not, speed up), then observed the traffic jams that resulted from the interactions. The students were shocked when the traffic jams began to move backward, even though all of the cars within the jams were moving forward.

Confusion of levels is not a problem restricted to scientifically naive high-school students. I showed the StarLogo traffic program to two visiting researchers, each of whom is involved in the cybernetics research community. They were not at all surprised that the traffic jams were moving backward. They were well aware of that phenomenon. But then one of the researchers said, "You know, I've heard that's why there are so many accidents on the freeways in Los Angeles. The traffic jams are moving backward and the cars are rushing forward, so there are lots of accidents." The other researcher thought for a moment, then replied, "Wait a minute. Cars crash into other cars, not into traffic jams." In short, he felt that the first researcher had confused levels, mixing cars and jams inappropriately. The two researchers then spent half an hour trying to sort out the problem.

5.4   A Traffic Jam Isn't Just a Collection of Cars

For most everyday objects, it is fair to think of the object as a collection of particular parts. (A particular chair might have four particular legs, a particular seat, a particular back.) But not so with objects like traffic jams. Thinking of a traffic jam as a collection of particular parts is a sure path to confusion. The cars composing a traffic jam are always changing, as some cars leave the front of the jam and others join from behind. Even when all of the cars in the jam are replaced with new cars, it is still the same traffic jam. A traffic jam can be thought of as an "emergent object"—it emerges from the interactions among lower-level objects (in this case, cars).

As students work on StarLogo projects, they encounter many emergent objects. In the termite example discussed earlier, the wood chip piles can be viewed as emergent objects. The precise composition of the piles is always changing, as termites take away some wood chips and add other wood chips. After a while, none of the original wood chips remains, but the pile is still there.

Students often have difficulty thinking about emergent objects. Two students, Frank and Ramesh, tried to use StarLogo to create "ant cemeteries." In their own (real) ant farms, they had observed ants gathering their dead colleagues into neat piles. They wondered how the ants did that. This problem is virtually identical to the problem of termites gathering wood chips into piles. But Frank and Ramesh resisted the simple decentralized approach that Callie and I used for the termites. They were adamant that dead ants should never be taken from a cemetery once placed there. They felt that the ants themselves defined the cemetary. How can a cemetery grow, they argued, if the dead ants in it are continually being taken away? In fact, if Frank and Ramesh had viewed the cemetary as an emergent object and allowed the composition of ant cemeteries to vary with time (as Callie and I allowed the composition of the wood chip piles to vary in the termite project), they probably would have been much more successful in their project.

5.5   The Hills are Alive

In *Sciences of the Artificial* [22], Simon describes a scene in which an ant is walking on a beach. Simon notes that the ant's path might be quite complex. But the complexity of the path, says Simon, is not necessarily a reflection of the complexity of the ant. Rather, it might reflect the complexity of the beach. Simon's point: don't underestimate the role of the environment in influencing and constraining behavior. People often seem to think of the environment as something to be *acted upon,* not something to be *interacted with.* People tend to focus on the behaviors of individual objects, ignoring the environment that surrounds (and interacts with) the objects.

A richer view of the environment is particularly important in thinking about decentralized and self-organizing systems. In designing StarLogo, I explicitly tried to highlight the environment. Most creature-oriented programming environments treat the environment as a passive entity, manipulated by the creature that move within it. In StarLogo, by contrast, the "patches" of the world have equal status with the creatures that move in the world. The environment is "alive"—it can execute actions even as creatures move within it. By reifying the environment, I hoped to encourage people to think about the environment in new ways.

Some students, however, resisted the idea of an active environment. When I explained a StarLogo ant-foraging program to one student, he was worried that pheromone trails would continue to attract ants even after the food sources at the ends of the trails had been fully depleted. He developed an elaborate scheme in which the ants, after collecting all of the food, deposited a second pheromone to neutralize the first pheromone. It never occurred to him to let the first pheromone evaporate away. In his mind, the ants had to take some positive action to get rid of the first pheromone. They couldn't rely on the environment to make the first pheromone go away.

6   Conclusions

The centralized mindset has undoubtedly affected many theories and trends in the history of science. Just as children assimilate new information by fitting it into their preexisting models and conceptions of the world, so do scientists. As Keller [9] puts it, "In our zealous desire for familiar models of explanation, we risk not noticing the discrepancies between our own predispositions and the range of possibilities inherent in natural phenomena. In short we risk imposing on nature the very stories we like to hear." In particular, we risk imposing centralized models on a decentralized world.

For many years, there has been a self-reinforcing spiral. People saw the world in centralized ways, so they constructed centralized tools and models, which further encouraged a centralized view of the world. Until recently, there was little pressure against this centralization spiral. For many things that people created and organized, centralized approaches tended to be adequate, even superior to decentralized ones. Even if someone wanted to experiment with decentralized approaches, there were few tools or opportunities to do so.

But the centralization spiral is now starting to unwind. As organizations and scientific models grow more complex, there is a greater need for decentralized ideas. At the same time, new decentralized tools (like StarLogo) are emerging that enable people to actually implement and explore such ideas. Still, many challenges lie ahead. We need to develop better explanations of why people are so committed to centralized explanations. And we need to develop better tools to help people visualize and manipulate decentralized interactions. Ultimately, we need to develop new tools and theories that avoid the simple dichotomy between centralization and decentralization, but rather find ways to integrate the two approaches, drawing on the best of both. Only then will we truly be ready to move beyond the centralized mindset.

Acknowledgments

Hal Abelson, Seymour Papert, Brian Silverman, Randy Sargent, Uri Wilensky, and Ryan Evans have provided encouragement, inspiration, and ideas for the StarLogo project. Steve Ocko, Fred Martin, Randy Sargent, Brian Silverman, and Seymour Papert have been major contributors to the LEGO/Logo project. Special thanks go to Chris Langton for his comments on a draft of this paper—and, more generally, for his continuing interest in this research. The LEGO Group and the National Science Foundation (Grants 851031-0195, MDR-8751190, and TPE-8850449) have provided financial support.

References

1. Arthur, W. B. (1990). Positive feedbacks in the economy. *Scientific American, 262*(2), 92–99.

2. Braitenberg, V. (1984). *Vehicles*. Cambridge, MA: The MIT Press.

3. Brooks, R. (1991). Intelligence without representation. *Artificial Intelligence, 47*, 139–160.

4. Cohen, M., & Hagan, P. (1981). Diffusion-induced morphogenesis in *Dictyostelium. Journal of Theoretical Biology, 93*, 881–908.

5. Deneubourg, J. L., & Goss, S. (1989). Collective patterns and decision-making. *Ethology, Ecology, & Evolution, 1*, 295–311.

6. Gleick, J. (1987). *Chaos: making a new science*. New York: Viking Penguin.

7. Holland, J. (1993). *Echoing emergence*. Santa Fe Institute Working Paper 93-04-023. Santa Fe, NM.

8. Karakotsios, K. (1992). *SimLife: the genetic playground*. Orinda, CA: Maxis Inc.

9. Keller, E. F. (1985). *Reflections on gender and science*. New Haven, CT: Yale University Press.

10. Keller, E. F., & Segel, L. (1970). Initiation of slime mold aggregation viewed as an instability. *Journal of Theoretical Biology, 26*, 399–415.

11. Langton, C. (Ed.) (1989). *Artificial life*. Redwood City, CA: Addison-Wesley.

12. Lindgren, K. (1991). Evolutionary Phenomena in Simple Dynamics. In C. Langton, C. Taylor, J. D. Farmer, & S. Rasmussen (Eds.), *Artificial life II*. Reading, MA: Addison-Wesley.

13. McCormick, J., & Wright, W. (1991). *SimAnt*. Orinda, CA: Maxis Inc.

14. Paley, W. (1802). *Natural theology—or evidences of the existence and attributes of the deity collected from the appearances of nature*. Oxford, UK: J. Vincent.

15. Palmiter, M. (1989). *Simulated evolution*. Bayport, NY: Life Sciences Associates.

16. Papert, S. (1980). *Mindstorms: children, computers, and powerful ideas*. New York: Basic Books.

17. Papert, S. (1991). Situating constructionism. In I. Harel & S. Papert (Eds.), *Constructionism*. Norwood, NJ: Ablex Publishing.

18. Resnick, M. (1989). LEGO, Logo, and Life. In C. Langton (Ed.), *Artificial life*. Redwood City, CA: Addison-Wesley.

19. Resnick, M. (1991). Animal simulations with *Logo: Massive parallelism for the masses. In J. A. Meyer & S. Wilson (Eds.), *From animals to animats*. Cambridge, MA: The MIT Press.

20. Resnick, M. (1992). *Beyond the centralized mindset: explorations in massively parallel microworlds*. Unpublished doctoral dissertation, Massachusetts Institute of Technology, Cambridge, MA.

21. Rumelhart, D., McClelland, J., & the PDP Research Group. (1986). *Parallel distributed processing*. Cambridge, MA: The MIT Press.

22. Simon, H. (1969). *The sciences of the artificial*. Cambridge, MA: The MIT Press.

23. Toffoli, T., & Margolus, N. (1987). *Cellular automata machines*. Cambridge, MA: The MIT Press.

24. Travers, M. (1989). Animal construction kits. In C. Langton (Ed.), *Artificial life*. Redwood City, CA: Addison-Wesley.

25. Wilson, E. O. (1971). *The insect societies*. Cambridge, MA: Harvard University Press.

Book Reviews

David G. Stork
Book Review Editor
Ricoh California
Research Center
2882 Sand Hill Road
Suite 115
Menlo Park, CA
94025-7022
stork@crc.ricoh.com

Books on Artifical Life and Related Topics

- *Adaptation in Natural and Artificial Systems: An Introductory Analysis with Applications to Biology, Control, and Artificial Intelligence.* J. Holland, (1992, Bradford Books/The MIT Press); $14.95 paper, $30 hardcover.

- *Artificial Life: Proceedings of an Interdisciplinary Workshop on the Synthesis and Simulation of Living Systems.* C. Langton (1989, Addison-Wesley); $24.95 paper, $41.95 hardcover.

- *Artificial Life II: Proceedings of the Workshop on Artificial Life.* C. Langton, D. Taylor, J. D. Farmer, & S. Rasmussen (Eds.) (1992, Addison-Wesley); $33.95 paper.

- *Toward a Practice of Autonomous Systems: Proceedings of the First European Conference on Artificial Life.* F. J. Varela & P. Bourgine (Eds.) (1992, MIT Press); $55.00 paper.

- *From Animals to Animats: Proceedings of the Second International Conference on Simulation of Adaptive Behavior.* J.-A. Meyer, H. L. Roitblat, & S. W. Wilson (Eds.) (1993, Bradford Books/The MIT Press); $55.00 paper.

- *Designing Automonous Agents.* P. Maes (Ed.) (1990, Bradford Books/The MIT Press); $22.95 paper.

- *Genetic Algorithms in Search, Optimization and Machine Learning.* D. Goldberg (1989, Addison-Wesley); $43.95 hardcover.

- *Genetic Programming: On the Programming of Computers by Means of Natural Selection.* J. Koza (1993, Bradford Books/The MIT Press); $55.00 hardcover.

- *Emergent Computation.* S. Forrest (Ed.) (1991, Bradford Books/The MIT Press); $32.50 paper.

- *The Algorithmic Beauty of Plants.* P. Prusinkiewicz & A. Lindenmayer (Springer Verlag, 1990); $39.95 hardcover.

- *Artificial Life: The Quest for a New Creation.* S. Levy (Random House, 1992); $25.00 hardcover.

The number of books on biology, evolutionary theory, learning, development, complex systems, neural networks, and other topics relevant to the study of Artificial Life is enormous, of course, but there is nevertheless a small, identifiable and growing number of books and conference proceedings available on topics most central to the field. A few books, such as John von Neumann's visionary *Theory of Self-Reproducing Automata* (1966), in which he explicitly put forth many key ideas in the field, are out of print and can best be found in better libraries. These older books appear in the reference lists in several of the books whose descriptions follow, and should be consulted whenever possible; the history of Artifical Life extends back longer than just the last 5 years! Here we consider a few of the more important books currently available, with particular attention to what they provide to newcomers to the field.

We can thank The MIT Press for reprinting John Holland's 1975 book, *Adaptation in Natural and Artificial Systems*, which deals with simulating evolution by genetic algorithms (which he referred to as "genetic" or "adaptive plans")—a fundamental theme in contemporary artificial life research. In the intervening years, the notation employed in the field has been simplified and some of the concepts refined and extended; nevertheless, many of Holland's central ideas remain vital and important. Even the particular demonstration problems he considered (e.g., maze running and the Prisoner's Dilemma) are common test cases in contemporary research. Particularly useful is his chapter, "Reproductive Plans and Genetic Operators," which clarifies and quantifies the computational power of genetic processes such as crossover, inversion, mutation, and so forth.

It should be noted, though, that there was work centered on simulated evolution almost a decade before the book came out, such as described in R. S. Rosenberg's *Simulation of Genetic Populations with Biochemical Properties* (1967). While Holland introduced many of the key ideas to the field, his greatest contributions were to clarify and add to the central concepts, and most importantly to have a vision of where they might lead.

Prospective readers of Holland's book would greatly profit from a preparation in elementary probability and combinatorics and should be prepared to work through a few derivations and technical discussions that are (in easy retrospect) a bit abstruse. A new chapter, "Interim and Prospectus," highlights topics such as combat, and mating strategies, illustrated by Holland's computer model system Echo. If the reader has only $15 to spend on Artifical Life, this book (in paperback) is the one to get.

Several conference and workshop proceedings are a source of information on the latest work. *Artificial Life*, from the 1987 Los Alamos workshop marking a renaissance of interest in the field, is an excellent place to start. Particularly valuable is the opening contribution by the book's editor, Chris Langton, which includes a review of the history and guiding concepts. The topics represented in the book are a bit scattered, with everything from simulating the origin of biological life to nanotechnology with Feynmann machines and artificial life for computer graphics. There are a number of "policy" papers, such as Hans Moravec's "Human Culture: A Genetic Takeover Underway" and Richard Laing's "Artificial Organisms: History, Problems, Directions," that are thought provoking. Richard Dawkins' lively style in "The Evolution of Evolvability" is one of the highlights in the book, and his simple simulations of "biomorphs" will serve to encourage anyone with a personal computer to try some experiments. The papers are significantly longer (roughly 30 pages, on average) than those from typical conference proceedings (and could even be considered chapters); they are long enough to get adequate detail for those interested in beginning work in the field.

The proceedings of the Second Workshop, *Artificial Life II*, preserves the enthusiasm and the diversity of the first. Neither can capture the lively discussions at the workshops themselves (e.g., over whether computer viruses are "really" alive or whether it is immoral to turn off some future computer simulation of artificial creatures). As J. D. Farmer and A. d'A. Belin point out in *Artificial Life II*, some people are deliberately provocative, and Eugene Spafford's "Computer Viruses—A Form of Artificial Life?" is productively provocative in just this way. Highlights in this book include a pair of papers on the "edge of chaos,"—one by Langton, the other by Stuart Kauffman and Sonke Johnson—as well as Danny Hillis' contribution on coevolving parasites, in which he describes methods for evolving one of the best algorithms for sorting numbers.

Papers from the First European Conference on Artificial Life, *Toward a Practice of Autonomous Systems*, reveal a slight emphasis on studying biological principles for creating autonomous robots. There are many papers on evolving robot navigation strategies, sensors, motor control systems, and so forth, and these (in the section "Autonomous Robots") provide the greatest value of the book. The other sections, "Swarm Intelligence," "Learning and Evolution," "Adaptive and Evolutionary Mechanisms," and "Issues and Conceptual Foundations," are of varied quality, although they provide a fairly good starting point for those new to the field. The papers are long enough (10 large-format pages, double column) for adequate detail and highlight the work going on in European laboratories.

Whereas these three Artificial Life proceedings just mentioned are quite broad, and what unity they possess centers on the exploration of the abstract, general strategies and principles underlying life, *From Animals to Animats* is a bit more focused on *organisms*. The majority of papers use the ideas from artificial life to create artificial autonomous systems based on biological principles or biological counterparts—"animats," as the editors define them. Several of the papers, such as S. Giszter's "Behavior Networks and Force Fields for Simulating Spinal Reflex Behaviors of the Frog," and R. Hartley's "Propulsion and Guidance in a Simulation of the Worm *C. Elegans*," are strongly influenced by "wet" biology. However, the majority are only loosely related to particular biological systems proper.

Designing Autonomous Agents: Theory and Practice from Biology to Engineering and Back contains 10 contributed chapters, generally exploring a methodological shift away from "deliberative" artificial intelligence, toward one based on sloppy "behavioral" and evolutionary methods. Perhaps its best spokesperson, and surely one of the most influential researchers in this approach, is Rodney Brooks, whose "Elephants Don't Play Chess" provides a good overview of his research program of developing "intelligent" systems through evolution and direct interaction with the physical world. The paper by Beer, Chiel, and Sterling, "A Biological Perspective on Autonomous Agent Design," describes how imposing biological constraints on a model insect can lead to interesting gates, a phenomenon studied by a number of groups reporting in the conference proceedings mentioned earlier. The Artificial Intelligence Laboratories at MIT and the Vrije U. Brussels, where editor Pattie Maes has affiliations, are strongly represented in the book, and if there is a drawback for the novice in the field, it is that a wide range of alternate groups and views on these topics lack representation.

Genetic algorithms are a recurring theme in many of the books, and David Goldberg's *Genetic Algorithms in Search, Optimization and Machine Learning*, the first full textbook on the subject, is a good place to learn about them. It could be used quite easily for a special course at the undergraduate level, or as supplemental reading for a course on control (or with less success, pattern recognition). There are but few subtle, challenging concepts or ones that rely on prerequisites beyond those required for simple programming. The problems he considers are, frankly, cooked up—useful pedagogically but not for convincing a skeptic of the power of the approach: the Prisoner's Dilemma, simple gambling tasks with a small number of choices, and so on. The most complicated is a 10-element planar truss in which the goal is to minimize the weight of the truss subject to load constraints. The explanations are generally clear and free of errors, and each chapter has problems and computer assignments; there are appendices with Pascal source code that make it easy to get started in programming and exploring on your own.

John Koza's *Genetic Programming* is closer to a research monograph on programming by means of natural selection and, frankly, at times reads like a manifesto. Koza clearly states his concepts and methodology, and he is by far more empirical (through numerous simulation studies) than theoretical. His basic approach is to use fragments of computer programs (e.g., Lisp strings) as the elements upon which variation and recombination occur. Although some genetic algorithm systems permit genes to change in length, in Koza's work it is essential that they do so, because the programs expand (or possibly contract) to solve a task. He provides a large number of simulation results on problems, such as the truck backer upper, trail following, and Pac Man, that show the effectiveness of the approach.

Koza notes that seven properties one typically desires in standard problem solving—correctness, consistency, justifiability, certainty, orderliness, parsimony, and decisiveness—are eschewed in genetic programming. Some programmers will cringe at the pages full of Lisp code that evolved to solve such "simple" problems as a broom balancer. Koza was right to include such code, though, because as programming by humans continues to stay expensive while hardware, memory, and computer speed continue their satisfying improvements, such "evolved" programs may appear more frequently. The issue of scalability will be crucial, however, and it is not yet clear how *large* code can be evolved by Koza's techniques. The appendixes provide the kernel and variations of some simple Lisp code for implementing genetic programming. Readers most concerned with Artificial Life proper should consult his sections on central place food foraging by ants, and the foraging strategy of the Anolis lizard. Here Koza shows computations of optimal foraging strategies in nature and how they can be duplicated by his genetic programming techniques—a very nice merging of ideas from biology and computer science.

A special 1990 issue of *Physica D* edited by Stephanie Forrest on *Emergent Computation* has been reprinted. There is a useful article by C. Langton, "Computation at the Edge of Chaos: Phase Transitions and Emergent Computation," on cellular automata studies of systems that evolve to the hazy condition between fully chaotic structurelessness and frozen order, that is, at the "edge" of chaos. Such work was influenced in part by Steve Wolfram's four-member categorization of cellular automata dynamics. A particularly valuable contribution is Stuart Kauffman's "Requirements for Evolvability in Complex Systems: Orderly Dynamics and Frozen Components," and, because it is long enough to explore important points in sufficient depth, this is the best place for the novice to read about his work on Boolean networks. A number of papers, while quite interesting, have little to do with Artificial Life proper. For instance, the quirky and interesting short paper, "Computer Arithmetic, Chaos and Fractals," by Julian Palmore and Charles Herring shows how the fact that computers necessarily employ finite precision calculations (as high as that precision might be) induces fractal structure on certain large computations.

In a qualitatively different vein, *The Algorithmic Beauty of Plants* by Przemyslaw Prusinkiewics and Aristid Lindenmayer stresses the *visual* ramifications of simple Artificial Life techniques. The numerous color photographs of simulated sunflowers, trees, and especially ferns will be an inspiration to many working in computer graphics.

The nature of the sources of fractal structure in plants and the modeling of cellular layers (especially during development) may be of greater interest to the general Artificial Life community. The book illustrates L systems (named after Lindenmayer), based on simple rewrite or "growing" models of plants. An example might be: take a short stalk and replace it by a forking branch; take each of these branches and replace each by another (smaller) forking branch, and so forth. It is really quite charming how trees and ferns can be simulated through such simple rules like these. Basic rules involving rate of cell division, structural forces, etc. can be run and compared closely with biological counterparts. For instance, by using L systems, cell lineage in *Microsorium linguaeforme* can be predicted and compared with micrographs.

Lindenmayer became seriously ill after beginning the book, and it was finished by his colleagues after his death. As such, it lacks a bit of unity and sweep, with somewhat abstract computer code juxtaposed with lovely computer graphs but without a textual analysis sufficiently deep to adequately inform the reader of the issues. Nevertheless, this is the best source of images derived from the principles of artificial life.

A good holiday present for a nontechnical spouse or an inquisitive high-school student would be Steven Levy's *Artificial Life: The Quest for a New Creation.* This trade book explains the field by following several seminal workers, and it blends biographical information (which typically provides the narrative structure) with the science, technology, and philosophy. Levy gets the science correct (although often after some appropriate simplifications) but occasionally succumbs to hype, especially in the earlier chapters. Some of the blame for this must be placed on a few scientists themselves, because Levy faithfully quotes their statements. It is just a bit harder to forgive Levy's dismissal of the skeptics of Artificial Life—some are thoughtful, careful and quite knowledgeable. (Artificial Life practitioners would do well, as many have, by taking these objections seriously.) In a similar vein, Levy attributes concepts or discoveries to the new Artificial Life people, whereas in some cases the ideas are much older. It adds drama, for instance, when recounting Danny Hillis' work on coevolution and punctuated equilibrium, to highlight the disagreements with "wet" biologists, although it is at the slight expense of veracity. But overall the book is quite enjoyable and can be recommended.

Space here does not permit mention of several other worthy books; reviews of these, and Artificial Life software, will have to await publication in subsequent issues of this journal.

Computer Viruses as Artificial Life

Eugene H. Spafford* †
Department of Computer
Sciences
Purdue University
West Lafayette, IN 47907-1398
spaf@cs.purdue.edu

Abstract   There has been considerable interest in computer viruses since they first appeared in 1981, and especially in the past few years as they have reached epidemic numbers in many personal computer environments. Viruses have been written about as a security problem, as a social problem, and as a possible means of performing useful tasks in a distributed computing environment. However, only recently have some scientists begun to ask if computer viruses are not a form of artificial life—a self-replicating organism. Simply because computer viruses do not exist as organic molecules may not be sufficient reason to dismiss the classification of this form of "vandalware" as a form of life. This paper begins with a description of how computer viruses operate and their history, and of the various ways computer viruses are structured. It then examines how viruses meet properties associated with life as defined by some researchers in the area of artificial life and self-organizing systems. The paper concludes with some comments directed toward the definition of artificially "alive" systems and experimentation.

Keywords
artificial life, ethics, computer virus

1 Introduction

There has been considerable interest in computer viruses during the last several years. One aspect of this interest has been to ask if computer viruses are a form of artificial life, and what that might imply. To address this, we must first understand something of the history and structure of computer viruses. Thus, we will begin with a condensed, high-level description of computer viruses—their history, structure, and how they relate to some properties that might define artificial life.

   A more detailed introduction to the topic of computer viruses may be found in the references, particularly [2, 3, 5, 9] and [15]. Also of use are references [10, 11, 14, 16] and [24], although the lists presented in the latter are somewhat out of date.

2 What Is a Computer Virus?

Computers are designed to execute instructions one after another. Those instructions usually do something useful—calculate values, maintain databases, and communicate with users and with other systems. Sometimes, however, the instructions executed can be damaging and malicious in nature. When that happens by accident, we call the code involved a software bug[1]—perhaps the most common cause of unexpected program behavior. If the source of the instructions was an individual who intended

---

∗ Portions of this paper are derived from Spafford [28, 30, 31].

† Copyright © 1989 ITAA, formerly ADAPSO, and 1991, 1993 by Eugene H. Spafford. Used with permission.

1 The original choice of the term bug is unfortunate in this context and is unrelated to the topic of artificial life.

that the abnormal behavior occur, then we consider this malicious coding; authorities have sometimes referred to this code as *malware* and *vandalware*. These names relate to the usual effect of such software.

There are many distinct forms of this software that are characterized by the way they behave, how they are triggered, and how they spread. In recent years, occurrences of malware have been described almost uniformly by the media as *computer viruses*. In some environments, people have been quick to report almost every problem as the result of a virus. This is unfortunate, because most problems are from other causes (including, most often, operator error). Viruses are widespread, but they are not responsible for many of the problems attributed to them.

The term computer virus is derived from and is in some sense analogous to a biological virus. The word *virus* itself is Latin for *poison*. Simplistically, biological viral infections are spread by the virus (a small shell containing genetic material) injecting its contents into a far larger organism's cell. The cell then is infected and converted into a biological factory producing replicants of the virus.

Similarly, a computer virus is a segment of machine code (typically 200–4,000 bytes) that will copy itself (or a modified version of itself) into one or more larger "host" programs when it is activated. When these infected programs are run, the viral code is executed, and the virus spreads further. Sometimes, what constitutes "programs" is more than simply applications: Boot code, device drivers, and command interpreters also can be infected.

Computer viruses cannot spread by infecting pure data; pure data files are not executed. However, some data, such as files with spreadsheet input or text files for editing, may be interpreted by application programs. For instance, text files may contain special sequences of characters that are executed as editor commands when the file is first read into the editor. Under these circumstances, the data files are "executed" and may spread a virus. Data files may also contain a "hidden" code that is executed when the file is used by an application, and this too may be infected. Technically speaking, however, pure data itself cannot be infected by a computer virus.

The first use of the term *virus* to refer to unwanted computer code was by the science fiction author David Gerrold. He wrote a series of short stories about a fictional G.O.D. machine (super computer) in the early 1970s that were later merged into a novel in 1972, titled *When Harlie Was One* [12]. The description of *virus* in that book does not fit the currently accepted, popular definition of computer virus—a program that alters other programs to include a copy of itself.

Cohen [2] formally defined the term *computer virus* in 1983. At that time, Cohen was a graduate student at the University of Southern California attending a security seminar. Something discussed in class inspired him to think about self-reproducing code. He put together a simple example that he demonstrated to the class. His advisor, Professor Len Adleman, thinking about the behavior of this creation, suggested that Cohen call his creation a computer virus. Dr. Cohen's doctoral thesis and later research were devoted to computer viruses.

Actual computer viruses were being written by individuals before Cohen, although not named such, as early as 1980 on Apple II computers [9]. The first few viruses were not circulated outside of a small population, with the notable exception of the "Elk Cloner" virus released in 1981 on several bulletin board systems.

Although Cohen (and others, including Adleman [1]) have attempted formal definitions of *computer virus*, none have gained widespread acceptance or use. This is a result of the difficulty in defining precisely the characteristics of what a virus is and is not. Cohen's formal definition includes any programs capable of self-reproduction. Thus, by his definition, programs such as compilers and editors would be classed as "viruses." This also has led to confusion when Cohen (and others) have referred to "good viruses"—something that most others involved in the field believe to be an oxymoron [4, 29].

Stubbs and Hoffman [32] quote a definition by John Inglis that captures the generally accepted view of computer viruses:

"He defines a virus as a piece of code with two characteristics:
1. At least a partially automated capability to reproduce.
2. A method of transfer which is dependent on its ability to attach itself to other computer entities (programs, disk sectors, data files, etc.) that move between these systems." (p. 145)

Several other interesting definitions are discussed in Highland [14, chap. 1].

After first appearing as a novelty, true computer viruses have become a significant problem. In particular, they have flourished in the weaker security environment of the personal computer. Personal computers were originally designed for a single dedicated user—little, if any, thought was given to the difficulties that might arise should others have even indirect access to the machine. The systems contained no security facilities beyond an optional key switch, and there was a minimal amount of security-related software available to safeguard data. Today, however, personal computers are being used for tasks far different from those originally envisioned, including managing company databases and participating in networks of computer systems. Unfortunately, their hardware and operating systems are still based on the assumption of single trusted-user access, and this allows computer viruses to spread and flourish on those machines. The population of users of PCs further adds to the problem, because many are unsophisticated and unaware of the potential problems involved with lax security and uncontrolled sharing of media.

Over time, the problem of viruses has grown to significant proportions. In the 7 years after the first infection by the *Brain* virus in January 1986, generally accepted as the first significant MS-DOS virus, the number of known viruses has grown to several thousand different viruses, most of which are for MS-DOS.

The problem has not been restricted to the IBM PC, however, and now affects all popular personal computers. Mainframe viruses may be written for any operating system that supports sharing of data and executable software, but all reported to date have been experimental in nature, written by serious academic researchers in controlled environments (e.g., [6]). This is probably a result, in part, of the greater restrictions built into the software and hardware of those machines, and of the way they are usually used. It may also be a reflection on the more technical nature of the user population of these machines.

2.1 Related Software

Worms are another form of software that is often referred to as a computer virus. Unlike viruses, worms are programs that can run independently and travel from machine to machine across network connections; worms may have portions of themselves running on many different machines. Worms do not change other programs, although they may carry other code that does, such as a true virus. It is their replication behavior that leads some people to believe that worms are a form of virus, especially those people using Cohen's formal definition (which incidentally would also classify standard network file transfer programs as viruses). The fact that worms do not modify existing programs is a clear distinction between viruses and worms, however.

In 1982, Shoch and Hupp [23] of Xerox PARC (Palo Alto Research Center) described the first computer worms. They were working with an experimental, networked environment using one of the first local area networks. While searching for something that would use their networked environment, one of them remembered reading *The Shock-wave Rider* by John Brunner, published in 1975. This science fiction novel described programs that traversed networks, carrying information with them. Those programs were called *tapeworms* in the novel. Shoch and Hupp named their own programs *worms*, because they saw a parallel to Brunner's tapeworms. The Xerox worms were actually useful—they would travel from workstation to workstation, reclaiming file space, shutting off idle workstations, delivering mail, and doing other useful tasks.

The Internet Worm of November 1988 is often cited as the canonical example of a damaging worm program [22, 26, 27]. The Worm clogged machines and networks as it spread out of control, replicating on thousands of machines around the Internet. Some authors (e.g., [7]) labeled the Internet Worm as a virus, but those arguments are not convincing (cf. the discussion in Spafford [25]). Most people working with self-replicating code now accept the Worm as a form of software distinct from computer viruses.

Few computer worms have been written in the time since then, especially worms that have caused damage, because they are not easy to write. Worms require a network environment and an author who is familiar not only with the network services and facilities but also with the operating facilities required to support them once they have reached their targets.

Worms have also appeared in other science fiction literature. Recent "cyberpunk" novels such as *Neuromancer* by William Gibson [13] refer to worms by the term virus. The media have also often referred incorrectly to worms as viruses. This paper focuses only on viruses as defined earlier. Many of the comments about viruses and artificial life may also be applied to worm programs.

Thimbleby [33] coined the term *liveware* to describe another form of self-propagating software that carries information or program updates. Liveware shares many of the characteristics of both viruses and worms but has the additional distinction of announcing its presence and requesting permission from the user to execute its intended functions. There have been no reports of liveware being discovered or developed other than by Thimbleby and his colleagues.

Other forms of self-reproducing and usually malicious software have also been written. Although no formal definitions have been accepted by the entire community to describe this software, there are some informal definitions that seem to be commonly accepted (cf. [21]). Several of these are often discussed by analogy to living organisms. This tendency toward anthropomorphism has perhaps led to some confusion about the nature of this software. Rather than discuss each of these software forms here, possibly adding to the confusion, the remainder of this paper will focus on computer viruses only; the interested reader may peruse the cited references.

3   Virus Structure and Operation

True viruses have two major components: one that handles the spread of the virus, and a "payload" or "manipulation" task. The payload task may not be present (has null effect), or it may await a set of predetermined circumstances before triggering.

For a computer virus to work, it somehow must add itself to other executable code. The viral code is usually executed before the code of its infected host (if the host code is ever executed again). One form of classification of computer viruses is based on the three ways a virus may add itself to host code: as a shell, as an add-on, and as intrusive code.

A fourth form, the so-called *companion virus*, is not really a virus at all, but a form of *Trojan horse* that uses the execution path mechanism to execute in place of a normal program. Unlike all other viral forms, it does not alter any existing code in

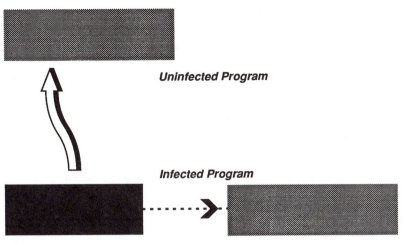

Figure 1. Shell virus infection.

any fashion: Companion viruses create new executable files with a name similar to an existing program, and they are chosen so that they are normally executed prior to the "real" program. Because companion viruses are not real viruses unless one uses a more encompassing definition of virus, they will not be described further here.

Shell viruses. A shell virus is one that forms a "shell" (as in "eggshell" rather than "Unix shell") around the original code. In effect, the virus becomes the program, and the original host program becomes an internal subroutine of the viral code. An extreme example of this would be a case where the virus moves the original code to a new location and takes on its identity. When the virus is finished executing, it retrieves the host program code and begins its execution. Almost all boot program viruses (described later) are shell viruses (Figure 1).

Add-on viruses. Most viruses are add-on viruses. They function by appending their code to the host code and/or by relocating the host code and inserting their own code to the beginning. The add-on virus then alters the start-up information of the program, executing the viral code before the code for the main program. The host code is left almost completely untouched; the only visible indication that a virus is present is that the file grows larger, if that can indeed be noticed (Figure 2).

Intrusive viruses. Intrusive viruses operate by overwriting some or all of the original host code with viral code. The replacement might be selective, as in replacing a subroutine with the virus, or inserting a new interrupt vector and routine. The replacement may also be extensive, as when large portions of the host program are completely replaced by the viral code. In the latter case, the original program can no longer function properly. Few viruses are intrusive viruses (Figure 3).

A second form of classification used by some authors (e.g., [24]) is to divide viruses into file infectors and boot (system start-up) program infectors. This is not particularly clear, however, because there are viruses that spread by altering system-related code that is neither boot code nor programs. Some viruses target file system directories, for example. Other viruses infect both application files *and* boot sectors. This second form of classification is also highly specific and only makes sense for machines that have infectable (writable) boot code.

Yet a third form of classification is related to how viruses are activated and select new targets for alteration. The simplest viruses are those that run when their "host" program is run, select a target program to modify, and then transfer control to the host.

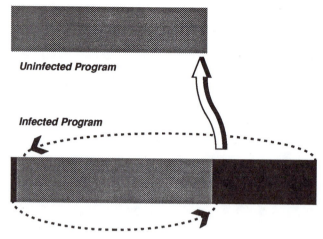

Figure 2. Add-on virus infection.

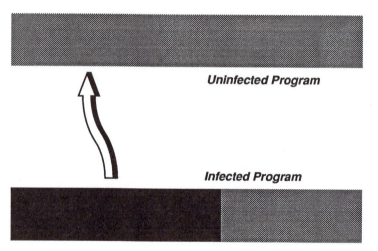

Figure 3. Intrusive virus infection.

These viruses are *transient* or *direct* viruses, known as such because they operate only for a short time, and they go directly to disk to seek out programs to infect.

The most "successful" PC viruses to date exploit a variety of techniques to remain resident in memory once their code has been executed and their host program has terminated. This implies that, once a single infected program has been run, the virus potentially can spread to any or all programs in the system. This spreading occurs during the entire work session (until the system is rebooted to clear the virus from memory), rather than during a small period of time when the infected program is executing viral code. These viruses are *resident* or *indirect* viruses, known as such because they stay resident in memory, and indirectly find files to infect as they are referenced by the user. These viruses are also known as TSR (**T**erminate and **S**tay **R**esident) viruses.

If a virus is present in memory after an application exits, how does it remain active? That is, how does the virus continue to infect other programs? The answer for personal computers running software such as MS-DOS is that the virus alters the standard

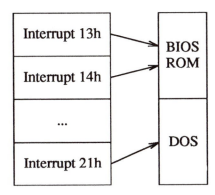

Figure 4. Normal interrupt usage.

interrupts used by DOS and the BIOS (Basic Input/Output System). The change to the environment is such that the virus code is invoked by other applications when they make service requests.

The PC uses many interrupts (both hardware and software) to deal with asynchronous events and to invoke system functions. All services provided by the BIOS and DOS are invoked by the user storing parameters in machine registers, then causing a software interrupt.

When an interrupt is raised, the operating system calls the routine whose address it finds in a special table known as the *vector* or *interrupt* table. Normally, this table contains pointers to handler routines in the ROM or in memory-resident portions of the DOS (see Figure 4). A virus can modify this table so that the interrupt causes viral code (resident in memory) to be executed.

By trapping the keyboard interrupt, a virus can arrange to intercept the **CTRL-ALT-DEL** soft reboot command, modify user keystrokes, or be invoked on each keystroke. By trapping the BIOS disk interrupt, a virus can intercept all BIOS disk activity, including reads of boot sectors, or disguise disk accesses to infect as part of a user's disk request. By trapping the DOS service interrupt, a virus can intercept all DOS service requests including program execution, DOS disk access, and memory allocation requests.

A typical virus might trap the DOS service interrupt, causing its code to be executed before calling the real DOS handler to process the request (see Figure 5.)

Once a virus has infected a program or boot record, it seeks to spread itself to other programs, and eventually to other systems. Simple viruses do no more than this, but most viruses are not simple viruses. Common viruses wait for a specific triggering condition and then perform some activity. The activity can be as simple as printing a message to the user or as complex as seeking particular data items in a specific file and changing their values. Often, viruses are destructive, removing files, or reformatting entire disks. Many viruses are also faulty and may cause unintended damage.

The conditions that trigger viruses can be arbitrarily complex. If it is possible to write a program to determine a set of conditions, then those same conditions can be used to trigger a virus. This includes waiting for a specific date or time, determining the presence or absence of a specific set of files (or their contents), examining user keystrokes for a sequence of input, examining display memory for a specific pattern, or checking file attributes for modification and permission information. Viruses also may be triggered based on some random event. One common trigger component is a counter used to determine how many additional programs the virus has succeeded in infecting—the virus does not trigger until it has propagated itself a certain minimum number of times. Of course, the trigger can be any combination of conditions, too.

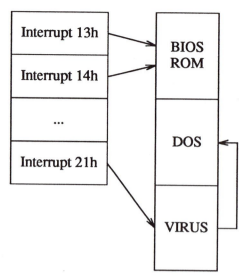

Figure 5. Interrupt vectors with TSR virus.

Computer viruses can infect any form of writable storage, including hard disk, floppy disk, tape, optical media, or memory. Infections can spread when a computer is booted from an infected disk, or when an infected program is run. This can occur either as the direct result of a user invoking an infected program, or indirectly through the system executing the code as part of the system boot sequence or a background administration task. It is important to realize that often the chain of infection can be complex and convoluted. With the presence of networks, viruses can also spread from machine to machine as executable code containing viruses is shared between machines.

Once activated, a virus may replicate into only one program at a time, it may infect some randomly chosen set of programs, or it may infect every program on the system. Sometimes a virus will replicate based on some random event or on the current value of the clock. The different methods will not be presented in detail because the result is the same: There are additional copies of the virus on the system.

4   Evolution of Viruses

Since the first viruses were written, we have seen what may be classified as five "generations" of viruses. Each new class of viruses has incorporated new features that make the viruses more difficult to detect and remove. Here, as with other classification and naming issues related to viruses, different researchers use different terms and definitions (cf. ref. [9, Appendix 10]). The following list presents one classification derived from a number of these sources. Note that these "generations" do not necessarily imply chronology. For instance, several early viruses (e.g., the "Brain" and "Pentagon" viruses) had stealth and armored characteristics. Rather, this list describes increasing levels of sophistication and complexity represented by computer viruses in the MS-DOS environment.

4.1   First Generation: Simple

The first generation of viruses were the simple viruses. These viruses did nothing very significant other than replicate. Many new viruses being discovered today still fall into this category. Damage from these simple viruses is usually caused by bugs or incompatibilities in software that were not anticipated by the virus author.

First-generation viruses do nothing to hide their presence on a system, so they can usually be found by means as simple as noting an increase in size of files or the presence of a distinctive pattern in an infected file.

4.2   Second Generation: Self-Recognition

One problem encountered by viruses is that of repeated infection of the host, leading to depleted memory and early detection. In the case of boot sector viruses, this could (depending on strategy) cause a long chain of linked sectors. In the case of a program-infecting virus, repeated infection may result in continual extension of the host program each time it is reinfected. There are indeed some older viruses that exhibit this behavior.

To prevent this unnecessary growth of infected files, second-generation viruses usually implant a unique *signature* that signals that the file or system is infected. The virus will check for this signature before attempting infection and will place it when infection has taken place; if the signature is present, the virus will not reinfect the host.

A virus signature can be a characteristic sequence of bytes at a known offset on disk or in memory, a specific feature of the directory entry (e.g., alteration time or file length), or a special system call available only when the virus is active in memory.

The signature presents a mixed blessing for the virus. The virus no longer performs redundant infections that might present a clue to its presence, but the signature does provide a method of detection. Virus sweep programs can scan files on disk for the signatures of known viruses or even "inoculate" the system by providing the viral signature in clean systems to prevent the virus from attempting infection.

4.3   Third Generation: Stealth

Most viruses may be identified on a contaminated system by means of scanning the secondary storage and searching for a pattern of data unique to each virus. To counteract such scans, some resident viruses employ stealth techniques. These viruses subvert selected system service call interrupts when they are active. Requests to perform these operations are intercepted by the virus code. If the operation would expose the presence of the virus, the operation is redirected to return false information.

For example, a common virus technique is to intercept I/O requests that would read sectors from disk. The virus code monitors these requests. If a read operation is detected that would return a block containing a copy of the virus, the active code returns instead a copy of the data that would be present in an uninfected system. In this way, virus scanners are unable to locate the virus on disk when the virus is active in memory. Similar techniques may be employed to avoid detection by other operations.

4.4   Fourth Generation: Armored

As antiviral researchers have developed tools to analyze new viruses and craft defenses, virus authors have turned to methods to obfuscate the code of their viruses. This "armoring" includes adding confusing and unnecessary code to make it more difficult to analyze the virus code. The defenses may also take the form of directed attacks against antiviral software, if present on the affected system. These viruses appeared starting in 1990.

Viruses with these forms of defenses tend to be significantly larger than simpler viruses and more easily noticed. Furthermore, the complexity required to significantly delay the efforts of trained antiviral experts appears to be far beyond anything that has yet appeared.

4.5   Fifth Generation: Polymorphic

The most recent class of viruses to appear on the scene are the polymorphic or self-mutating viruses. These are viruses that infect their targets with a modified or encrypted version of themselves. By varying the code sequences written to the file (but still functionally equivalent to the original), or by generating a different, random encryption key, the virus in the altered file will not be identifiable through the use of simple byte matching. To detect the presence of these viruses requires that a more complex algorithm be employed that, in effect, reverses the masking to determine if the virus is present.

Several of these viruses have become quite widespread. Some virus authors have released virus "toolkits" that can be incorporated into a complete virus to give it polymorphic capabilities. These toolkits have been circulated on various bulletin boards around the world and incorporated in several viruses.

5   Defenses and Outlook

There are several methods of defense against viruses. Unfortunately, no defense is perfect. It has been shown that any sharing of writable memory or communications with any other entity introduces the possibility of virus transmission. Furthermore, Cohen, Adleman [1, 2], and others have shown proofs that the problem of writing a program to exactly detect all viruses is formally undecidable: It is not possible to write a program that will detect every virus without any error.

Of some help is the observation that it is trivial to write a program that identifies all infected programs with 100% accuracy. Unfortunately, this program must identify *every* (or nearly so) program as infected, whether it is or not! This is not particularly helpful to the user, and the challenge is to write a detection mechanism that finds most viruses without generating an excessive number of false positive reports.

Defense against viruses generally takes one of three forms:

Activity monitors are programs that are resident on the system. They monitor activity and either raise a warning or take special action in the event of suspicious activity. Thus, attempts to alter the interrupt tables in memory or to rewrite the boot sector would be intercepted by such monitors. This form of defense can be circumvented (if implemented in software) by viruses that activate earlier in the boot sequence than the monitor code. They are further vulnerable to virus alteration if used on machines without hardware memory protection—as is the case with all common personal computers.

Another form of monitor is one that emulates or otherwise traces execution of a suspect application. The monitor evaluates the actions taken by the code and determines if any of the activity is similar to what a virus would undertake. Appropriate warnings are issued if suspicious activity is identified.

Scanners have been the most popular and widespread form of virus defense. A scanner operates by reading data from disk and applying pattern matching operations against a list of known virus patterns. If a match is found for a pattern, a virus instance is announced.

Scanners are fast and easy to use, but they suffer from many disadvantages. Foremost among the disadvantages is that the list of patterns must be kept up-to-date. In the MS-DOS world, new viruses are appearing by as many as several dozen each week. Keeping a pattern file up-to-date in this rapidly changing environment is difficult.

A second disadvantage to scanners is one of false positive reports. As more patterns are added to the list, it becomes more likely that one of them will match some otherwise legitimate code. A further disadvantage is that polymorphic viruses cannot be detected with scanners.

To the advantage of scanners, however, is their speed. Scanning can be made to work quite quickly. Scanning can also be done portably and across platforms [17], and pattern files are easy to distribute and update. Furthermore, of the new viruses discovered each week, few will ever become widespread. Thus, somewhat out-of-date pattern files are still adequate for most environments. Scanners equipped with algorithmic or heuristic checking may also find most polymorphic viruses. It is for these reasons that scanners are the most widely used form of antiviral software.

Integrity checkers/monitors are programs that generate checkcodes (e.g., checksums, cyclic redundancy codes (CRCs), secure hashes, message digests, or cryptographic checksums) for monitored files [20]. Periodically, these checkcodes are recomputed and compared against the saved versions. If the comparison fails, a change is known to have occurred to the file, and it is flagged for further investigation. Integrity monitors run continuously and check the integrity of files on a regular basis. Integrity shells recheck the checkcode prior to every execution [3].

Integrity checking is an almost certain way to discover alterations to files, including data files. Because viruses must alter files to implant themselves, integrity checking will find those changes, Furthermore, it does not matter if the virus is known or not—the integrity check will discover the change no matter what causes it. Integrity checking also may find other changes caused by buggy software, problems in hardware, and operator error.

Integrity checking also has drawbacks. On some systems, executable files change whenever the user runs the file or when a new set of preferences is recorded. Repeated false positive reports may lead the user to ignore future reports or disable the utility. It is also the case that a change may not be noticed until after an altered file has been run and a virus spread. More importantly, the initial calculation of the checkcode must be performed on a known unaltered version of each file. Otherwise, the monitor will never report the presence of a virus, probably leading the user to believe the system is uninfected.

Several vendors have begun to build self-checking into their products. This is a form of integrity check that is performed by the program at various times as it runs. If the self-check reveals some unexpected change in memory or on disk, the program will terminate or warn the user. This helps to signal the presence of a new virus quickly so that further action may be taken.

If no more computer viruses were written from now on, there would still be a computer virus problem for many years to come. Of the thousands of reported computer viruses, several hundred are well established on various types of computers around the world. The population of machines and archived media is such that these viruses would continue to propagate from a rather large population of contaminated machines.

Unfortunately, there appears to be no lessening of computer virus activity, at least within the MS-DOS community. Several new viruses are appearing every day. Some of these are undoubtedly being written out of curiosity and without thought for the potential damage. Others are being written with great purpose and with particular goals in mind—both political and criminal. Although it would seem of little interest to add to the swelling number of viruses in existence, many individuals seem to be doing exactly that.

6 Viruses as Artificial Life

Now that we know what computer viruses are and how they spread, we can examine the question of whether they represent a form of artificial life. The first, and obvious, question is "What is life?" Without an answer to this question, we will be unable to say if a computer virus is "alive."

One very reasonable list of properties associated with life was presented in Farmer and Belin [8]. That list included:

- *life is a pattern in space-time* rather than a specific material object.

- *self-reproduction*, in itself or in a related organism.

- *information storage of a self-representation.*

- *a metabolism* that converts matter/energy.

- *functional interactions with the environment.*

- *interdependence of parts.*

- *stability under perturbations* of the environment.

- *the ability to evolve.*

- *growth or expansion*

Let us examine each of these characteristics in relation to computer viruses.

6.1   Viruses as Patterns in Space-Time

There is a near match to this characteristic. Viruses are represented by patterns of computer instructions that exist over time on many computer systems. Viruses are not associated with the physical hardware but with the instructions executed (sometimes) by that hardware. Computer viruses, like all functional computer code, are simply manifestations of algorithms. The algorithms themselves also represent an underlying pattern.

It is questionable if these patterns exist in space, however, unless one extends the definition of space to "cyberspace," as represented by a computer system. The patterns of the viruses are a temporary set of electrical and magnetic field changes in the memory or storage of computer systems. The existence of the virus is only within these patterns of energy. Arguably, the code for each virus could be printed in ink on paper, resulting in a more substantiative existence. That, however, is merely a representation of the true virus and should not be viewed as existence any more than a picture of a person is itself the person.

6.2   Self-Reproduction of Viruses

One of the primary characteristics of computer viruses is their ability to reproduce themselves (or an altered version of themselves). Thus, this characteristic seems to be met. One of the key characteristics is their ability to reproduce.

However, it is perhaps more interesting to examine this aspect in light of the agent of reproduction. The virus code is not itself the agent—the computer is. It is questionable if this can be considered sufficient for purposes of classification as artificial life. To do so would imply that, for instance, the blueprints for a Xerox machine are capable of self-reproduction: When outside agents follow the instructions therein, it is possible to produce a new machine that can then be used to make a copy of them. It is not the blueprint (algorithm; virus) that is the agent of change but the entity that interprets it.

6.3   Information Storage of a Self-Representation

This is the most obvious match for computer viruses. The code that defines the virus is a template that is used by the virus to replicate itself. This is similar to the DNA molecules of what we recognize as organic life.

6.4   Virus Metabolism

This property involves the organism taking in energy or matter from the environment and using it for its own activity. Computer viruses use the energy of computation expended by the system to execute. They do not convert matter but make use of the electrical energy present in the computer to traverse their patterns of instructions and infect other programs. In this sense, they have a metabolism.

Again, however, we are forced to change this view if we examine the case more closely. The expenditure of energy is not by the virus but by the underlying computer system. If the virus were not active, and an interactive game were being run instead, the same amount of energy would be used. In most systems, even if no program is being run, the energy use remains constant. Thus, we must conclude that viruses do not actually have a metabolism.

6.5   Functional Interactions with the Virus's Environment

Viruses perform examinations of their host environments as part of their activities. They alter interrupts, examine memory and disk architectures, and alter addresses to hide themselves and spread to other hosts. They very obviously alter their environment to support their existence. Many viruses accidentally alter their environment because of bugs or unforeseen interactions. The major portion of damage from all computer viruses is a result of these interactions.

6.6   Interdependence of Virus Parts

Living organisms cannot be arbitrarily divided without destroying them. The same is true of computer viruses. Should a computer virus have a portion of its "anatomy" excised, the virus would probably cease to function normally, if at all. Few viruses are written with superfluous code, and, even so, the working code cannot be divided without disabling the virus.

However, it is interesting to note that the virus can be reassembled later and regain its functional status. If a living organism (as we know it) were to be divided into its component parts for a period of time, then reassembled, it would not become "alive" again. In this sense, computer viruses are more like simple machines or chemical reactions rather than instances of living things.

6.7   Virus Stability Under Perturbations

Computer viruses run on a variety of machines under different operating systems. Many of them are able to compromise (and defeat) antiviral and copy protection mechanisms. They may adjust on the fly to conditions of insufficient storage, disk errors, and other exceptional events. Some are capable of running on most variants of popular personal computers under almost any software configuration—a stability and robustness seen in few commercial applications.

6.8   Virus Evolution

Here, too, viruses display a difference from systems we traditionally view as "alive." No computer viruses evolve as we commonly use the term, although it is conceivable that a very complex virus could be programmed to evolve and change. However, such a virus would be so large and complex as to be many orders of magnitude larger than most host programs and probably bigger than the host operating systems. Thus, there is some doubt that such a virus could run on enough hosts to allow it to evolve. (Note that "evolve" implies a change in function or attributes; polymorphic viruses represent cases of random changes in structure but not functionality.)

Higher-level mutations of viruses do exist, however. There are variants of many known viruses, with over a dozen known for some IBM PC viruses. The variations involved can be very small, on the order of two or three instructions' difference, to major changes involving differences in messages, activation, and replication. The source of these variations appears to be programmers (the original virus authors or otherwise) who alter the viruses to avoid antiviral mechanisms or to cause different kinds of damage. Polymorphic viruses alter their copies to avoid detection, but the pattern of alteration is ultimately a human product. These changes do not constitute evolution, however.

Interestingly, there is also one case where two different strains of a Macintosh virus are known to interact to form infections unlike the "parents," although these interactions usually produce "sterile" offspring that are unable to reproduce further. This likewise does not appear to be evolution as we know it [19].

6.9 Growth

Viruses certainly do exhibit a form of growth, in the sense that there are more of them in a given environment over time. Some transient viruses will infect every file on a system after only a few activations. The spread of viruses through commercial software and public bulletin boards is another indication of their widespread replication. Although accurate numbers are difficult to derive, reports over the last few years indicate an approximate yearly doubling in the number of systems infected by computer viruses. Clearly, computer viruses are exhibiting significant growth.

6.10 Other Behavior

As already noted, computer viruses exhibit "species" with well-defined ecological niches based on host machine type and variations within these species. These species are adapted to specific environments and will not survive if moved to a different environment.

Some viruses also exhibit predatory behavior. For instance, the DenZuk virus will seek out and overwrite instances of the Brain virus if both are present on the same system. Other viruses exhibit territorial behavior—marking their infected domain so that others of the same type will not enter and compete with the original infection. Some viruses also exhibit self-protective behavior, including camouflage techniques.

It is important to note, however, that none of these characteristics came from the viruses themselves. Rather, each change and addition to virus behavior has been wrought by an outside agency: the programmer. These changes have been in reaction to a perceived need to "enhance" the virus—usually to make it more difficult to find.

It might well be argued that more traditional living organisms may also undergo change from without. As an example, background radiation may cause occasional random mutations. However, programmers are the only source of change to computer viruses, and this distinction is worth noting; other living systems undergo changes to themselves and their progeny without obvious outside agencies.

7 Concluding Comments

Our study of computer viruses at first suggests they are close to what we might define as "artificial life." However, upon closer examination, a number of significant deficiencies can be found. These lead us to conclude that computer viruses are not "alive," and it is not possible to refine them so as to make them "alive" without drastically altering our definition of "life."

To suggest that computer viruses are alive also implies that some part of their environment—the computers, programs, or operating systems—also represents artificial life. Can life exist in an otherwise barren and empty ecosystem? A definition of "life" should probably include something about the environment in which that life exists.

Undoubtedly, we could adjust our definitions and characteristics to encompass computer viruses or to better exclude them. This illustrates one of the fundamental difficulties with the entire field of artificial life: how to define essential characteristics in such a way as to unambiguously define living systems. Computer viruses provide one interesting example against which such definitions may be tested.

From this, we can observe that computer viruses (and their kin) provide an interesting means of modeling life. For at least this reason, research into computer viruses (using the term in a broader sense, a là Cohen) may be of some scientific interest. By modeling behavior using computer viruses, we may be able to gain some insight into systems with more complex interactions. Research into competition among computer viruses and other software, including antiviral techniques, is of practical interest as well as scientific interest. Modified versions of viruses such as Thimbleby's Liveware may also prove to be of ultimate value. Research into issues on virus defense methods, epidemiology, and on mutations and combinations also could provide valuable insight into computing.

The problem with research on computer viruses is their threat. True viruses are inherently unethical and dangerous. They operate without consent or knowledge; experience has shown that they cannot be recalled or controlled, and they may cause extensive losses over many years. Even viruses written to be benign cause significant damage because of unexpected interactions and bugs. To experiment with computer viruses is akin to experimenting with smallpox or anthrax microbes—there may be scientific knowledge to be gained, but the potential for disasterous consequences looms large.

In one sense, we use "computer viruses" every day. Editors, compilers, backup utilities, and other common software meet some definitions of viruses. However, their general nature is known to their users, and they do not operate without at least the implied permission of those users. Furthermore, their replication is generally under the close control or observation of their users. It is these differences from the colloquial computer virus that makes the latter so interesting, however. These differences are also precisely what suggest that computer viruses approach a form of artificial life.

If we are to continue to research computer viruses, we need to find fail-safe ways of doing so. This is a major research topic in itself. The danger of creating and accidentally releasing more sophisticated viruses is too great to risk, especially with our increasing reliance on computers in critical tasks. One approach might be to construct custom computing environments for study, different enough from all existing computer systems that a computer virus under study would be completely nonfunctional outside it. This is an approach similar to what has been taken with Core Wars [18]. Another approach is to only study existing viruses in known environments.

Ultimately, it would be disappointing if research efforts resulted in widespread acceptance of computer viruses as a form of artificial life. It would be especially dangerous to attract the untrained, the careless, and the uncaring to produce them. Already, contests have been announced for virus writers to produce a "useful" or "shortest" virus. Self-reproducing code is easier to write than to control, and encouraging its production in uncontrolled environments is irresponsible; accidents happen all too frequently with computers.

The origin of most computer viruses is one of unethical practice. Viruses created for malicious purposes are obviously bad; viruses constructed as experiments and released into the public domain would likewise be unethical, and poor science besides: experiments without controls, strong hypotheses, and the consent of the subjects. Facetiously, I suggest that if computer viruses evolve into something with artificial consciousness, this might provide a doctrine of "original sin" for their theology.

More seriously, I would suggest that there is something of great importance already to be learned from the study of computer viruses: the critical realization that experimentation with systems in some ways (almost) alive can be hazardous. Computer viruses have caused millions of dollars of damage and untold aggravation. Some of them have been written as harmless experiments that "got away" and others as malicious mischief. A great many of them have firmly rooted themselves in the pool of available computers and storage media, and they are likely to be frustrating users and harming systems for years to come. Similar but considerably more tragic results could occur from careless experimentation with organic forms of artificial life. We must never lose sight of the fact that "real life" is of much more importance than "artificial life," and we should not allow our experiments to threaten our experimenters. This is a lesson we all would do well to learn.

References

1. Adleman, L. (1990). An abstract theory of computer viruses. In S. Goldwasser (Ed.), *Lecture notes in computer science* (Vol. 403). Berlin, NY: Springer-Verlag.

2. Cohen, F. (1985). *Computer viruses*. Pittsburgh: ASP Press.

3. Cohen, F. B. (1990). *A short course on computer viruses*. Pittsburgh: ASP Press.

4. Cohen, F. B. (1991, September/October). Friendly contagion: harnessing the subtle power of computer viruses. *The Sciences*, 22–28.

5. Denning, P. J. (Ed.) (1990). *Computers under attack: intruders, worms and viruses*. New York: ACM Press (Addison-Wesley).

6. Duff, T. (1989). Experiences with viruses on Unix systems. *Computing Systems, 2*(2), 155–171. Usenix Association.

7. Eichin, M. W., & Rochlis, J. A. (1989). With microscope and tweezers: an analysis of the internet virus of November 1988. In *Proceedings of the Symposium on Research in Security and Privacy* (pp. 326–343), Oakland, California. IEEE-CS.

8. Farmer, J. D., & Belin, A. d'A. (1991). Artificial life: the coming evolution. In *Proceedings of the Second Conference on Artificial Life* (pp. 815–838).

9. Ferbrache, D. (1992). *A pathology of computer viruses*. Berlin, NY: Springer-Verlag.

10. Feudo, C. V. (1992). *The computer virus desk reference*. Homewood, IL: Business One Irwin.

11. Fites, P., Johnson, P., & Kratz, M. (1992). *The computer virus crisis* (2nd ed.) New York: Van Nostrand Reinhold.

12. Gerrold, D. (1972). *When Harlie was one*. Garden City, NY: Doubleday.

13. Gibson, W. (1984). *Neuromancer*. New York: Ace/The Berkeley Publishing Group.

14. Highland, H. J. (Ed.) (1990). *Computer virus handbook*. Oxford: Elsevier Advanced Technology.

15. Hoffman, L. J. (Ed.) (1990). *Rogue programs: viruses, worms, and Trojan horses*. New York: Van Nostrand Reinhold.

16. Hruska, J. (1990). *Computer viruses and anti-virus warfare*. Chichester, UK: Ellis Horwood.

17. Kumar, S., & Spafford, E. H. (1992). A generic virus scanner in C++. In *Proceedings of the 8th Computer Security Applications Conference* (pp. 210–219). Los Alamitos, California. ACM and IEEE, IEEE Press.

18. Levy, S. (1992). *Artificial life: the quest for a new creation*. New York: Pantheon.

19. Norstad, J. (1990). *Disinfectant on-line documentation*. Evanston, IL: Northwestern University. 1.8 edition.

20. Radai, Y. (1991, September). Checksumming techniques for anti-viral purposes. *1st Virus Bulletin Conference* (pp. 39–68).

21. Russell, D., & Gangemi, Sr. G. T. (1991). *Computer security basics*. Cambridge, MA: O'Reilly & Associates.

22. Seeley, D. (1990). Password cracking: a game of wits. *Communications of the ACM, 32*(6), 700–703.

23. Shoch, J. F., & Hupp, J. A. (1982). The "worm" programs—early experiments with a distributed computation. *Communications of the ACM, 25*(3), 172–180.

24. Solomon, A. (1991). *PC VIRUSES Detection, Analysis and Cure*. London: Springer-Verlag.

25. Spafford, E. H. (1989). An analysis of the Internet Worm. In C. Ghezzi & J. A. McDermid (Eds.), *Proceedings of the 2nd European Software Engineering Conference* (pp. 446–468). Springer-Verlag.

26. Spafford, E. H. (1989). The Internet Worm: crisis and aftermath. *Communications of the ACM, 32*(6), 678–687.

27. Spafford, E. H. (1989). The Internet Worm program: an analysis. *ACM Computer Communication Review, 19*(1), 17–57; also issued as Purdue CS Technical Report TR-CSD-823.

28. Spafford, E. H. (1991). Computer viruses: a form of artificial life? In D. Farmer, C. Langton, S. Rasmussen, & C. Taylor (Eds.), *Artificial life II, studies in the sciences of complexity* (pp. 727–747). Redwood City, CA: Addison-Wesley. *Proceedings of the Second Conference on Artificial Life.*

29. Spafford, E. H. (1992, January/February). Response to Fred Cohen's "contest." *The Sciences*, p. 4.

30. Spafford, E. H. (1994). Viruses. In John Marciniak (Ed.), *Encyclopedia of software engineering*. New York: John Wiley & Sons.

31. Spafford, E. H., Heaphy, K. A., & Ferbrache, D. J. (1989). *Computer viruses: dealing with electronic vandalism and programmed threats*. Arlington, VA: ADAPSO.

32. Stubbs, B., & Hoffman, L. J. (1990). Mapping the virus battlefield. In L. J. Hoffman (Ed.), *Rogue programs: viruses, worms, and Trojan horses* (pp. 143–157). New York: Van Nostrand Reinhold.

33. Witten, I. H., Thimbleby, H. W., Coulouris, G. F., & Greenberg, S. (1991). Liveware: a new approach to sharing data in social networks. *International Journal of Man-Machine Studies, 34*(3), 337–348.

Genetic Algorithms and Artificial Life

Melanie Mitchell
Santa Fe Institute
1660 Old Pecos Tr., Suite A
Santa Fe, NM 87501
mm@santafe.edu

Stephanie Forrest
Department of Computer
Science
University of New Mexico
Albuquerque, NM 87131-1386
forrest@cs.unm.edu

Abstract Genetic algorithms are computational models of evolution that play a central role in many artificial-life models. We review the history and current scope of research on genetic algorithms in artificial life, giving illustrative examples in which the genetic algorithm is used to study how learning and evolution interact, and to model ecosystems, immune system, cognitive systems, and social systems. We also outline a number of open questions and future directions for genetic algorithms in artificial-life research.

1 Introduction

Evolution by natural selection is a central idea in biology, and the concept of natural selection has influenced our view of biological systems tremendously. Likewise, evolution of artificial systems is an important component of artificial life, providing an important modeling tool and an automated design method. Genetic algorithms (GAs) are currently the most prominent and widely used models of evolution in artificial-life systems. GAs have been used both as tools for solving practical problems and as scientific models of evolutionary processes. The intersection between GAs and artificial life includes both, although in this article we focus primarily on GAs as models of natural phenomena. For example, we do not discuss topics such as "evolutionary robotics" in which the GA is used as a black box to design or control a system with lifelike properties, even though this is certainly an important role for GAs in artificial life. In the following, we provide a brief overview of GAs, describe some particularly interesting examples of the overlap between GAs and artificial life, and give our view of some of the most pressing research questions in this field.

2 Overview of Genetic Algorithms

In the 1950s and 1960s several computer scientists independently studied evolutionary systems with the idea that evolution could be used as an optimization tool for engineering problems. In Goldberg's short history of evolutionary computation ([42], chap. 4), the names of Box [21], Fraser [39, 40], Friedman [41], Bledsoe [18], and Bremermann [22] are associated with a variety of work in the late 1950s and early 1960s, some of which presages the later development of GAs. These early systems contained the rudiments of evolution in various forms—all had some kind of "selection of the fittest," some had population-based schemes for selection and variation, and some, like many GAs, had binary strings as abstractions of biological chromosomes.

In the later 1960s, Rechenberg [89] introduced "evolution strategies," a method first designed to optimize real-valued parameters. This idea was further developed by Schwefel [96, 97], and the field of evolution strategies has remained an active area of research, developing in parallel to GA research, until recently when the two communities have begun to interact. For a review of evolution strategies, see [9]. Also in the 1960s Fogel, Owens, and Walsh [36] developed "evolutionary programming." Candidate solutions to given tasks are represented as finite-state machines, and the evolutionary operators are selection and mutation. Evolutionary programming also remains an area of active research. For a recent description of the work of Fogel et al., see [34].

GAs as they are known today were first described by John Holland in the 1960s and further developed by Holland and his students and colleagues at the University of Michigan in the 1960s and 1970s. Holland's 1975 book, *Adaptation in Natural and Artificial Systems* [55], presents the GA as an abstraction of biological evolution and gives a theoretical framework for adaptation under the GA. Holland's GA is a method for moving from one population of "chromosomes" (e.g., bit strings representing organisms or candidate solutions to a problem) to a new population, using selection together with the genetic operators of crossover, mutation, and inversion. Each chromosome consists of "genes" (e.g., bits), with each gene being an instance of a particular "allele" (e.g., 0 or 1). Selection chooses those chromosomes in the population that will be allowed to reproduce and decides how many offspring each is likely to have, with the fitter chromosomes producing on average more offspring than less fit ones. Crossover exchanges subparts of two chromosomes (roughly mimicking sexual recombination between two single-chromosome organisms); mutation randomly changes the values of some locations in the chromosome; and inversion reverses the order of a contiguous section of the chromosome, thus rearranging the order in which genes are arrayed in the chromosome. Inversion is rarely used in today's GAs, at least partially because of the implementation expense for most representations. A simple form of the GA (without inversion) works as follows:

1. Start with a randomly generated population of chromosomes (e.g., candidate solutions to a problem).

2. Calculate the fitness of each chromosome in the population.

3. Apply selection and genetic operators (crossover and mutation) to the population to create a new population.

4. Go to step 2.

This process is iterated over many time steps, each of which is called a "generation." After several generations, the result is often one or more highly fit chromosomes in the population. It should be noted that the previous description leaves out many important details. For example, selection can be implemented in different ways—it can eliminate the least fit 50% of the population and replicate each remaining individual once, it can replicate individuals in direct proportion to their fitness (fitness-proportionate selection), or it can scale the fitness and replicate individuals in direct proportion to their scaled fitnesses. For implementation details such as these, see [42].

Introducing a population-based algorithm with crossover and inversion was a major innovation. Just as significant is the theoretical foundation Holland developed based on the notion of "schemata" [42, 55]. Until recently, this theoretical foundation has been the basis of almost all subsequent theoretical work on GAs, although the usefulness of this notion has been debated (see, e.g., [45]). Holland's work was the first attempt to put computational evolution on a firm theoretical footing.

GAs in various forms have been applied to many scientific and engineering problems, including the following:

- *Optimization.* GAs have been used in a wide variety of optimization tasks, including numerical optimization (e.g., [63]), and combinatorial optimization problems such as circuit design and job shop scheduling.

- *Automatic programming.* GAs have been used to evolve computer programs for specific tasks (e.g., [69]) and to design other computational structures, for example, cellular automata [80] and sorting networks [52].

- *Machine and robot learning.* GAs have been used for many machine-learning applications, including classification and prediction tasks such as the prediction of dynamical systems [75], weather prediction [92], and prediction of protein structure (e.g., [95]). GAs have also been used to design neural networks (e.g., [15, 25, 47, 48, 67, 77, 81, 94, 105]) to evolve rules for learning classifier systems (e.g., [54, 57]) or symbolic production systems (e.g., [46]), and to design and control robots (e.g., [29, 31, 50]). For an overview of GAs in machine learning, see De Jong [64, 65].

- *Economic models.* GAs have been used to model processes of innovation, the development of bidding strategies, and the emergence of economic markets (e.g., [3–5, 58]).

- *Immune system models.* GAs have been used to model various aspects of the natural immune system [17, 38], including somatic mutation during an individual's lifetime and the discovery of multi-gene families during evolutionary time.

- *Ecological models.* GAs have been used to model ecological phenomena such as biological arms races, host-parasite coevolution, symbiosis, and resource flow in ecologies (e.g., [11, 12, 26, 28, 52, 56, 61, 70, 71, 83, 87, 88, 101]).

- *Population genetics models.* GAs have been used to study questions in population genetics, such as "under what conditions will a gene for recombination be evolutionarily viable?" (e.g., [16, 35, 74, 93]).

- *Interactions between evolution and learning.* GAs have been used to study how individual learning and species evolution affect one another (e.g., [1, 2, 13, 37, 53, 76, 82, 84, 102, 103]).

- *Models of social systems.* GAs have been used to study evolutionary aspects of social systems, such as the evolution of cooperation [7, 8, 73, 78, 79], the evolution of communication (e.g., [72, 104]), and trail-following behavior in ants (e.g., [27, 68]).

This list is by no means exhaustive, but it gives a flavor of the kinds of things for which GAs have been used, both for problem solving and for modeling. The range of GA applications continues to increase.

In recent years, algorithms that have been termed *genetic algorithms* have taken many forms and in some cases bear little resemblance to Holland's original formulation. Researchers have experimented with different types of representations, crossover and mutation operators, special-purpose operators, and approaches to reproduction and selection. However, all of these methods have a "family resemblance" in that they take some inspiration from biological evolution and from Holland's original GA. A new term,

Evolutionary Computation, has been introduced to cover these various members of the GA family, evolutionary programming, and evolution strategies [66].

In the following sections we describe a number of examples illustrating the use of GAs in Artificial Life. We do not attempt to give an exhaustive review of the entire field of GAs or even that subset relevant to Artificial Life, but rather concentrate on some highlights that we find particularly interesting. We have provided a more complete set of pointers to the GA and Artificial-Life literature in the "Suggested Reading" section at the end of this article.

3   Interactions Between Learning and Evolution

Many people have drawn analogies between learning and evolution as two adaptive processes—one taking place during the lifetime of an organism, and the other taking place over the evolutionary history of life on earth. To what extent do these processes interact? In particular, can learning that occurs over the course of an individual's lifetime guide the evolution of that individual's species to any extent? These are major questions in evolutionary psychology. GAs, often in combination with neural networks, have been used to address these questions. Here we describe two artificial-life systems designed to model interactions between learning and evolution, and in particular the "Baldwin effect."

3.1   The Baldwin effect

Learning during one's lifetime does not directly affect one's genetic makeup; consequently, things learned during an individual's lifetime cannot be transmitted directly to its offspring. However, some evolutionary biologists (e.g., [98]) have discussed an indirect effect of learning on evolution, inspired by ideas about evolution due to Baldwin [10] (among others). The idea behind the so-called Baldwin effect is that if learning helps survival, then organisms best able to learn will have the most offspring and increase the frequency of the genes responsible for learning. If the environment is stable so that the best things to learn remain constant, then this can lead indirectly to a genetic encoding of a trait that originally had to be learned. In short, the capacity to acquire a certain desired trait allows the learning organism to survive preferentially and gives genetic variation the possibility of independently discovering the desired trait. Without such learning, the likelihood of survival—and, thus, the opportunity for genetic discovery—decreases. In this indirect way, learning can affect evolution, even if what is learned cannot be transmitted genetically.

3.2   Capturing the Baldwin Effect in a Simple Model

Hinton and Nowlan [53] used a GA to model the Baldwin effect. Their goal was to demonstrate this effect empirically and to measure its magnitude, using the simplest possible model. A simple neural-network learning algorithm modeled learning, and the GA played the role of evolution, evolving a population of neural networks with varying learning capabilities. In the model, each individual is a neural network with 20 potential connections. A connection can have one of three values: "present," "absent," and "learnable." These are specified by "1," "0," and "?," respectively, where each ? connection can be set during the learning phase to 1 or 0. There is only one correct setting for the connections (i.e., only one correct set of 1s and 0s). The problem is to find this single correct set of connections. This will not be possible for networks that have incorrect fixed connections (e.g., a 1 where there should be a 0), but those networks that have correct settings in all places except where there are ?s have the capacity to learn the correct settings. This is a "needle-in-a-haystack" search problem, because there is only one correct setting in a space of 2^{20} possibilities. However, allowing learning to take place changes the shape of the fitness landscape, changing the single spike to a smoother "zone of increased fitness," within which it is possible to learn the correct connections.

Hinton and Nowlan used the simplest possible "learning" method: random guessing. On each learning trial, a network guesses a 1 or 0 at random for each of its learnable connections. This method has little to do with the usual notions of neural-network learning. Hinton and Nowlan presented this model in terms of neural networks so as to keep in mind the possibility of extending the example to more standard learning tasks and methods.

In the GA population, each network is represented by a string of length 20 over the alphabet {0, 1, ?}, denoting the settings on the network's connections. Each individual is given 1,000 learning trials. On each learning trial, the individual tries a random combination of settings for the ?s. The fitness is an inverse function of the number of trials needed to find the correct solution. An individual that already has all of its connections set correctly has the highest possible fitness, and an individual that never finds the correct solution has the lowest possible fitness. Hence, a tradeoff exists between efficiency and flexibility: having many ?s means that, on average, many guesses are needed to arrive at the correct answer, but the more connections that are fixed, the more likely it is that one or more of them will be fixed incorrectly, meaning that there is no possibility of finding the correct answer.

Hinton and Nowlan's experiments showed that learning during an individual's "lifetime" does guide evolution by allowing the mean fitness of the population to increase. This increase is due to a Baldwin-like effect: Those individuals that are able to learn the task efficiently tend to be selected to reproduce, and crossovers among these individuals tend to increase the number of correctly fixed alleles, increasing the learning efficiency of the offspring. With this simple form of learning, evolution could discover individuals with all of their connections fixed correctly, and such individuals were discovered in these experiments. Without learning, the evolutionary search never discovered such an individual.

To summarize, learning allows genetically coded partial solutions to get partial credit, rather than the all-or-nothing reward that an organism would get without learning. A common claim for learning is that it allows an organism to respond to unpredictable aspects of an environment—aspects that change too quickly for evolution to track genetically. Although this is clearly one benefit of learning, the Baldwin effect is different: It says that learning helps organisms adapt to genetically predictable, but difficult, aspects of the environment, and that learning indirectly helps these adaptations become genetically fixed. Consequently, the Baldwin effect is important only on fitness landscapes that are hard to search by evolution alone, such as the needle-in-a-haystack example given by Hinton and Nowlan.

As Hinton and Nowlan point out, the "learning" mechanism used in their experiments—random guessing—is completely unrealistic as a model of learning. Hinton and Nowlan point out that "a more sophisticated learning procedure only strengthens the argument for the importance of the Baldwin effect" ([53], p. 500). This is true insofar as a more sophisticated learning procedure would, for example, further smooth the original "needle-in-the-haystack" fitness landscape in Hinton and Nowlan's learning task. However, if the learning procedure were *too* sophisticated—that is, if learning the necessary trait were too easy—then there would be little selection pressure for evolution to move from the ability to learn the trait to a genetic encoding of that trait. Such tradeoffs occur in evolution and can be seen even in Hinton and Nowlan's simple model. Computer simulations such as theirs can help us to understand and to measure such tradeoffs. More detailed analyses of this model were performed by Belew [13] and Harvey [49].

3.3 Evolutionary Reinforcement Learning (ERL)

A second computational demonstration of the Baldwin effect was given by Ackley and Littman [1]. In their Evolutionary Reinforcement Learning (ERL) model, adaptive individuals ("agents") move randomly on a two-dimensional lattice, encountering food, predators, hiding places, and other types of entities. Each agent's state includes the entities in its visual range, the level of its internal energy store, and other parameters. Each agent possesses two feed-forward neural networks: (1) an evaluation network that maps the agent's state at time t to a number representing how good that state is, and (2) an action network that maps the agent's state at time t to the action it is to take on that time step. The only possible actions are moving from the current lattice site to one of the four neighboring sites, but actions can result in eating, being eaten, and other less radical consequences. The architectures of these two networks are the same for all agents, but the weights on the links can vary between agents. The weights on a given agent's evaluation network are fixed from birth—this network represents innate goals and desires inherited from the agent's ancestors (e.g., "being near food is good"). The weights on the action network change over the agent's lifetime according to a reinforcement-learning algorithm.

An agent's genome encodes the weights for the evaluation network and the initial weights for the action network. Agents have an internal energy store (represented by a real number) that must be kept above a certain level to prevent death; this is accomplished by eating food that is encountered as the agent moves from site to site on the lattice. An agent must also avoid predators, or it will be killed. An agent can reproduce once it has enough energy in its internal store. Agents reproduce by cloning their genomes (subject to mutation). In addition to cloning, two spatially nearby agents can together produce offspring via crossover. There is no "exogenous" *a priori* fitness function for evaluating a genome as there was in Hinton and Nowlan's model and in most engineering applications of GAs. Instead, the fitness of an agent (as well as the rate at which a population turns over) is "endogenous": it emerges from many actions and interactions over the course of the agent's lifetime. This feature distinguishes many GAs used in artificial-life models from engineering applications.

At each time step t in an agent's life, the agent evaluates its current state, using its evaluation network. This evaluation is compared with the evaluation it produced at $t - 1$ with respect to the previous action, and the comparison gives a reinforcement signal used in modifying the weights in the action network. The idea here is for agents to learn to act in ways that will improve the current state. After this learning step, the agent's modified action network is used to determine the next action to take.

Ackley and Littman observed many interesting phenomena in their experiments with this model. The main emergent phenomena they describe are a version of the Baldwin effect and an effect they call "shielding." Here we will describe the former; see Ackley and Littman [1] for details on other phenomena. They compared the results of three different experiments: (1) EL: both evolution of populations and learning in individual agents took place, (2) E: evolution of populations took place but there was no individual learning, and (3) L: individual learning took place but there was no evolution. The statistic that Ackley and Littman measured was roughly the average time until the population became extinct, averaged over many separate runs. They found that the best performance (longest average time to extinction) was achieved with EL populations, closely followed by L populations, and with E populations trailing far behind. More detailed analysis of the EL runs revealed that with respect to certain behaviors, the relative importance of learning and evolution changed over the course of a run. In particular, Ackley and Littman looked at the genes related to food-approaching behavior for both the evaluation and action networks. They found that in earlier generations, the genes encoding evaluation of food proximity (e.g., "being near food is good") remained relatively constant across the population, while the genes encoding initial weights in the action network were more variable. This indicated the importance of maintaining the goals for the learning process and, thus, the importance of learning for survival. However, later in the run the evaluation genes were more variable across the population, whereas the genes encoding the initial weights of the action network remained more constant. This indicated that inherited behaviors were more significant than learning during this phase. Ackley and Littman interpreted this as a version of the Baldwin effect. Initially, it is necessary for agents to *learn* to approach food; thus, maintaining the explicit knowledge that "being near food is good" is essential for the learning process to take place. Later, the genetic knowledge that being near food is good is superseded by the genetically encoded behavior to "approach food if near," so the evaluation knowledge is not as necessary. The initial ability to learn the behavior is what allows it to eventually become genetically coded.

This effect has not been completely analyzed, nor has the strength of the effect been determined. Nevertheless, results such as these, and those of Hinton and Nowlan's experiments, demonstrate the potential of artificial-life modeling: biological phenomena can be studied with controlled computational experiments whose natural equivalent (e.g., running for thousands of generations) is not possible or practical. And when performed correctly, such experiments can produce new evidence for and new insight into these natural phenomena. The potential benefits of such work are not limited to understanding natural phenomena. A growing community of GA researchers is studying ways to apply GAs to optimize neural networks to solve practical problems—a practical application of the interaction between learning and evolution. A survey of this work is given in Schaffer, Whitley, and Eshelman [94]. Other researchers are investigating the benefits of adding "Lamarckian" learning to the GA and have found in some cases that it leads to significant improvements in GA performance [2, 44].

4   Ecosystems and Evolutionary Dynamics

Another major area of artificial-life research is modeling ecosystem behavior and the evolutionary dynamics of populations. (Ackley and Littman's work described earlier could fit into this category as well.) Here we describe two such models that use GAs: Holland's Echo system, meant to allow a large range of ecological interactions to be modeled, and Bedau and Packard's Strategic Bugs system, for which a measure of evolutionary activity is defined and studied. As in the ERL system, both Echo and Strategic Bugs illustrate the use of endogenous fitness.

4.1   Echo
Echo is a model of ecological systems formulated by Holland [55, 56, 62]. Echo models ecologies in the same sense that the GA models population genetics [56]. It abstracts away virtually all of the physical details of real ecological systems and concentrates on a small set of primitive agent–agent and agent–environment interactions. The extent to which Echo captures the essence of real ecological systems is still largely undetermined, yet it is significant because of the generality of the model and its ambitious scope. The goal of Echo is to study how simple interactions among simple agents lead to emergent high-level phenomena such as the flow of resources in a system or cooperation and competition in networks of agents (e.g., communities, trading networks, or arms races). Echo extends the GA in several important ways: resources are modeled explicitly in the system, individuals (called agents) have a geographical location that affects their (implicit) fitness, certain types of interactions between agents are built into the system (e.g., trade, combat, and mating), and fitness is endogenous.

Similar to Ackley and Littman's ERL model, Echo consists of a population of agents distributed on a set of sites on a lattice. Many agents can cohabit the same site, and there is a measure of locality within each site. Also distributed on the lattice are different types of renewable resources; each type of resource is encoded by a letter (e.g., "a," "b," "c," "d"). Different types of agents use different types of resources and can store these resources (the letters) internally.

Agents interact by mating, trading, or fighting. Trading and fighting result in the exchange of internal resources between agents, and mating results in an offspring whose genome is a combination of those of the parents. Agents also self-reproduce (described later), but mating is a process distinct from replication. Each agent has a particular set of rules that determines its interactions with other agents (e.g., which resources it is willing to trade, the conditions under which it will fight, etc.). "External appearance" can also be coded in these rules as a string tag visible to other agents. This allows the possibility of the evolution of social rules and potentially of mimicry, a phenomenon frequently observed in natural ecosystems. The interaction rules use string matching, and it is therefore easy to encode the strings used by the rules onto the genome.

Each agent's genome encodes the details of the rules by which it interacts (e.g., the conditions under which the rules are applied) and the types of resources it requires. As in many other artificial-life models (e.g., ERL and the Strategic Bugs model described below), Echo has no explicit fitness function guiding selection and reproduction. Instead, an agent reproduces when it accumulates sufficient resources to make an exact copy of its genome. For example, if an agent's genome consists of 25 a's, 13 b's, and 50 c's, then it would have to accumulate in its internal storage at least 25 a's, 13 b's, and 50 c's before cloning itself. As is usual in a GA, cloning is subject to a low rate of mutation, and, as was mentioned earlier, genetic material is exchanged through mating.

In preliminary simulations, the Echo system has demonstrated surprisingly complex behavior (including something resembling a biological "arms race" in which two competing species develop progressively more complex offensive and defensive combat strategies), ecological dependencies among different species (e.g., a symbiotic "ant-caterpillar-fly" triangle), and sensitivity (in terms of the number of different phenotypes) to differing levels of renewable resources [55].

Some possible directions for future work on Echo include (1) studying the evolution of external tags as mechanisms for social communication; (2) extending the model to allow the evolution of "metazoans"—connected communities of agents that have internal boundaries and reproduce as a unit; this capacity will allow for the study of individual agent specialization and the evolution of multicellularity; (3) studying the evolutionary dynamics of schemata in the population; and (4) using the results from (3) to formulate a generalization of the well-known Schema Theorem based on endogenous fitness [56]. The last is a particularly important goal, because there has been very little mathematical analysis of artificial-life simulations in which fitness is endogenous.

4.2 Measuring Evolutionary Activity

How can we decide if an observed system is evolving? And how can we measure the rate of evolution in such a system? Bedau and Packard [11] developed an artificial-life model, called "Strategic Bugs," to address these questions. Their model is simpler than both ERL and Echo. The Strategic Bugs world is a two-dimensional lattice, containing only adaptive agents ("bugs") and food. The food supply is renewable; it is refreshed periodically and distributed randomly across the lattice. Bugs survive by finding and eating food, storing it in an internal reservoir until they have enough energy to reproduce. Bugs use energy from their internal reservoir in order to move. A bug dies when its internal reservoir is empty. Thus, bugs have to find food continually in order to survive.

Each bug's behavior is controlled by an internal look-up table that maps sensory data from the bug's local neighborhood to a vector giving the direction and distance of the bug's next foray. For example, one entry might be, "If more than 10 units of food are two steps to the northeast and the other neighboring sites are empty, move two steps to the northeast." This look-up table is the bug's "genetic material," and each entry is a gene. A bug can reproduce either asexually, in which case it passes on its genetic material to its offspring with some low probability of mutation at each gene, or sexually, in which case it mates with a spatially adjacent bug, producing offspring whose genetic material is a combination of that of the parents, possibly with some small number of mutations.

Bedau and Packard wanted to define and measure the degree of "evolutionary activity" in this system over time, where evolutionary activity is defined informally as "the rate at which useful genetic innovations are absorbed into the population." Bedau and Packard assert that "persistent usage of new genes is what signals genuine evolutionary activity," because evolutionary activity is meant to measure the degree to which useful new genes are discovered and persist in the population.

To measure evolutionary activity, Bedau and Packard began by keeping statistics on gene usage for every gene that appeared in the population. Recall that in the Strategic Bugs model, a bug's genome is represented as a look-up table, and a gene is simply an entry in the table—an input/action pair. Each gene is assigned a counter, initialized to 0, which is incremented every time the gene is used—that is, every time the specified input situation arises and the specified action is taken. When a parent passes on a gene to a child through asexual reproduction or through crossover, the value of the counter is passed on as well and remains with the gene. The only time a counter is initialized to 0 is when a new gene is created through mutation. In this way, a gene's counter value reflects the usage of that gene over many generations. When a bug dies, its genes (and their counters) die with it.

Bedau and Packard [11] plot, for each time step during a run, histograms of the number of genes in the population displaying a given usage value (i.e., a given counter value). These histograms display "waves of activity" over time, showing that clusters of genes are continually being discovered that persist in usage over time—in other words, that the population is continually finding and exploiting new genetic innovations. This is precisely Bedau and Packard's definition of evolution, and according to them, as long as the waves continue to occur, it can be said that the population is continuing to evolve. Bedau and Packard define a single number, the *evolutionary activity* at a given time, $A(t)$, that roughly measures the degree to which the population is acquiring new and useful genetic material at time t—in short, whether or not such activity waves are occurring at time t and what their characteristics are. If $A(t)$ is positive, then evolution is occurring at time t. Claiming that life is a property of populations and not of individual organisms, Bedau and Packard ambitiously propose A(t) as a test for life in a system— if A(t) is positive, then the system is exhibiting life at time t. Bedau, Ronneburg, and Zwick [12] have extended this work to propose several measures of population diversity and to measure them and characterize their dynamics in the context of the Strategic Bugs model.

The important contribution of Bedau and Packard's paper is the attempt to define a macroscopic quantity such as evolutionary activity. It is a first step at such a definition, and the particular definition of gene usage is no doubt too specific to the Strategic Bugs model, in which the relationship between genes and behavior is completely straightforward. In more realistic models it will be considerably harder to define such quantities. However, the formulation of macroscopic measures of evolution and adaptation, as

well as descriptions of the microscopic mechanisms by which the macroscopic quantities emerge, is essential if artificial life is to be made into an explanatory science and if
it is to contribute significantly to real evolutionary biology.

5   Learning Classifier Systems

Learning classifier systems [57] are one of the earliest examples of how GAs have been
incorporated into models of living systems, in this case cognitive systems. Classifier systems have been used as models of stimulus-response behavior and of more complex
cognitive processes. Classifier systems are based on three principles: learning, intermittent feedback from the environment, and hierarchies of internal models that represent
the environment. Classifier systems have been used to model a variety of "intelligent"
processes, such as how people behave in economic and social situations (playing the
stock market, obeying social norms, etc.), maze running by rats, and categorization
tasks.

Like neural networks, classifier systems consist of a parallel machine (most often
implemented in software) and learning algorithms that adjust the configuration of the
underlying machine over time. Classifier systems differ from neural networks in the
details of the parallel machine, referred to as the *internal performance system*, and
in the details of the learning algorithms. Specifically, the classifier system machine is
more complex than most neural networks, computing with quantities called "messages"
and controlling its state with if-then rules that specify patterns of messages. The GA
is used to discover useful rules, based on intermittent feedback from the environment
and an internal credit-assignment algorithm called the *bucket brigade*. Thus, a classifier
system consists of three layers, with the performance system forming the lowest level.
At the second level, the bucket-brigade learning algorithm manages credit assignment
among competing classifiers. It plays a role similar to that of back-propagation in neural
networks. Finally, at the highest level are genetic operators that create new classifiers.

Associated with each classifier is a parameter called its strength. This measure reflects
the utility of that rule, based on the system's past experience. The bucket-brigade
algorithm is the mechanism for altering each rule's strength. The algorithm is based on
the metaphor of an economy, with the environment acting both as the producer of raw
materials and the ultimate consumer of finished goods, and each classifier acting as an
intermediary in an economic chain of production. Using the bucket brigade, a classifier
system is able to identify and use the subset of its rule base that has proven useful in
the past. However, a classifier system's initial rule base usually will not contain all of
the classifiers necessary for good performance. The GA interprets a classifier's strength
as a measure of its fitness, and periodically (after the strengths have stabilized under the
bucket brigade), the GA deletes rules that have not been useful or relevant in the past
(those with low strength) and generates new rules by modifying existing high-strength
rules through mutation, crossover, and other special-purpose operators. Similarly to
conventional GAs, these deletions and additions are all performed probabilistically.
Under the definition of induction as "all inferential processes that expand knowledge
in the face of uncertainty" [57, p. 1], the GA plays the role of an inductive mechanism
in classifier systems.

An important motivation in the formulation of classifier systems was the principle that
inductive systems need the ability to construct internal models. Internal models should
allow a system to generate predictions even when its knowledge of the environment
is incomplete or incorrect, and further, to refine its internal model as more information
about the environment becomes available. This leads naturally to the idea of a default
hierarchy in which a system can represent high-level approximations, or defaults, based

on early information, and, over time, refine the defaults with more specific details and exceptions to rules. In classifier systems, default hierarchies are represented using clusters of rules of different specificities. In [57], the concept of a "quasi-morphism" is introduced to describe this modeling process formally.

There have been several modeling efforts based on learning classifier systems, including [19, 20, 32, 90, 91, 106, 107]. Each of these is a variation on the standard classifier system as described earlier, but each of the variations captures the major principles of classifier systems. For example, Riolo [90] used a classifier system to model the kind of latent learning and look-ahead behavior of the type observed in rats. For this work, Riolo designed a simple maze, similar to those in latent-learning experiments on rats. The maze has one start point and several endpoints. At each endpoint there is a box, which may or may not be filled with food, and the various endpoint boxes may or may not be distinguishable (e.g., by color) from one another. In these kinds of experiments, the procedure is roughly as follows: (1) before food is placed in the boxes, nonhungry rats are placed in the maze and allowed to explore; (2) the rats are not fed for 24 hours; (3) the rats are placed in the maze (at one of the endpoints) and allowed to eat from one of the boxes; and (4) the rats are placed at the start location of the maze, and their behavior is observed. If the boxes are distinguishable, then the rats reliably choose the path through the maze leading to the box from which they ate.

Riolo makes several points about these experiments: (1) in the "pre-reward" phase, the rats learn the structure of the maze without explicit rewards; (2) they learn to use an internal model to perform a look-ahead search that allows them to predict which box was in which part of the maze; (3) the rats are able to use this look-ahead search once they associate food with a particular box; and (4) this type of inference cannot be made by a simple reactive (stimulus-response) system. It is commonly believed that the task requires the use of internal models and look-ahead prediction.

To model these experiments using a classifier system, Riolo augmented the basic classifier system model to include a look-ahead component. The extensions included (1) allowing the classifier system to iterate several cycles of its performance system (the rule base) before choosing an action, in effect "running" an internal model before acting; (2) choosing special-purpose genetic operators to coordinate the internal model-building (i.e., to distinguish predictions from suggested actions); and (3) using three different kinds of strength to measure the utility of rules (to measure predictive ability vs. real-time ability, to produce a reward from an action, and to measure long-term vs. short-term utility). With these modifications, the classifier system achieved results comparable with the latent-learning results reported for rats. Further, the classifier system with the look-ahead component outperformed the unmodified version significantly. Riolo's experiment is one of the best demonstrations to date of the necessity of internal models for classifier systems to succeed on some tasks.

6 Immune Systems

Immune systems are adaptive systems in which learning takes place by evolutionary mechanisms similar to biological evolution. Immune systems have been studied by the artificial-life community both because of their intrinsic scientific interest and because of potential applications of ideas from immunology to computational problems (e.g., [17]). The immune system is capable of recognizing virtually any foreign cell or molecule. To do this, it must distinguish the body's own cells and molecules that are created and circulated internally (estimated to consist of on the order of 10^5 different proteins) from those that are foreign. It has been estimated that the immune system is capable of recognizing on the order of 10^{16} different foreign molecules [60]. From a pattern-recognition perspective, these are staggering numbers, particularly when one considers that the human genome, which encodes the "program" for constructing the immune system, only contains about 10^5 genes, and further, that the immune system is distributed throughout the body with no central organ to control it.

Different approaches to modeling the immune system have included differential-equation-based models (e.g., see [85, 86]), cellular-automata models [24], classifier systems [33], and GAs [38]. In the last, GAs are used to model both somatic mutation (the process by which antibodies are evolved during the lifetime of an individual to match a specific antigen) and the more traditional type of evolution over many individual lifetimes of variable-, or V-, region gene libraries (the genetic material that codes for specific receptors).

The GA models of Forrest, Javornik, Smith, and Perelson [38] are based on a universe in which antigens (foreign material) and antibodies (the cells that perform the recognition) are represented by binary strings. More precisely, the binary strings are used to represent receptors on B cells and T cells and epitopes on antigens, although we refer to these (loosely) as antibodies and antigens. Recognition in the natural immune system is achieved by molecular binding—the extent of the binding being determined by molecular shape and electrostatic charge. The complex chemistry of antigen recognition is highly simplified in the binary immune system and modeled as string matching. The GA is used to evolve populations of strings that match specific antigens well. For strings of any significant length, a perfect match is highly improbable, so a partial matching rule is used that rewards more specific matches (i.e., matches on more bits) over less specific ones. This partial matching rule reflects the fact that the immune system's recognition capabilities need to be fairly specific in order to avoid confusing self molecules with foreign molecules.

In the models of Forrest et al., one population of antibodies and one of antigens is created, each randomly. For most experiments, the antigen population is held constant, and the antibody population is evolved under the GA. However, in some experiments the antigen population is allowed to coevolve with the antibodies (i.e., antigens evolve away from the antibodies while the antibodies are evolving toward the antigens). Antigens are "presented" to the antibody population sequentially (again, by analogy with the natural immune system), and high-affinity antibodies (those that match at many bit positions) have their fitnesses increased.

This binary immune system has been used to study several different aspects of the immune system, including (1) its ability to detect common patterns (schemas) in the noisy environment of randomly presented antigens [38]; (2) its ability to discover and maintain coverage of the diverse antigen population [99]; and (3) its ability to learn effectively, even when not all antibodies are expressed and not all antigens are presented [51]. This last experiment is particularly relevant to the more general question of how selection pressures operating only at the global, phenotypic level can produce appropriate low-level, genetic structures. The question is most interesting when the connection between phenotype and genotype is more than a simple, direct mapping. The multigene families (V-region libraries) of the immune system provide a good subject for experimentation from this point of view—the phenotype is not a direct mapping from the genotype, but the connection is simple enough that it can be studied analytically. In [51], all antigens were exactly 64 bits. The V-region library was modeled as a set of four libraries, each with eight entries of length 16 (producing a genome with 512 bits). Antibodies were expressed by randomly choosing one entry from each library and concatenating them together to form one 64-bit antibody.

Recent work on the kind of genotype–phenotype relations that might be expected between a sequence (e.g., an RNA sequence) and its corresponding higher-order structure (e.g., its secondary structure) may also apply to modeling the immune system

	Player B	
	Cooperate	Defect
Player A Cooperate	3, 3	0, 5
Defect	5, 0	1, 1

Figure 1. The payoff matrix for the Prisoner's Dilemma. The pairs of numbers in each cell give the respective payoffs for players A and B in the given situation.

[59]. For example, the interaction between the immune system and a rapidly evolving pathogen can be regarded as a system with rapidly changing fitness criteria at the level of the secondary structure. Yet, the immune system and pathogen are both coevolving through mutations at the genetic level. In a coevolutionary system such as this, the populations evolve toward relatively uncorrelated parts of the phenotype landscape where mutations have a relatively large effect on the secondary structure, thus facilitating the process of continuous adaptation itself. This is a similar point to that raised in [51]. The idea of exploiting variations in the phenotype through mutations at the genetic level is a recurring theme in evolution, and the immune system provides a clear example of where such exploitation might occur.

7 Social Systems

Understanding and modeling social systems, be they insect colonies or human societies, has been a focus of many artificial-life researchers. GAs have played a role in some of these models, particularly those modeling the evolution of cooperation. Here we describe how the GA was used to evolve strategies for interaction in the context of the Prisoner's Dilemma.

The Prisoner's Dilemma (PD) is a simple two-person game that has been studied extensively in game theory, economics, and political science because it can be seen as an idealized model for real-world phenomena such as arms races [6]. On a given turn, each player independently decides whether to "cooperate" or "defect." The game is summarized by the payoff matrix shown in Figure 1. If both players cooperate, they each get three points. If player A defects and player B cooperates, then player A gets five points, and player B gets zero points; vice versa if the situation is reversed. Finally, if both players defect, they each get one point. What is the best strategy to take? If there is only one turn to be played, then clearly the best strategy is to defect: the worst consequence for a defector is to get one point and the best is to get five points, which are better than the worst score and the best score, respectively, for a cooperator. The dilemma is that if the game is iterated, that is, if two players play several turns in a row, the strategy of always defecting will lead to a much lower total payoff than the players would get if they both cooperated. How can reciprocal cooperation be induced? This question takes on special significance when the notions of "cooperating" and "defecting" correspond to actions in the real world, such as a real-world arms race.

Axelrod [6] has studied the PD and related games extensively. Early work, including the results of two tournaments that played pairs of human-designed strategies against each other, suggested that the best strategy for playing the iterated PD is one of the simplest: TIT FOR TAT. TIT FOR TAT cooperates on the first move and then, on subsequent moves, does whatever the other player did last. That is, it offers cooperation and then reciprocates it, but if the other player defects, TIT FOR TAT will retaliate with a defection.

Axelrod [8] performed a series of experiments to see if a GA could evolve strategies to play this game successfully. Strategies were encoded as look-up tables, with each entry (C or D) being the action to be taken given the outcomes of three previous turns. In Axelrod's first experiment, the evolving strategies were played against eight human-designed strategies, and the fitness of an evolving strategy was a weighted average of the scores against each of the eight fixed strategies. Most of the strategies that evolved were similar to TIT FOR TAT, having many of the properties that make TIT FOR TAT successful. Strikingly, the GA occasionally found strategies that scored substantially higher than TIT FOR TAT.

It is not correct to conclude that the GA evolved strategies that are "better" than any human-designed strategy. The performance of a strategy depends very much on its environment, that is, the other strategies with which it is playing. Here the environment was fixed, and the highest-scoring strategies produced by the GA were ones that discovered how to exploit specific weaknesses of the eight fixed strategies. It is not necessarily true that these high-scoring strategies would also score well in some other environment. TIT FOR TAT is a generalist, whereas the highest-scoring evolved strategies were more specialized to their given environment. Axelrod concluded that the GA is good at doing what evolution often does: developing highly specialized adaptations to specific characteristics of the environment.

To study the effects of a dynamic environment, Axelrod carried out another experiment in which the fitness was determined by allowing the strategies in the population to play with each other rather than with the fixed set of eight strategies. The environment changes from generation to generation because the strategies themselves are evolving. At each generation, each strategy played an iterated PD with the other members of the population, and its fitness was the average score over all these games. In this second set of experiments, Axelrod observed the following phenomenon: the GA initially evolves uncooperative strategies, because strategies that tend to cooperate early on do not find reciprocation among their fellow population members and, thus, tend to die out. But after about 10–20 generations, the trend starts to reverse: the GA discovers strategies that reciprocate cooperation and that punish defection (i.e., variants of TIT FOR TAT). These strategies do well with each other and are not completely defeated by other strategies, as were the initial cooperative strategies. The reciprocators score better than average, so they spread in the population, resulting in more and more cooperation and increasing fitness.

Lindgren [70] performed a series of experiments similar to Axelrod's second experiment but included the possibility of noise, in which players can make mistakes in following their strategies. He also allowed a more open-ended kind of evolution in which a "gene duplication" operator allowed the amount of memory available to a given strategy to increase. He observed some very interesting evolutionary dynamics, including periods of relative stasis with one or two strategies fairly stable in the population, punctuated by mass extinction events. Other work using computational evolution to discover PD strategies in the presence of noise or imperfect information about the past (both making the PD a more realistic model of social or political interactions) has been done by Miller [79] and Marks [73], among others.

8   Open Problems and Future Directions

In the previous sections we have briefly described some representative examples of artificial-life projects that use GAs in a significant way. These examples, and many others that we do not have space to discuss, point the way to several open problems in GAs. Some of these are quite technical (e.g., questions about genetic operators and representations), and some are more general questions, relevant to many areas of Artificial Life.

It is difficult to distinguish between "yet another cute simulation" and systems that teach us something important and general, either about how to construct artificial life or about the natural phenomena that they model. We suggest that artificial-life research should address at least one of these two criteria and that it is important to be explicit about what any specific system teaches us that was not known before. This is a much more difficult task than may be readily appreciated, so difficult in fact that we consider it an open problem to develop adequate criteria and methods for evaluating artificial-life systems.

On the modeling side it can be very difficult to relate the behavior of a simulation quantitatively to the behavior of the system it is intended to model. This is because the level at which Artificial-Life models are constructed is often so abstract that they are unlikely to make numerical predictions. In GAs, for example, all of the biophysical details of transcription, protein synthesis, gene expression, and meiosis have been stripped away. Useful Artificial-Life models, however, may well reveal general conditions under which certain qualitative behaviors arise, or critical parameters in which a small change can have a drastic effect on the behavior of the system. What is difficult is to distinguish between good qualitative modeling and simulations that are only vaguely suggestive of natural phenomena.

More specific to GAs is the central question of representation. For any given environment or problem domain, the choice of which features to represent on the genotype and how to represent them is crucial to the performance of the GA (or any other learning system). The choice of system primitives (in the case of GAs, the features that comprise the genotype) is a design decision that cannot be automated. GAs typically use low-level primitives such as bits, which can be very far removed from the natural representation of environmental states and control parameters. For this reason, the representation problem is especially important for GAs, both for constructing artificial life and in modeling living systems.

Although the representation problem has been acknowledged for many years, there have been surprisingly few innovative representations, the recent work on genetic programming [69] and messy GAs [43] being notable exceptions. In genetic programming, individuals are represented as S-expressions—small programs written in a subset of LISP. Although S-expressions can be written as linear strings, they are naturally viewed as trees, and the genetic operators operate on trees. Crossover, for example, swaps subtrees between S-expressions. Messy GAs were developed by Goldberg, Korb, and Deb [43] to allow variable-length strings that can be either over- or underspecified with respect to the problem being solved. This allows the GA to manipulate short strings early in a run, and over time, to combine short, well-tested building blocks into longer, more complex strings. New versions of the crossover operator (e.g., uniform crossover [100]) can reduce the inherent bias in standard crossover of breaking up correlated genes that are widely separated on the chromosome (referred to as "positional bias"). These approaches are promising in some cases, especially because the strong positional dependence of most current representations is an artifact introduced by GAs. In natural genetic systems, one gene (approximately) codes for one protein regardless of where it is located, although the expression of a gene (when the protein is synthesized) is indirectly controlled by its location. In spite of the foregoing, the vast majority of current GA implementations use a simple binary alphabet linearly ordered along a single haploid string. It should be noted that researchers interested in engineering applications have long advocated the use of simple "higher-cardinality alphabets," including, for example, real numbers as alleles [30]. Given the fact that GA performance is heavily dependent on the representation chosen, this lack of diversity is surprising.

The representation issues described earlier primarily address the question of how to engineer GAs. Moving away from this question toward more realistic models of evolution are more extended mappings between the genotypic representation and the phenotype. Buss [23], among others, has pointed out that the principle of evolution by natural selection is applicable at many levels besides that of the individual, and in particular, that natural selection controls development (e.g., embryology) that interacts with selection at the level of the individual. Related to this point, and to the observation that evolution and learning can interact, are several recent studies of GAs that include a "development" cycle, which translates the genotype through a series of steps into the phenotype. The most common example of this is to let the genotype specify a grammar (as in L-systems). The grammar is then used to produce a legal object in the language it specifies (the development step), and this string (the phenotype) is then evaluated by the fitness function. Examples of this exploratory work include Belew [14], Gruau [47], Kitano [67], and Wilson [108]. Although this work is only a crude approximation of development in living systems, it is an important first step and represents a promising avenue for future research.

Related to the question of representation is the choice of genetic operators for introducing variation into a population. One reason that binary linearly ordered representations are so popular is that the standard mutation and crossover operators can be applied in a problem-independent way. Other operators have been experimented with in optimization settings, but no new general-purpose operators have been widely adopted since the advent of GAs. Rather, the inversion operator, included in the original proposals for theoretical reasons, has been largely abandoned. We believe it deserves more study. In addition, during the past several decades, molecular biology has discovered many new mechanisms for rearranging genetic material (e.g., jumping genes, gene deletion and duplication, and introns and exons). It would be interesting to know if any of these is significant algorithmically.

Explicit fitness evaluation is the most biologically unrealistic aspect of GAs. Several of the examples described in the previous sections (e.g., ERL, Echo, Strategic Bugs, and some of the PD work) move away from an external, static fitness measure toward more coevolutionary and endogenous evaluations. Although it is relatively easy to implement endogenous or coevolutionary fitness strategies, there is virtually no theory describing the behavior of GAs under these circumstances. In particular, a theory about how building blocks are processed (cf. [42, 55]) under these circumstances would be helpful.

Perhaps the most obvious area for extending the GA is to the study of evolution itself. Although ideas from evolution have provided inspiration for developing interesting computational techniques, there have been few attempts to use these techniques to understand better the evolutionary systems that inspired them. GAs, and the insights provided by analyzing them carefully, should help us to understand better natural evolutionary systems. This "closing of the modeling loop" is an important area of future research on evolutionary computational methods.

Acknowledgments

The authors gratefully acknowledge the Santa Fe Institute Adaptive Computation Program and the Alfred P. Sloan Foundation (grant B1992-46). Support was also provided to Forrest by the National Science Foundation (grant IRI-9157644). We thank Ron Hightower, Terry Jones, and Chris Langton for suggestions that improved this paper.

Suggested Reading

1. Belew, R. K., & Booker, L. B. (Eds.) (1991) *Proceedings of the Fourth International Conference on Genetic Algorithms*. San Mateo, CA: Morgan Kaufmann.

2. Farmer, J. D., Lapedes, A., Packard, N. H., & Wendroff, B., (Eds.) (1986). *Evolution, games, and learning*. Special issue of *Physica D, 22*.

3. Forrest, S. (Ed.) (1990). *Emergent computation*. Cambridge, MA: The MIT Press. Also published as *Physica D, 42*.

4. Forrest, S. (Ed.) (1993) *Proceedings of the Fifth International Conference on Genetic Algorithms*. San Mateo, CA: Morgan Kaufmann.

5. Forrest, S. (1993). Genetic algorithms: Principles of natural selection applied to computation. *Science, 261*, 872–878.

6. Goldberg, D. E. (1989). *Genetic algorithms in search, optimization, and machine learning*. Reading, MA: Addison-Wesley.

7. Grefenstette, J. J. (Ed.) (1985). *Proceedings of an International Conference on Genetic Algorithms and Their Applications*. Hillsdale, NJ: Lawrence Erlbaum Associates.

8. Grefenstette, J. J. (Ed.) (1987). *Proceedings of the Second International Conference on Genetic Algorithms*. Hillsdale, NJ: Lawrence Erlbaum Associates.

9. Holland, J. H. (1992). *Adaptation in natural and artificial systems*. 2nd ed. Cambridge, MA: The MIT Press. (1st ed., 1975).

10. Holland, J. H. (1992). Genetic algorithms. *Scientific American*, July, pp. 114–116.

11. Holland, J. H., Holyoak, K. J., Nisbett, R. E., & Thagard, P. (1986). *Induction: Processes of inference, learning, and discovery*. Cambridge, MA: The MIT Press.

12. Langton, C. G. (Ed.) (1989). *Artificial life*. Reading, MA: Addison-Wesley.

13. Langton, C. G. (Ed.) (1993). *Artificial life III*. Reading, MA: Addison-Wesley.

14. Langton, C. G., Taylor, C., Farmer, J. D., & Rasmussen, S. (Eds.) (1992). *Artificial life II*. Reading, MA: Addison-Wesley.

15. Männer, R., & Manderick, B. (Eds.) (1992). *Parallel problem solving from nature 2*. Amsterdam: North Holland.

16. Meyer, J.-A., Roitblatt, H. L., and Wilson, S. W. (Eds.) (1993). *From animals to animats 2: Proceedings of the Second International Conference on Simulation of Adaptive Behavior*. Cambridge, MA: The MIT Press

17. Meyer, J.-A., & Wilson, S. W. (Eds.) (1991). *From animals to animats: Proceedings of the First International Conference on Simulation of Adaptive Behavior*. Cambridge, MA: The MIT Press

18. Mitchell, M. (1993). Genetic algorithms. In L. Nadel and D. L. Stein (Eds.), *1992 lectures in complex systems*. Reading, MA: Addison-Wesley.

19. Schaffer, J. D. (ed.) (1989). *Proceedings of the Third International Conference on Genetic Algorithms*. Los Altos, CA: Morgan-Kaufmann.

20. Schwefel, H.-P., & Männer, R. (Eds.) (1990). *Parallel problem solving from nature*. Berlin: Springer-Verlag (Lecture Notes in Computer Science, Vol. 496).

21. Varela, F. J., and Bourgine, P. (Eds.) (1992). *Toward a practice of autonomous systems: Proceedings of the First European Conference on Artificial Life*. Cambridge, MA: The MIT Press.

References

1. Ackley, D. H., & Littman, M. L. (1992). Interactions between learning and evolution. In C. G. Langton, C. Taylor, J. D. Farmer, & S. Rasmussen (Eds.), *Artificial life II*, (pp. 487–507). Reading, MA: Addison-Wesley.

2. Ackley, D. H., & Littman, M. L. (1993). A case for Lamarckian evolution. In C. G. Langton (Ed.), *Artificial life III*. Reading, MA: Addison-Wesley.

3. Andreoni, J., & Miller, J. H. (1991). *Auctions with adaptive artificial agents* (Working Paper 91-01-004). Santa Fe, NM: Santa Fe Institute.

4. Andreoni, J., & Miller, J. H. (in press). Auction experiments in artificial worlds. *Cuadernos*.

5. Arthur, W. Brian (1993). On designing economic agents that behave like human agents. *Evolutionary Economics, 3*, 1–22.

6. Axelrod, R. (1984). *The evolution of cooperation*. New York, NY: Basic Books.

7. Axelrod, R. (1986). An evolutionary approach to norms. *The American Political Science Review, 80*.

8. Axelrod, R. (1987). The evolution of strategies in the iterated Prisoner's Dilemma. In L. D. Davis (Ed.), *Genetic algorithms and simulated annealing*. Research Notes in Artificial Intelligence. Los Altos, CA: Morgan Kaufmann.

9. Bäck, T., Hoffmeister, F., & Schwefel, H.-P. (1991). A survey of evolution strategies. In R. K. Belew & L. B. Booker (Eds.), *Proceedings of the Fourth International Conference on Genetic Algorithms* (pp. 2–9). San Mateo, CA: Morgan Kaufmann.

10. Baldwin, J. M. (1896). A new factor in evolution. *American Naturalist, 30*, 441–451.

11. Bedau, M. A., & Packard, N. H. (1992). Measurement of evolutionary activity, teleology, and life. In C. G. Langton, C. Taylor, J. D. Farmer, & S. Rasmussen (Eds.), *Artificial life II* (pp. 431–461). Reading, MA: Addison-Wesley.

12. Bedau, M. A., Ronneburg, F., & Zwick, M. (1992). Dynamics of diversity in an evolving population. In R. Männer & B. Manderick (Eds.), *Parallel problem solving from nature 2* (pp. 95–104). Amsterdam: North Holland.

13. Belew, R. K. (1990). Evolution, learning, and culture: Computational metaphors for adaptive algorithms. *Complex Systems, 4*, 11–49.

14. Belew, R. K. (1993). Interposing an ontogenic model between genetic algorithms and neural networks. In J. Cowan (Ed.), *Advances in neural information processing (NIPS5)*. San Mateo, CA: Morgan Kaufmann.

15. Belew, R. K., McInerney, J., & Schraudolph, N. N. Evolving networks: Using the genetic algorithm with connectionist learning. In C. G. Langton, C. Taylor, J. D. Farmer, & S. Rasmussen (Eds.), *Artificial life II* (pp. 511–547). Reading, MA: Addison-Wesley.

16. Bergman, A., & Feldman, M. W. (1992). Recombination dynamics and the fitness landscape. *Physica D, 56*, 57–67.

17. Bersini, H., & Varela, F. J. (1991). The immune recruitment mechanism: A selective evolutionary strategy. In R. K. Belew & L. B. Booker (Eds.), *Proceedings of the Fourth International Conference on Genetic Algorithms* (pp. 520–526). San Mateo, CA: Morgan Kaufmann.

18. Bledsoe, W. W. (1961). The use of biological concepts in the analytical study of systems. Paper presented at the ORSA-TIMS National Meeting, San Francisco, CA, November 1961.

19. Booker, L. (1991). Instinct as an inductive bias for learning behavioral sequences. In J.-A. Meyer & S. W. Wilson (Eds.), *From animals to animats: Proceedings of the First International Conference on Simulation of Adaptive Behavior* (pp. 230–237). Cambridge, MA: MIT Press.

20. Booker, L. B. (1982). *Intelligent behavior as an adaptation to the task environment*. Ph.D. thesis, The University of Michigan, Ann Arbor, MI, 1982.

21. Box, G. E. P. (1957). Evolutionary operation: A method for increasing industrial productivity. *Journal of the Royal Statistical Society C, 6*, 81–101.

22. Bremermann, H. J. (1962). Optimization through evolution and recombination. In M. C. Yovits, G. T. Jacobi, & G. D. Goldstein (Eds.), *Self-organizing systems* (pp. 93–106). Washington, DC: Spartan Books.

23. Buss, L. W. (1987). *The evolution of individuality*. Princeton, NJ: Princeton University Press.

24. Celada, F., & Seiden, P. E. (1992). A computer model of cellular interactions in the immune system. *Immunology Today, 13*, 56–62.

25. Chalmers, D. J. (1990). The evolution of learning: An experiment in genetic connectionism. In D. S. Touretzky et al. (Eds.), *Proceedings of the 1990 Connecionist Models Summer School*. San Mateo, CA: Morgan Kaufmann.

26. Collins, R. J., & Jefferson, D. R. (1991). Selection in massively parallel genetic algorithms. In R. K. Belew & L. B. Booker (Eds.), *Proceedings of the Fourth International Conference on Genetic Algorithms* (pp. 249–256). San Mateo, CA: Morgan Kaufmann.

27. Collins, R. J., & Jefferson, D. R. (1992). AntFarm: Towards simulated evolution. In C. G. Langton, C. Taylor, J. D. Farmer, & S. Rasmussen (Eds.), *Artificial life II* (pp. 579–601). Reading, MA: Addison-Wesley.

28. Collins, R. J., & Jefferson, D. R. (1992). The evolution of sexual selection and female choice. In F. J. Varela & P. Bourgine (Eds.), *Toward a practice of autonomous systems: Proceedings of the First European Conference on Artificial Life* (pp. 327–336). Cambridge, MA: The MIT Press.

29. Davidor, Y. (1992). *Genetic algorithms and robotics*. Robotics and Automated Systems. Singapore: World Scientific.

30. Davis, L. D. (Ed.) (1991). *Handbook of genetic algorithms*. New York: Van Nostrand Reinhold.

31. Dorigo, M. & Sirtori, E. (1991). Alecsys: A parallel laboratory for learning classifier systems. In R. K. Belew & L. B. Booker (Eds.), *Proceedings of the Fourth International Conference on Genetic Algorithms* (pp. 296–302). San Mateo, CA: Morgan Kaufmann.

32. Dumeur, R. (1991). Extended classifiers for simulation of adaptive behavior. In J. A. Meyer & S. W. Wilson (Eds.), *From animals to animats: Proceedings of the First International Conference on Simulation of Adaptive Behavior* (pp. 58–65). Cambridge, MA: The MIT Press.

33. Farmer, J. D., Packard, N. H., & Perelson, A. S. (1986). The immune system, adaptation, and machine learning. *Physica D, 22*, 187–204.

34. Fogel, D. B. (1992). *Evolving artificial intelligence*. Ph.D. thesis, University of California, San Diego, CA.

35. Fogel, D. B., & Atmar, J. W. (1990). Comparing genetic operators with Gaussian mutations in simulated evolutionary processes using linear search. *Biological Cybernetics, 63*, 111–114.

36. Fogel, L. J., Owens, A. J., & Walsh, M. J. (1966). *Artificial intelligence through simulated evolution*. New York: John Wiley.

37. Fontanari, J. F., & Meir, R. (1990). The effect of learning on the evolution of asexual populations. *Complex Systems, 4*, 401–414.

38. Forrest, S., Javornik, B., Smith, R., & Perelson, A. (1993). Using genetic algorithms to explore pattern recognition in the immune system. *Evolutionary Computation, 1*, 191–211.

39. Fraser, A. S. (1957). Simulation of genetic systems by automatic digital computers: I. introduction. *Australian Journal of Biological Science, 10*, 484–491.

40. Fraser, A. S. (1957). Simulation of genetic systems by automatic digital computers: II. effects of linkage on rates of advance under selection. *Australian Journal of Biological Science, 10*, 492–499.

41. Friedman, G. J. (1959). Digital simulation of an evolutionary process. *General Systems Yearbook, 4*, 171–184.

42. Goldberg, D. E. (1989). *Genetic algorithms in search, optimization, and machine learning*. Reading, MA: Addison-Wesley.

43. Goldberg, D. E., Korb, B., & Deb, K. (1990). Messy genetic algorithms: Motivation, analysis, and first results. *Complex Systems, 3,* 493–530.

44. Grefenstette, J. J. (1991). Lamarckian learning in multi-agent environments. In R. K. Belew & L. B. Booker (Eds.), *Proceedings of the Fourth International Conference on Genetic Algorithms* (pp. 303–310). San Mateo, CA: Morgan Kaufmann.

45. Grefenstette, J. J., & Baker, J. E. (1989). How genetic algorithms work: A critical look at implicit parallelism. In J. D. Schaffer (Ed.), *Proceedings of the Third International Conference on Genetic Algorithms.* San Mateo, CA: Morgan Kaufmann.

46. Grefenstette, J. J., Ramsey, C. L., & Schultz, A. C. (1990). Learning sequential decision rules using simulation models and competition. *Machine Learning, 5,* 355–381.

47. Gruau, F. (1992). Genetic synthesis of Boolean neural networks with a cell rewriting developmental process. In L. D. Whitley & J. D. Schaffer (Eds.), *International Workshop on Combinations of Genetic Algorithms and Neural Networks* (pp. 55–72). Los Alamitos, CA: IEEE Computer Society Press.

48. Harp, S. A., & Samad, T. (1991). Genetic synthesis of neural network architecture. In L. D. Davis (Ed.), *Handbook of genetic algorithms* (pp. 202–221). New York: Van Nostrand Reinhold.

49. Harvey, I. (1993). The puzzle of the persistent question marks: A case study of genetic drift. In S. Forrest (Ed.), *Proceedings of the Fifth International Conference on Genetic Algorithms* (pp. 15–22). San Mateo, CA: Morgan Kaufmann.

50. Harvey, I., Husbands, P., & Cliff, D. (1993). Issues in evolutionary robotics. In J.-A. Meyer, H. L. Roitblat, & S. W. Wilson (Eds.), *From animals to animats 2: Proceedings of the Second International Conference on Simulation of Adaptive Behavior* (pp. 364–373). Cambridge, MA: The MIT Press.

51. Hightower, R., Forrest, S., & Perelson, A. (in press). The evolution of secondary organization in immune system gene libraries. In *Proceedings of the Second European Conference on Artificial Life.* (Working Paper 92-11-054). Santa Fe, NM: Santa Fe Institute.

52. Hillis, W. D. (1990). Co-evolving parasites improve simulated evolution as an optimization procedure. *Physica D, 42,* 228–234.

53. Hinton, G. E., & Nowlan, S. J. (1987). How learning can guide evolution. *Complex Systems, 1,* 495–502.

54. Holland, J. H. (1986). Escaping brittleness: The possibilities of general-purpose learning algorithms applied to parallel rule-based systems. In R. S. Michalski, J. G. Carbonell, & T. M. Mitchell (Eds.), *Machine learning II* (pp. 593–623). San Mateo, CA: Morgan Kaufmann.

55. Holland, J. H. (1992). *Adaptation in natural and artificial systems* (2nd ed.). Cambridge, MA: The MIT Press (1st ed., 1975).

56. Holland, J. H. (1993). *Echoing emergence: Objectives, rough definitions, and speculations for Echo-class models* (Working Paper 93-04-023). Santa Fe Institute. To appear in G. Cowan, D. Pines, & D. Melzner (Eds.), *Complexity: Metaphors, models, and reality.* Reading, MA: Addison-Wesley.

57. Holland, J. H., Holyoak, K. J., Nisbett, R. E., & Thagard, P. (1986). *Induction: Processes of inference, learning, and discovery.* Cambridge, MA: The MIT Press.

58. Holland, J. H., & Miller, J. H. (1991). *Artificial adaptive agents in economic theory* (Working Paper 91-05-025). Santa Fe, NM: Santa Fe Institute.

59. Huynen, M. (1993). *Evolutionary dynamics and pattern generalization in the sequence and secondary structure of RNA.* Ph.D. thesis, Universiteit Utrecht, The Netherlands.

60. Inman, J. K. (1978). The antibody combining region: Speculations on the hypothesis of general multispecificity. In G. I. Bell, A. S. Perelson, & G. H. Pimbley, Jr. (Eds.), *Theoretical immunology* (pp. 243–278). New York: Marcel Dekker.

61. Jefferson, D., Collins, R., Cooper, C., Dyer, M., Flowers, M., Korf, R., Taylor, C., & Wang,

A. (1992). Evolution as a theme in artificial life: The Genesys/Tracker system. In C. G. Langton, C. Taylor, J. D. Farmer, & S. Rasmussen (Eds.), *Artificial life II* (pp. 549–577). Reading, MA: Addison-Wesley.

62. Jones, T., & Forrest, S. (1993). *An introduction to SFI Echo* (Working Paper 93-12-074). Santa Fe, NM: Santa Fe Institute.

63. De Jong, K. A. (1975). *An analysis of the behavior of a class of genetic adaptive systems.* Ph.D. thesis, The University of Michigan, Ann Arbor, MI.

64. De Jong, K. A. (1990). Genetic-algorithm-based learning. In Y. Kodratoff & R. Michalski (Eds.), *Machine learning* (vol. 3, pp. 611–638). San Mateo, CA: Morgan Kaufmann.

65. De Jong, K. A. (1990). Introduction to second special issue on genetic algorithms. *Machine Learning, 5,* 351–353.

66. De Jong, K. A. (1993). Editorial introduction. *Evolutionary Computation, 1,* iii–v.

67. Kitano, H. (1990). Designing neural networks using genetic algorithms with graph generation system. *Complex Systems, 4,* 461–476.

68. Koza, J. R. (1992). Genetic evolution and co-evolution of computer programs. In C. G. Langton, C. Taylor, J. D. Farmer, & S. Rasmussen (Eds.), *Artificial life II* (pp. 603–629). Reading, MA: Addison-Wesley.

69. Koza, J. R. (1993). *Genetic programming: On the programming of computers by means of natural selection.* Cambridge, MA: MIT Press.

70. Lindgren, K. (1992). Evolutionary phenomena in simple dynamics. In C. G. Langton, C. Taylor, J. D. Farmer, & S. Rasmussen (Eds.), *Artificial life II* (pp. 295–312). Reading, MA: Addison-Wesley.

71. Lindgren, K., & Nordhal, M. G. (1993). Artificial food webs. In C. G. Langton (Eds.), *Artificial life III.* Reading, MA: Addison-Wesley.

72. MacLennan, B. (1992). Synthetic ethology: An approach to the study of communication. In C. G. Langton, C. Taylor, J. D. Farmer, & S. Rasmussen (Eds.), *Artificial life II* (pp. 631–655). Reading, MA: Addison-Wesley.

73. Marks, R. E. (1992). Breeding hybrid strategies: Optimal behavior for oligopolists. *Journal of Evolutionary Economics, 2,* 17–38.

74. Menczer, F., & Parisi, D. (1992). A model for the emergence of sex in evolving networks: Adaptive advantage or random drift? In F. J. Varela & P. Bourgine (Eds.), *Toward a practice of autonomous systems: Proceedings of the First European Conference on Artificial Life.* Cambridge, MA: MIT Press/Bradford Books.

75. Meyer, T. P., & Packard, N. H. (1991). Local forecasting of high dimensional chaotic dynamics (Tech. Rep. CCSR-91-1). Center for Complex Systems Research, Beckman Institute, University of Illinois at Urbana Champaign.

76. Miller, G. F., & Todd, P. M. (1990). Exploring adaptive agency: I: Theory and methods for simulating the evolution of learning. In D. S. Touretzky et al. (Eds.), *Proceedings of the 1990 Connectionist Models Summer School.* San Mateo, CA: Morgan Kaufmann.

77. Miller, G. F., Todd, P. M., & Hegde, S. U. (1989). Designing neural networks using genetic algorithms. In J. D. Schaffer (Ed.), *Proceedings of the Third International Conference on Genetic Algorithms* (pp. 379–384). San Mateo, CA: Morgan Kaufmann.

78. Miller, J. H. (1988). *Two essays on the economics of imperfect information.* Ph.D. thesis, The University of Michigan, Ann Arbor, MI.

79. Miller, J. H. (1989). The coevolution of automata in the repeated prisoner's dilemma (Tech. Rep. 89-003). Santa Fe, NM: Santa Fe Institute.

80. Mitchell, M., Crutchfield, J. P., & Hraber, P. T. (in press). Evolving cellular automata to perform computations: Mechanisms and impediments. *Physica D.*

81. Montana, D. J., & Davis, L. D. (1989). Training feedforward networks using genetic algorithms. In *Proceedings of the International Joint Conference on Artificial Intelligence.*

San Mateo, CA: Morgan Kaufmann.

82. Nolfi, S., Elman, J. L., & Parisi, D. (1990). Learning and evolution in neural networks (Tech. Rep. CRL 9019). San Diego: Center for Research in Language, University of California.

83. Packard, N. H. (1989). Intrinsic adaptation in a simple model for evolution. In C. G. Langton (Ed.), *Artificial life* (pp. 141–155). Reading, MA: Addison-Wesley.

84. Parisi, D., Nolfi, S., & Cecconi, F. (1992). Learning, behavior, and evolution. In F. J. Varela & P. Bourgine (Eds.), *Toward a practice of autonomous systems: Proceedings of the First European Conference on Artificial Life.* Cambridge, MA: The MIT Press.

85. Perelson, A. S. (1989). Immune network theory. *Immunological Review, 110,* 5–36.

86. Perelson, A. S., Weisbuch, G., & Coutinho, A. (1992). *Theoretical and experimental insights into immunology.* New York: Springer-Verlag.

87. Ray, T. S. (1991). Is it alive, or is it GA? In R. K. Belew & L. B. Booker (Eds.), *Proceedings of the Fourth International Conference on Genetic Algorithms* (pp. 527–534). San Mateo, CA: Morgan Kaufmann.

88. Ray, T. S. (1992). An approach to the synthesis of life. In C. G. Langton, C. Taylor, J. D. Farmer, & S. Rasmussen (Eds.), *Artificial life II* (pp. 371–408). Reading, MA: Addison-Wesley.

89. Rechenberg, I. (1973). *Evolutionstrategie: optimierung technischer systeme nach prinzipien der biologischen evolution.* Stuttgart: Frommann-Holzboog.

90. Riolo, R. (1991). Lookahead planning and latent learning in a classifier system. In J. A. Meyer & S. W. Wilson (Eds.), *From animals to animats: Proceedings of the First International Conference on Simulation of Adaptive Behavior* (pp. 316–326). Cambridge, MA: The MIT Press.

91. Riolo, R. (1991). Modeling simple human category learning with a classifier system. In R. K. Belew and L. B. Booker (Eds.), *Proceedings of the Fifth International Conference on Genetic Algorithms* (pp. 324–333). San Mateo, CA: Morgan Kaufmann.

92. Rogers, D. (1990). Weather prediction using a genetic memory (Tech. Rep. 90.6). Moffett Field, CA: Research Institute for Advanced Computer Science, NASA Ames Research Center.

93. Schaffer, J. D., & Eshelman, L. J. (1991). On crossover as an evolutionarily viable strategy. In R. K. Belew & L. B. Booker (Eds.), *Proceedings of the Fourth International Conference on Genetic Algorithms* (pp. 61–68). San Mateo, CA: Morgan Kaufmann.

94. Schaffer, J. D., & Whitley, D., & Eshelman, L. J. (1992). Combinations of genetic algorithms and neural networks: A survey of the state of the art. In L. D. Whitley & J. D. Schaffer (Eds.), *International Workshop on Combinations of Genetic Algorithms and Neural Networks* (pp. 1–37). Los Alamitos, CA: IEEE Computer Society Press.

95. Schulze-Kremer, S. (1992). Genetic algorithms for protein tertiary structure prediction. In R. Männer & B. Manderick (Eds.), *Parallel problem solving from nature 2* (pp. 391–400). Amsterdam: North Holland.

96. Schwefel, H.-P. (1975). *Evolutionsstrategie und numerische Optimierung.* Ph.D. thesis, Technische Universität Berlin, Berlin, 1975.

97. Schwefel, H.-P. (1977). *Numerische Optimierung von Computer-Modellen mittels der Evolutionsstrategie* (vol. 26 of *Interdisciplinary Systems Research*). Basel: Birkhäuser.

98. Maynard Smith, J. (1987). When learning guides evolution. *Nature, 329,* 761–762.

99. Smith, R., Forrest, S., & Perelson, A. S. (1993). Searching for diverse, cooperative populations with genetic algorithms. *Evolutionary Computation, 1,* 127–149.

100. Syswerda, G. (1989). Uniform crossover in genetic algorithms. In J. D. Schaffer (Ed.), *Proceedings of the Third International Conference on Genetic Algorithms* (pp. 2–9). San Mateo, CA: Morgan Kaufmann.

101. Taylor, C. E., Jefferson, D. R., Turner, S. R., & Goldman, S. R. (1989). RAM: Artificial life

for the exploration of complex biological systems. In C. G. Langton (Ed.), *Artificial life* (pp. 275–295). Reading, MA: Addison-Wesley.

102. Todd, P. M., & Miller, G. F. (1990). Exploring adaptive agency III: Simulating the evolution of habituation and sensitization. In H.-P. Schwefel & R. Männer (Eds.), *Parallel problem solving from nature* (Lecture Notes in Computer Science). Berlin: Springer-Verlag.

103. Todd, P. M., & Miller, G. F. (1991). Exploring adaptive agency II: Simulating the evolution of associative learning. In J.-A. Meyer & S. W. Wilson (Eds.), *From animals to animats: Proceedings of the First International Conference on Simulation of Adaptive Behavior* (pp. 306–315). Cambridge, MA: The MIT Press.

104. Werner, G. M., & Dyer, M. G. (1992). Evolution of communication in artificial organisms. In C. G. Langton, C. Taylor, J. D. Farmer, & S. Rasmussen (Eds.), *Artificial life II* (pp. 659–687). Reading, MA: Addison-Wesley.

105. Whitley, L. D., Dominic, S., & Das, R. (1991). Genetic reinforcement learning with multilayer neural networks. In R. K. Belew & L. B. Booker (Eds.), *Proceedings of the Fourth International Conference on Genetic Algorithms* (pp. 562–569). San Mateo, CA: Morgan Kaufmann.

106. Wilson, S. W. (1985). Knowledge growth in an artificial animal. In J. Grefenstette (Ed.), *Proceedings of the First International Conference on Genetic Algorithms and Their Applciations.* Hillsdale, NJ: Lawrence Erlbaum Associates.

107. Wilson, S. W. (1987). Classifier systems and the animat problem. *Machine Learning, 2,* 199–228.

108. Wilson, S. W. (1989). The genetic algorithm and simulated evolution. In C. G. Langton (Ed.), *Artificial life* (pp. 157–165). Reading, MA: Addison-Wesley.

Artificial Life as Philosophy

Daniel Dennett
Cognitive Studies
Tufts University
Medford, MA 02115
ddennett@pearl.tufts.edu

There are two likely paths for philosophers to follow in their encounters with Artificial Life: They can see it as a new way of doing philosophy, or simply as a new object worthy of philosophical attention using traditional methods. Is Artificial Life best seen as a new philosophical method or a new phenomenon? There is a case to be made for each alternative, but I urge philosophers to take the leap and consider the first to be more important and promising.

Philosophers have always trafficked in thought experiments, putatively conclusive arguments about what is possible, necessary, and impossible under various assumptions. The cases that philosophers have been able to make using these methods are notoriously inconclusive. What "stands to reason" or is "obvious" in various complex scenarios is quite often more an artifact of the bias and limitations of the philosopher's imagination than the dictate of genuine logical insight. Artificial Life, like its parent (aunt?) discipline, Artificial Intelligence, can be conceived as a *sort* of philosophy—the creation *and testing* of elaborate thought experiments, kept honest by requirements that could never be imposed on the naked mind of a human thinker acting alone. In short, Artificial Life research is the creation of prosthetically controlled thought experiments of indefinite complexity. This is a great way of confirming or disconfirming many of the intuitions or hunches that otherwise have to pass as data for the sorts of conceptual investigations that define the subject matter of philosophy. Philosophers who see this opportunity will want to leap into the field, at whatever level of abstraction suits their interests, and gird their conceptual loins with the simulational virtuosity of computers.

But perhaps some philosophers won't see the field this way. They will disagree with this assessment of mine or will worry about some of its presuppositions and implications, and, for them, Artificial Life will appear to be just one more controversial object in the world in need of philosophical analysis, criticism, defense, categorization. What are the *n* defining doctrines of the Artificial Life creed, and what can be said in defense or criticism of them? Already the stirrings of discussion about whether one wants to distinguish "strong AL" from one or another variety of "weak AL" can be heard in the corridors of philosophy. No doubt there is some useful work to be done identifying the popular misconceptions of the field and exposing them, scolding the overambitious partisans on both sides, and clarifying the actual products, as well as the prospects, of work in the field. It would be a shame, however, if this conceptual policeman role were to be the dominant contribution philosophers make to the field.

If we draw the boundaries of Artificial Life rather broadly, there are many quite traditional philosophical issues in the philosophy of biology, of science, of mind, and even metaphysics and ethics on which AL explorations have already begun to yield important insights. Even such a relatively simple ancestor as Conway's Life game provides a host of insights into traditional questions about causation, levels of explanation, identity over time, ceteris paribus reasoning and other topics [1]. Are Hobbesian just so stories about the possibility of the evolution of cooperation defensible? Certainly Axelrod's pioneering competitions point the way to a rich future of exploration. Under what conditions does (could, would, must, might) communication arise as a feature of interaction between individuals in groups? Can we build a gradualist bridge from simple amoeba-like automata to highly purposive intentional systems, with identifiable goals, beliefs, and so forth? These questions of manifest philosophical interest merge seamlessly with the delicious conceptual questions of biology: Why is there sex? Are there fixable scales or measures of complexity or designedness or adaptativeness that we can use to formulate hypotheses about evolutionary trends? Under what conditions does the fate of groups as opposed to individuals play a decisive role in evolution? What *is* an individual? The list goes on and on.

Artificial Life has already provided philosophers with a tidy batch of examples that challenge or illustrate points that have figured prominently in contemporary philosophy. I anticipate that as philosophers acquaint themselves with the field and actively enter into its explorations, the philosophical progeny of the early work will multiply like fruitflies. After all, the field could hardly be better designed to appeal to a philosopher's habits: You get to *make up* most of the facts! This, as any philosopher knows, is perfectly kosher in a conceptual investigation.

References

1. Dennett, D. C. (1991). Real patterns. *Journal of Philosophy, 88*, 27–51.

Levels of Functional Equivalence in Reverse Bioengineering

Stevan Harnad
Laboratoire Cognition
et Mouvement
URA CNRS 1166 I.B.H.O.P.
Universite d'Aix Marseille II
13388 Marseille cedex 13, France
harnad@princeton.edu

Abstract   Both Artificial Life and Artificial Mind are branches of what Dennett has called "reverse engineering": Ordinary engineering attempts to build systems to meet certain functional specifications; reverse bioengineering attempts to understand how systems that have already been built by the Blind Watchmaker work. Computational modeling (virtual life) can capture the formal principles of life, perhaps predict and explain it completely, but it can no more *be* alive than a virtual forest fire can be hot. In itself, a computational model is just an ungrounded symbol system; no matter how closely it matches the properties of what is being modeled, it matches them only formally, with the mediation of an interpretation. Synthetic life is not open to this objection, but it is still an open question how close a functional equivalence is needed in order to capture life. Close enough to fool the Blind Watchmaker is probably close enough, but would that require molecular indistinguishability, and if so, do we really need to go that far?

Keywords
computationalism, evolution, functionalism, reverse engineering, robotics, symbol grounding, synthetic life, virtual life, Turing test

In Harnad [13] I argued that there was a fundamental difference between virtual and synthetic life, and that whereas there is no reason to doubt that a synthetic system could really be alive, there *is* reason to doubt that a virtual one could be. For the purposes of this inaugural issue of *Artificial Life*, I will first recapitulate the argument against virtual life (so as to elicit future discussion in these pages), and then I will consider some obstacles to synthetic life.

1   What Is Life?

First, What is it to be "really alive"? I'm certainly not going to be able to answer this question here, but I can suggest one thing it's *not*: It's not a matter of satisfying a definition, at least not at this time, for such a definition would have to be preceded by a true theory of life, which we do not yet have. It's also not a matter of arbitrary stipulation, because some things, like plants and animals, are indeed alive, and others, like stones and carbon atoms, are not. Nor, by the same token, is *everything* alive, or *nothing* alive (unless the future theory of life turns out to reveal that there is nothing unique to the things we call living that distinguishes them from the things we call nonliving). On the other hand, the intuition we have that there is something it is *like* to be alive—the animism that I suggested was lurking in vitalism [13]—may be wrong. And it would be a good thing, too, if it turned out to be wrong, for otherwise the problem of life would inherit the mind/body problem [22,23]; more about this shortly.

Here's a quick heuristic criterion for what's really alive (although it certainly doesn't represent a necessary or sufficient condition): Chances are that whatever could slip by the Blind Watchmaker across evolutionary generations undetected is alive [15]. What

I mean is that whatever living creatures are, they are what has successfully passed through the dynamic Darwinian filter that has shaped the biosphere. So if there are candidates that can comingle among the living indistinguishably (to evolution, if not to some other clever but *artificial* gadget we might use to single out imposters), then it would be rather arbitrary to deny they were alive. Or rather, lacking a theory of life, we'd be hard put to say *what* it was that they weren't, if they were indeed not alive, though adaptively indistinguishable from things that were alive.

This already suggests that life must have something to do with functional properties: the functional properties we call *adaptive*, even though we don't yet know what those are. *We* don't know, but the Blind Watchmaker presumably knows, or rather, whatever it is that He *cannot* know can't be essential to life. Let me be more concrete: If there were an autonomous, synthetic species (or a synthetic subset of a natural species) whose individuals were either manmade or machine-made—which pretty well exhausts the options for "synthetic" versus "natural," I should think—yet could eat and be eaten by natural species, and could survive and reproduce amongst them, then someone might have a basis for saying that these synthetic creatures were not *natural*, but not for saying that they were not *alive*, surely.

We might have the intuition that those ecologically indistinguishable synthetic creatures differed from living ones in some essential way, but without a theory of life we could not say what that difference might be. Indeed, if it turned out that all natural life was without exception based on left-handed proteins and that these synthetic creatures were made of right-handed proteins (which in reality would block any viable prey/predator relation, but let's set that aside for now as if it were possible), even that would fail to provide a basis for denying that they were alive. So invariant correlates of natural life do not rule out synthetic life.

The animism lurking in our intuitions about life does suggest something else that might be missing in these synthetic creatures, namely, a mind, someone at home in there, actually being alive [4]. At best, however, this would make them *mindless* zombies, but not *lifeless* ones—unless of course mind and life *do* swing together, in which case we would fall back into the mind/body problem, or, more specifically, its other incarnation, the "other minds" problem [10]. For the Blind Watchmaker is no more a mind reader than we are; hence, neither He nor we could ever *know* whether or not a creature was a zombie (because the zombie is functionally indistinguishable from its mindful counterpart). So if life and mind swing together, the question of what life is is empirically undecidable, and a synthetic candidate fares no better or worse than a functionally equivalent natural one.

2   Virtual Life

All this has been about synthetic life, however, and synthetic life of a highly lifelike order: capable of interacting adaptively with the biosphere. What about virtual life? Virtual life, let's not mince words, is computational life, and computation is the manipulation of formal symbols based on rules that operate on the shapes of those symbols. Not just any manipulations, to be sure; the ones of interest are the ones that can be systematically interpreted: as numerical calculations, as logical deductions, as chess moves, as answers to questions, as solutions to problems. What is critical to computation is that even though the symbols are systematically interpretable as *meaning* something (numbers, propositions, chess positions), their *shape* is arbitrary with respect to their meaning, and it is only on these arbitrary shapes that the rules operate. Hence, computation is purely syntactic; what is manipulated is symbolic *code*. The code is interpretable by us as meaning something, but that meaning is not "in" the symbol system any more than the meaning of the words in a book is in the book. The meaning is in the heads of the interpreters and users of the symbol system.

This is not to minimize the significance and power of formal symbol manipulation, for that power is in fact the power of computation as it has been formalized by the fathers of modern computational theory: Turing, Goedel, Church, von Neumann (see Boolos & Jeffrey [1]). According to the Church-Turing Thesis, computation, in the sense of formal symbol manipulation, captures what it is that a mathematician means intuitively by a mechanical procedure. So far, every formalization of this notion has turned out to be equivalent. A natural generalization of the Church-Turing Thesis to the physical world is that every physically realizable system is formally equivalent to a symbol system (at least in the case of discrete physical systems, and to as close an approximation as one wishes in the case of continuous physical systems).

What all this means is that formal symbol manipulation is no mean matter. It covers a vast territory, both mathematical and physical. The only point at which it runs into some difficulty is when it is proposed as a candidate for what is going on in the mind of the interpreter or the user of the symbol system. It is when we suppose that *cognition* itself is *computation* that we run into a problem of infinite regress that I have dubbed "the symbol grounding problem" [7]. For whatever it might be that is really going on in my head when I think, my thoughts certainly don't mean what they mean merely because they are interpretable as so meaning by you or anyone else. Unlike the words in a static book or even the code dynamically implemented in a computer, my thoughts mean what they mean autonomously, independently of any external interpretation that can be or is made of them. The meanings in a pure symbol system, in contrast, are ungrounded, as are the meanings of the symbols in a Chinese/Chinese dictionary, symbols that, be they ever so systematically interpretable, are useless to someone who does not already know Chinese, for all one can do with such a dictionary is to pass systematically from one arbitrary, meaningless symbol to another: Systematically interpretable to a Chinese speaker, but intrinsically meaningless in itself, the symbol system neither contains nor leads to what it is interpretable as meaning. The meaning must be projected onto it from without.

The arbitrariness of the shapes of the symbols—the shape of the code—and the fact that computational algorithms, the rules for manipulating these meaningless symbols, can be described completely independently of their physical implementation, was exploited by the philosopher John Searle [24] in his celebrated "Chinese Room Argument" against the hypothesis that cognition is just computation:

Computation is implementation independent; the details of its physical realization are irrelevant. Every implementation of the same formal symbol system is performing the same computation and, hence, must have every purely computational property that the symbol system has. Searle accordingly pointed out that the hypothesis that cognition is just computation can only be sustained at the cost of being prepared to believe that a computer program that can pass the Turing Test [25] in Chinese—that is, correspond for a lifetime as a pen pal indistinguishably from a real pen pal—would understand Chinese even though Searle, implementing exactly the same program, would not. The source of the illusion on which Searle had put his finger was the systematic interpretability of the symbol system itself: Given that the symbols can bear the weight of a systematic interpretation, it is very hard for us to resist the seductiveness of the interpretation itself, once it is projected onto the system. More specifically, once we see that the symbols are interpretable as meaningful messages from a pen pal, it is hard to see our way out of the hermeneutic hall of mirrors this creates, in which the interpretation keeps sustaining and confirming itself over and over: We keep seeing the reflected light of the interpretation that we ourselves have projected onto the system [8,9].

Searle simply reminded us that *in reality* all we have in this case is a systematically interpretable set of symbols. We would not mistake a computer simulation of, say, a forest fire—that is, a virtual forest fire: a set of symbols and symbol manipulations that were systematically interpretable as trees, burning—for a real forest fire because, among other things, the symbol system would lack one of the essential properties of a real forest fire: heat. Even a full-blown, virtual-world simulation of a forest fire, one that used transducers to simulate the sight, heat, sound, and smell of a forest fire, would not be called a forest fire (once the true source of the stimulation was made known to us), because "computer-generated forest fire stimuli to human senses" on the one hand and "forest fires" on the other are clearly not the same thing. In the case of the "virtual pen pal," in contrast, there was nothing to curb the fantasies awakened by the systematic interpretability, so we were prepared to believe that there was really someone home in the (implemented) symbol system, understanding us. It required Searle, as yet another physical implementation of the same symbol system, to point out that this too was all done with mirrors, and that there was no one in there understanding Chinese in either case.

Between the purely symbolic forest fire and the one supplemented by "virtual-world" transducers traducing our senses, however, are important differences that are pertinent to the difference between the virtual and the synthetic [6]. The hypothesis that Searle attacked, stated in full, would be that cognition is *only* computation, that is, just implementation-independent symbol manipulation. Transduction, of course, is *not* just implementation-independent symbol manipulation. In this case, however, when the transduction is being driven by a symbol system and used only to fool our senses, the objection is the same: A real forest fire is clearly not the same as either (a) a pure symbol system systematically interpretable as if it were a forest fire (a virtual forest fire), or (b) a symbol system driving transducers in such a way as to give the sensory impression of a forest fire (a virtual-world forest fire). A real forest fire is something that happens to real trees, in the real woods. Although a real forest fire may be contained, so as not to incinerate the whole earth, there is in a real sense no barrier between it and the rest of the real world. There is something essentially interactive ("nonadiabatic") about it, "situated" as it is, in the real world of which it is a part. A real forest fire is not, in short, an ungrounded symbol system, whereas that is precisely what a virtual forest fire is.

Now any implementation of a virtual forest fire—whether a purely symbolic one, consisting of interpretable code alone, or a hybrid "virtual-worlds" implementation, consisting of a symbol system plus sensorimotor transducers that generate the illusion of a forest fire to the human senses—is of course also a part of the real world, but it is immediately obvious that it is the *wrong* part. To put it in the terms that were already used earlier in this paper: the purely symbolic virtual forest fire may be equivalent to a real forest fire to our intellects, when mediated by the interpretation occurring in our brains, and the hybrid sensory simulation may be equivalent to our senses, when mediated by the perception occurring in our brains, but *in the world* (the only world there is), neither of these virtual forest fires is functionally equivalent to a real forest fire. Indeed, virtual forest fires are truly "adiabatic": They are incapable of spreading to the world, indeed of affecting the world in any way *qua* fire (as opposed to food for thought or sop for the senses).

I write all this out longhand, but of course there is no "Artificial Fire" Movement, some of whose adherents are arguing that virtual forest fires are really burning. It is simply obvious that real forest fires and virtual ones are radically different kinds of things, and that the kind of thing a virtual forest fire is in reality, setting aside interpretations, whether symbolic or sensory, is a symbol system that is capable of having a certain effect on a human mind. A real forest fire, too, can have an effect on a human mind (perhaps even the same effect), but that's not *all* a real forest fire is, nor is that its essential property, which has nothing to do with minds.

What about synthetic forest fires? Well, synthetic trees—the functional equivalents of trees, manmade or machine-made, possibly out of a different kind of stuff—might be possible, as discussed earlier in the case of synthetic creatures. Synthetic fire is harder to conceive: some other kind of combustive process perhaps? I don't know enough physics to be able to say whether this makes sense, but it's clearly a question *about physics* that we're asking: whether there is a physical process that is functionally equivalent to ordinary fire. I suspect not, but if there is, and it can be engineered by people and machines, let's call that synthetic fire. I see no reason for denying that, if it were indeed functionally indistinguishable from fire, such synthetic fire would be a form of real fire. The critical property would be its functional equivalence to fire in the real world.

So that would be a synthetic forest fire, functionally equivalent to a real one in the world. In the case of the virtual forest fire, another form of equivalence is the one usually invoked, and it too is sometimes called "functional," but more often it is referred to, more accurately, as computational, formal, or Turing equivalence [1]. This is really an instance of the physical version of the Church-Turing Thesis mentioned earlier: Every physical system can be simulated by (that is, is formally equivalent to) a symbol system. The relationship is not merely illusory, however, for the computer simulation, formally capturing, as it does, the functional principles of the real system that it is computationally equivalent to, can help us understand the latter's physical as well as its functional properties. Indeed, in principle, a virtual system could teach us everything we need to know in order to build a synthetic system in the world or to understand the causal properties of a natural system. What we must not forget, however, is that the virtual system is *not* the real system, synthetic or natural, and in particular—as in the case of the virtual forest fire as well as the virtual pen pal—it lacks the *essential* properties of the real system (in the one case, burning, and in the other, understanding).

The virtual system is, in other words, a kind of "oracle" (as I dubbed it in Harnad [13]), being systematically interpretable as if it were the real thing because it is computationally equivalent to the real thing. Hence, the functional properties of the real thing should have symbolic counterparts in the simulation, and they should be predictable and even implementable (as a synthetic system) on the basis of a translation of the formal model into the physical structures and processes it is simulating [3]. The only mistake is to think that the virtual system *is* an instance of the real thing, rather than what it really is, namely, a symbol system that is systematically interpretable as if it were the real thing.

Chris Langton was making an unwitting appeal to the hermeneutic hall of mirrors a few years ago at a robotics meeting in Flanders [17] when he invited me to suppose that, in principle, all the initial conditions of the biosphere at the time of the "primal soup" could be encoded, along with the requisite evolutionary algorithms, so that, in real or virtual time, the system could then evolve life exactly as it had evolved on earth: unicellular organisms, multicellular organisms, invertebrates, mammals, primates, humans, and then eventually even Chris and me, having that very conversation (and perhaps even fast-forwardable to decades later, when one of us would have convinced the other of the reality or unreality of virtual life, as the case may be). If I could accept that all of this was possible in principle (as I did and do), so that not one property of real life failed to be systematically mirrored in this grand virtual system, how could I, Chris asked, continue to insist that it wasn't really alive? For whatever I claimed the crucial difference might be, on the basis of which I would affirm that one was alive and the other not, could not the virtual version capture that difference too? Isn't that what Turing Indistinguishability and computational equivalence guarantee?

The answer is that the virtual system could not capture the critical (indeed the essential) difference between real and virtual life, which is that the virtual system is and always will be just a dynamical implementation of an implementation-independent symbol system that is systematically interpretable as if it were alive. Like a highly realistic, indeed oracular book, but a book nonetheless, it consists only of symbols that are systematically construable (by us) as meaning a lot of true and accurate things, but without those meanings actually being *in* the symbol system: They are merely projected onto it by us, and that projected interpretation is then sustained by the accuracy with which the system has captured formally the physical properties it is modeling. This is not true of the real biosphere, which really *is* what I can systematically interpret it as being, entirely independent of me or my interpretation.

What makes it so unnecessary to point out this essential distinction in the case of a virtual forest fire, which no one would claim was really burning, yet so necessary in the case of virtual life, to which some people want to attribute more than meets the eye, again arises from something that Artificial Life has in common with Artificial Mind: The *essential* property each is concerned with (being alive and having a mind, respectively) is *unobservable* in both cases, either to the human senses or to measuring instruments. So this leaves our fantasy unconstrained when it infers that a virtual system that is systematically interpretable as if it were living (or thinking) really *is* living (or thinking). This temptation does not arise with virtual forest fires or virtual solar systems, because it is *observable* that they are not really burning or moving [16].

There clearly *is* an unobservable essence to having a mind (one whose presence each of us is aware of in his own case, but in no other, in knowing at first hand that one is not a zombie), but is there a corresponding unobservable essence to being alive? I think not. There is no *elan vital*, and whatever intuition we have that there is one is probably parasitic on intuitions about having a mind. So what we are projecting onto virtual life—what we are really saying when we say that virtual creatures are really alive—is probably the same thing we are projecting onto virtual mind when we believe there's really someone home in there, thinking, understanding, meaning, etc. And when we're wrong about it, we are probably wrong for the same reason in both cases, namely, that we have gotten trapped in the hermeneutic circle in interpreting an ungrounded symbol system [21].

3 Synthetic Life

Can there be a *grounded* symbol system? The answer will bring us back to the topic of synthetic life, about which I had promised to say more. And here again there will be a suggestive convergence and a possible divergence between the study of Artificial Life and the study of Artificial Mind: One way out of the hermeneutic circle in mind modeling is to move from symbolic modeling to hybrid analog/symbolic modeling [19,20], and from the pen pal version of the Turing Test (TT or T2) [12,25] to the robotic version (the Total Turing Test, T3). To remove the external interpreter from the loop, the robot's internal symbols and symbol manipulations must be grounded directly in the robot's autonomous capacity to discriminate, categorize, manipulate, and describe the objects, features, events, and states of affairs in the world that those symbols are interpretable as being about [5,11,14]. T2 called for a system that was indistinguishable from us in its symbolic (i.e., linguistic capacities). T3 calls for this too, but it further requires indistinguishability in all of our robotic capacities: in other words, total indistinguishability in external (i.e., behavioral) function. (I will consider indistinguishability in both external *and* internal [i.e., neural] function, T4, shortly.)

A T3 system is grounded, because the connection between its internal symbols and what they are about is direct and unmediated by external interpretation. The grounding, however, is purchased at the price of no longer being a pure symbol system. Hence, a robotic mind would be a synthetic mind rather than a virtual one. There is, of course, still the possibility that the robot is a zombie, and there are still ways to tighten the degrees of freedom still further: T4 would call for internal indistinguishability, right down to the last neuron and neurotransmitter. These could be synthetic neurons, of course, but they would have to be functionally indistinguishable from real ones.

My own guess is that if ungrounded T2 systems are underdetermined and open to overinterpretation, T4 systems are overdetermined and include physical and functional properties that may be irrelevant to cognition. I think T3 is just the right empirical filter for mind modeling, because not only is it the one we use with one another, in our day-to-day solutions to the other-minds problem (we are neither mind readers nor brain experts), but it is the same filter that shaped us phylogenetically: The Blind Watchmaker is no mind reader either and harks only to differences in adaptive function. So the likelihood that a T3 robot is a zombie is about equal to the likelihood that we might ourselves have been zombies.

Or is it? Let us not forget the "robotic" functions of sustenance, survival, and reproduction. Are these not parts of our T3 capacity? Certainly a failure of any of them *would* be detectable to the Blind Watchmaker. A species that could not derive the energy needed to sustain itself or that failed to reproduce and maintain continuity across generations could not pass successfully through the Darwinian filter. And to be able to do that might turn out to call for for nothing less than molecular continuity with the rest of the biosphere—in which case T4 alone would narrow the degrees of freedom sufficiently to let through only life/mind. And synthetic life of *that* order of functional indistinguishability from real life would have to have such a high degree of verisimilitude as to make its vitality virtually as certain as that of genetically engineered life.

Yet I am still betting on T3: The life-modeler's equivalent to the mind-modeler's T3 equivalence (lifelong robotic indistinguishability) is transgenerational ecological indistinguishability, and it is not yet clear that this would require molecular indistinguishability (T4). Certainly our model falls so far short of T3 right now that it seems safe to aim at the external equivalence without worrying unduly about the internal—or at least to trust the exigencies of achieving external equivalence to pick out which internal functions might be pertinent rather than to assume a priori that they all are.

That, at least, appears to be a reasonable first pass, methodologically speaking, as dictated by applying Occam's Razor to these two particular branches of inverse applied science: reverse cognitive engineering and reverse bioengineering, respectively. Ordinary forward engineering applies the laws of nature and the principles of engineering to the design and building of brand new systems with certain specified functional capacities that we find useful: bridges, furnaces, airplanes. Reverse engineering [2] must discover the functional principles of systems that have already been designed and built by nature—plants, animals, people—by attempting to design and build systems with equivalent functional capacities. Now in the case of natural living systems and natural thinking systems, "life" (whatever that is) and "mind" (we all know what that is) seem to have "piggybacked" on those functional capacities; it accordingly seems safe to assume they will also piggyback on their synthetic counterparts [18].

The only point of uncertainty is whether external functional equivalence (T3) is a tight enough constraint to fix the degree of internal functional equivalence that ensures that life and mind will piggyback on it, or whether internal functional equivalence (T4) must be captured right down to the last molecule. I'm betting on T3, in part because it is more readily attainable, and in part because even if it is not equivalence enough, we can never hope to be any the wiser.

References

1. Boolos, G. S., & Jeffrey, R. C. (1980). *Computability and logic*. Cambridge, UK: Cambridge University Press.

2. Dennett, D. C. (in press). Cognitive science as reverse engineering: several meanings of "top down" and "bottom up." In D. Prawitz, B. Skyrms, & D. Westerstahl (Eds.), *Proceedings of the 9th International Congress of Logic, Methodology, and Philosophy of Science*. North Holland. In press.

3. Harnad, S. (1982a). Neoconstructivism: a unifying theme for the cognitive sciences. In T. Simon & R. Scholes (Eds.), *Language, mind and brain* (pp. 1–11). Hillsdale, NJ: Erlbaum.

4. Harnad, S. (1982b). Consciousness: an afterthought. *Cognition and Brain Theory, 5*, 29–47.

5. Harnad, S. (ed.). (1987) *Categorical perception: the groundwork of cognition*. New York: Cambridge University Press.

6. Harnad, S. (1989). Minds, machines and Searle. *Journal of Theoretical and Experimental Artificial Intelligence, 1*, 5–25.

7. Harnad, S. (1990a). The symbol grounding problem. *Physica D, 42*, 335–346.

8. Harnad, S. (1990b). Against computational hermeneutics (invited commentary on Eric Dietrich's computationalism). *Social Epistemology, 4*, 167–172.

9. Harnad, S. (1990c). Lost in the hermeneutic hall of mirrors (invited commentary on Michael Dyer, Minds, machines, Searle and Harnad). *Journal of Experimental and Theoretical Artificial Intelligence, 2*, 321–327.

10. Harnad, S. (1991). Other bodies, other minds: a machine incarnation of an old philosophical problem. *Minds and Machines, 1*, 43–54.

11. Harnad, S. (1992a). Connecting object to symbol in modeling cognition. In A. Clarke & R. Lutz (Eds.), *Connectionism in context*. New York: Springer Verlag.

12. Harnad, S. (1992b). The Turing test is not a trick: Turing indistinguishability is a scientific criterion. *SIGART Bulletin, 3*(4), 9–10.

13. Harnad, S. (1993a). Artificial life: synthetic versus virtual. Artificial life III. In *Proceedings, Santa Fe Institute Studies in the Sciences of Complexity* (Vol. XVI).

14. Harnad, S. (1993b). Grounding symbols in the analog world with neural nets. *Think, 2*(1), 12–78 (special issue on "Connectionism versus Symbolism," D. M. W. Powers & P. A. Flach [Eds.]).

15. Harnad, S. (1993c). *Turing indistinguishability and the Blind Watchmaker*. Paper presented at Conference on "Evolution and the Human Sciences," London School of Economics Centre for the Philosophy of the Natural and Social Sciences, June 24–26, 1993.

16. Harnad S. (1993d). Discussion (passim) In G. R. Bock & J. Marsh (Eds.), *Experimental and Theoretical Studies of Consciousness*. CIBA Foundation Symposium 174. Chichester: Wiley.

17. Harnad, S. (1993e). Grounding symbolic capacity in robotic capacity. In L. Steels & R. Brooks (Eds.), *The "artificial life" route to "artificial intelligence": building situated embodied agents*. Hillsdale, NJ: Lawrence Erlbaum.

18. Harnad, S. (1994). Does the mind piggy-back on robotic and symbolic capacity? In H. Morowitz (Ed.), *The mind, the brain, and complex adaptive systems*. Los Alamos: Santa Fe Institute Series.

19. Harnad, S., Hanson, S. J., & Lubin, J. (1991). Categorical perception and the evolution of supervised learning in neural nets. In D. W. Powers & L. Reeker (Eds.), *Working Papers of the AAAI Spring Symposium on Machine Learning of Natural Language and Ontology* (pp. 65–74). Presented at Symposium on Symbol Grounding: Problems and Practice, Stanford University, March 1991.

20. Harnad, S., Hanson, S. J., & Lubin, J. (in press). Learned categorical perception in neural nets: implications for symbol grounding. In V. Honavar & L. Uhr (Eds.), *Symbol processors and connectionist networks for artificial intelligence and cognitive modelling: steps toward principled integration*. San Diego: Academic Press.

21. Hayes, P., Harnad, S., Perlis, D., & Block, N. (1992). Virtual symposium on virtual mind. *Minds and Machines, 2,* 217–238.

22. Nagel, T. (1974). What is it like to be a bat? *Philosophical Review, 83,* 435–451.

23. Nagel, T. (1986). *The view from nowhere.* New York: Oxford University Press.

24. Searle, J. R. (1980). Minds, brains and programs. *Behavioral and Brain Sciences, 3,* 417–424.

25. Turing, A. M. (1964). Computing machinery and intelligence. In A. Anderson (Ed.), *Minds and machines.* Engelwood Cliffs, NJ: Prentice-Hall.

Why Do We Need Artificial Life?

Eric W. Bonabeau
CNET Lannion B-RIO/TNT
22301 Lannion Cedex France
bonabeau@lannion.cnet.fr

G. Theraulaz
CNRS-URA 1837
Laboratoire d'Ethologie
et de Psychologie Animale
Universite Paul Sabatier
31062 Toulouse France
guy.theraulaz@cict.fr

Abstract In this paper, we ask the question of whether we need artificial life (AL) at all. We find a lot of convincing arguments in favor of AL, but we also point out some dangers AL is exposed to. This careful epistemological review reveals the potential richness of AL without being either too reductionist or too holistic. We give some examples showing how this can be done in practice, and conclude that almost everybody needs AL.

Keywords
AL and Art, AL and theoretical biology, AL and engineering, AL and You, boundary conditions, epistemology, levels of analogy, reductionism, synthesis

1 The Many Lives of Artificial Life

It is sometimes beneficial to ask critical questions. One such critical question is to know why we are doing artificial life (AL). Our heads of departments seem to be waiting for an answer, especially when it comes to money: Why should they fund us to do something that doesn't look serious? Well, the possible answers are multiple, but never satisfy them. If ever you are faced with the same kind of "hierarchical" problem, this contribution is aimed at helping you in finding the right things to say to your boss. But things are never that simple. Whatever justification you might use, there are always associated dangers. Therefore, this contribution is also aimed at helping you avoid the numerous traps you could find when starting a discussion on artificial life with your boss. But we also hope to be able to convince not only your boss but also yourself. In order to do so, let us start with a very brief, somewhat provocative, compact "definition" of artificial life: We consider it as a general method consisting in generating at a macroscopic level, from microscopic, generally simple, interacting components, behaviors that are *interpretable as lifelike*. This statement is general enough that it can be applied to 99% of what is done within the artificial life framework. However, depending on the field to which it applies, this framework leads to very different results. For example, biologists do not have the same vision of artificial life as, say, computer scientists, artificial intelligence (AI) researchers, engineers or even artists. Hence, one should speak of artificial lives rather than of artificial life.

2 Artificial (Way of) Life

Before proceeding, we should explain in depth our definition of artificial life. It is based on the observation that most of what has been (or is being) done in AL relies on the following simple assumption: Synthesis is the most appropriate approach to the study of complex systems in general and of living complex systems in particular. Because it seems to be more difficult to start from manifestations of life and try to find its fundamental principles by top-down analysis than to start from computational and physical simulations and try to synthesize more and more complex behaviors, which in turn might capture the nature of some aspects of life, AL thus focuses on ways of achieving emergence to generate these more and more complex behaviors [25]. Apparently, AL's object of study is in essence not different from the object of study of biology: Only the methodology is different. Actually, the methodological aspects constitute the true essence of AL. Note that these aspects are not purely technical and are not as trivial as they may sound: They raise very specific issues, and synthesis, although certainly powerful, must be handled with care. We shall return to this topic later, because it is important that the power of synthesis be directed toward the right channels. Let us note also that AL's methodology is a completely reductionist one, because it is aimed at explaining high-level behaviors from low-level causes.

While the first inspirations of AL's simulations, theories, and models are living things and behaviors, life-as-we-know-it, synthesis naturally allows one to create a much wider spectrum of behaviors, life-as-it-could-be. The only way one can decide whether or not the synthesized behaviors fall within the framework of AL is by judging how well they reproduce some aspects of life, life-as-we-know-it, at the macroscopic level. In order to do this, one has to interpret the obtained behaviors as lifelike. This is a crucial point: There are numerous ways of interpreting these behaviors. One can resort to experimental biological data, to additional criteria of plausibility, or to whatever criterion available.

Let us take an example: trail following in ants. We know through experiments that in some species, ants lay a certain amount of pheromone on their way to a food source and much more pheromone on their way back to the nest, and that they tend to follow pheromone gradients. When one is simulating on a computer a colony of artificial foraging ants following these elementary individual behavioral rules, the observed exploratory patterns can be interpreted in the framework of a theory, whereby the simulation constitutes a test to know if the previously mentioned factors could be sufficient to explain the exploratory patterns of real ant colonies. It is not to say that real ants have anything else in common with artificial ants than this way of locally processing data from their environment and of responding to it. But one knows that the features implemented in the simulations correspond to something real, and that, as advocated in Langton et al. [26], both types of exploratory patterns are two instances of the same phenomenon: The self-organization of collective activities in space and time. Besides experimental data, the simulation is also constrained by a certain form of biological plausibility: In effect, if artificial ants have to deposit 10 (artificial!) tons of pheromone to reproduce the experimentally observed behavior, they do not constitute a good model of real ants. But artificial lifers are not all biologists and do not all seek models to explain biological phenomena. If they just want to reproduce exploratory patterns, they can resort to ants capable of depositing 10 tons of pheromone. Then, the synthesized patterns can no longer be interpreted in the rigid framework of a biological theory: They are interpreted as lifelike if they are similar to biological patterns at a purely phenomenological level. This phenomenological level becomes art if the only constraints one accepts to satisfy are of an aesthetic nature. Engineers, on the other hand, have a different point of view: They need to create efficient, robust, adaptive systems capable of solving problems; the constraint they have to satisfy is a constraint of viability.

To summarize, let us say that more than a scientific field, AL is a way of practicing science. And it is an exciting new way of practicing science, especially for young scientists tired of the boring daily practice of traditional sciences. Moreover, AL goes beyond its application to science: For instance, as we shall try to show, art is inherently associated with AL. But AL is synthetic and reductionist: This makes it quite dangerous, especially for the excited young scientists. In the next two sections, we will take some time to make a review of criticisms that can be made against AL. Most of these criticisms can be wiped out by cautious use of AL, but we have to remain constantly conscious of their existence. This will help in discussions with your boss. We will end with a section explaining why we need artificial life. Don't worry: The reasons are numerous so that you'll have plenty of arguments.

3 Synthesis

Any science having to deal with complex systems can feel the attraction of synthesis. Living systems are undoubtedly complex. The most commonly shared definition of a complex system states that it is a network of interacting objects, agents, elements, or processes that exhibit a dynamic, aggregate behavior. The action of an object (possibly) affects subsequent actions of other objects in the network, so that the action of the whole is more than the simple sum of the actions of its parts. In other words, a system is complex if it is not reducible to a few degrees of freedom or to a statistical description. A complex system has many degrees of freedom that strongly interact with each other, keeping us from either of the two classical reductions: It exhibits what Weaver [47] called organized complexity (as opposed to organized simplicity and disorganized complexity). Besides, the complementary idea of chaos taught us that unpredictability can also arise in low-dimensional deterministic systems, showing that even "reducible" systems can be very hard to deal with. In any case, synthesis, that is, a bottom-up approach generally based on simulation, seems to be a good candidate, if not the only one, to explore the behavioral space of complex systems. Thus, the reason why the sciences of complex systems did not emerge before is simple: There was a sort of unexplored niche in the gigantic scientific ecology. Complex systems, be they low-dimensional chaotic or high-dimensional, could not be studied before the last decades because they require high computational power—far beyond the (unaided) human brain's capabilities. Synthesis has strong computational requirements.

Unfortunately, the synthetic approach, although certainly useful if one does not want to "miss emergent properties" [40], implies weakened explanatory status of models, huge spaces of exploration, absence of constraints. By using synthetic exploration, AL deals with all the phenomena such an exploration may allow. It results in a space of possible behaviors that is too huge: Otherwise stated, life-as-it-could-be is dramatically ill-defined. With such a program, AL tends to forget higher-level sciences (see e.g., "AI has for the most part neglected the fundamental biology of the nervous system. This criticism will undoubtedly be aimed at AL as well" [29]). It should, on the contrary, accept the empirical constraints provided by the observations of these higher-level sciences, even if the ultimate hope is to go beyond the study of what exists toward the study of what could have existed—the latter providing (of course!) no observation at all. Moreover, how can one scientifically assess the validity of models without resorting to constraints? If we resort to synthesis with only the goal of phenomenologically reproducing observed behaviors, it is hard to determine the extent to which a model explains the phenomenon it reproduces. But even when one has appropriate criteria, the level of explanation reached by a given *synthetic* model remains uncertain, and most of epistemology until today has focused on analysis rather than on synthesis.

3.1 A Matter of Levels
Putnam [32] reached an interesting conclusion by making first a difference between "to deduce" and "to explain": Being able to deduce the properties of a phenomenon from a set of causes is not equivalent to explaining this phenomenon, because only a few among the many possible causes may be relevant, "certain systems can have behaviors to which their microstructure is largely irrelevant" [32]. Explaining the phenomenon

amounts to determining what the relevant causes are. Note that the number of such causes might be very high in the case of complex living systems, making explanation intractable. Further, it may simply be impossible to deduce the properties of a phenomenon from a set of causes originating from one single discipline: This is so because "the laws of the higher-level discipline are deducible from the laws of the lower-level discipline together with 'auxiliary hypotheses' that are accidental from the point of view of the lower-level discipline" [32]. The laws of the higher-level discipline, therefore, depend on both the laws of the lower-level discipline and "boundary conditions" that are "accidental from the point of view of physics but essential to the description of" [32] the higher level. It is through the huge space of possibilities allowed by physics and through the many possible accidental causes that higher-level phenomena are somewhat autonomous relative to other levels. Moreover, even when no accidental cause is needed, it may take too long a time to deduce the higher-level properties from the lower-level ones.

Thus, if we summarize Putnam's ideas, we may state the following (using Putnam's terminology): A great number of laws of the lower-level are irrelevant to the understanding of higher-level phenomena; yet, the remaining relevant causes can be intractably numerous. Other laws originating from other perspectives are essential for the understanding of the higher-level phenomena but are purely accidental at the lower level.

In the same spirit, one can see a major obstacle appear: Any kind of higher-level structure can be very hard to deal with, due to the fact that explanation is not transitive (i.e., explanations at one level are not of the same nature as explanations at another level), which gives some unpleasant autonomy to higher levels relative to (explanations at) lower levels. If we say, as in Weidlich, [48] that "a level is a stratum of reality of a certain self-contained organization," that is with a "quasi autonomous dynamics," then (1) the *immensity* of the phase space allowed by the physics of level 1 can make the behavior of level 2 unpredictable, that is, it may be impossible to have any idea about shapes and structures appearing at the higher level given the laws of physics; (2) each passage from one level to another has its *own* boundary conditions; and (3) external boundary conditions (external causes) are *accidental*. (It is worth noticing that these external boundary conditions may also be generated by the higher levels in which the level under study is embedded.) As a consequence, it can be very hard to find tools to deal with higher levels when starting from a given level, and usually, "it appears that the lower level provides the constituent units for the next higher level only" [48].

It is also natural to speak of emergence in the present context. The notion of emergence, often debated within AL, is of high interest in its own right and would justify a separate review. To summarize, we shall say that emergence is generally defined as a process through which entirely new behaviors appear, whose properties cannot be derived from a given model of how the system behaves, so that another model has to be built in order to deal with these new behaviors. Usually, but not necessarily, the new behaviors appear at a macroscopic level while one has only a model of the microscopic level, so that a new model—possibly phenomenological—must be developed for the macroscopic level. The major disagreements about emergence stem from different interpretations of what it means to "derive the properties of the new behaviors" [4,7,8,12,23–27,29,34,35]. In any case, the synthetic nature of AL also explains why people in artificial life share an irrational faith in the power of emergence, although everybody acknowledges that "the concept of emergence in itself offers neither guidance on how to construct such a[n emergent] system nor insight into why it would work" [21]: This also makes AL even more reductionist than most classical reductionist sciences, because for AL the laws of physics within a given system are almighty; not only must the system comply with physical rules, it is also defined by them because they generate sufficient "boundary conditions" by themselves. In other words, the system has to exhibit a highly specific but surprising behavior at the macroscopic level given only the laws of microphysics.

3.2   On the Nature of Phenomenological Analogies

Let alone the danger of outrageously worshipping emergence, the transversality of concepts that is central to AL can also be dangerous when it is not appropriately applied: "a direct comparison of physical and social systems on the phenomenological level can only lead to a superficial, short breathed analogy lacking structural depth," "deep and rather universal analogies between social and physical systems (. . .) reflect the fact that, due to the universal applicability of certain mathematical concepts to multi-component systems, all such systems exhibit an indirect similarity on the macroscopic collective level, which is independent of their possible comparability on the microscopic level" [48]. All natural objects, be they physical, biological, social, or else, are modeled through systems: Only a limited set of observables is chosen, and syntactic relationships are looked for between these observables to account for their (experimentally observed) behaviors. Two systems can share some similarities with respect to some set of observables, while they completely diverge when it comes to other observables. Thus, one must be very cautious when dealing with resemblances not to confuse these necessarily partial resemblances with global analogy at all levels of description and with respect to all possible sets of observables. An example is in order here. Diffusion-limited growth (DLG) [3] is a good illustration of limited resemblances that do not cross levels. DLG is a formalism that is used to model the growth of many different types of patterns, from the growth of bacterial colonies to the growth of electro-chemical deposition, solidification from a supersaturated solution, solidification from an undercooled liquid, etc. Such growth phenomena result in fractal patterns, especially when the concentration of the diffusing field (nutrient in the case of bacterial colonies) is insufficient. Although these many different systems can be described by the same type of equations, and develop the same type of spatial pattern, they cannot be compared at any other level: A bacterial colony has little in common with electrochemical deposition. Besides, there is a functional relevance in the case of the bacterial colony that does not exist in other cases: Growing fractally is a way of achieving a perfect compromise between the surface explored and the density of individuals (see Figure 1).

In artificial life in particular, due to the lack of constraints, phenomenological relationships are almost the only criterion that can be used to judge simulations and models ("simulations are metaphorical, not literal" [27]). It could give the wrong impression that the nature of the simulated processes is essentially the same as the phenomenon they reproduce. While this might be true at the global level, it is certainly false at the level of the constituent units. Let us take the example of the colony of robots built by Beckers and colleagues [18] in Brussels. They reproduce some interesting behaviors at the collective level that are reminiscent of patterns of activities found in insect societies. Yet, the interactions implemented between the robots (particular nonlocal communication processes) are very different from the interactions actually existing in insect colonies. Therefore, although there is a phenomenological similarity at the global level, neither the interactions nor the constituent units are similar.

Our judgment is largely based on our intuitions, experiences, and even emotions, which is in contradiction with AL's ambition to synthesize life-as-it-could-be: We judge simulations based on how well they meet our aesthetic requirements, which themselves rely on our experience of life-as-we-know-it. (What other experience could we have?) As a consequence, we will never be able to recognize or synthesize forms of "life" that are really far from life-as-we-know-it. Thus, instead of ambiguously and dangerously refusing constraints by defining a self-contradictory program, AL should make clear what constraints it chooses to be based upon. All this reminds us of an artistic approach:

a   **b**

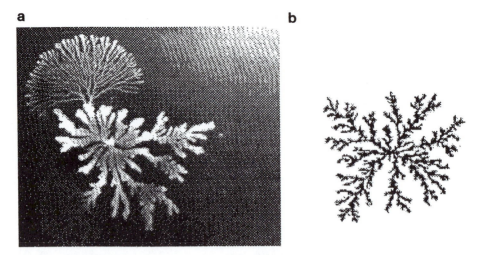

Figure 1. (Modified from Ben-Jacob et al. [3]): (a) represents the growth of a bacterial colony in two different nutrient environments; when nutrient is in sufficient quantity, growth is denser than when nutrient is lacking, in which case the pattern becomes fractal; (b) represents a pattern obtained by electrochemical deposition.

Building an AL's creature, be it a cellular automaton, amounts to making some set of equations and our subconscious meet, just as an artist makes his or her imagination wander around with the help of some technical tools until he or she reaches a state of aesthetic satisfaction. If we are particularly appealed by, say, 1D-CA rule 18, it is because it generates interesting patterns, while most other cellular automata (CA) rules generate uninteresting behavior. By tuning a set of parameters, namely, the values of the associated rule table, we eventually meet a rule that gives us a certain satisfaction. This parallel between art and AL is not surprising if one remembers the importance of sensorial media (like videotapes or computer graphics) in AL demos.

3.3   AL Lost in Immensity

Apart from the contradiction it contains, the life-as-it-could-be program may constitute an intractable task; all the more as "real life," life-as-we-know-it, already covers a large spectrum of possible behaviors: "Life is self-organizing in the sense that it leads to very special forms, that is, from a wide basin of attraction it leads to a much narrower set of meaningful states. But this alone would not yet be surprising: The surprising aspect is that this attraction is not at all rigid. Although the attractor is very small compared with full-phase space, it is still huge, and, therefore, it allows for a wide spectrum of behaviors" [19]. That is why we should follow Sober's [37] suggestion to approach the general questions on the "nature of mind or the nature of life" by "focusing on more specific psychological and biological properties ... this strategy makes the general questions more tractable." By using Putnam's [33] words, the only way for AL not to be "one damned thing after another" is to accept empirical constraints and eventually have one or several "Master Programs," otherwise AL researchers would be tinkers—like evolution—and the number of "damned things" we may think of may be astronomical. Such Master Programs can be, for example, the study of the emergence of self-replicating molecules, of coevolutionary dynamics, of the interplay between evolution, adaptation and learning, of autonomous systems, of collective problem-solving and decision-making abilities in natural and artificial systems, etc. There are other fields dealing with life, adaptation, and evolution that can provide sufficient constraints. The best bottom-up approach needs some kind of validation by top-down data. Most of serious AL-based research is being carried out following such a Master Program with the right constraints, be they experimental or else, but let us emphasize that not everything is serious in the AL community.

4 Reductionism and the Nature of Artificial Life

Following Wimsatt [49], we shall say that "... a reductionist is interested in understanding the character, properties, and behavior of the studied system in terms of the properties of its parts and their interrelations and interactions. This means that the reductionist is primarily interested in the entities and relations internal to the system under study." But Wimsatt added, "This is a sufficiently inclusive description that it probably captures any analytic method in general...." unnecessarily restricting the scope of reductionism to the realm of analytic methodologies, while its definition does not refer to any kind of analysis. And from this definition, it is clear that AL, although synthetic, is 100% reductionist. It is often believed that reductionism goes together with analysis: The sciences of complex systems in general, and AL in particular, offer beautiful counterexamples. Hence, being reductionist is not necessarily a bad thing! The reductionist nature of AL manifests itself in combination with its synthetic nature under some peculiar forms we shall describe.

Artificial life's synthetic exploration procedure is partly motivated by the reductionist hope that simple (most often formal) elements in interactions will generate a sufficient richness of behaviors peculiar to life. Yet, as was pointed out in papers warning against computational reductionism [see, e.g., 7,8], one may miss important phenomena because some external variables or conditions, accidental from the point of view of the model (i.e., not taken into consideration by the model), may turn out to be crucial to the generation of behaviors constituting the essence of life. These conditions, which are essential to the generation or the understanding of a particular phenomenon, are thereafter called "boundary conditions." They can be internal as well as external. We all hope that a lot of "interesting" behaviors can be generated "internally." While doing so, we must be aware of the theoretical limitations such a purely "internal" approach has, and we are indeed if one judges by all the efforts that are being made to incorporate external factors in models. Besides, as all scientists, we are condemned to resort to models, which are necessarily partial images of the world. No science does better in this respect.

4.1 Boundary Conditions

Coming back to Wimsatt's general definition, we see that being reductionist leads to a particular interest in the "entities and relations internal to the system." This constitutes the essence of AL's reductionist side: One tries not to resort to explanations external to the system, or external boundary conditions, in order to make things emerge. The idea behind boundary conditions [31] is the following: although it is true that a higher level has a behavior that is compatible with lower-level laws, lower-level laws alone are *unspecific*. They cannot determine the behavior of the higher level: Boundary conditions make the link between the two levels by "directing lower-level processes to definite channels" [23]. Vitalistic conclusions may easily be drawn from these considerations, if one believes that irreducible boundary conditions underlie the appearance of life: In effect, among the *immense* [13] number of possible states of the world allowed by physics, only a few are compatible with life, and such compatibility may not be deducible from the laws of physics. The idea of boundary condition is closely linked to Elsasser's [13] immensity, to Pattee's nonholonomic constraints, and to Rössler's privileged zero property, nicely summarized in Kampis [23]. The notion of self-generated boundary condition is easy to visualize: We use this terminology to describe the property of some systems that generate boundary conditions from inside (when nonlinear laws of interaction are present), that is, which exhibit a highly specific behavior without the help of any exogenous phenomenon. Such a phenomenon would be "purely accidental" from the point of view of the internal dynamics [32]. It is important to notice that in a case where boundary conditions are generated internally, the dynamics of the system drives it toward a functionally relevant state. If, for instance, the system is composed of interacting processes, it will evolve toward a state where the interactions between the processes will allow it to implement a function without the need of any external, environmental tuning. The systems we are studying are obviously open systems that interact with their surroundings by exchanging matter, energy, (physical) entropy, or "information," and they cannot be entirely described by purely internal mechanisms: We all know this very simple fact and try to incorporate such exchanges in our models and simulations, but at the same time we try to find a minimal set of factors that would account for a particular phenomenon. Let us not forget that such factors may exist inside as well as outside the system.

4.2   More on Reductionists and Environments

As emphasized in Wimsatt [49], reductionists usually tend to look for internal explanations (intrasystemic mechanisms) rather than for external causes (intersystemic mechanisms), and in any case internal mechanisms are very often considered more "fundamental." Extreme reductionists "simplify the description of the environment before simplifying the description of the system" and "construct experimental arrangements so as to keep environment variables constant"; in a nutshell, they "ignore, oversimplify, or otherwise underestimate the importance of the context of the system under study" [49]. But, for example, "evolution depends on a result of microstructure (variation in genotype) but it also depends on conditions (presence of oxygen) that are accidental from the point of view of physics and chemistry" [32]. This last remark in particular reminds us of the multitude of "frozen accidents" that have certainly occurred during evolution (note that there are undoubtedly other mechanisms in evolution): These frozen accidents were mainly caused by external conditions (external relative to a given system's laws of functioning). Thus, the task of reproducing evolution (i.e., to synthesize *artificial life*) by purely self-generated boundary conditions seems hopeless, because at certain points in evolution, external causes have produced crucially relevant changes. Although we do not believe that anyone in AL exhibits such a form of extreme reductionism—once again, environments are certainly considered important, and one should even say more and more important in AL-related simulations and models—it is a good thing to remain conscious of the full complexity of the world around us, of the infinite, open-ended richness of real environments: Artificial Lifers are confronted with the challenging task of translating that complexity and this richness into working simulations and models.

Also of utmost importance is the fact that the complexity of an organism is often believed to reflect the complexity of its environment, at least to some extent. The idea of enaction [45,46] is based on the statement that an organism and its environment are mutually defined. Even if one does not believe in complete mutual specification, it raises the issue of evaluating the influence of environmental structures on an organism's structures. One cannot hope to do so without embodying artificial creatures in somewhat realistic, varying environments. A way of taking external causes into account is by making embodiment a clear goal of all AL's theories and simulations [5,6]—which it is already to a large extent: Let us make it even clearer. Embodying an artificial creature in some kind of environment (with the ultimate goal of plunging it into a real one) implies making a thorough investigation of the notion of external boundary condition. AL constitutes an important first step toward this goal, in the sense that it is an attempt to delimit the power of self-generated boundary conditions and, therefore, to locate the frontiers beyond which it is the realm of accidental causes.

Taking environments into account is anyway very useful if adaptivity is a desirable goal to achieve: In effect, adaptivity is by definition relative to modifications of the environment. The richer the environment, the more adaptive a system has to be in order to keep up with such variations. It has been advocated many times by Brooks that building one robot is worth 100 simulations, not only because technical details of the implementation must be tackled with, but also and, we believe, most importantly, because this is the only way to be confronted to the actual complexity of the world. Certainly, richer environments make things harder: They make the fully nonlinear relationship between GTYPE and PTYPE [25] much more complex. Thus, it is acceptable, *as a first step*, to simulate limited environments. We must remark that the notion of environment is different depending on the level at which one is located, for example, in a swarm of insects (be they natural or artificial), the environment of the swarm as a whole is the physical space that surrounds it, while the environment of one particular individual comprises both the environment of the swarm *and* the other members of the swarm with which this individual interacts. The dynamically varying pattern of interactions constitutes an environment that is *internal* to the swarm system and, thus, provides it with internal boundary conditions. Such internal boundary conditions may be sufficient to generate functionally relevant patterns in (a) a highly simplified external environment, (b) a fixed external environment, or (c) a complex, varying external environment.

We (in AL) show a tendency to test our (collective) systems in case (a) or (b). Sometimes it is because it is hard or/and computationally expensive to do otherwise. Sometimes, we do so without being aware of it. Yet, many natural systems, if not all, live in a case (c) environment: There, internal boundary conditions may very well be at the same level of importance as external boundary conditions in most cases.

4.3   Function as a Side Effect of Structure?

There is often a focus of interest on the notion of structure while functional aspects are quite often neglected. Sometimes, these two aspects are confused with one another, because one does not see the purpose of making separate studies on structure and on function, the latter being considered a side effect of the former. (In effect, a function is just the consequence of plunging a structure into an environment.) But, this side effect can have dramatic consequences: "any adaptation has systematically specifiable conditions under which its employment will actually decrease the fitness of the organism" [49]. Let us take a look at the collective foraging behavior of army ant colonies [10,17]. The Ecitons live in tropical rain forests in colonies containing up to 2,000,000 individuals. Each individual is practically blind, and each day a great number of ants leave the nest to explore a new area to find preys. They constitute a swarm-raiding system that adopts a specific configuration. Moreover, this pattern is species-specific. Such a structure emerges spontaneously from individual trail-laying and trail-following behaviors, through interactions between individuals going toward the edge of the swarm, individuals flowing back to the nest, and the distribution of preys in the environment. But in some cases, when rain erased the pheromone trail, a swarm following the same elementary behavioral rules may be trapped in an unended circular mill, as it was described by Schneirla [17,36]. With this example we can see that biological structures, different foraging ant patterns that emerge under different environmental conditions, may possess functional value for the colony in one case and none in the other (Figure 2). Deneubourg and Goss [10] have proposed a probabilistic lattice

a

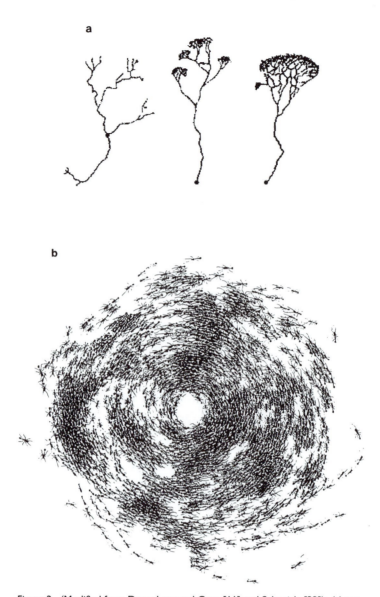

b

Figure 2. (Modified from Deneuborg and Goss [11] and Schneirla [32]): (a) represents the functionally efficient exploratory pattern of army ants having a trail-following/trail-laying behavior; the three different patterns correspond to three different distributions of preys in the environment (more precisely they correspond to different species that hunt for different types of preys, whence different distributions); (b) schematically represents a circular mill of army ants—they move faster and faster as the trail gets stronger, and continue to turn until exhausted.

model of foraging taking into account some environmental changes. Not only does this model account for the different foraging patterns found for different distributions of preys, it is also capable of reproducing circular mills in appropriate conditions.

Let us clarify the differences between structure and function (not to be taken literally): A function F is specified by its effects on a given (finite) subset of environmental variables, and a structure S is functionally defined by its effects (when plunged into a given environment) with respect to all possible environmental variables in their whole ranges. That's the difference. In the previous example, the structure implementing the foraging function in a normal environment is compactly represented by the behavioral rules that army ants follow (mostly trail laying and trail following). But the same structure, that is, the same behavioral rules, plunged into another environment does not at all implement the same function. Moreover, the colony is no longer viable. More precisely, let (X_i) be all possible environmental variables (i can be a continuous index, but that's not important to get the idea), and let $E = \{X_1, \ldots, X_n\}$ be a subset of these variables, acted upon by F: $F(X_1, \ldots, X_n) = (Y_1, \ldots, Y_n)$. For instance, F can represent the modification of the states of some variables in time: in continuous time $(dX_1/dt, \ldots, dX_n/dt) = F(X_1, \ldots, X_n)$, or in discrete time, $F(X_1[t], \ldots, X_n[t]) = (X_1[t+1], \ldots, X_n[t+1])$. F is a function of these n variables. Then S is said to implement function F in environment $\{X_i\}$ iff $S(X_1, \ldots, X_n$, and all other $X_i) = F(X_1, \ldots, X_n)$. What is usually assumed by reductionists is $\{$all other $X_i\}$ = constant, which is incorrectly derived into $\delta S/\delta X_i = 0$ for $i \neq 1 \ldots n$. This can be true for some X_i and for some range of values, but this is generally false. What we can see here is that many different structures can implement the same function and that the same structure can implement many different functions if different values of "irrelevant" variables are assumed. Moreover, the function implemented by S in a given environment depends on what variables we have chosen to look at: S can also have an effect on other variables, accidental from the point of view of the chosen variables.

Because we thought it was essential, we have emphasized a lot the importance of environments: By plunging AL-based "creatures" in more and more realistic environments, we will be naturally confronted with the complexity of life. We would be delighted if this appeared obvious to everybody in AL.

4.4 Computational Reductionism

It is true that AL as well as the sciences of complex systems have greatly benefited from the advances of computers in the last decades: These advances have enabled a "time compression" allowing for the simulation of processes that would otherwise have taken years and years. But there are some questions: (1) Is time compression powerful enough to explore all possible behaviors (including interesting ones) of a formally defined system? (2) Can finite specifications lead to open-endedness? Computational reductionism stands on the idea that any phenomenon that obeys the *laws* of physics can be simulated on a computer. Thus, while classical reductionism conjectures the reducibility of any biological process to the laws of physics, computational reductionism goes further by "transitivity of reduction": Any biological process can be simulated on a computer. But [7,8,12,13,34,35]:

- What if life can be "explained" only by an immense dimensional model, such that the number of relevant degrees of freedom itself is not even tractable and cannot be acted upon with present-day computers? Practical computers are not Turing machines, nor do human programmers live more than a billion years.

- The algorithmically based notion of logical depth showed us that some (very deep) objects can be simulated only by themselves, in the sense that there exists no shortcut to generating them; thus, if evolution is depth-generating, it may be very hard to reproduce its latest products on a computer by using a synthetic procedure very similar to an "artificial evolution." (This is a philosophical objection that does not jeopardize such simulations—they will obviously teach us something—but which questions their power.)

- If it is tempting to say that any process that obeys physical laws can be simulated (on a Turing machine, that is, provided enough space, memory, and time are available), nothing can be said about synthesis, because simulation and synthesis have two very different statuses. The laws of physics (in this context) have finite specifications, they are defined with respect to a set of chosen observables (properties of the object) that are transformed into variables to form a system, together with relationships between them (not to say that physics is restricted to laws). Given one phenomenon, we can look for laws (with the meaning defined earlier) governing its behavior, and, once this is done, it is likely that the phenomenon can be simulated. Now, if we synthesize some behavior with a computer, this behavior will be bound to obey the "physical" laws expressed in the specifications of the system. It is now a completely unresolved question to know whether or not these derivable behaviors are open-endedly diversified.

- Close in spirit to these issues is the question of understanding the influence exerted by the medium of "implementation" through the boundary conditions it provides to the "simulated" process. For example, an infinitely complex medium can provide open-endedness to the processes it implements, although the processes themselves are not open-ended. These boundary conditions are sometimes difficult to deal with, because they may be essential to the implementation without being clearly taken into account in the model, or simply because they are hard to track down due to the high complexity of the medium [29].

Yet one shouldn't be too pessimistic about all these theoretical limitations of AL's computational reductionism. Rather than true limitations, they constitute questions asked to AL. And AL is precisely a constructive way of checking whether these limitations are real obstacles.

4.5   The Pride of Being Reductionist

Reductionism does not only have drawbacks. In effect one could argue that AL models are the simplest ones in some sense, because they rely on simple elements in interactions, and that it is epistemological common sense to start with simple models rather than with complicated ones, with internal rather than with too many external causes. Although this is not completely true for at least two reasons: (1) when doing, for example, biological modeling, one often starts with many more variables than necessary, and gradually simplifies the model to retain only relevant variables; (2) simplicity is not necessarily a quality as regards biological sciences—being reductionist is thus not necessarily a negative thing, on the contrary. Common wisdom holds that being reductionist implies tracking the causes of macroscopic phenomena down to the level of elementary particles or more loosely down to the level of physical laws, which, for instance, any biological system ultimately obeys or seems to obey. But one can be ontologically, methodologically, or epistemologically reductionist, depending on the extent to which one accepts and/or practices reductionist principles. AL is methodologically reductionist in essence, not more, not less. And using reductionist methods is actually a safe way of practicing science, provided one doesn't forget high-level sciences. Let us recall an anecdote reported by Putnam [32]: A lot of biology departments fired their naturalists after Watson and Crick's discovery of the structure of DNA, because it was believed at that time that one would be able to explain everything with DNA. This, one should remember.

5   Why Do We Need AL?

It is time for us now to confess that we love AL. It may not be clear for the reader yet. Too many people in AL think that being critical means being an enemy. On the contrary, constructive criticisms will enhance AL's diffusion while making it more and more resistant to external attacks. If all the things we said in the previous sections were obvious to you, if you agree with them, then we are happy, because they were not at all obvious to us.

5.1   AL and Theoretical Biology

The objectives of AL should be stated without ambiguity: AL is not in competition with theoretical biology, although there is a nonempty intersection between AL and theoretical biology. On the contrary, it can contribute to theoretical biology because it allows one to go beyond pure biological modeling. If one quotes Emmeche [12], AL may contribute to theoretical biology by "(i) simulating developmental and evolutionary phenomena of life on Earth, (ii) simulating life as it could have evolved in non earthly environments given some set of realistic boundary conditions, (iii) providing new concepts and models of emergent phenomena belonging to a general set of complex systems of which biological systems (under particular kinds of description) may be a subset" [12]. Although we do not believe that point (ii) is so important because it falls within the life-as-it-could-be program, it is obvious to us that AL can contribute to many fields of theoretical biology, like ecological modeling and evolutionary modeling as well as to the understanding of collective behaviors in animal societies [42,43]. To have more applications, see the paper by Taylor and Jefferson [41] in this volume. It is not to say that biologists did not resort to synthesis or self-organization as modeling tools before AL: Rather, AL is a unified, transdisciplinary attempt to make these tools systematic.

Let us give an example [39] of how AL-based tools of investigation can be applied to the understanding of biological phenomena. Consider the immune system: It has to perform the task of discriminating between self and nonself, that is, it has to protect the organism against external aggressors (antigens) but at the same time has to be tolerant with the molecules of the organism. A wrong functioning of immune tolerance leads to autoimmune diseases, which in many cases can be lethal or at least have severe consequences. The classical paradigm of immunology is the theory clonal selection, whereby external antigens stimulate the production of specific molecules (antibodies produced by lymphocytes) against them. These specific antibodies proliferate thanks to a combined process involving a rapid reproduction of the corresponding lymphocytes leading the creation of a clone (a set of cells with common genetic characteristics) and an enhanced secretion of the antibody that stimulates the reproduction of the secreting cell in a positive feedback, and so on. But antibodies are molecules, which could as well be attacked by other antibodies and be eliminated. But this is fortunately not the case, except in the case of diseases. How can one explain such a tolerance? Certainly, the immune system is too complex to be completely and thoroughly modeled. And analytic approaches are certainly doomed because the immune system is a highly interacting system functioning as a network: Breaking things down and separating constituent units is not a good solution. On the other hand, resorting to synthesis may help. One can use a somewhat abstract but inspiring representation of the antibodies in a two-dimensional shape space [30]: Clones that are divided in two families according to their (abstract) stereochemical properties (represented by two parameters in the case of a two-dimensional shape space). Two clones taken from two different families will strongly interact if they are close on the two-dimensional shape space. The affinity, or strength of interaction is given by $m_i = \exp(-d_i^2)$, where d is the distance between them. Let us assume that two clones belonging to the same family don't interact at all. New clones are constantly presented to the network for recruitment, in order to mimic the constant production of lymphocytes in the bone marrow. Let the "field" a clone feels from other clones of the complementary family be given by $h = \sum_i m_i$: This

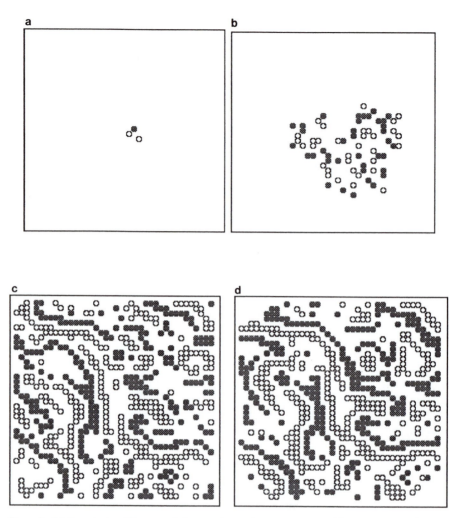

Figure 3. (a) One starts with a central clone, and new clones are proposed for recruitment; the two families are represented respectively by filled and empty circles; (b) the system after a few time steps. (c,d) The system eventually converges to a state where there are intertwined stripes of cells from the two families.

represents the total strength of the interactions, in a mean-field manner. Now, a clone is recruited if the field it feels falls within a window. This corresponds to the experimental observation that the activity of clones falls off rapidly outside of that window. All the basic ingredients are gathered. One can simulate such an (over)simplified model of the immune system in the absence of any external antigen and see how it evolves (see Figure 3[a–d]).

One finds that such a system evolves toward a rather stationary state (in a statistical sense) where there are intertwined stripes of cells from the two families. This constitutes a very improbable pattern. But even more interesting is the way this state responds to perturbations. Assume that we put in this system a molecule (say of the self) that is not subjected to the field-window condition, at least for a certain amount of time. You can see in Figure 4 that this molecule (a black square in our case—we randomly chose that it had a big affinity for clones represented by filled circles) starts in a "hostile" environment because it is surrounded by filled circles, but it is progressively integrated

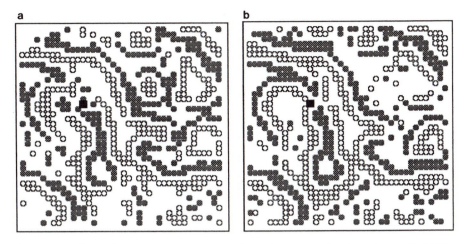

Figure 4. (a) The black square being sensitive to filled circles, it is in a hostile environment. (b) The black square has finally been integrated within a stripe of empty circles through deformations of the system.

into a stripe of more friendly clones (empty circles). The system locally deforms in order to do so. If one measures the sizes of the reorganizations needed to integrate the molecule, one even finds that they are power-law distributed (up to a cut-off size), which is reminiscent of self-organized criticality, a property of some dissipative many-body systems to evolve toward a statistically stationary state where events of any size and duration can take place, allowing for reorganizations at all scales.

What do we learn from this experiment, and what does it have to do with AL? The answer to the first is far from obvious in a biological setting: The model is more than simple compared with the complexity of the immune system, and almost no experimentalist will consider it a good model of what may actually happen in the immune system. Yet, if one sees it as a simple clue, it may constitute an inspiring metaphor, showing the importance of the network aspect of the immune system. It can be integrated in a theory postulating the existence of a central immune system, based on the activity of lymphocytes B alone, which is distinct from the peripheral immune system involving lymphocytes T, which by the way appeared much later in the course of evolution. This model, although simple, then represents a first step toward the modeling of the very basic mechanisms of the central immune system as it grows before birth. And it is indeed being used as a starting point for the design of more complex models involving many more features of the immune system. As regards the second question, why is it AL? The answer is disputable, but let us put it this way: This model is too far from any biological reality to belong to genuine biological modeling as it is practiced in most laboratories. Yet, as we just argued, it teaches something: It is useful. Moreover, it is based on synthetic techniques (more or less CAs), that is, AL techniques. As you can see in the references, the paper reporting these results has been published in the *Journal of Theoretical Biology*. We consider this as AL's influence, which has allowed such marginal research in biology to be diffused to the large audience it deserves. We also believe it does not suffer from the criticisms of the previous sections, because it is clearly biologically inspired and perfectly defines its limit of applicability.

Let us now give another type of example from which generally applicable conclusions can be drawn, showing the power of AL techniques to explore biological models beyond their crude biological application. To make things clear, let us start from general considerations about modeling. Starting from experimental observations, one generally wants to build a model belonging to a given class of models to account for these observations. The choice of the model class is both a matter of taste and more importantly a matter of relevance in the context of the observed phenomenon: The model parameters must have a biological significance, be it assumed or explicit. Once the relevant parameters have been found, they are generally tuned until the model can explain the observations: that is, the model must at least reproduce the data and be able to make some predictions (e.g., if the biological system is perturbed, the corresponding perturbation in the model must lead to the same consequences as in the real system). Let us assume we have such a wonderful model at hand. In certain ranges of values, the parameters will induce a behavior close to the observations. But if these parameters are set out of the "biologically adequate" range of values, how can the model be interpreted? Some will argue [27] that exploring the model's behavior by tuning its parameters amounts to exploring life-as-it-could-be. Well, it is true that sometimes one finds new kinds of behaviors that, although not directly relevant to biology, can have some interest for other disciplines (see the examples to follow). But, more surprisingly, these apparently nonbiological behaviors can tell a lot to biologists: Some ensemble of constraints certainly led to the particular set of parameters allowing our model to reproduce the experimentally observed data. But were these values of the parameters unavoidable? Is it possible that other (environmental) constraints could have evolved other values for the parameters? A thorough understanding of the nature of the parameters is made possible by applying AL's bottom-up concepts (systematic synthetic exploration), and such an understanding is invaluable when it comes to looking for constraints likely to lead to a particular behavioral form. Take, for example, the building behavior of wasps [42,43]. One of the important questions ethologists ask is whether the architectural forms observed in nature (and more generally social organizations and behavioral forms) are unavoidable. We have tested a model of building behavior in order to reproduce wasps' nests found in *Vespa* genera. The basic hypotheses underlying the model are quite simple: Each wasp is capable of acting on its local environment by depositing a brick according to the state of this local environment. The space in which the nest is constructed is a $10 \times 10 \times 10$ cubic lattice, and the local environment of each wasp consists of a $3 \times 3 \times 3$ cube ($\sim 1/40$ of the total volume), the center of which is occupied by the wasp. The behavioral rules that we use can be deterministic, stochastic, epochal. In Figures 5 and 6 we show two nests generated using these rules. In Figure 5, the rules have been adjusted to reproduce patterns actually found in the *Vespa* genera. By slightly modifying the behavioral rules, we got the pattern in Figure 6, which is never found in nature. Hence, the question of knowing whether the behavioral rules used to generate the nest in Figure 5 could be an "attractor" of evolution, given some set of environmental conditions. For some reasons, the nest in Figure 5 is viable (while the one in Figure 6 is certainly not, at least in the environment-as-we-know-it). Thus, to make our question more accurate, we should ask why, among viable types of nests, only one type (or a highly restricted number of types) seems to have been selected. Although accidental causes are still possible, we can propose a tentative answer: The behavioral rules used to generate the rules of Figure 5 are the simplest possible. Any other behavioral rule is unavoidably more complex. This simplicity property might make it more easily reachable by evolution. We will not continue this speculative discussion too far: We just meant to illustrate that AL synthetic methodologies were the only solution to explore the space of architectural patterns and find other possible viable architectures.

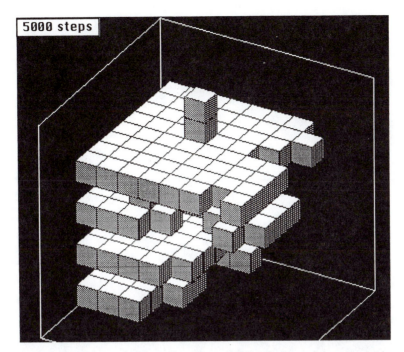

Figure 5. "Artificial nest" generated by a swarm of 10 "artificial wasps" depositing bricks according to the state of their local environments. The behavioral rules have been chosen so as to reproduce nest architectures that can be found in nature in the *Vespa* genera. Note, for instance, the little piece on the top of the nest, which corresponds very closely to natural pedicels, and the succession of horizontal planes that represent the combs of natural nests.

5.2   The Interplay of AL and Philosophy

A "philosophy of AL" is under way. If philosophy can somewhat "guide" the quest of AL, mutual enrichment is also possible, because AL is precisely a scientific attempt to clarify some old philosophical issues about the nature of life, and other issues... it raises! AL "promises to be of significant philosophical interest. AL has relatively straightforward relevance to issues in metaphysics, philosophy of science, philosophy of biology, and philosophy of mind, but it also bears centrally on more distant issues in social and political philosophy, economic philosophy, and ethics" [1]. But because we are not philosophers, we urge you to read Harnad and Dennett [11,20]!

5.3   Designing Artificial Problem-Solvers

We believe that the idea of AL giving rise to engineering applications is fundamental. Taylor [40] gave some examples about such applications, like in the field of ecology (simulations of populations of insects leading to the development of control tools for agriculture). AL as a toolbox is precisely at the interface between many disciplines and as such serves as a multidirectional communication channel. In particular, AL builds bridges between natural sciences and the sciences of the artificial: This makes it unique and indispensable. We can give many more examples based on AL's methodologies.

Algorithms. The design of algorithms is a booming domain of activity in AL. AL tools have led to the development of many interesting algorithms that often perform better than classical algorithms within a shorter time, all the more as they generally contain much explicit or implicit parallelism, like in swarm-inspired algorithms or genetic algorithms. They resort to distributed agents, or to evolutionary algorithms, or often to

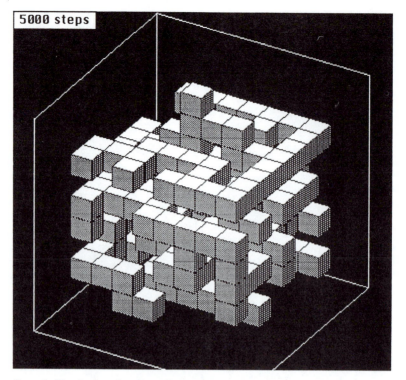

Figure 6. "Artificial nest" generated by a swarm of 10 "artificial wasps" depositing bricks according to the state of their local environments. The behavioral rules have been found by a systematic exploration of the space of possible architectures. We selected this one because it can be derived from the preceding one through a slight modification only, while yielding a strikingly different pattern that is never encountered in nature. Could it have become functionally viable with another evolutionary history (including the evolution of the environment)?

both. For instance, Packard used a genetic algorithm to evolve cellular automata to make them reproduce electrochemical deposition patterns. In very much the same spirit, one of us (EWB) is currently developing a genetic algorithm to evolve coupled map lattices (CMLs) for time series prediction: CMLs compete to survive in an environment composed of a times series; the coexisting, fit CMLs may be able to predict very efficiently in some specific region of the state space, and one eventually ends up with a population of CMLs capable of predicting the whole series. Hillis evolved sorting algorithms by making them coevolve with parasites, and found a very good solution [22]: parasites modify the fitness landscape and make it harder for algorithms to perform well; thus, both the parasites and the algorithms become more and more complex, and one finally obtains a very efficient algorithm. We all know Koza's genetic programming technique, in which LISP-like programs are evolved to solve particular problems [in 26]. Deneubourg and Goss [10] have designed a distributed sorting algorithm in which artificial ants can realize global clustering with only local information and a small memory: Roughly, the rules consist in taking an object of type A with a high probability if the artificial ant is surrounded by objects of type B, and in dropping this object with a high probability if it is surrounded by objects of the same type; the same holds for objects of type B; artificial ants are allowed to move randomly, and after a certain amount of time, one gets clusters of objects A and clusters of objects B, and finally, one can get only one cluster of each type. Bersini [described in 5] de-

320

veloped a control algorithm inspired by the metadynamics of the immune system (i.e., the dynamics of recruitment of new clones in the system): In a few words, the idea is that many solutions are generated, and only the most adapted ones are recruited. Colorni and colleagues [9] proposed a combinatorial optimizer based on the trail-laying and trail-following behavior of ants and applied it successfully to the traveling salesman problem. The basic principle of this algorithm is directly inspired by ants; in effect, due to the volatility of the deposited pheromone, the pheromone present on the longer path to the food source will disappear more rapidly than the pheromone on the shorter path because the longer path necessarily has a lower density of ants on it, and, thus, the corresponding pheromone trail will be reinforced more rarely; this process is amplified until the shortest path is eventually selected by the whole colony (although "explorers" still exist). Note that many refinements of this crude principle are possible, for instance, this "mass recruitment" of ants through pheromone can be a disadvantage when a new, closer source is introduced, in that the colony will be unable to switch to this better source. By allowing different types of recruitment, like tandem, group, and mass recruitments to be combined, one gets a much more flexible swarm, capable of responding efficiently to modifications of the environment. Finally, Snyers and Kuntz [personal communication, 1994] developed an optimization algorithm dedicated to the graph partitioning problem, using pheromone-like tracers combined with a genetic algorithm. We have to stop here for lack of room, many more examples could be given, and we chose the ones we are the most familiar with because of our backgrounds. To know more, for example, about computer viruses, see Spafford [38].

Robotic systems. Many robotic systems are currently being developed in the spirit of artificial life [15,16,18]. They are devoted to harvesting, mining, and ecological sampling, and many other tasks are to be announced. The artificial wasps we presented in a previous paragraph also constitute good candidates for the design of robots exhibiting an asynchronous, emerging collective building ability, whereby they can generate very complex, highly structured architectures without any central controller and complying only with simple local rules. Note that all the examples of robots share essential similarities: Each individual robot is usually simple, and the collective intelligence appearing at the colony level is the result of interactions between the robots. These interactions can either be direct, through some kind of communication process [1], or indirect through modifications in the environment by one individual that induce subsequent changes in the behavior of the other individuals ("stigmergic script") [42]. All this has rather interesting consequences: The colony of robots is more flexible and more robust (if one robot gets out of order, the global task performed by the colony is generally not affected) than one individual complicated robot, and the cost of developing a colony of simple agents is eventually less than that of designing the complicated robot. (Besides, losing it in an accident would have many more aftermaths than losing a poor little agent of a colony.) To know more about autonomous agents, see Maes [28].

Most existing colonies of robots have been inspired by natural systems, systems exhibiting collective intelligence: insect societies. One of us (GT) has developed the concept of *swarm intelligence* [44] to help build bridges between biological and artificial contexts: "A swarm is a group of active and mobile elements which can communicate with each other and thereby influence each other's actions. Each unit interacts locally with its environment and in particular has access to only local information." If the task to be performed by a biological swarm has a biological relevance (efficient, flexible, optimized foraging, adaptive division of labor) at the level of the colony, the corresponding task performed by an artificial swarm has a relevance with respect to the engineer's goals (gathering and transport of objects, exploring new areas, synchronizing activity, sorting objects, building or allocating an appropriate number of units to different tasks whose demand is variable). Central to the idea of swarm intelligence is the coexistence of individual simplicity and collective complexity. Such systems, often relying on competing positive feedbacks as an organizing force, have three important properties: simplicity, reliability, and flexibility. The units make no complex decision based on knowledge or environmental representation and are allowed a high degree of randomness in their movements. However, they are spread out in their environment and are influenced by local environmental cues that could have been modified by their own or other units' past actions. Because a particular configuration is adopted dynamically (and not imposed a priori) in response to a large number of environmental cues, any change in the environment leads to an appropriate reconfiguration, conferring a lot of adaptivity and flexibility to the swarm.

Cellular robotic systems [2], although they are *simulated* robotic systems, are aimed at exploring the possible problem-solving abilities of robotic colonies. They serve as a first step in the process of designing such colonies. In particular, Beni and colleagues [private communication] introduced an asynchronous cyclic swarm capable of solving very simple ordinary differential equations in a distributed manner. We improved this cyclic swarm and designed a two-dimensional swarm capable of solving partial differential diffusion-like equations [5].

Let us also briefly mention that a parallel can be drawn between AL and cybernetics (the study of control and communication in the animal and the machine) [see, e.g., [25], but one of the main differences is the nature of the tools available to AL, compared with those that were available to cybernetics. Given the impact of cybernetics on science in general and on engineering sciences in particular, despite this lack of a truly powerful tool ("the science of feedback"), one can expect an atomic impact from AL.

5.4 AL and Art

Let us end this brief review with the relationship between AL and art. As we already advocated, art inheres in the very foundations of AL. Synthesis, which is the central method in the AL toolbox, becomes artistic creation when the Artificial Lifer, like the "Zoosystemician" Bec [26], is free from any constraint (especially the unpleasant constraints imposed by reality) and is only limited by the power of his or her imagination. Sims even proposed to everyone to become an artist by allowing people to interact with his "genetically" generated pictures in real time. (To have an idea of Sims' ideas, see, e.g., [6] or even better the video proceedings of the second AL workshop.) By choosing such or such a picture, they contribute to the development of a new type of art, based on the interaction between their imagination and computationally generated images. This new form of art, although controversial because the artist sort of lets the computer do all the work, is full of promises: For the first time, it is possible to convey the bottom of our dreams—for the first time it is possible to really visualize the creatures that *live* in there.

6 Conclusion

In conclusion, if you have to justify your AL activity, you should first remember that AL is a particular way of looking at things that can be fruitfully applied to many domains. If you are dealing with systems that are too complex to be studied with traditional scientific tools, AL can certainly help. You should not forget your primary goals and get lost in AL's immensity. While top-down approaches usually forget to obey lower-level constraints and laws, purely bottom-up approaches usually forget to look at higher-level constraints, and this leads in both cases to considerable flaws. Artificial life, being "very bottom-up," needs constraints. Both empirical constraints originating from biology and other natural sciences, and pragmatic constraints oriented by the design of useful, viable, efficient, robust, flexible, decentralized, lifelike systems, can channel your AL energy into extraordinary accomplishments. If you are a biologist (you are certainly hard to convince, and it must be even worse for your boss) seeking new modeling tools, AL is a general toolbox that offers you a broad spectrum of new techniques of experimentation, from computer simulations of evolution to models of how decentralized systems can collectively perform biologically relevant tasks. If you are looking for ways of getting out of classical AI's dead-end, AL can help by providing you with ways of making symbols emerge out of low-level sensory-motor processes. If you are a computer scientist, not necessarily involved in AI, AL gives you the pleasure not only of playing god, but also of finding new distributed algorithms for optimization, control, or prediction. If you are a philosopher, AL will give you the opportunity to think about new issues in ethics, epistemology, and so on and will provide you with years of work to unravel the ontological status of life: you will be able to think over life as no other philosopher before. If you are an engineer, AL constitutes an almost inexhaustible source of ideas for the design of a bunch of new machines. In all these cases, cooperation is crucial: biologists do not necessarily master the thermodynamics of cooperative structures, while physicists usually have only little knowledge about biological systems; ethologists do not always master computer programming, while gifted programmers are generally not familiar with animal societies. One can draw wrong conclusions when working in somebody else's field: communication is essential, and AL is a powerful medium of communication for diffusing transdisciplinary concepts. Let alone the fact that concepts originating from other disciplines often have an exotic flavor, they can also serve as a source of inspiration in one's own field. Finally, if you are an artist, AL opens a world of new experiences to you: it complements the traditional artistic techniques by extending the scope of art-as-it-is to the wider scope of art-as-it-could-be, where everything which is in your imagination, even deep inside your subconscious, can be recreated in alternative media. With all this in mind, you should definitely be able to reassure your boss and hopefully yourself if ever you needed to be reassured.

Acknowledgments

Many thanks go to Paul Bourgine, Jean-Louis Deneubourg, Jacques Gervet, Chris Langton, and John Stewart for many exciting debates and discussions, and to Mark Bedeau, Peter Cariani, Claus Emmeche, George Kampis, and Bill Wimsatt for fruitful intellectual exchanges. We gratefully acknowledge Emmanuel Sardet for writing the software, allowing for the visualization of artificial nests, and Christian Vidal for writing the cyclic swarm program.

References

1. Bedeau, M. (1992). Philosophical aspects of artificial life. In F. J. Varela & P. Bourgine (Eds.), *Toward a Practice of Autonomous Systems, Proceedings of the First European Conference on Artificial Life* (pp. 494–503). Cambridge, MA: The MIT Press/Bradford Books.

2. Beni, G. (1988). The concept of cellular robotic system. In H. E. Stephanou, A. Meystel, J. Herath, & J. Y. S. Luh (Eds.), *Proceedings of 1988 IEEE Int. Symposium on Intelligent Control*. Arlington, VA: IEEE Computer Society Press.

3. Ben-Jacob, E., Shmueli, H., Shochet, O., & Tenenbaum, A. (1992). Adaptive self-organization during growth of bacterial colonies. *Physica A, 187*, 378–424.

4. Bonabeau, E. (1993). On the appeals and dangers of synthetic reductionism. In *Proceedings of ECAL'93, Self-organisation and life: from simple rules to global complexity*, Brussels, May 24–26, (pp. 86–102).

5. Bonabeau, E., & Theraulaz, G. (1994). *Collective intelligence*. Paris: Hermes.

6. Bourgine, P., & Varela, F. J. (1992). Towards a practice of autonomous systems. In F. J. Varela & P. Bourgine (Eds.), *Toward a Practice of Autonomous Systems, Proceedings of*

the First European Conference on Artificial Life (pp. xi–xvii). Cambridge, MA: The MIT Press/Bradford Books.

7. Cariani, P. 1989. *On the design of devices with emergent semantic functions.* Ph.D. dissertation, State University of New York at Binghamton.

8. Cariani, P. (1991). Adaptivity and emergence in organisms and devices. In *World Futures*, vol. 31 (pp. 49–70). New York: Gordon and Breach Science Publishers S.A.

9. Colorni, A., Dorigo, M., & Maniezzo, V. (1992). Distributed optimization by ants colonies. In F. J. Varela & P. Bourgine (Eds.), *Toward a Practice of Autonomous Systems, Proceedings of the First European Conference on Artificial Life* (pp. 134–142). Cambridge, MA: The MIT Press.

10. Deneubourg, J.-L., & Goss, S. (1989). Collective patterns and decision making. *Ethology Ecology & Evolution, 1*, 295–311.

11. Dennett, D. (1994). Artificial life as philosophy. *Artificial Life, 1*, 291–292.

12. Emmeche, C. (1992). Life as an abstract phenomenon: Is AL possible? In F. J. Varela & P. Bourgine (Eds.), *Toward a Practice of Autonomous Systems, Proceedings of the First European Conference on Artificial Life* (pp. 466–474). Cambridge, MA: The MIT Press/Bradford Books.

13. Elsasser, W. (1981). Principles of a new biological theory: A summary. *Journal of Theoretical Biology, 89*, 131–150.

14. Forrest, S. (1990). Emergent computation. *Physica D, 42*, 1–11.

15. Fukuda, T., & Ueyama, T. (1992). Self-evolutionary robotic system? Sociology and social robotics. *Journal of Robotics and Mechatronics, 4*, 96–103.

16. Fukuda, T., Ueyama, T., Sugiura, T., Sakai, A., & Uesugi, T. (1992). Self-organization and swarm intelligence in the society of robot being. In *Proceedings of the Second International Symposium on Measurement and Control in Robotics (ISMCR '92)* (pp. 787–794). Tsukuba Science City, Japan, November 15–19, 1992.

17. Goss, S., Deneubourg, J. L., Aron, S., Beckers, R., & Pasteels, J. M. (1990). How trail laying and trail following can solve foraging problems for ant colonies. In R. N. Hughes (Ed.), *Behavioural mechanisms of food selection* (pp. 661–678). NATO ASI Series, Vol. G20. Berlin Heidelberg: Springer Verlag.

18. Goss, S., Deneubourg, J.-L., Beckers, R., & Henrotte, J.-L. (1993). Recipes for collective movement. In *Proceedings of the Second Conference on Artificial Life*, Universite Libre de Bruxelles: Brussels, pp. 400–410.

19. Grassberger, P. (1989). Problems in quantifying self-generated complexity. *Helvetica Physica Acta, 62*, 489–511.

20. Harnad, S. (1994). Levels of functional equivalence in reverse bioengineering. *Artifical Life, 1*, 293–301.

21. Hillis, D. (1988). Intelligence as an emergent behavior; or, the songs of Eden. In S. R. Graubard (Ed.), *The artificial intelligence debate*. Cambridge, MA: The MIT Press.

22. Hillis, W. D. (1991). Co-evolving parasites improve simulated evolution as an optimization procedure. In C. G. Langton, C. Taylor, J. D. Farmer, & S. Rasmussen (Eds.), *Artificial life II*, pp. 313–324. Redwood City: Addison-Wesley.

23. Kampis, G. 1991. Emergent computations, life and cognition. In *World Futures*, vol. 31 (pp. 33–48). New York: Gordon and Breach Science Publishers S.A.

24. Langton, C. (1986). Studying artificial life with cellular automata. *Physica D, 22*, 120–149.

25. Langton, C. (Ed.) (1988). *Artificial Life*. Reading, MA: Addison-Wesley.

26. Langton, C., Taylor, C., Farmer, D., & Rasmussen, S. (Eds.) (1991). *Artificial life II*. Reading, MA: Addison-Wesley.

27. Langton, C. G. (1992). Artificial Life. In L. Nadel & D. Stein (Eds.), *Lectures in Complex Systems*. Reading, MA: Addison-Wesley.

28. Maes, P. (1994). Modeling adaptive autonomous agents. *Artificial Life, 1*, 135–162.

29. Pattee, H. (1988). Simulations, realizations, and theories of life. In C. G. Langton (Ed.), *Artificial life*. Reading, MA: Addison-Wesley, 63–77.

30. Perelson, A. (Ed.) (1988). *Theoretical Biology*, 2 vol. Reading, MA: Addison-Wesley.

31. Polanyi, M. (1968). Life's irreducible structure. *Science, 160*, 1308–1312.

32. Putnam, H. (1973). Reductionism and the nature of psychology. *Cognition, 2*, 131–146.

33. Putnam, H. (1988). Much ado about not very much. In S. R. Graubard (Ed.), *The artificial intelligence debate*. Cambridge, MA: The MIT Press.

34. Rosen, R. (1978). *Fundamentals of measurement and representation of natural systems*. New York: North Holland.

35. Rosen, R. (1985). *Anticipatory systems*. New York: Pergamon Press.

36. Schneirla, T. C. (1944). A unique case of circular milling in ants, considered in relation to trail following and the general problem of orientation. *American Museum Novitates*, Number 1253, 1–26 (The American Museum of Natural History, New York).

37. Sober, E. (1991). Learning from functionalism—prospects for strong AL. In C. G. Langton, C. Taylor, J. Doyne Farmer & S. Rasmussen (Eds.), *Artificial life II*. Reading, MA: Addison-Wesley, 749–765.

38. Spafford, E. H. (1994). Computer viruses as artificial life. *Artificial Life, 1*, 249–265.

39. Stewart, J., & Varela, F. J. (1991). Morphogenesis in shape space. *Journal of Theoretical Biology, 153*, 477–498.

40. Taylor, R. (1991). Fleshing out artificial life II. In C. G. Langton, C. Taylor, J. Doyne Farmer & S. Rasmussen (Eds.), *Artificial life II*. Reading, MA: Addison Wesley, 25–38.

41. Taylor, C., & Jefferson, D. (1994). Artificial life as a tool for biological inquiry. *Artificial Life, 1*, 1–13.

42. Theraulaz, G., & Deneubourg, J. L. (1994). Swarm intelligence in social insects and the emergence of cultural swarm patterns. In R. A. Gardner, A. B. Chiarelli, B. T. Gardner, & F. X. Ploojd (Eds.), *The ethological roots of culture*. NATO ASI Series, Amsterdam: North-Holland.

43. Theraulaz, G., Goss, S., Gervet, J., & Deneubourg, J. L. (1991). Task differentiation in Polistes wasp colonies: a model for self-organizing groups of robots. In J. A. Meyer & S. W. Wilson (Eds.), *Simulation of adaptive behavior: from animals to animats* (pp. 346–355). Cambridge, MA: The MIT Press/Bradford Books.

44. Theraulaz, G., Goss, S., Gervet, J., & Deneubourg, J.-L. (1990). Swarm intelligence in wasp colonies: An example of task assignment in multi-agent systems. In A. Meystel, J. Herath, & S. Gray (Eds.), *Proceedings of 5th IEEE International Symposium on Intelligent Control*. Philadelphia.

45. Varela, F. J. (1979). *Principles of biological autonomy*. Amsterdam: North-Holland.

46. Varela, F. J., Thompson, E., & Rosch, E. (1991). *The Embodied Mind*. Cambridge, MA: The MIT Press.

47. Weaver, W. (1968). Science and complexity. *American Scientist, 36*, 536–544.

48. Weidlich, W. (1991). Physics and social science—the approach of synergetics. *Physics Reports, 204*, 1–163.

49. Wimsatt, W. C. (1986). Heuristics and the study of human behavior. Ch. 13 in W. Fiske & K. Scwheder (Eds.), chap 13. Chicago: University of Chicago Press.

Index